John Wolcott Phelps, Lucien de La Hodde

The cradle of rebellions

A history of the secret societies of France

John Wolcott Phelps, Lucien de La Hodde

The cradle of rebellions
A history of the secret societies of France

ISBN/EAN: 9783337206178

Printed in Europe, USA, Canada, Australia, Japan

Cover: Foto ©ninafisch / pixelio.de

More available books at **www.hansebooks.com**

THE
CRADLE OF REBELLIONS.

THE

CRADLE OF REBELLIONS.

A HISTORY

OF THE

SECRET SOCIETIES OF FRANCE.

BY

LUCIEN DE LA HODDE,

REPORTER FOR THE "CHARIVARI," MEMBER OF THE DETECTIVE
POLICE, ETC. ETC.

NEW YORK:
PUBLISHED BY JOHN BRADBURN,
(SUCCESSOR TO M. DOOLADY.)
49 WALKER STREET.
1864.

Entered, according to the Act of Congress, in the year 1864, by
JOHN BRADBURN,
In the Office of the Clerk of the District Court of the United States in and for the Southern District of New York.

PREFACE.

The object in translating this work, the production of a sparkling and witty French writer, De La Hodde, is to show the dangerous consequences, to society and government, arising from the practices of secret associations. It gives a perfect illustration of the operations of these associations in bringing about the present unprincipled rebellion in the United States. French characters, similar to the leading conspirators against our own government, are set forth in a way that gives the reader a clear insight into the science of demagogism, and lays open that nefarious class of political transactions which must tend to the ruin of any country whatever, and especially to one which is governed by republican institutions. New light is shed upon the darkling work of secret societies; their demoralizing consequences to society are exposed, and their deeds of subterraneous deceit and treachery brought to the contempt and detestation of all good, true, and loyal men.

The reader will see the agencies by which the government of Louis Philippe was overthrown and a military despotism established in its place, the same agencies which Joel R. Poinsett had previously established in Mexico under the name of the Secret Societies of the *Escoseces* and *Yorkinos*, which hastened the ruin of republican government in that country, and prepared the way for the admission of despotic government from France. They were the same agencies that contributed largely toward the annexation of Texas, that have sustained slavery so long against the moral convictions of an unsophisticated people, and without which the present rebellion could hardly have been incepted. Even those so called charitable institutions, designed as means of secret benevolence, the Freemasons and Odd-Fellows, have been used, often against their own knowledge or consent, by the great masters of secret political associations, as so many subordinate cog-wheels in the great machinery of insurrection and rebellion. Even many of the industrial pursuits of the free States were overruled, unconsciously, to the same end. It is a merit, a charitable act, to protect the weak against the strong.

Slavery, in its contest against the virtues of a republican people, was weak; and it was therefore right and just in the knight of subterraneous craft to labor for its defence! Slavery was as weak as it was just; and every act, therefore, done in its behalf, however villainous it might be, was sanctified by the end proposed, and sanctified the knight who did it! Such has come to be the spirit of secret associations in the United States.

The American people, animated by that candor and openness which flows naturally from their all-benevolent institutions, are unsuspecting as yet, in the mass, of those dark and covert machinations by which their liberties are endangered, and of which this History gives a striking example. Indeed, it is believed that political education has become necessary, to every voter, for the preservation of our government, and that it can hardly be completed, at the present day, unless by some such insight of political baseness and craft as is herein disclosed. None, we may say, can so readily understand the present rebellion, the immorality, political depravity and infamy that have led to it, as they who, through the perusal of these pages, shall become acquainted with those mainsprings of action that brought about the French revolution of 1848.

With regard to the translation we may say a word: it has been done in haste; yet much of it is not without purity of English style and diction. But it is chiefly from the great importance of the facts to the American people that we recommend it to their careful perusal.

MARCH 28, 1864.

CONTENTS.

	PAGE
INTRODUCTION	17

BOOK I.

CHAPTER I.

Enumeration of the elements which constitute the mob—The students—The imbeciles—The gypsies—The sovereign people—The fly-catchers—The disaffected—Political refugees—The bandits . 27

CHAPTER II.

The Carbonari 33

CHAPTER III.

Scheme for expelling the deputies and peers—The republican party—Its numerical strength—Plagiarism from '93—A sketch of the popular societies after the period of July, 1830 . . . 41

CHAPTER IV.

The friends of the people—The bourgeoisie drive them from their club—A mob—Schemes for assassinating the king and ex-ministers—Old Wooden-leg—Libellous handbills—Complot of the Parisian artillery—Its chiefs 51

CHAPTER V.

Trial of the ministers—A mob—A complot in the National Guard—Messrs. G. Cavaignac, Guinard, Trelat, Sambuc, Audry de Puyraveau—Their trial—Mobs upon mobs—The artillery of Marshal Lobau 59

CHAPTER VI.

Permanence of the mob—M. Carlier and the cudgellers of the Bastile—The bull-dogs of the populace vanquished—M. Gisquet—Suggestions concerning the re-establishment of the ministry of police . . 69

CHAPTER VII.

Complot of the towers of Notre Dame—Trial of members of the *Friends of the People*—Messrs. Bonnias, Raspail, Blanqui, Antony Thouret—The chiefs of the popular societies boil over—Messrs. Rittiez, Toussaint Bravard, Cahaigne, Avril, Imbert. . . 77

CHAPTER VIII.

The mob of the rag-pickers—The cholera, and the pretended poisoners—Credulity of the people—Odious machinations of the republicans—The legitimist party—Affair of the street of Prouvaires—A patriot writer 85

CHAPTER IX.

Preparations for an insurrection—Order of battle of the secret societies—Political Refugees—An attempt at assassinating General Bem—Young Italy—M. Mazzini—A secret tribunal—A frightful drama 95

CHAPTER X.

The revolt of the 5th and 6th of June—A theory of insurrections—Why the plan of General Cavaignac is a bad one . . . 105

CHAPTER XI.

Shows that the advisers are not the payers—M. Jeanne—Decadence of the republican party—The affair of the bridge of Arcole—The good faith of the demagogues—The pistol-shot of the Pont Royal—The *Rights of Man*—A remarkable similitude—The necessity of putting a stop to anarchy 113

CHAPTER XII.

Formation of the Society of the *Rights of Man*—Names of the members of the committee—M. Millon, a publicist coachman—Orders of the day—The detached forts—A complot—Why it proved a failure—A trial—Violence of the accused, and especially of M. Viguerte . 123

CHAPTER XIII.

Robespierre's Declaration of the rights of man, published as the republican gospels—The Committee of Action—Its chief—Reviews of the sections—Morality of the conspirators—The law respecting associations—Battle is decided upon 135

CHAPTER XIV.

A great patriot—M. Cavaignac devoted to the dagger—Preparations for the insurrection.—The forces of the Republican party in 1834 146

CHAPTER XV.

The effective strength for war of the *Rights of Man*—The forces of the government—Preparations for the conflict—Review of the *Society of Action*—Arrest of Captain Kersausie—Insurrection of the 13th and 14th of April—Why the rout of the republicans proved complete 152

CHAPTER XVI.

The *Rights of Man* and the *Mutualists* of Lyons—Insurrection—The theatrical part of M. Lagrange—Eclipse of the principal chiefs . 159

CHAPTER XVII.

The conspiracies of Luneville, Saint Etienne, Chalons, Clermont. Grenoble, Vienne, and Marseilles—The trials of April—The accused—Their defenders—The escape from Sainte Pelagie—Verdict—M. Marrast in prison—An odious illumination—The revolt of the cells—An attempt to assassinate M. Carrel 168

CHAPTER XVIII.

PAGE

Still another mob—M. Raspail and M. Gisquet—The complot of Neuilly—The Chaveau family—The attempt of Fieschi—M. Recurt and Pepin—The part played by the *Rights of Man* . . 178

CHAPTER XIX.

The laws of September—Their necessity—Bad newspapers do more harm than good ones do good—It is not true that the shutting up of the clubs induces secret societies—The folly of unrestricted liberty 189

CHAPTER XX.

The *Revolutionary Legions*—Political assassination—Aliband—M. Sobrier—M. Recurt—M. Flocon—M. Barbès—M. Martin-Bernard . 195

CHAPTER XXI.

Organization of the *Society of the Families*—The form of reception —Despotism of the chiefs—Secret details 203

CHAPTER XXII.

A clandestine manufactory—The powder affair—Complot of the Arc de Triomphe—Project against the Tuileries—M. Gisquet retires— The affair of Strasbourg 210

CHAPTER XXIII.

Organization of the *Seasons*—A new personality of conspirators— Reviews—Prudential measures—M. Martin Bernard—Regicides— An amnesty—Its effect—Recrudescence of propagandism—A new formula of reception—Hatred against the bourgeoisie . . 218

CHAPTER XXIV.

The *Republican Monitor*—The *Free Man*—M. Joigneaux—Seizure of powder—Skill of the committee of the *Seasons*—Preliminaries of the 12th of May—M. Barbès hesitates—How he is decided by M. Blanqui—Counter order of the battle—The choice of ground . 228

CHAPTER XXV.

The chiefs of the *Seasons* and their general staff—The inspection by M. Blanqui—Everything in readiness—Call to arms—The store of Lepage—The committee called for—Perplexity of M. Blanqui—M. Barbès—The post of the Palace of Justice—Proclamation—Mialon, the galley-slave—M. Tisserant—Suspected courage of some of the chiefs 238

BOOK II.

CHAPTER I.

Reorganization of the *Seasons*—The provisional committee—The four *Revolutionary Agents*—Orders of the day again brought in use—My course of proceeding with the patriots 250

CHAPTER II.

Two adventures—M. Dourille—He becomes chief of the *New Seasons*—*The Journal of the People*—M. Dupoty—His portrait. . . 256

CHAPTER III.

M. Cabet and communism—The banquet of Chatillon—The republicans show signs of life—The banquet of Belleville in reply to that of Chatillon 262

CHAPTER IV.

A strike—Revolutionary petulance—The communists of action—Messrs. Rozier, Lionne and Vellicus—M. Dourille parades his troops—An harangue upon the boulevards—The equipment of M. Rozier—Arrests 271

CHAPTER V.

The attempt of Darmès—Abominable instigations—A pistol fired at the princes—New free and accepted judges—Sentence of death—Its consequences 278

CHAPTER VI.

The revolutionary congress at Lyons—The wife of a conspirator—M. Callès—M. Bonnardel—M. Jailloux—A session of the conspirators 286

CHAPTER VII.

Details of the plan—Examination of localities—A nocturnal conventicle—Repast of the conspirators—Decision—Why the conspiracy proved a failure—Reflections 295

CHAPTER VIII.

M. Flocon becomes a conspirator again—A meeting at the coffeehouse of Saint Agnès—A Revolutionary decision—Fear of the laws of September—Nomination of a committee—A failure . . 303

CHAPTER IX.

Retirement of M. Dourille—The new committee—A few words upon secret agents—New orders of the day—Honorable proceedings of M. Delessert—The communists of Toulouse—A delegate sent to Paris—Simplicity of the *Icarians*—M. Flocon becomes a committeeman of the *New Seasons*—Review of the groups . . 309

CHAPTER X.

History of the establishment of the *Reform*—Tyranny exercised over M. E. Baune—The poor M. Grandménil—M. Flocon becomes dictator of the Journal. 319

CHAPTER XI.

Don Quixote-Lagrange—His great enterprises—His decadence—The rather queer but very edifying commercial transactions of M. Caussidière 324

CHAPTER XII.

The democratic press before February—The *National* and M. Marrast—The man who never pays his debts, and the toothless lion—The *Charivari*—M. Altaroche—M. Albert Clerc—M. Félix Pyat . 333

CHAPTER XIII.

Systematic enfeeblement of the *Seasons*—A new committee—Messrs. Caussidière, Léoutre, Grandménil, Leroux—An effort at reorganization—The reason of its failure—An extraordinary contest . 340

CHAPTER XIV.

Continuation of the history of the *Reform*—The Polish subscription—The talents of M. Caussidière—Impuissance of the journal . 346

CHAPTER XV.

M. Albert becomes one of the committee—Orders of the day abolished—The dissenting society—Its chiefs—Patriotic theft—Another dismemberment—A plan of insurrection 353

CHAPTER XVI.

The bomb plot—M. Caussidière forms a revolutionary congress—The check given him—Interview of members of the congress with M. Ledru-Rollin—Their disappointment—Portrait of M. Ledru-Rollin 361

CHAPTER XVII.

Profiles in charcoal—Messrs. Proudhon, Louis Blanc, Considérant, Thoré, Sarrut, Miot, Xavier Durrieu, Bareste . . . 370

CHAPTER XVIII.

The effective strength of the republican party in the beginning of 1848—The bourgeoisie and the royalty of July . . . 382

CHAPTER XIX.

The banquets—What the republicans first thought of them—Great wrath of the Left—The banquet of the twelfth arrondissement—The disdain of the *Reform*—Assembling of the students—The decision that they came to—The committee of the banquet—The backing out of the Left 389

CHAPTER XX.

State of the public mind on the 21st of February—A council of war held at the *Reform*—The strange opinions of M. Louis Blanc, and M. Ledru-Rollin—A wonderful decision—The revolution is a trick of the police 400

CHAPTER XXI.

The *Dissenting Society* begins the movement—The morals of this Society—Scenes at the *Place de la Concorde*—The gamins of Paris—Barricades—An attempt at assassination—Opinion of the chiefs—Council of war—Pillage—A conflagration—Result of the day of the 22d 410

CHAPTER XXII.

The intrigue of the *Reform*—All the patriots don the uniform of the National Guards—The bourgeoisie of the *Siècle*—Disastrous mediation—The *Seasons* in the boulevard of Saint Martin—Arms given!—M. Albert accused of treason—Concession to the revolt . . 419

CHAPTER XXIII.

Ferocity—The popular wolf let loose in Paris—The *Reform* and the *National* organize a catastrophe—A seditious peregrination—M. Lagrange—The pistol-shot of the Boulevard des Capucines . 426

CHAPTER XXIV.

The course that ought to have been pursued on the 24th—Hesitation at the barricades—Royalty takes measures for safety—General Bedeau—Disastrous concession—The Hôtel-de-Ville taken—Combat of the Palais-Royal—Heroism and ferocity—Scene at the Tuileries—Abdication—The palace abandoned 436

CHAPTER XXV.

The true heroes of 1848—The nomination of three Provisional Governments 449

CHAPTER XXVI.

The Hôtel-de-Ville—The delegates of the people—A new provisional government—General Lagrange—The prefecture of police—M. Sobrier—The companions of the prefect—Order for the arrest of the Duchess of Orleans—Organization of the Montagnards . . 459

CHAPTER XXVII.

Records of the prefecture—The secret tribunal of the Luxembourg—The eight barrelled revolver—Poison—Orgies at the Luxembourg—The band of the Tuileries—Finale 471

INTRODUCTION.

It is not by concealing our errors that we avoid the commission of new ones; nor can anything be gained from their concealment—not even the lesson which they teach.

Let us, then, admit, that if the party of order had remained true to itself on the 24th of February [1848], and had presented its resistance like a wall of brass to the popular avalanche, nothing would have been lost, not even after the evacuation of the Tuileries, the complete occupation of Paris, and the proclamation of the Republic. Had a firm and decided declaration of the fundamental principles of the monarchy been made, and a military chief appointed to rally the troops who were deeply chagrined by the insolence of their pretended conquerors, nothing more would have been necessary to have determined the provinces to a movement which would have nipped the reckless insurrection of the capital in the bud. But this would have been civil war, it is said; let us, however, give things their true names, and it would have been a revolt suppressed; it would have been a country wrested from a degrading invasion; it would have been the principle of authority saved from a shipwreck without example, and perhaps without remedy.

The mob, on the faith of their Fontanaroses, may magisterially declare that all the men of order are cowards, and that the mere presence of republicans has sufficed to reduce them to submission; but that is an old story. How was it in June, 1848, when the insurrectionists were ten times more numerous than they had been in February; when nothing failed them, neither organization, nor chiefs, nor material means; when General Cavaignac had allowed them to take the advantage of ground, and to get more than half a day's start in their works of attack; when Paris had been dismantled of its troops, and all authority deprived of its moral force; when, in fine, never had a more favorable opportunity been left to a sedition—how was it then? Why, this party of order, which is so cowardly, seized the insurrection by the throat and strangled it at once; and it was because, having learned their power, they doubted not their right, and were animated by a profound concern for the dangers of society. In February all this was wanting; for, previous to the insurrection of February, for a period of fifteen years, the party of order had never made a test of their strength. The elections having been exceedingly restricted, it was impossible to ascertain positively the real opinion of the country; and it was imagined that France, having been quietly republicanized, was giving an expression of long cherished wishes, in the execution of which she had become resolved and determined. And, above all, there was not the least suspicion of the horrible evils that were preparing for us. Other and more powerful causes, moreover, tended to the demoralization of the masses; among which may be mentioned the defection of M. de Lamartine, who, in offering the Republic to the bourgeoisie, inspired them with a confidence which was due rather to their respect for his character than to their appreciation of that form of government; and then, as to the provinces, the idea prevailed there that the triumph of the revolt in Paris had arisen from an irresistible fact of war—from a battle in which the authorities had been overwhelmed.

Now although all these causes are known by our statesmen, yet they have not been brought to the knowledge of the people, and it is proper that every one should understand them. It is not imagined that an occurrence like that of the 24th of February will ever take place again, and for the excellent reason that the admiration of the spectators will never become so inordinate as to task the performers of such a farce with the necessity of a repetition: but it must not be inferred, therefore, that all danger is past, and that there is no longer need of our care and attention. As a principal condition of success against every renewed attempt on the part of demagogues, we must have confidence in ourselves and that serenity which is the attribute of confidence; and then, should occasion call, with well understood unanimity, we must seize the musket and rush to the fight. Let no one trust to his neighbor; for if his neighbor should do the same, the enemy will remain master of the ground. As to the departments, it has become their sacred duty, when men offer them a new form of government, to reply—We don't know you; then to form their battalions immediately, hasten to the capital, and suppress the revolution. In this way the success of the anarchists would be rendered impossible; for they become formidable only from the negligence or indecision of the friends of order.

There are certain logicians who will tell us that all this is useless; that revolutions are the result of ideas which have arrived at the point of practical execution, and that, like steam, they burst the vessel in which they were contained. This comparison appears sufficiently just; but the true inferences to be derived from it are quite different from those intended. For if a revolution is compared to a bursting boiler, then the results in both cases ought to be the same, viz: carnage and ruin. But is the bursting of the boiler in fact anything but an accident? There was a flaw in the metal or in the constitution; the conductor of the machinery, either industrial, mechanical, or governmental, was guilty of a moment's negligence; the boiler burst—and, what does that prove? Why nothing, unless it is that by a more careful choice of materials and greater attention on the part of agents, the catastrophe may be avoided. The comparison of the boiler is really then not a bad one; for the nicest pieces of mechanism, as well as the most admirable institutions, are destroyed solely either from some little defect or from the imprudence which we have just mentioned.

Of one thing we may rest assured, that the greater part of our revolutions signify nothing. Our barricades are no more the expression of the national will, than is the poisoned cup of the Russian or the bowstring of the Turk. Unexpected and astounding events take place; the first come are the first served; the mob of Paris, delighted with every change, cries Bravo! the bewildered provinces allow things to take their course, and the *Moniteur* proclaims that a great act of national sovereignty has been accomplished. Between a king of France thus crushed beneath barricades, and a strangled sultan, or a poisoned czar, we ask where is the difference? If it exists at all, it is only in this, that in Turkey or Russia the conspirators who destroy the incumbents of sovereignty, become themselves the inheritors of its power, whereas, those among us who inherit the power are never those by whom that power is overthrown.

The revolution of Thermidor, which drowned the terrorists in a sea of blood of their own digging, is the only one of our revolutions which entire France has applauded. The one which has been the most national bears the date of 1789; not that it was unmixed with disadvantages, for it deprived the laboring classes of those guaranteed securities of well-being which they have never recovered since; but it placed influence and power where they rightly belong, in the bosom of the nation.

The Directory, the Consulate, the Empire, were all the consequences of the revolution of Thermidor. If the Empire went too far in acts of repression, it was only because '93 had run too far into license; for a reaction will as surely transcend its just limits as the ball will rebound. The Committee of Public Safety gave us the manners of bedlamites, while, on the other hand, the Directors gave us those of an Aspasia. Robespierre inundated the country with demoralizing newspapers, and Napoleon restricted the action of the press, even at a time when there was no longer any occasion for it, for it had done its work. Without responding to an absolute necessity, the Empire frankly met and satisfied the necessity of the times.

What was the revolution of March, 1814, and that of June, 1815? Mere caprices. The lower class adored Napoleon; the middle class loved him, and the old aristocracy respected him; but notwithstanding all this, and even at the very time while he is fighting like a lion in his prodigious campaign of France, the gates of Paris are thrown open to the allies. The battle of Waterloo finally takes place, and France looks on trembling with anxiety; the prayers of every one accompany that man of genius during the fight; but he falls, and the wave closes over him forever. A few months after, in his exile, three or four soldiers are the only courtiers left to him of his once imperial estate.

France, it is said, had become tired out; her sacrifices were too frequent and too great. What was she tired of? Of imposts and taxes? The Emperor compelled the enemy to pay the expenses of war. Was she tired of furnishing soldiers? Is France ever tired of that? No; the truth is that Napoleon had ceased to be the representative of the great middle class of the nation, that class which is not averse to war in its proper time, but which, above all others, is addicted to peace. Napoleon had come to be regarded by them as a man of eternal warfare. Nevertheless, this man in his last struggles had become identified with our national independence, and every body felt it an imperative duty to prevent his fall. There was not a soul who did not entertain this idea; there was not one who could conceal a blush at the idea of his natal soil being invaded; but nevertheless Napoleon was abandoned, and Europe rushed down like an avalanche upon him and upon France.

But is the nation to blame for his fall? Has she coldly surrendered to annihilation that man who had raised her to a height of grandeur and glory above that of all other nations? Alas! she repented her of her act as soon as it was done. What then is the mystery of this immortal drama? It is a love affair—a mistress, in a moment of coldness, abandons her dying lover, and receives in return a legacy of despair!

But under the Restoration we enjoyed a noble and dignified peace. Those Bourbons who returned to France in the suite of the allies, by whom they were little cared for, knew how, under all circumstances, to maintain a favorable position in the face of Europe. They were moreover fond of the arts, of grandeur and display, which, to the people of France, are matters of necessity. It could not be said of them that they were bad men possessed of the instincts of tyranny; for their manners were mild, and their dispositions generous and loyal. The last king of the oldest branch of the family, a serious, pious, and chivalric old man, could not have failed to do honor to the throne by the qualities of his heart. But on one fine day he was overthrown, because, forsooth, being careful of his power, and believing that the design was to ruin it, or usurp it, he took some means to protect it. Paris, like an uplifted hammer, ever ready to strike against any power legitimate or not, fell upon the old king, and he sank to rise no more.

Without doubt the printers, the journalists, the getters up of agitation, and all that class of men must suffer a few stringent ordinances on the return of the Bourbons, but then that real France which is composed of a rural population, and of those industrious laborers of the cities—all those in fine who either repose after their labor, or labor in search of repose, those calm and serious men who look upon life through a different medium than that presented by the impure columns of daily papers—all that class of persons never demanded the fall of a family which they regarded as the very incarnation of the national sovereignty.

It is true that, besides the pretext of offensive ordinances, there prevailed the false idea that the allies had come into France at the call of the Bourbons; and to this was added the fact that the power which had been placed in the hands of the aristocracy was not consistent with the idea of '89. But was the revolution of February brought about on account of these considerations? Not at all; for it is only Paris, and always Paris that, at a signal given, by no matter whom, and against no matter what, rushes into the streets, intoxicates itself with powder and blood, and stops only when everything is overthrown, pavements, positions, and power.

This part which Paris plays, destroying from the mere pleasure of destruction, and then imposing her work upon France, and striking every surrounding state with the terror of its consequences, is the most lamentable fact of contemporaneous history; and it has become a question of the gravest importance to ascertain how long the worthy people of the capital, the inhabitants of the provinces, and the states of Europe, are to be held at the mercy of these workshops of insurrection, which lie in the suburbs of Paris.

The fall of the Empire was the work of caprice, and the fall of the Restoration the result of a fit of passion. Neither of these acts was the consequence of a fixed determination of the country.

They who are considered the ablest of historians, generally give us the philosophy of every important event; and though with the best disposition in the world to follow their example, it would yet be impossible to discover any trace of philosophy in many of the astonishing events that occur among us. It is a sad fact, it must be confessed, for the honor of humanity, but a fact, nevertheless, which confirms this celebrated saying, that, though man acts, it is God who leads him—a saying, by the way, that was uttered by Fenelon, and not by Bossuet, as M. Louis Blanc has it.

The old dynasty having disappeared, a new one arose in its place. It was of the same family, but with antecedents, character, and tastes quite different. It represented as nearly as practicable that portion of the nation which is called the bourgeoisie, and which might truly be termed the heart of the people; for it is a common centre which stimulates with the healthy energies of life the members of the community which are above it, as well as those which are below. The mind of France naturally conformed to the course of things; an inclination to peace began to take the place of a fondness for war; to our military enthusiasm there succeeded the sober work of developing the material resources of the country. Everything which could tend to this result, necessarily imposed upon us by the condition of things in Europe, found example and encouragement in our new reigning family, which was renowned for its love of order, moderation, and peace. The gypsy vagabonds of society; the men who live by the groans which they utter upon the miseries of the people; the rampant apostles of the mob; all that race who work the mines of ignorance by the instrumentality of falsehood and deception; all this class of men saw at a glance that their reign was threatened. And what a howl did they not set up against the new power! With what furious and incessant attacks did they not assail it! But from open struggles they finally felt compelled to resort to murder and assassination, until at length, rejected by the disapprobation of the country, they drew off their forces and disappeared amidst the impenetrable shades of oblivion. For a period of twelve years, their existence was never disclosed, except by a few attempts at revolt, which were so feeble as to excite rather pity than contempt; and they were dead at last—stone dead.

Freed from this incumbrance, society renewed its work. Our workshops opened their doors, our storehouses were filled, and our widely disseminated products inundated Europe and covered the globe. A general increment of well-being showed itself at every turn; and even the poorest of the poor began to conceive the flattering ideas of a better fortune. But, unfortunately, among the idle and worthless, these ideas excited nothing but criminal hopes. For, let us not deceive ourselves, this socialism, as it is called, does not spring from the misery of the people, but from a growing improvement in their condition. If those intermeddlers who got up the disturbances of July had not come in to trouble the working classes, these classes would have gladly followed the career of new advantages which labor opened up to them; and they would have clearly understood that therein lay their true and only emancipation, but, thanks to our evil geniuses, extravagant desires have been infused in the place of just hopes; and those men to whom society offered a fair chance of a part of its wealth, took it into their heads to seize upon everything by force.

Let us look, then, for a moment at the picture which this view of things presents us. We see the royalty of the new dynasty enthroned amidst the national riches. Renowned throughout the world for its wisdom, it is bound to the country by a community of manners, instincts, and interests. The king, himself, is in fact only the first citizen among a great nation of citizens. He is surrounded by a family of princes, young, simple minded, brave, and intelligent, whose nobility is rather an attribute of their personal character than of their exalted rank. The factious, tired out by their useless efforts, have fallen at his feet powerless and desperate. His power seems to be unshakable. But all of a sudden there comes a storm—a gust—a flurry—a puff of wind; a few battalions of the National Guard raised the cry of reform! and this king, who seemed so powerful, is seized with a vertigo; he thinks that the whole class of the bourgeoisie have deserted him; he gives up in despair and falls—leaving a handful of republicans in the attitude of having hurled him from his throne.

Every attempt at giving a philosophical explanation of such a fact as this, must, of course, prove fruitless. We have said that the insurrection of 1814 was a caprice, and that that of 1830 was a fit of passion; but as to this of 1848, what can it be called but a political trick?

In conclusion, the reader will please understand that though I speak in all freedom of the actors in our revolutions, I do not intend thereby to strike at the existing Republic. On the contrary, I refrain not only from insulting, but even from treating as they deserve those men who, composing only a small faction before the affair of February, have, nevertheless, for a space of eighteen years, infested society with their pernicious schemes of insurrection and blood. I intend to show, as clearly as possible, how the existing Republic has been brought about, how many partisans it had, and by what artifices and by what men it has been planned, and sprung upon us; for I have a *"right"* to do this, and I choose to exercise my right. That the affair of February, however, appears to me perfectly inexplicable, is true; and that it will appear so to the public from the details which I shall give, is highly probable; but that is not my fault. The moment has arrived for telling the truth, and it offers us a lesson full of instruction. The times of gagging and fear which were imposed upon us by the demagogues have passed away, and one may venture to express his sentiments freely without being gagged as a traitor.

I submit with all due loyalty to the existing form of government; but as no one is *obliged*, so far as I know, to fall desperately in love with a very ugly woman who may have been imposed upon him in marriage, I shall not, therefore, probably become very much smitten with the Republic. I am ready to respect her, however, if she deserves it, as a legitimate connection.

HISTORY

OF

SECRET SOCIETIES.

BOOK I.

CHAPTER I.

Enumeration of the elements which constitute the mob—The students—The imbeciles—The gypsies—The sovereign people—The fly-catchers—The disaffected—Political refugees—The bandits.

WHATEVER may be done to the contrary, it is very certain that no form of government among us will ever escape the pest of conspiracies; for there is always a large class of men who think that the government under which they live is the worst one that they could have; and as these men also think that all our insurrections have been the work of secret societies, these societies are hence held by them in very particular esteem.

But, in fact, not one of our revolutions, during the last sixty years, has been the work of conspirators. However blasphemous this assertion may appear to the grumblers of the mob, we hold it to be irrefragably true.

There is but one maker of revolutions in France, and that is Paris; idle, sophistical, disappointed, restless, evil-minded Paris. We all know her. But this Paris does not overthrow the government on a fixed day, and according to a settled plan; for every time she takes the initiative she is crushed at once. Witness the affair of June, 1832; of May, 1839;

and several other similar affrays. To meet with success, it is necessary that the bourgeoisie, either in a fit of passion, as in 1830, or from a misdirection of ideas, as in 1848, should set the insurrection in motion. And above all, Providence itself must permit one of those incomprehensible contingencies—such, for instance, as that of sovereign power giving way to a revolt without the test of a combat.

This Paris, which is always lying in wait to seize power by the throat and strangle it, is composed of the following elements, viz:—

1. *The Youth of the Schools*, as they are called.—It is the nature of these gentlemen to be opposed to the government. The most of them would consider it ridiculous to have the same ideas as their neighbor, the bourgeois, who defends the existing order of things, because they give him and his family the means of an honest livelihood. And then, schoolboys, we know, are fond of noise, fracas, and sudden events, and, indeed, they expect to be recognized by such traits. Every one has heard of their traditions of the Pré aux Clercs; they are a species of puerility which would be amusing if these young men, as well by their real courage as from the prestige which is accorded them, and from the facility with which they become instruments in the hands of the factious, did not, in fact, possess a considerable weight in our revolutions. The majority of students, it is well known, are occupied in the study of law, of medicine, or some other science, and not in reforming the government at the point of the bayonet; hence, in speaking of the youth of the schools, we mean only those of whom the anarchical journals take it upon themselves to be the interested flatterers—those who parade at the clubs, political meetings, and other rude places. The students who are occupied with their studies, have never had the honor of attracting the attention of our patriot editors.

The youth of the schools have their chiefs; some of whom have never taken the papers, and others have ceased to take them for the last ten years, for they go directly to the *pure* fountain-head, to the offices of the papers themselves, and there receive their instructions. When an order of the day is given, they hasten to all the estaminets in the Latin quarter of the town, where they are sure to meet with their fellows—some of the youths of the schools frequent such places, too; the leaders resort thither, also, and then are distributed those documents which, at one and the same time, enlighten the faithful, and invite the curious.

Rumors have spread, that the schools are to be removed beyond the limits of Paris; and it is certain that the government might thus cut off *one* of the arms of the insurrectional Briareus. The English, who have a genius for order and public tranquillity, have long since excluded from their capital this interesting but rather dangerous portion of the community. Besides the political question involved, it is a sufficient reason for the government, that those students who now spend their time at billiards, or in revolutionary manœuvres, would be much better off in the provinces, under the eyes of their parents, than at Paris; and that those who really wish to devote themselves to study, have no need of the too numerous distractions of the capital.

2. *The Imbeciles.*—In this class are included lawyers without clients, doctors without patients, writers without readers, merchants without customers, and all that troup of hopeful men, who, having studied their parts in the politics of the newspapers, aspire to enact them as men of the State. Some few of them are indeed capable of the posts to which they aspire, but they find it intolerable to arrive at them like the rest of the crowd, by diligence and perseverance. Others of their number are not capable, and these are by far the most ardent and ambitious. They are all imbecile, for they fail in the first evidence of strength, which is patience. The organizers of secret societies, and schemers of insurrection, come from this class.

3. *The Gypsies.*—These exist everywhere, and, especially among us—a class of imaginative persons, who have an utter horror of ordinary life. The generality of mortals usually understand that pleasure and repose are the rewards only of labor and privation; but the gypsies expect never to work,

and always to enjoy. As this kind of life, however, in order to be conveniently practised, requires some fat rents, which they have not, they are obliged to have recourse to the expedient of establishing a sort of vagrancy, of which the obscurest estaminets become the courts of miracles. The provinces count but a few of these individuals; for they generally alight upon the capital, the only place where idleness flourishes, and where certain wickednesses thrive at their ease. To determine from what quarter this variety of the social world comes, is not easy; it comes, from no matter where, from the highest as well as the lowest. Some few of them remain very nearly honest men, especially if they are not of too excitable a temperament, or are wanting in the courage of crime; but the greater part of them have the instincts of debauchees, which they gratify at all hazards.

It is in this class that are found the chiefs of sections, the commandants of barricades, etc.

4. *The Sovereign People*—that is to say, the workmen of Paris, either native or those who have become acclimated in the suburbs.—Brave by nature, and a fighter by habit, the workman expects to make a fortune out of every political tumult. A lofty sentiment of independence, acquired by the reading of revolutionary rhapsodies, renders him impatient of the restraints of authority. He never likes the master by whom he is employed, generally detests all others; and the rich and the dignitaries of the government he considers himself bound to execrate. This is not a mere portrait of our own inventing, for M. Louis Blanc, who will recognize some of his own workmanship in it, declares that the people is gross and brutal. Now there is but one people for M. Louis Blanc, and men of his like, and that people is the people of Paris. This organizer of labor adds, it is true, that it is not the fault of the people that they are so. Agreed. But it is something very astonishing, that with two such important qualities, courage and intelligence, the people of Paris should remain so deplorably deficient in polish. Those socialists who are candid, frankly confess the fact, and if they would

open their eyes and confess the whole truth, they would acknowledge that they themselves are the cause of it.

It is useless to deny that this workman, gross, brutal, quarrelsome, ignorant of his duty, in opposition always to the law, is not in the majority in Paris; we mean, of course, of those who are wheedled by the patriots—those who are told, and really believe it themselves, that they alone are the masters of the destinies of the country.

5. *The Fly-Catchers.*—This is a class of persons who are rather to be pitied than condemned. They are good men at bottom, but they listen to M. Bareste, maker of almanacs, who tells them that the country is horribly governed; to M. Proudhon, that detestable mystifier, who tells them that property is theft; to M. Ledru-Rollin, a millionaire overwhelmed with debts, who tells them that the patriots are dying from hunger. Through foolish or shameless newspapers, they are made to see every day that black is white, and white black; the same falsehood presented in a hundred different ways, the same deception practised in a hundred different forms, is offered to them every morning, in the most natural manner in the world—with the most perfect air of assurance; the friends are near to support the cause; the papers of the opposite opinion are never read, because *they are sold;* if good advice happens to be given, *that* comes from a renegade or a spy; and thus a large mass of honest men give themselves up to foolish schemes, harassing miserably their own lives, and those of others. From the National Guard which introduces the Republic with the shout of "Hurrah for reform!" down to the innocent citizen who swallows everything that is told him, they are Fly-Catchers, political and socialist, from every class of society, and of every shade and variety of color and complexion.

These honest souls serve as the lever, as the plastron, or as the make-weights of the revolutions.

6. *The Disaffected.*—This class, also, is composed of an infinitude of elements; but we design especially to speak of those persons who, by the fall of former governments, have been injured either in their fortunes or affections. They

never take a part in the insurrection as mere common soldiers; some are led into it for the sake of excitement, and others for a consideration. These latter, men practised in the routine of political life, are too skilful to leave any traces of their manœuvres. Instructions, advice, material aid, everything of this kind, reaches its destination among them only from the third or fourth person. The police alone has been able to follow this train of bribes and intrigues into its obscure shades; but thus far it has seldom been able to detect the plotters in the fact.

These men, who are the very leprosy of the body politic, are incontestably the most dangerous of all others to every government.

7. *Political Refugees.*—This class of men is a virus with which France has become inoculated, and which adds to her revolutionary maladies. The abettors of revolt from all countries, drawn among us by an imprudent generosity on our part, are constantly busied in fomenting insurrections; knowing well that a disturbance in France is a signal to other countries.

8. *The Bandits.*—The social condition of a country is always very much disturbed during revolutionary times, and it is then, in particular, that malefactors have rare picking. A few good men, it is true, during the disturbances of February, posted up notices of—"Death to Robbers!" but this did not prevent the Duchess of Orleans' shawls from being stolen, nor the wine-casks of M. Duchatel from being emptied, nor the jewels of the family of Orleans from being sold throughout Europe. That some few of the mob endeavored to preserve the police cannot be denied; we render justice to whom it is due. But what a fine pretension is here set up! Ah! we must know these fellows who live upon the wealth of others. No sooner does the disturbance break forth, than, seized with patriotic zeal, they rush with a lantern in one hand and a musket in the other, demanding only to be posted at the best places, reserving the time and mode of action to themselves.

But robbers are not the only ones who profit by an insurrection. There are a few well-meaning men, it is true, who, after having shouted, "Hurrah for the charter! Hurrah for reform!" and having borne the brunt of the fight, then withdraw, in all the pride of integrity, to die in their garrets; but there are some very accomplished rascals, on the other hand, who, when the revolution is over, are found living in comfortable ease on their suddenly acquired rents. Indeed, it is beyond a doubt that the thieves, robbers, and assassins of Paris never fail to furnish some of the *heroes* of our revolutions.

Such, then, are the eight divisions of the forces which are usually employed in an insurrection. Sometimes they may be seen all assembled together; but this depends upon circumstances; for, if the affair appears to be badly managed, some of the forces draw off, but when things take a favorable turn, and success seems probable, then the whole army may be found drawn up in line.

CHAPTER II.

The Carbonari.

FROM what has been said, an idea may be formed of the sphere in which the revolutionary influence usually operates. But the whole of the revolutionists, it will be understood, do not take a part in conspiracies, for many of them are deterred, either from fear or a want of confidence in success. I have said, in another place, in substance, that secret societies may raise a mob, but can never accomplish a revolution.

Not being much inclined, myself, to retrospective science, it appears to me that any attempts at systematizing history, such as are made by certain writers, would be but so much time thrown away; for, though mere ideas may be combined and arranged according to pleasure, yet stubborn facts admit only of a combination which is peculiar to themselves. Hence, in taking up the clue, such as it is, of our modern conspiracies, I do not propose to go further back than the affair of July, 1830.

There is, however, one secret society of the period of the Restoration, which must be taken into consideration, because it has become pretty directly enlinked with those of modern times. I allude to the Carbonari.

About the year 1820, two young men, whose first appearance upon the political stage was not made till 1848, Messrs. Buchez and Fottard, assisted by two others—Messrs. Bazard and Joubert—established, with the name of *The Friends of Truth*, a masonic lodge, the object of which was wholly political. It had nothing to do with socialism or republicanism; for these matters, at that time, were but little thought of. The leading idea of these young men was, firstly, to play a part, and, secondly, to upset the government of the Bourbons. What kind of government they would have established in the place of the one which they intended to overthrow, was not fully settled; but, as the prestige of Napoleon was then at its height, we may suppose that Napoleon II. would have been placed upon the throne.

The *Friends of Truth* were the sons of citizens, students, clerks, artists, etc. In their meetings they declaimed a great deal, and especially against the Bourbons, who had been returned to them, they said, in the baggage-wagons of the enemy. The government might easily have refuted a charge of this kind by the fact, that the restoration of the Bourbons was but little in accordance with the wishes of the Allies; that Austria was interested in preserving the throne to the son of one of her arch-duchesses; that the Emperor Alexander had no desire to despoil the son of a man of whom he was a great admirer; that Prussia had no other design than that of prostrating Napoleon, and that, in fine, the reinstallation of the Bourbons was the result of a great and sudden necessity of public order, precisely as was the elevation to power of Louis Napoleon, on the 10th of December. But, as all these arguments were not offered, the speakers and writers were left a fine chance to denaturalize facts and excite the passions.

The career of the *Friends of Truth*, though not very illustrious, was signalized by a single event. The Chamber of Deputies was discussing the law of elections (on which occasion, the opposition press declared that the charter was violated, for violations of the Constitution had already become the fashionable slang of the day), and the minds of men, and the streets of the capital, were buzzing with rumors, when the lodge conceived the occasion a favorable one for making its appearance. It assembled its members, besieged the Chamber, and filled the air with their cries of "Hurrah for the charter!" Some young men of family being informed of what was going on, and thinking it proper to take upon themselves the championship of good order, assailed the mob with their canes. In the scuffle which ensued, a young man by the name of Lallemand was killed.

This death became the subject of recriminations fruitful beyond conception. The newspapers; the speakers of the Chamber; all those men who make it a business to abuse the authorities; all those who believe whatever is told them, raised a concert of croaking, the echoes of which were repeated and prolonged till the very last days of the Restoration. The unfortunate Lallemand, whose death was very much to be regretted, without doubt, but who was killed in a mob, nevertheless, became one of the phantoms which the opposition for fifteen years conjured up, on all occasions, to the eyes of the Bourbons.

In this, one of their last spasms, the *Friends of Truth* nearly terminated their existence. And we shall see in the sequel, that every one of the secret societies has met with the same fate, coming to its end after a fruitless attempt. Like wasps, they leave their sting and die. However, the conspirators themselves are not got rid of so easily; from an old conspiracy they proceed to a new one.

As a result of the prosecution of the *Friends of Truth*, Messrs. Joubert and Dugied, being forced to expatriate themselves, sought refuge in Naples; and, as usual with refugees, they became instrumental in the troubles of the country which offered them an asylum. The city being in a state of insurrection, they mingled in its revolts; but without preventing, however, the disaster that befell the descendants of Masaniello. Not knowing where to bend their steps, they returned again to their own country, upon which they wished to bestow their valuable services.

M. Dugied, during his stay in Naples, had been initiated into the mysteries of the Carbonari, and he conceived the idea of applying this association to France. Having, therefore, made known his views to M. Flottard, they decided upon carrying them into an immediate execution, and to take as a nucleus the remnants of the *Friends of Truth*. With some few indispensable modifications of the Italian society, the organization was arranged upon the following plan :—

An upper lodge (vente), central lodge, and special lodge.

The upper lodge was the committee of direction and action: everything centred there, and became subordinate by the following combinations :—

Two members of the committee, having found an adept, came to an understanding with him without disclosing their connection with the committee, and agreed to form a lodge. The adept was named president, one of the initiators, censor, and the other a deputy. The part of the deputy was to correspond with the committee, giving the president to understand that this committee was only a superior degree of the society. The part of the censor was to inspect the labors of the lodge. These three chiefs took to themselves seventeen recruits, which raised the number of the members to twenty. Thus constituted, this group was called a central lodge. Two members of this lodge, proceeding in the same way that we have just described, formed a lodge, which was called a special lodge of the first order, and this lodge, repeating the operation, formed an ordinary special lodge, thus extending their ramifications without limit.

To make the explanation clearer, perhaps, conceive a tree bottom upwards; the trunk is the upper lodge, the branches are the central lodge, the twigs the special lodge of the first order, and the buds the special ordinary lodge.

An organization identical with this, but under different

names, was adapted to the army. The upper lodge was called the legion; the central lodge, cohortes; the special lodge of the first order, centuries, and the special ordinary lodges, maniples.

The object of this double form of organization was to throw the police off the scent by making them believe that there was a distinct and separate society in the army. As another measure of precaution, it was prohibited to every member, *under the pain of death*, to become affiliated in any other lodge than the one to which he belonged; for by entering into a considerable number of the lodges, a member might discover and make known the secrets of the society. All the lodges were to operate in unison, but without being aware of it, under one and the same controlling power.

The Carbonari had no fixed principles; they received men of all opinions, provided that these opinions tended to the fall of the Bourbons. However, two important nuclei became separated from their midst; the imperialists and the liberals. The character of the first is sufficiently defined by their name; the second were the sons of citizens, animated against the government by the patriotism of youth, and the jealousy of class; wishing, in fact, only to get possession of the titles or the influence of the old families. As to what is called the people, they were not known among the Carbonari; for the illustrious part which has been attributed to them in our days, had not yet been invented.

The object to be attained appeared rather vague to some of the members; but the means to be employed were clear to all; they were to cover France with a multitude of small detachments of the main army, which, at a signal given by an invisible power, were to rush in from all quarters and crush the Bourbons. In order to be always in readiness for action, every member, after having given his oath of implicit obedience, was bound to furnish himself with a musket and fifty cartridges.

At the origin of the society, the upper lodge consisted only of seven members: Messrs. Dugied, Flottard, Bazard, Buchez, Joubert, Cariol and Limperani; four of whom, we find, had been chiefs of the *Friends of Truth*. And we shall often meet with cases in the sequel, of this shifting of the conspirators from one society to another. At every period of disturbance, all the disorder hinges upon some two or three dozens of such incorrigible ringleaders, whom the government, if it does not wish to be destroyed itself, ought to have learned by this time to get rid of at once.

The Carbonari having grown to a considerable extent, the upper lodge thought that it would be useful to add to their number some persons of distinction; for by extending their organization to men of character, they would add to their strength, and diminish their responsibility. General Lafayette, who preserved till his last days an itching for popularity which was perfectly juvenile, accepted the offer which they made him of being misled into the conspiracy; and his example was followed by several deputies.

Towards the close of the year 1821 the society recapitulated its forces; and it was found that in Paris, the young men of the schools, the clerks, and the sons of citizens generally, having been unremittingly worked upon, had become initiated in the lodges in large numbers. In the provinces, the principal cities, such as Bordeaux, Nantes, Toulouse, La Rochelle, Poitiers, Colmar, Béfort, etc., all had their affiliated battalions. The zeal of the members arose to the highest pitch, and the inspectors who visited the lodges found them almost all armed, and waiting only for the signal of attack.

The committee, then, decided that the attack should be made; but the majority having resolved to commence by a *coup-de-main*, Paris was thus deprived of the initiative, and the dangerous honor of beginning the affair was accorded to Béfort. Some forty resolute young men were dispatched thither with the mission of organizing the uprising and assuming the direction of it.

In order to be prepared for every contingency, and according to the classical usages in such cases, a provisional government was appointed; and Messrs. Lafayette, de Corcelles, senior, Yoyez-d'Argenson, Dupont (de l'Eure) and Koecklin, were presented in advance with the spoils of power. But the skins of a great many unkilled lions have been divided in the same way before.

To do General Lafayette justice, although he was led into these sad affairs by flatteries addressed to his self-love, yet in the part which he took in them he was governed by a perfect sincerity. Hence, when informed that his presence was necessary at Béfort in order to set things agoing, he set out immediately. But from a rather singular circumstance, however, he did not arrive in the evirons of Béfort until the moment when, after a miserable affray, his accomplices were making their escape in a general disbandment. Judging that every effort to rally this fugitive army would be useless, he wheeled about and returned to Paris. The government allowed his conduct to pass unnoticed.

M. Flottard had been appointed chief of the movement of the west, which was to break out in La Rochelle; but every thing terminated there as it did in the east—in a fruitless attempt, which, being known in advance, was suppressed at once.

And happy would it have been if this double check had opened the eyes of the younger chiefs of the upper lodges, and convinced the oldest members of their madness and folly. The police had an eye upon all their movements and an ear in all their meetings; and every attempt at an insurrection led to a catastrophe. We are aware that some of the old Carbonari relate with much complacency that the secrets of the lodges were admirably kept, although confided to so large a number of young men; and we have no desire to dissipate their pleasant illusions; but unfortunately history is rather against them. At Béfort, the commandant Foustain had been so well prepared beforehand that he was able to crush the insurrection at its very birth; at Nantes, General Despinois followed step by step the proceedings of General Berton, and the plot of Colonel Caron for delivering up the general was baffled before its execution. And besides, the *Moniteur* states that M. Grandménil (who afterwards established the *Reform*, and played a part in the affair of February) passed as one of the denouncers of the conspiracy, while it is well known that in the Chamber of Deputies he was considered as one of its instigators.

M. Flottard resolved to have satisfaction for his failure; he hastened to Paris, declared the check at La Rochelle a matter of no consequence, and announced that if he were permitted to have the assistance of some person of distinction, he would engage to arouse the West. General Lafayette, rather ashamed of having arrived too late the first time, offered his services again, and promised this time to be more punctual. He was thanked for his zeal, but his services were not accepted. M. Flottard, therefore, had to content himself with Colonel Deutzel, a notability of rather doubtful character, but who was sufficient, however, for the result as it turned out. In fact, this second expedition did not even arrive at the beginning of an execution. The grain of sand which had prevented Cromwell from upsetting the world, turned up again at La Rochelle, and prevented the conflagration of France; for as General Berton, in making his escape from the first affair, had lost his uniform, he was obliged to go to Saumur to look for it, and that took five days; but during those five days the police arrested the civil chiefs of the Carbonari on the one part, and four non-commissioned officers, chiefs of the military branch of the conspiracy, on the other. On receiving this news, M. Flottard made his escape in all haste, leaving to the sword of justice General Berton, Colonel Caron, and the four sergeants of La Rochelle.

The axe which cut off the heads of these unfortunate victims, gave also the death-blow to the society of the Carbonari.

CHAPTER III.

Scheme for expelling the deputies and peers—The republican party—Its numerical strength—Plagiarism from '93—A sketch of the popular societies after the period of July, 1830.

THOSE persons who are persuaded that the fall of every government is due to a conspiracy, will not be convinced, even at the present day, that the restoration was not overthrown by the Carbonari. But the truth is, that, with the exception of a few obstinate old men, such as M. Charles Teste, and M. Buonarotti, the Carbonari have been nearly destitute of reliable adherents and insurrectional influence ever since the year 1822. The society had nothing to do with the revolution of July.

And it cannot be claimed that any other secret societies prepared and fought the battle of the three days; for, between the times of Carbonarism and the year 1830, there is but one society—the society of *Aid-thyself*—which makes its appearance upon the scene; and as this was under the direction of Messrs. Guizot, de Broglie, etc., it will hardly be accused of conspiracy; and besides, its measures were open to every one and its object known, viz: the organization of elections.

The immediate cause of the revolution of July was a strong opposition on the part of the bourgeoisie against the influence of the aristocracy—this opposition being incidentally exasperated by the ordinances. The conflict of influences between the tradition of the old families and the liberation of the middle classes, presented a question which it was certainly very difficult to settle, but the government of the elder branch of the Bourbons was sufficiently honorable to have given the disputants a fair field if the coup d'état of the 25th of July had not cut every thing short. The middle classes did not send the workmen into the streets with the view of creating a revolution, for every day of revolution is for them a day of doubt and anxiety; they had no intention of overthrowing royalty; for they recognized royalty as a necessary part in our social mechanism; but when once engaged, they became excited with the game, and their cry for the charter became equivalent to " Down with the Bourbons."

Besides, the impulse having been once given, it was not easy to stop the movement. The young men who had become enthusiastic with the renown of the wars of the empire, rushed to arms; the imbeciles, the gypsies, the disaffected, were all agog; the workingmen of the suburbs, always ready for a fight, and the more peaceable workingmen who had been discharged by their employers, swelled the throng, and an overthrow was the consequence, of which, however, the bourgeoisie were the cause—which the bourgeoisie alone had commenced and directed, but which, after all, the bourgeoisie did not desire.

These things appear strange and unaccountable; but they are not the only example which we have of such incredible inconsistency.

It will be astonishing to some, perhaps, and even some may be indignant that we do not give the republicans a place in the line of battle of the three days; but let them have a little patience, and we shall come, in due time, to speak of the republicans; it would not be proper to hurry these heroes upon the stage before they had donned their uniforms. Every body knows that the republicans, at that day, formed but a very small and insignificant party, both at Paris and in the provinces; and hence it is impossible that their influence could have been very great in the affair of July. However, it must be confessed, that the few republicans who were actually then in existence, made themselves very busy, both during and after the fight.

The democrats are not proverbial for their modesty; and no sooner had the fight ended, than they conceived the idea that it was all their work, and that France ought to be delivered up to their sway. From a letter in the *Tribune*, we learn that Messrs. Flocon and l'Heritier (de l'Ain) were among the number of those who entertained this idea; but, as they could not make it be believed at that time, it was not till eighteen years afterwards, that M. Flocon had the good luck of becoming elevated to a membership of the government. M. l'Heritier (de l'Ain) has not yet met with much good luck, having figured thus far in the ceremonials of our republic only as one of the commission of the conquerors of February, and of the socialist committee, which has been one of the valuable results to us of the 13th of June.

We mention these two personages in particular, because the above-mentioned letter of the *Tribune* seems to have placed them in a prominent relief; but it must be admitted that a body of youths did, from that time, make a part of all the republican mobs, pursuing with fury the invasion of power.

Their first act was to demand the expulsion of the deputies and a convocation of the primary assemblies. The bourgeoisie, having become the masters, perceived clearly that the powers which had fallen into their hands, had need of some form of consecration; and justly frightened by the responsibilities of their position, their chief concern became, that authority should not be compromised by being allowed to fall into the streets. These men were, therefore, everything considered, the best representatives of the country. And why, indeed, should their quality as true representatives of the nation be annulled by the *coup de main* of Paris?

This is the way that the bourgeoisie of the country argued; but, of course, it was not much to the liking of a certain class of men who had their own reasons for demanding the vacation of power. The mode of argument of this class of men was naturally this: a violent attack has thrown Paris into commotion, and destroyed authority; hence, the only thing to be done is, to deliver up the State to those who, by surprising the city, have overthrown the government. Such is, has been, and always will be, the logic of the revolutionists. But, fortunately, this manner of looking upon this is beginning to fall into discredit.

At the close of the three days, seeing that the deputies still remained as the guardians of power, the small faction of republicans, composed of audacious and enterprising men, drew together a mob of the combatants yet reeking from the fight, and, on the 4th of August, pushed them upon the Chamber. Their object was to summon the deputies to vacate their seats, and, in case of a refusal, to put them out of doors. Three or four thousand individuals allowed themselves to be hurried away, wittingly or not, into this enterprise. Messrs. Flocon, l'Heritier, and other leaders, penetrated into the hall of Pas-Perdus, and summoned several of the members who were passing there, with all the due formality of authority; but not much attention was paid to them. Nevertheless, no inconsiderable uneasiness was felt in the hall, for fear that the crowd without might go to extremes. But the men of good faith were finally appeased by Messrs. Benjamin Constant and Lafayette, who happened to come in. As to the others, they rushed into the hall in a rage; taxed the people with cowardice if they did not turn out the deputies on the spot, and then spread themselves about in the vicinity, crying: "To arms!"

But the cry was not heeded; for though the population of Paris breaks out into sudden and unexpected fights, yet the time for these fights is neither advanced nor retarded a single moment by a call to arms.

The abortive attempt against the Chamber of Deputies was to be renewed the next day against the Chamber of Peers. The word was given to assemble at the Hôtel de Ville, and from there to march upon the Luxembourg, uttering cries in order to arouse the people. The palace was to be invaded, pillaged, and then locked up. The leaders were promptly at the rendezvous; but, unfortunately for them, as nobody else was there, the enterprise was given up.

The next attempt was by moral suasion. The republicans threatened, in a few days, to return to the Chamber with an overwhelming petition. Everything was brought in play in order to get it up—promises, management, solicitations; but after all their labors, the result was a cipher of scarcely five thousand signatures.

Now, everybody knows that after a revolution, all the partisans of the victorious cause alight at once upon the capital; not from any motives of avarice, certainly not, but for lending their valuable services to the new order of things, in the characters of prefects, receivers, justices of the peace, etc.; and hence, we may presume, that the republican party, in almost its entire strength, was then in Paris and had signed their names to the petition, and that a small body of five thousand individuals had thus endeavored to impose their wishes upon thirty-two millions of Frenchmen!

And in giving the number of republicans as five thousand, we make none of those reductions which are usually considered allowable in such cases; for we exclude neither Flycatchers, Gypsies, nor Bandits, whose names gave as much length to the petition as any others. We might then, in fact, be justified in making a very considerable reduction of this five thousand of republicans, which we are willing to admit, however, were in existence in those times.

The attack upon the Chambers commenced the series of republican complots. It was a wild, tumultuous affair, and, in some respects, one of revolutionary fervor. Although the spirit of '93 was not particularly noticeable in it, yet we shall soon see that spirit revealing itself, in a servile imitation of the peculiar mode of proceeding of that model epoch.

We are forced to confess that neither a genius for invention, any more than modesty, is a characteristic trait of the republicans. By referring to the commencement of the existing republic, we see that M. Marrast proposed to establish a kind of Venetian oligarchy, of which he hoped to become the Doge; and M. Ledru-Rollin suggested a popular democracy, of which he was to be the Danton. The latter, remaining master of the ground, set busily at work to hunt up and copy, with great care, the divers proceedings, customs, and usages, of the first period of the revolution. Except the scaffold, which fortunately has been allowed to remain in its shed, there is not a Jacobinical rag or fritter which was not turned up, not a foolish invention that has not been reproduced, even from the red cap, which signifies a great deal too much, down to the tree of liberty, which signifies nothing at all. It was not forgotten to establish by decree, not only liberty and equality, something which we may understand, but also fraternity, something which is not quite so comprehensible; for it is not easy to see how a relation or sentiment like that of fraternity, can be made the subject of an obligation or a decree. In the names of parties there was the same imitation. The famous word aristocrat, which was elongated into *aristocrusliers* by the sans-culotte of '93, became shortened into *aristos*, by the communists of 1848. The chiefs, the leading spirits of the throng, have not even been able to invent their own names. The word Montagnard, which lay rotting in blood, they gathered out from the gutters, never seeming to think that everything great and worthy is original, and that it demands, and will receive only a name peculiar to itself.

After the days of July, this imbecility, which struts in the name of tradition, appeared in the re-establishment of the clubs and popular societies; which were formed precisely upon the model of the first revolution.

The student Sambuc got up a society, which was called the *Society of Order and Progress*, rather an inappropriate title, it would seem, for every member was bound to have a musket and cartridges, things which generally have more to do with disorder than order; and as the society, wholly composed of students, intended to direct the state according to the ideas of the Latin quarter of the town, it is not easy to perceive how the state could have made much progress.

The students soon got up another society, which was directed by Messrs. Marc, Dufraisse, and Eugene l'Heritier. Its object was to abolish the University. From that time the claim was set up for a system of education, free, gratuitous, obligatory, and purely laical.

Soon afterwards appeared the *Union;* a society established with the view of compelling every one, at the point of the bayonet, to acknowledge the sovereignty of the people, as interpreted by certain bullies. But this society, in its fraternal efforts, was subject to so much *dis*-union in itself, that it died of the fits at the very commencement of its career.

Then came the society of *Political Convicts*. These consisted of men who demanded a recompense for having disturbed public order under an old form of government, thus setting an example to adventurers to pursue the same course under a new form of government, with the view of gaining the reward which the new form of government would not fail to bestow. Fieschi having presented himself to this society as a political victim, received a pension from it until the year 1834, at which period it was discovered that this rascal had been prosecuted for any other cause than that of his political opinions.

Next came the *Claimers* of July, commanded by M. O'Reilly, their number ultimately amounting to nearly five thousand. Every one of its members pretended to have displaced at least one paving stone; fancied himself the author of the revolution, and demanded a corresponding recompense. From a want of means to meet all these demands, many of them very excessive, the government had to bear the charge of the blackest ingratitude, and be threatened with the wrath of heroes yet unknown.

At the same time appeared the *Gallic Society*, whose chief was M. Thielmans. It was an association both hierarchic and armed, its designs being to overthrow the government by force.

The *Friends of the Country*, and the *Regenerated Franks*, had the same object; but these were only simple clubs, got up for gratifying the ambition of their founders.

Still another association looms up to view, called the *Constitutional Society*, designed by M. Cauchois Lemaire to operate against the heredity of the peerage; but as this was restricted to legal limits, we shall say nothing further of it.

We may mention again, also, the ancient society of *Aid Thyself*, which was continued by M. Garnier Pages. But it had no republican complexion, and its prudent course was hardly observable amidst the more turbulent proceedings of its contemporaries.

The most important association of that period was the society of the *Friends of the People*. Its influence soon extended throughout the whole republican party; by this society the party was organized, directed and kept in motion until the affair of June, 1848, when it finally disappeared in a tempest of blood. It was the successor of that masonic lodge of which we have already spoken, called the *Friends of Truth*. On parting with this lodge, we may describe its closing scene.

On the 21st of September the *Friends of Truth* presented a spectacle in the streets of Paris, which, for dramatic effect, probably stands solitary and alone. The anniversary of the execution of the four sergeants of La Rochelle having arrived, all the societies determined to celebrate it with funeral ceremonies; and the *Friends of Truth* particularly distinguished themselves on the occasion by the display which they made. They assembled at their place of meeting in the street of Grenelle-Saint-Honoré; there they arranged their programme, put on their insignia, and then proceeded in a procession to the Place de Grêve, where the four conspirators had been executed. The very venerable M. Cahaigne, covered with the insignia of his dignity, headed the procession with that very particular solemnity which his friends so much admired. During their passage the guards, yielding to the pitiable spirit of disorganization of the times, came out of their guard-houses, and, at the sound of the drum, saluted the aprons and red ribbons of the masons.

Arrived upon the Place de Grêve, the *Friends of Truth* arranged themselves in a very serious circle in the midst of a large multitude of people. There had assembled together the most of the patriots of the period, together with a very considerable contingent of the great army of simpletons of Paris. Such a spectacle as this was a little too rare not to be made the occasion of a festivity by the curious. Some orators of the old Carbonari raised their voice to celebrate the heroism of the sergeants and to curse the government, which, in executing them, had only exercised the legitimate right of self-defence. It appertained, undoubtedly, to these gentlemen, among whom we meet again with M. Buchez, to bewail the fate of their old companions; but the way they should have done it was not to glorify a crime justly punished, but to ask pardon of the shades of the four celebrated victims of whose untimely deaths their pernicious counsels had been partly the cause.

All this passed under the eye of the police, who had orders to let it go on, the prefect, M. Girod de l'Ain, having declared that he saw no objection to it.

This was the last sign of life exhibited by the *Friends of Truth;* soon afterwards it became lost in the association of the *Friends of the People.*

We are certainly indebted to a purely republican idea for the creation of this society. It was directed from its very birth against the new government, and even before, we may say, for it had made a double attempt against the national representation. The affair of July had fallen, like a bomb, in the midst of a generation of young men whose fathers had been the actors in our first political troubles. The Restoration, in finding them grown to be men, could only regard them with repugnance as the sons of revolutionists. The bourgeoisie, after the affair of July, received them with pleasure, but as these young men wished to impose upon the bourgeoisie their violent opinions, a secession became the immediate consequence. Hence, they finally fell into the hands of men who were notable on more accounts than one, and became the most dangerous characters of the opposition.

Among the chiefs, such as were the most capable or the most audacious, became distinguished at once. In their intemperate writings and speeches, they refused to recognize the new order of things, claiming the exercise of the same right by which the new government had come into power, that is, the right of revolution. The government allowed a great many attacks to pass unnoticed; but as, in fact, it was obliged to defend itself, even for the good of society, of which it was the head, it finally commenced a series of prosecutions against such transgressions as were the most gross, and against such offenders as were the most bold.

In the latter category, are included several persons whose names will be frequently met with in all the subsequent disturbances, viz: Messrs. Godefroy Cavaignac, Guinard, Marrast, Raspail, Trelat, Flocon and Blanqui, and, we may add as of secondary importance, Messrs. Antony Thouret, Charles Teste, the two Vignerte, Cahaigne, Bonnias, Bergeron, Imbert, Fortoul, Delescluze, Felix Avril, etc., being almost all young men without position in society, who took up at that time the business of agitators, and have not abandoned it since. The most of them were writers of greater or less ability, and the poison that distilled from their pens was sure to have a greater effect, inasmuch as it fell upon minds already disposed to the revolutionary fever. Every day it was but the repetition of the same bravado attacks on the part of these writers against the law, the same insults against the government, and the same efforts directed against the very foundations of society. A journal was established—everybody knew the *Tribune*—which became the organ and the very incarnation of the genius of demagogism. It was aided by another paper, which was called the *Revolution of* 1830, but which was not so open in its hatred, nor so venomous in its attacks. There was also still another paper, the *Movement*, which endeavored to gain subscriptions by the force of scandal; but in this it was surpassed by several little sheets, whose coarse jests and rude sketches filled the imbeciles and other such patriots with delight.

Those of our young agitators who were not writers for the papers, issued little sheets of their own at two sous a piece, which, by the agency of the lowest order of booksellers, were scattered all over France. M. Paguere is one of the propagandists, who commenced his fortune in this way, and which he has gone on increasing, probably, through every turn of the political wheel—it being understood, of course, that we should never attribute any increment of his fortune to the works of the Messrs. Cabet, which he at that time edited.

To the writings of the day may be added the speeches of

the clubs, which were the wildest declaration of anarchical principles and the perpetual incentives of revolutionary passions. The very air of Paris seemed to be infected by an odor which can be compared to nothing but an explosion of mephitic gas. And such is always the case after every revolution; and of all the bad consequences that follow the overthrow of a government, this is not the least detestable of those to which certain men wish to accustom us. But these men have their way, and demoralization prevails like a pestilence.

With all our fine courage, and our clear intellect, we are, in certain cases—we Frenchmen—beings of the strangest weaknesses and of the most inconceivable inconsistency; and there was no need of the affair of February to show it, because we had already given abundant proofs of it in the affair of July. Was it not then seen that the magistracy, dropping the sanctions of their office, affected to encourage the violations of law? Whether from connivance, from fear, or an exaggerated respect for the letter of the code, certain it is that acquittals took place which tended to nothing short of the most unlimited impunity. And hence we are not to be astonished at the audacity of anarchical ideas and the rapidity of strength which was acquired by the *Friends of the People.*

CHAPTER IV.

The friends of the people—The bourgeoisie drive them from their club—A mob—Schemes for assassinating the king and ex-ministers—Old Woodenleg—Libellous handbills—Complot of the Parisian artillery—Its chiefs.

THE society of the *Friends of the People* being permitted to proceed openly, in the face of article 291 of the penal code, which the authorities declined applying to them, were enabled to dispense with a rigorous organization. The affiliation had none of those mysterious ceremonies designed for making an impression upon the mind and imposing secrecy which are necessary when societies are prohibited. Admission into the society was gained either from notoriety or by declaration of patriotism. The word patriotism was not tacitly understood among them as absolutely one and the same thing with republicanism, but it fell but little short of it. Several worthy men might have imagined at that time, as they have since, that the best way to serve the government is by making violent attacks upon it; but such absurd notions were not generally prevalent.

The leaders and the greater part of the members labored knowingly and resolutely for a republican revolution; and their mode of proceeding was as follows: To absorb in themselves all the various elements of the party; to control the secondary societies and individual democrats by means of a large central public society and an extensive plan of democratic writings; to affiliate all the patriots that presented themselves, and especially men of influence or talent whose popularity or character might be turned to account in propagating the sentiments of the society; to allow no occasions of discord, over and above those produced by writings and speeches, to pass without stirring up the minds of the people; to keep the government constantly in a precarious condition, and finally, after a series of successive shocks, to devise the first favorable moment for overthrowing it altogether.

This system of continual agitation, which became very practicable immediately after a revolution, was carried into operation with unremitted zeal. The chiefs, conceiving that insurrections abroad might be made to react powerfully in furtherance of their projects at home, dispatched emissaries into the neighboring countries with orders to try the chance of exciting commotions there. The governments of the greater powers were sufficiently on their guard to thwart such manœuvres as these; but the smaller nations, such as the Belgians and the Poles, ventured upon the hazard of an insurrection. The Belgians gained a nationality by it, and the Poles lost everything national that they had left.

With regard to Belgium, the *Friends of the People* were not content with sending their speech makers there; for a battalion, organized by their cares, had gone from France with the design of determining and supporting the movement. The success of this expedition of 1830, naturally led our revolutionists of 1848 to follow the example; but they found the Belgians in the enjoyment of a pretty good monarchy, which they had no desire to exchange for a very bad republic.

The central society *of the Friends of the People* installed itself in the riding school of Peltier, Montmartre Street, under the presidency of M. Hubert (John Lewis). The members took their seats within the inclosure of the riding ground, the extensive corridors which surround it being left open to the public. Tumultuous scenes, in which violence and burlesque, talent and no talent, held alternate sway, were enacted there every day. Some of its members, great admirers of revolutionary parodies, would have gladly introduced the female knitters, and all the rest of the panoply of the ancient Jacobins.

As the idea of dispersing the national representation still remained uppermost, and as, moreover, agitation of some kind was necessary, it was decided, towards the close of September, to get up a grand discussion on the legality of the powers of the Assembly. During three days this question, discussed in open public and amidst a people still warm from the combat, kept Paris in a constant ferment. The decision arrived at by this discussion was: That the powers of the deputies had expired; that the people demanded the vacation of their seats; and that a notice to this effect should be posted up upon the walls of Paris. The articles of this resolution were voted in actual session, and the manuscript notice was immediately sent to the printer. However indulgent the police were at that time, they perceived that this was an occasion for them to act; and the notice was seized at the office of the press. Messrs. Hubert and Thierry, the first as president, and the second as treasurer of the society, and M. David as printer of the notice, were sent to the correctional police. M. Hubert, in commencing that series of scandals which characterized the political prosecutions of the period, made a revolutionary speech, the substance of which was, that justice changes with the government, and that the magistrates of the Restoration had no right to judge him, a delinquent under the government of July. This piece of folly, or effrontery, or whatever else it may be called, has been repeated a great many times since, and always to the very great admiration of the patriots.

M. Hubert, and M. Thierry, were sentenced to three months imprisonment; the printer was acquitted. The tribunal, by decision, declared the society dissolved.

This commencement of action on the part of the authorities seemed to promise an efficient suppression of disorders; but the judiciary soon afterwards changed its course, and gave an interpretation to the law which was as false as it was dangerous.

After the vote upon the resolutions of the grand discussion, there took place a significant manifestation; the bourgeoisie, become impatient of an agitation which was ruinous to their interests, resolved to restore order; and they assembled for this purpose in large numbers before the riding-school in the street of Montmartre. The cry was raised of—"Down with the clubs!" At the same time, some of the National Guards entered the hall and declared that the traders could not stand being continually troubled any longer as they had been; and that in the name of their companions they had come to summons the *Friends of the People* to cease their anarchical course of proceedings. Upon this there arose a mingled outburst of protestations, clamors, and abuse; but as the shop-keepers showed themselves resolved, and determined to have peace, the club finally gave up, left the hall, and dispersed.

This energetic act, together with the legal decision which dissolved the society, compelled the *Friends of the People* to assume a new phase.

The public club became transformed into a secret society; not under the conditions of such absolute secrecy as we shall see hereafter, but in this respect that the affiliated members alone could take a part in the meetings, and that these meetings were no longer announced through the newspapers, nor posted up by notices upon the walls. In other respects, the society, far from hastening to its dissolution, increased rapidly day by day, both in the number of its members and in its spirit of propagandism. The emanations from the press multiplied without limit, treating upon every variety of subject and in every variety of way; the order of the day was communicated by circulars; decrees were issued; affiliations went on in the provinces, and France, and especially Paris, felt the workings of anarchy like the approach of an earthquake which threatened to engulf her.

As the *Friends of the People* saw clearly that they were not strong enough to throw the Chambers, or in other words the government out of the windows, they sought some other occasion of disorder. The trial of the ministers, which was about to take place, came exactly to their purpose.

On the 17th of October, some noisy bands, commanded by members of the *Friends of the People* and of the *Society of Order and Progress*, made their appearance upon the place of the Palais Royal. When arrived under the windows of the king, who at that time was residing in that ancient palace, these apostles of fraternity set up the shout at the top of their voices—"Death to the ministers!" The National Guards came in and cleared the place. But the next day, the word having been communicated the night previous, the crowd made its appearance again, more numerous than before. It was preceded by the most alarming rumors. It was noised about that the clubists were going to Vincennes; and that they were going to wrest the ministers from prison and assassinate them. This fine project was effectively defeated; but it had been preceded by an attempt upon the Palais Royal. Was it really the design to have butchered the king before proceeding to assassinate the ex-ministers? There can be but very little room for a doubt; all that was wanting was a favorable occasion. Louis Philippe has had, from the very beginning of his reign, the unenviable honor of giving too much offence to men of disorder, to expect anything but destruction at their hands, by any and every means by which they could accomplish it. The republicans will not probably regard this allegation as a calumny made upon themselves; and, indeed, we make it in order to give them an occasion of applauding themselves for it—now that the *sovereignty of the end to be gained* not only permits it but even renders it their duty.

It is certain, however, that, on the 18th of October, some members of the *Friends of the People* hurried through the different quarters of the city, exciting the people to move upon the Palais Royal, and declaring that it must be entered at all hazards. About a thousand persons responded to the call and proceeded in a tumult towards the abode of the king; but finding there a large guard with a determined air of resistance, their courage became disconcerted, and they concluded to turn their attention to some other quarter. The project of attack upon Vincennes was rather difficult of execution; but when it was announced by the leaders as the second part of the programme, everybody seemed ready for the work. On their way, however, and by the time they had reached the barrier du Trone, three-fourths of their number had either disbanded themselves or lagged behind, so that the expedition was reduced to about three hundred men. On they went, however, and when arrived at Vincennes, they sent a summons to General Daumenil, commandant of the fortress, to deliver up the prisoners. The old soldier shrugged his shoulders and replied that such things were not done in that way. The mob then burst out into cries of fury, and threatened to take the fort. "As to that matter," said Old Wooden-Leg, "you can try it; but I advise you not to."

Perceiving the force of the remark, the would-be killers of ministers beat a retreat and returned to Paris, frightening the people with their cries of death. The National Guard stood waiting for them, and, judging that this odious parade had lasted long enough, it surrounded them, and bore one hundred and thirty-six of their number to the prefecture of the police.

But this was only the beginning of the play; for a month afterwards, on the trial of the ministers, the same ferocity, so well in accord with the fraternal phraseology of the clubs, was exhibited again, filling France with indignation, and exciting the inquiry in Europe if we really were that exceedingly humane and civilized people which we pretended to be.

As a satisfaction for their double check at the Palais Royal and Vincennes, the mob posted up, during the night, some libellous placards against the royal family; a species of vengeance perfectly in keeping with the cause and the men; the dagger had failed, and the alternative was abuse.

Several days afterwards, some other placards, clandestinely posted up, announced that an indemnity of two hundred thousand francs had been granted to M. de Quelen; and, "without doubt," said the anonymous patriot, "to indemnify him for the powder and poniards found in his house, and which were to have been employed against the brave combatants of July." The statement that arms and ammunition had been found at the house of the Archbishop of Paris was an odious invention which it is useless to repeat. It is well known that such allegations are the special adroitness of the brutified populace, and the intelligent men of the party know the falsehood of them as well as their opponents.

The republicans did not rely solely upon mere popular societies, whose groups are comparatively insignificant, and whose action in the streets presents nothing formidable; they counted upon a support of much more serious importance.

The National Guard of Paris, then at the height of its zeal, formed a magnificent army in the service of good order. A single arm, however, the artillery, became invaded by the republicans of the *Friends of the People.* The hierarchy of the society were also members of an armed body; that is to say, the high priests, or chiefs of the *Friends of the People,* held also the principal grades of office in the artillery; so that the society, which was proscribed as a political association, was found legally organized, and armed as a body of militia. This incompatible state of things was known by the authorities, and was the just occasion of much disquietude; but a simple reason of state was hardly sufficient at that time for dissolving a national guard. Such a measure would have given rise to a tempest of vociferations, the very idea of which would have been terrible. Besides, after every revolution, a part of the power falls to the share of men who, issuing from a state of disorder, naturally make their conditions with the government. From weakness, therefore, on the one hand, and from connivance on the other, the republicans of the *Friends of the People* possessed an armed organization under the guise of the artillery of Paris.

The exaltation and impatience of the clubists, pushed them to a prompt use of the extraordinary advantage which had thus been left to them; and they were determined to act on the first occasion. The disturbances of the month of October had appeared premature to the chiefs, and they had taken no active part in them, leaving them to the populace. However, this question of the ex-ministers had been worked upon with so much care, that the moment of the trial, it was thought, might be made a good pretext for a disturbance.

Of the four batteries of which the artillery of the National Guard was composed, there were chiefs of the second battery, Messrs. Guinard and Godefroy Cavaignac, and of the third battery, Messrs. Bastide and Thomas, all leading members of the society of the *Friends of the People*. In the other two batteries there were a great many patriot officers, who spared no pains to gain over their men.

Well persuaded that the ideas of blood with which the people had been excited on the subject of the ex-ministers, could be worked upon with advantage, the chiefs of the *Friends of the People* and of the *Society of Order and Progress* decided that a new attempt should be made during the trial. The scheme was, to move upon the Luxembourg, there to put in execution that idea which had become so dear to the patriots, viz: the assassination of the ex-ministers; and then, having done this, to return to the Palais Royal and make an end of the monarchy, after having proceeded in a due revolutionary manner with respect to the king. The means reckoned upon to carry out this scheme were to be furnished through the treason of the corps of artillery, who were to deliver up their guns.

An act of so grave a character as that of giving guns to a mob required to be skilfully executed; but Messrs. Cavaignac, Guinard, Bastide, etc., were intelligent men, incapable of any ordinary miscarriage. As a preparatory measure, a rumor was quietly spread that the suburbs had formed a complot against some portion of the National Guard, which was supposed to be the artillery;· but that, however, the artillery were true and faithful, and would remain so. A pretty clever invention; but however that may be, the con· nivance of the artillery was formally denied; and as a proof of their attachment to order, it was even urged that M. Cavaignac had issued cartridges to his men, for the purpose of repelling an attack. Now, without dwelling too long upon M. G. Cavaignac, a man exceptional to his own party, and to whom we shall render the justice which he deserves, we may be permitted to believe that this distribution of cartridges was made with any other object than that which was pretended; the result will then show if we are wrong.

CHAPTER V.

Trial of the ministers—A mob—A complot in the National Guard—Messrs. G. Cavaignac, Guinard, Trelat, Sambuc, Audry de Puyraveau—Their trial—Mobs upon mobs—The artillery of Marshal Lobau.

FROM the first day of the trial of the ex-ministers, some young men of the *Society of Order and Progress*, led by M. Sambuc, together with others from the *Friends of the People*, were seen in groups around the Court of Peers. Their numbers being increased by the usual contingent of curious persons and malefactors, they soon became a very considerable assemblage. The clamors began, grew louder and louder, and finally ended in an awful chorus—a diapason of hideous voices, growling forth the frenzied refrain of—"Death to the ministers!"

An honest man, M. Odilon-Barrot, prefect of the Seine, justly indignant at such proceedings, caused a proclamation to be posted up, in which were these courageous words:—

"I declare that the first act of aggression will be considered as a crime. If there is among you a man so guilty as to attempt the life of his fellow citizens, let him not imagine that he may escape by the chances of a combat; for he will be considered as a murderer, and judged as such by the Court of Assizes, according to the rigor of the law. Is, then, the reparation which our generous country demands, the blood of a few unfortunate persons?"

The republican faction assembled around the Luxembourg, not to await the decrees of justice, but to dictate them, and to dictate them in blood. Such men as Messrs. Cavaignac and Guinard had no desire, probably, to see the ministers butchered; but the idea would serve to excite the mob, and favor a plan of revolution already in the way of execution.

Every day, during the continuance of the trial, the mob took up its position, in a threatening attitude, before the palace of Medicis. True to the hour, these pretended disciples of humanity returned to their posts, giving Paris an idea of a charnel house, besieged by ferocious beasts.

As soon as the arguments were finished, and before the delivery of the sentence, some carriages, which had been made ready in the garden of the palace, received the prisoners, who hurried back, with a strong escort, to Vincennes.

The judgment of the court was to be given that day; and every means were taken in order to exasperate the populace for the announcement of the verdict, which it was known would be lenient. The crowd, therefore, were in a greater ferment than ever. Suddenly a discharge of cannon was heard, announcing that the prisoners were in safety.

"To arms!" cried some of the chiefs, who were looking for an occasion. The signal was given.

The crowd was thrown into a tumult of agitation and fury; all it wanted was direction; the leaders were there; and by a single word—"To the Louvre!" an electrical spark seemed to be sent through the mass—the expected guns were at the Louvre.

Upon the route, some of the National Guards and agents of the authorities experienced the first effect of the explosion;

some were overthrown and trampled under foot, while others were assailed with daggers and pistols.

Always, in like cases, when the affair miscarries, the cunning and the foolish alike will swear by everything that is holy, that the manifestation was wholly and entirely pacific; and always, too, at the beginning of these affairs there will be seen the flash of daggers and the gleams of pistols, which the possessors have certainly not had far to go to find.

While the column was proceeding towards the Louvre, the authorities, having been informed of their coming, closed the gates and made ready for a defence.

All the artillery was shut up within the inclosures of the palace, where a singular spectacle was presented to the view. Some of the companies of artillery were devoted to the government, and others to the revolutionists. There were other companies in which the opinions were divided; some having a majority in favor of order, and some in favor of disorder. All these men, young, ardent, and equally resolved upon maintaining their respective parties, were there, face to face, exchanging looks of distrust and defiance. The artillerists who were faithful, standing by their guns, were determined to defend them to the last, and to spike them sooner than allow them to be taken. They knew that the men of the Cavaignac and Guinard batteries had their musketoons loaded, and that the republicans of the societies where ready to rush upon them in order to seize their guns. The position was a critical one; but the *bourgeois*, as the aristocratic disdain of the Democrats already began to designate them, showed both the disposition and the courage to make an effective resistance.

The mob continuing to increase on the outside of the inclosure, some detachments of the National Guards entered the interior and joined their comrades. The scene then became more serious; altercations arose which threatened to end in violence. The commandant Barré, addressing himself to M. Bastide, one of his captains, accused him and his men of treason. The artillerists of each party sided with their chiefs; and the moment had arrived when the musketoons were brought to the shoulder ready to fire. However, the quarrel was quieted. In the mean time, the National Guard on the outside of the inclosure cleared the ground, and things remained in this state until night. At about ten o'clock the Duke of Orleans came to join his battery, in full uniform, and he was received with such marks of devotion that the opposite party was completely silenced. The republican artillerists abandoned their cause, leaving the guns to those who would use them, not for the encouragement, but for the suppression of disorder.

In this manner the matter ended; and such scenes, it might be thought, had been repeated often enough; but the spirit of anarchy and discord is tenacious. The next day the *Friends of the People* and the members of the *Society of Order and Progress* made their appearance again in the streets. But on this occasion the swell-mobs, such as the *Fly-Catchers*, and those patriots in general who have some little pretensions to good sense, concluded that the *manifestation* had already been quite sufficient, and they abstained from taking a part in it. The clubists, therefore, seeing that their presence produced a most unfavorable effect, directed their course towards the Latin quarter of the town, where, in the midst of a region renowned for the secrets which it furnishes for mobs, they expected a better reception. But there, a new disappointment awaited them. Some of the students of that class which is devoted to study, worn out by the vain efforts made to win them over to the cause of disorder, and disgusted with a reputation which the majority of their number by no means deserved, took it into their heads to get up a meeting, and an assemblage of pupils soon came together amounting to fifteen hundred. The republicans, deceived by their own habits of disorder, hastened in delight to assume the command of what they thought a magnificent reinforcement in favor of agitation; but what was their astonishment, or rather their indignation, on seeing this column pursue its course, in good order, towards the Palais Royal and there request permission to pay their compliments to the king! Of course, nothing was left to the republicans but to beat a retreat, and return to the depths of their clubs to await some better occasion.

These disturbances, alike dangerous in their tendency and disgusting in character, resulted in bringing before the Court of Assizes nineteen persons, whose names were as follows: Messrs. Godefroy Cavaignac, Guinard, and Trelat, the first two captains, and the third private soldier of the Parisian Artillery; Sambuc and Audry, students, and Messrs. Francfort, Penard, Ronhier, Pecheux d'Herbinville, Chassarre, Gourdin, Guilley, Chaurin, Le Cartard, the brothers Garnier, Danton, Lenoble, and Pontois.

We give a hasty sketch of a few of these personages, such as are deserving of it; and first that of M. Godefroy Cavaignac.

A son of one of those sombre men who bear the responsibility of the days of terror, he entered upon public life full of paternal recollections and revolutionary ambition. It is but bare justice to say that he was a man of great mind, generous soul, and loyal disposition. He was both a poet and an artist; and he loved to live in a world of fancy. His error consisted, like that of all dreamers in general, in looking upon things only within that sphere of the imagination where, although the mere individual may stroll at his leisure, yet the citizen stumbles and the statesman loses all authority. M. Godefroy Cavaignac was destined, by his brilliant qualities, to arrive at the head of his party, and, in spite of his good intentions, to do much mischief to his country. And from those very qualities of head and heart which gave him a commanding influence over others, he was also doomed to a miserable struggle against the jealousy and ignorance of his own party. That extraordinary hatred of which he soon became the object on the part of the republicans—a hatred which went to the extreme of devoting him to the dagger—arose, doubtlessly, from no other cause than the superiority of his talents, character, and personal appearance. He entertained to a high degree, but without affectation or bitterness, a perfect contempt for all little things, and a profound pity for all little men. His personal appearance commanded respect. A tall and graceful figure, a firm eye with a shade of sadness, features perfectly regular, a military bearing, and, not last, a heavy pair of black moustaches, gave him an impress of nobleness which awakened, at a glance, the strongest prepossessions in his favor. He was the very type of a political hero—such as would be conceived by the artist.

If the France of 1848 had found this man at her head, we may readily conceive that she would have had to experience the consequences of many generous follies, but no miserable parodies, stupendous inaptitudes, or shameless dilapidations. How long he might have remained in power is very conjectural; but, according to every probability, he would have soon experienced the fate of those serious minds which stoop to meddle with extravagant facts. He would have been seized upon and torn by all the blind or interested impulses of the moment. Just think of the vain-glory of M. Ledru-Rollin, the roguery of M. Caussidiere, the poison of M. Blanqui, the prattle of Louis Blanc, the frenzy of M. Sobrier, and above all, the jealousy of those ridiculous or imbecile geniuses, such as Flocon, Lamartine, Marrast, etc., by which he would have been assailed and annoyed!

I have some right to speak of the characters of the republicans; for I have happened to have a close view of them; and some credit, therefore, may be given to this panegyric upon M. Godefroy Cavaignac. He was, in my opinion, the only man of the republican party of 1830, who was, at one and the same time, possessed of a high order of abilities and governed by a perfect sincerity. I may add, that though strongly devoted to his party, yet he had no respect for it, and that, on the other hand, though they yielded him their respect, he had none of their love.

Concerning M. Guinard, there is but little to be said; unless it is that he might be considered as a counterpart of M. G. Cavaignac. In comparison with that gentleman he bore the same relation to him that a good copy bears to its original. Though recommended by a great many good qualities, yet these qualities were all of an ordinary elevation: his character being of that kind where nothing appears prominent. But he must not, therefore, be confounded with the rest of the republican crowd, to which he was rendered far superior by his loyalty and firmness.

The pock-fretted physiognomy of M. Trelat, radiant with benignity, gave the idea of an organization where the ruling qualities were mildness and affection. He was, in fact, a very good and kind mannered man, and in every way well fitted for the office which he filled as physician to the old women of the Salpêtrière. His goodness amounted to a weakness; and weakness, in political matters, leads to such results as—the establishment of national workshops. We need say no more.

M. Sambuc was one of those brawling students whose ambition was not satisfied with the glory of reaming pots and jovial suppers. Under the double influence of the fashion of the times and the patriotic fever of youth, he became a revolutionist; but cured at last by the attentions of the officers of justice, he left Paris, and never made his appearance again during the long period of our political troubles.

As to M. Audry de Puyraveau, son of a former deputy, he was a young man of mediocre abilities, who considered himself bound to maintain in the Latin quarter the republican reputation of his father. We shall meet with him more than once hereafter, either before the correctional police, or Court of Assizes, a confirmed conspirator, whose part, however, never surpassed that of one of the rank and file.

The trial of the disturbers of the peace attracted public attention, and made a great noise in the party. M. Godefroy Cavaignac made an exposition of his republican principles remarkable for its energy. There was a certain grandeur in his attitude and manner of speaking, which it would be impossible to deny. It must be confessed, it smelt of powder; and the interest excited by a proud young man, son of a revolutionist, thus confessing his revolutionary principles, can be readily imagined. But his own efforts, as well as those of his confederates, who were also ambitious of a scene at the tribunal, ended only in an aggravation of their offence. More than one of their number, being far below the part to which they aspired, produced quite a shrugging of the shoulders among men of good sense. For instance, M. Pecheux d' Herbinville, who had been charged with having distributed arms to the mob, declared, emphatically, that he had taken those arms from the Swiss Guards in 1830. What did he mean by that? Why, doubtlessly, that the spoils of one revolution should be appropriated to the use of getting up another. Such is the mode of argument usually pursued by the demagogues. Every individual who has had the honor, by the discharge of a musket, to contribute to the disturbance of France and Europe, thinks that he has thus acquired the right to do the same thing again whenever he pleases.

Besides the principles of political subversion, which were made the subject of the trial, there began to be perceived, during the proceedings, some of those notions which, at the present day, are called socialism. They attracted but little notice at that time; for even the most fearful could hardly have imagined that such Utopian fancies would go beyond the limits of theory; but we have since seen that there is no doctrine however absurd that may not, at some time or another, take possession of the fancies of the most intellectual people of the world.

From some cause or another, notwithstanding the circumstances of the case, and the scandal of the trial, all the accused were acquitted.

In consequence, the republican party claimed the victory, and considered itself master of the ground. And, to profit by their success, they got up a mob the very next day, April 16, 1831. But it was soon put down by the National Guards and other troops.

There was in power, from that period, a man who had no idea of admitting such a condition of things as a permanent state of revolution, and, knowing to what lengths factions were capable of going, he determined upon a course of repression, both active and energetic. This man was M. Casimir

Perrier. The prefecture had not yet become invested with a sufficient force of officials to meet the exigencies of the times, but in the character of M. Carlier, chief of the municipal police, it possessed a functionary of the most decided spirit and indefatigable activity. The government of July, therefore, which had thus far been bandied about at the mercy of the revolutionary whirlwind, was to enter into a new phase, not of perfect tranquillity—by no manner of means, but of firm unshaken determination.

It was impossible to be mistaken in one thing, to wit, that the chiefs of the republican faction, being also at the head of the *Friends of the People*, had decided upon a scheme of permanent agitation with the view of arriving at some favorable occasion for overthrowing the government; a scheme which was only too easy of execution, in the excited state in which the minds of men then were; and hence we shall see disturbance after disturbance, succeeding each other without interruption.

On the 2d of March, there was a mob around the Palais Royal, consisting of several hundreds of that class of laborers with which national workshops are established. Having taken up their position under the windows of the king, they set up the ravenous cry of—" Give us work or bread!" The papers of the period shed tears of pity over the lot of these very worthy citizens, who were, in fact, nothing less than their own instruments, and those of the *Friends of the People;* for the honest workingman, he who has energy and good sense, knows better than to mingle in manifestations the immediate tendency of which is to injure his interests.

Several days later, the insurrection of Poland served as the pretext for another disturbance. On the 10th of March, a couple of individuals began the disorders by firing pistols into the windows of the Russian embassy: a blind fury which, in beating the air for an object, attacked the representative inviolability of a nation with which we were on terms of amity and peace. On the 11th and 12th, assemblages took place which occasioned the arrest of several men who were armed. Five weeks afterwards, a mob arose which continued for three days. It then returned to its recesses, but only to make its appearance again, at the end of one month, day for day. On this occasion its acts were of a serious consequence; the cry of—"Down with the National Guard!" was raised; some gunsmiths' shops were pillaged, lanterns broken in pieces, and one of the guard stations threatened.

But these scenes served rather to excite the indignation of the people than to alarm the government. Sure of the support of all reasonable and industrious men, the government wished to restore order to Paris by some effective means, yet without the shedding of blood. Marshal Lobau, a perfect soldier, proposed a measure, which, though it evinced some contempt for the folks of the mob, possessed, nevertheless, the merit of originality. The *Friends of the People* having learned that the cross of honor of July would bear the inscription of, "*Given by the King*," thought that they could make it the occasion of a mob. Hence, orders were immediately issued for assembling at the Place Vendome for the purpose of organizing a manifestation. Manifesting had become a business with some few hundreds of ambitious and idle persons, and they were always ready to obey a call on every occasion. Prompt to the hour, therefore, they assembled around the column of Vendome, and resolutely awaited the arrival of the public force. When the force came, they were rather roughly handled; but still they kept a pretty good countenance until the arrival of Marshal Lobau with a new kind of artillery, with which he had furnished himself, and which was not perceived by the mob. On the first summons, which was stoically resisted, the old general unmasked his pieces and gave a command which was not exactly "fire," but which in an instant set half a dozen vigorously played fire engines at work, spitting their aqueous grape shot upon the astonished crowd, and producing the most wonderful effect; for a general disbandment took place, mingled with cries and confusion, a devil-take-the-hindmost sort of a ramble-scramble, worse than if it had rained bullets. The place was cleared as if by enchantment.

These several disturbances gave occasion to a series of

prosecutions which were remarkable solely for this—that the leaders of the party seldom or never made their appearance in them. The accused, as usual, were either reckless men or poor devils, whose credulous enthusiasm rendered them the ready instruments of designing men. As to the directors of these movements, they contented themselves with giving their instructions, taking particular care to keep out of the way whenever the disorder broke out, and the hard knocks began to be given.

CHAPTER VI.

Permanence of the mob—M. Carlier and the cudgellers of the Bastile—The bull-dogs of the populace vanquished—M. Gisquet—Suggestions concerning the re-establishment of the ministry of police.

It were useless to repeat all the reasons by which the *Tribune* and other papers of that kind sought to justify the disorder of the streets. One of those reasons was the misery of the people: too true, indeed, as is always the case after every political commotion, but imputable, it must be acknowledged, to any other cause rather than to the government. For it is evident that a new government could have no interest in making itself hated; interest alone, to say nothing of conscience, would teach it to have a regard for the necessities of the people. But the opposition of the radicals, though very ready to bestow upon royalty all kinds of mean names, was not willing to grant it the most simple of all, that of rendering itself popular without the aid of the purse. Not content with reproaches of tyranny and avarice which it bestowed upon the new government, it declared that the government had determined to do nothing for the working classes. But the government, nevertheless, could show, by figures, that it had employed in a single month seven millions of francs upon the public works.

The mob, by the instigation of the republicans, had become permanent; every pretext for a disturbance was seized upon with avidity; and when no pretext presented itself, it was a very easy matter to make one. Several days before the 14th of July, 1831, it was announced that the anniversary of the destruction of the Bastile would be celebrated by planting liberty trees; and the initiated were moreover informed that there would be *something*—for which every one of course was to hold himself in readiness. The police, which began to have an ear in the secret conventicles of mischief, being informed of the *something*, thought it high time to show a mere handful of republicans in Paris that the country was not to remain forever at the mercy of their tyranny, and measures were taken to suppress the intended disorder at its very commencement. A proclamation was, therefore, issued, prohibiting the forming of assemblages, and planting liberty trees. But, notwithstanding this, the clubists, having the *Friends of the People* at their head, made their appearance in the streets at the hour appointed. They separated into two bands, which proceeded in opposite directions, one towards the Champ Elysées, and the other towards the Bastile. At the Champ Elysées, as the mayor of the first arrondissement was entering among the mob in order to address them some observations, he was stopped by M. Desirabode, a dentist, who presented two pistols at his throat. This furious dentist, being repulsed at the point of the bayonet by the National Guards, paid dear for his temerity; for, grievously wounded, he owed his life to the interposition of the very man whom he had threatened to assassinate.

As to the scene which took place at the Bastile, there was no end to the discussion which followed it, nor to the versions which were given of it. According to the papers of the period, the police had forever disgraced themselves in the affair by launching a body of policemen, robbers, and galley slaves upon poor, unarmed victims. Such was the republican version of the affair; everybody knows it; but the one which we give has the double misfortune of being both much less discreditable to the police, and at the same time much more true.

Some workingmen of the suburb Saint Antoine—real workingmen—those who desired to work, but were prevented by the perpetual brawls of the republicans, called upon M. Carlier, chief of the municipal police, and offered to keep order themselves in their quarter of the town, if the *Friends of the People* should make their appearance there. They were told that the proceeding which they proposed was a very delicate matter; that it would be a fight between citizens, for no regular authority could be given them for the suppression of disturbances; but that, after all, the offer which they had made was very honorable to them, and the tranquillity of their quarter a matter of sufficient importance to receive their care and attention. They asked for nothing more, and returned to their suburb.

The next day, when the republicans arrived and were making ready to begin their noise, the officious defenders of order, men by nature rather brutal, and who were perfectly disposed to become more brutal still, fell upon the mob with their cudgels, upset the Fly-catchers, pommelled the clubists, and thus made a vigorous clearance of the place.

It was unpleasant, undoubtedly, to be belabored in that style; but the *Friends of the People* had such a strange manner of showing their love for the workingmen, that it was no more than fair that the workingmen should have an opportunity of showing their gratitude in a similar way.

Such is, in a few words, the famous history of the cudgellers taken from the bagnio. It changes character materially when not related by the patriots. In the accounts of it by the patriots, there are, as usual, only affirmations based upon idle gossips or barefaced invention; but on the part of the police, there are positive proofs, which M. Caussidière and others have been able to see if they wished it.

The lesson thus given at the Bastile had its effect; there was not another mob for the space of a month. In those times Paris had an occasion to thank God for a period of tranquillity of four weeks. It can hardly be believed, at this day, that a few hundreds of rascals could take it into their heads to make a periodic disturbance of the peace of the country, and succeed in it; yet such is the history of but yesterday.

In the month of September the news of the fall of Poland presented too fine an occasion for a disturbance to be neglected. The smaller emanations from the press spat fire and flames; the *Tribune* foamed, and the chiefs of the *Friends of the People* turned blue with indignation. Those terrible men who, when finally in power themselves, had the prudence not to devour a single tyrant, have never failed in their opposition to demand a general war in Europe for any cause whatever, and no matter what. The refusal on the part of the government of July to embark in an undertaking, the impracticability of which they themselves admitted seventeen years afterwards, was, according to their way of thinking, the basest of treasons. Up with the mob, then! Two or three hundred patriots first go to the Palais Royal and insult the king; then they proceed to the Hôtel des Capucines, shouting—"Hurrah for Poland! Down with the ministers!" Then stones are let loose into the windows. From the Hôtel des Capucines they repair to the boulevard Saint Denis, a gunsmith's shop on the way being sacked and pillaged. Such was the bill of fare that day. The next day—as usual—the same thing over and over again; for these wretched melo-dramas always had, at least, their five acts. The groups assembled again in front of the Hotel of Foreign Affairs; and while uttering their menacing cries, a carriage, in which were recognized the president of the council, M. Casimir Perrier and another minister, was coming out of the inclosure. It was immediately surrounded and stopped; however, a few firm words from the minister sufficed to clear a passage, and it proceeded on its way. But the mobbers soon recovered themselves and pursued their enemy. Overtaking the carriage at the place Vendome, they stopped the horses, and set up the most violent vociferations. M. Casimir Perrier got out and addressed the crowd:—

"What do you want?" said he, "the ministers? Here we are. But you, who are you? pretended friends of liberty threatening the men who are charged with the execution of the law!"

By these words, uttered in a tone of lofty assurance, the audacity of the malefactors was completely subdued. They stood aside, and the courageous functionary passed on, as the master passes in the midst of dogs, whose mischievous eyes fall beneath his rebukeful look.

For a moment they remained as if perfectly crushed by this lordly bearing; but, spurred on by pride and vexation, they spread themselves through Paris, invaded the theatres, which they ordered to be closed in sign of mourning, and then set to work at the edge of the suburb of Montmartre, in tearing up paving stones. A considerable body of troops had to be brought out to disperse them. But for two days afterwards, the reverberations, as it were, of their discord still continued, like the howling of the waves after the tempest has subsided.

In November, 1831, M. Gisquet was appointed prefect of the police. During the sixteen months which had elapsed since the revolution, three incumbents had succeeded to the office of prefect, Messrs. Girod de l'Ain, Baude, and Vivien; M. Gisquet made the fourth. These changes in the management of the prefecture, added to the indecision and indulgence of functionaries who had risen by the revolution, had evidently tended to encourage the audacity and perseverance of the anarchists. To some extent it might be said, in the words of the *Reform*, that the first three prefects had worked at the preservation of order by means of disorder, or, in other words, they had not had either the disposition or the capacity to establish a regular and coherent system of order. To play the part of a Sartine or a Fouche requires not only the disposition to maintain order, but a high degree of skill accompanied by untiring zeal, and indefatigable activity; and there are occasions when it requires a man of very extraordinary ability. By referring to the period immediately after our first revolution, it will be seen that there never was a society more completely disorganized; and yet, under the skilful management of a man of the police, the Duke of

Otranto, aided by a natural reaction, all the elements of order were made at once to assume their proper form and condition. When Napoleon designed to assume the head of affairs, knowing that the art of governing is the art of leading, and with that penetrating glance of his, he began by addressing himself to Talleyrand, the leader of the chancelleries, and to the Duke of Otranto, the leader of the masses. The police is not, indeed, a mere matter of supervision and repression; it should be considered as the initiative, and the direction of the public mind. Those supple, acute, penetrating men, who are delving every day into the secrets of life, and the knowledge of human well-being—why should they not become the conductors as well as the inspectors of the masses? What is to prevent their chief, that man of omniscience, from giving a counterpoise to the extravagances of popular opinion, and in thus preserving the public mind in a state of equilibrium? He could easily do it if he were a man of superior abilities, practised in the business, and free in his action. By freedom of action, we mean to imply that the present functions of the police are too much restricted, and that they can be made really effective only by being extended to embrace all France. Under a state of things such as we are now actually experiencing, we believe that the re-establishment of the ministry of police would render the effect of supervision and control much more intense and active than it now is. But, under the present system, how is it? Why, the minister of the interior, merely a man of administration, or of parliamentary consequence, finds himself suddenly at the head of a service of the first importance, which requires long experience, and particular aptitude, and which becomes a matter of only secondary consideration among his other functions. Hence there results, on the one hand, a want of experience and especial capacity, and, on the other, an insufficiency or slackness in the action of the machine. Since the service of the police is one and the same for Paris and the provinces, why divide it? Since unity is the first principle of power, why not organize the police according to this principle? Why, in fine, impose upon a functionary already overcharged with duties, a service which claims by itself all the attention of a man of genius? Inasmuch as the complots of Paris extend into the provinces, the ramifications of the police should extend there also. It very often happens, indeed, that the prefects of the provinces are advised of what is going on among them by information received from Paris. But this information, as it now is, has to go through the ministry of the interior, a useless formality, which occasions an unnecessary loss of time. Besides, impediments in the way of execution may now arise from a difference of opinion between the minister of the interior and the prefect of police, in which, although the inferior is in a much better position for seeing and judging, yet he must yield to his superior.

And the inconvenience of our present system of police is not less when regarded with respect to the direction which it might give to the mind of the masses. The prefect of police has to deal with the head, and not with the members of the country. He is, from the nature of the case, the principal agent in everything that concerns the police; but as it now is, if he wishes to make his action felt by the members, which he might do by bringing it to bear upon a single point, he has to go and consult with an unpractised superior; and hence, the effect which might be produced at once and with co-ordination, has to be done in detail, with all the useless delays occasioned by passing through an unnecessary and irregular channel.

The establishment of a ministry of the police, although not absolutely essential, would prove, nevertheless, in those feverish moments of disorganization which sometimes seize upon a people, a means of cure of very considerable efficacy. At the present day, for instance, it would furnish the quickest means of attaining an end, which, in our opinion, ought to be pursued by everybody, viz: the destruction of socialism.

The summary, then, of the system of police which we propose, is as follows: a ministry of police, to supervise and direct the public mind throughout France; commissaries general to act under its orders in the principal centres of population: these functionaries to act in co-operation with, and independently of, the prefects within their limits, who are to be occupied solely with the affairs of administration; then under the commissaries general, commissaries central, to be stationed in every town of importance. The commissaries general should be taken from Paris, men experienced in their business, and be furnished with secret service money and agents for establishing a police in the provinces—something which does not now exist. There should be agents for the city and agents for the country; and the office of these latter should be marked out with particular intelligence and care: for the most difficult part of their duties would not consist in the performance of a mere supervision, but in eradicating from the thoughts of simple minded men those mischievous ideas which are inspired by the demagogues.

A general plan of this kind, made up of numerous details which it is unnecessary to mention, and resolutely directed by large and comprehensive views, would bring socialism to its last shift by the end of a year. And this could be the more easily accomplished, inasmuch as the doctrine is by no means firmly rooted in the country; its principal disciples are only either fools or knaves: and it has become developed only at a time of moral subversion, and of corresponding weakness, on the part of the authorities. It is an epidemic, however, against which great precautions should be taken; but which can nevertheless be effectively cured by the means of intelligently and energetically prescribed remedies: and among those remedies, the system of police which we have proposed would certainly be the most effectual.

CHAPTER VII.

Complot of the towers of Notre Dame—Trial of members of the *Friends of the People*—Messrs. Bonnias, Raspail, Blanqui, Antony Thouret—The chiefs of the popular societies boil over—Messrs. Rittiez, Toussaint Bravard, Cahaigne, Avril, Imbert.

At the commencement of the year 1832, the *Friends of the People* had the principal direction of the republican party. There were other societies still, pursuing the same course, such as the *Claimers of July*, commanded by M. O'Reilly, the *Gallic Society*, under the direction of M. Thielmans, and various other groups, under different denominations; but the preponderance of the *Friends of the People* was acknowledged and respected.

M. Casimir Perrier, on assuming the management of the police, had taken measures with respect to this society, which had partly effected their object: that is to say, the conspiracy had been forced to abate somewhat of its audacity, and to become more circumspect in its proceedings. But though thus repressed, its work was not the less ardently prosecuted: the propagandism was continued by speeches and newspaper articles, and especially by pamphlets, the employment of this latter means being pursued with the most extraordinary zeal.

Although the society, since its dissolution, had become secret, yet it had not yet assumed that organization and discipline which had characterized carbonarism, and which we shall find it possessed of at a later period. To a certain degree its meetings might still be considered public; for, as the greater part of its discussions were published, and as the committee professed only a moral propagandism, the sections taking good care, at the same time, to avoid meetings larger than the legal number of twenty persons, a sort of respect was thus shown for the law, by which the tribunals of those days were fain to rest content.

But the *Friends of the People*, though united in their object, the overthrow of royalty, were far from being unanimous either as to the course to be pursued, or the day for delivering battle. Though in the mobs which had harassed Paris since the period of July, there is perceived a premeditated scheme of agitation, yet the odious responsibility of this scheme should not be imputed entirely to men of such serious cast of mind as Messrs. Cavaignac and Guinard; it rests chiefly with leaders of secondary importance, by whom the plan was conceived, and by whom it was executed with the most detestable perseverance. The leaders of secret societies, we repeat it, never preserve their influence except under the condition of submitting to the tyranny of the reckless and hair-brained, who are in a hurry to rush at once to the conclusion of their schemes; and such was the character of those men who, from the first days of 1832, impatient to arrive at the end of their designs, declared that mobs were useless, and urged that an attack should be made in mass. With their heads turned by the noise of the clubs, and blinded by their own exaltation, they persuaded themselves that Paris was all on their side, and that they had only to make their appearance in order to destroy the government, root and branch. It was in vain that some of the republicans endeavored to give them a more moderate view of things; to show them that the bourgeoisie were in favor of the new reign, and that the great mass of the workingmen were interested in preserving peace. In reply to such arguments as these they only grumbled, and hastened to effect a schism. But then, perceiving their isolation and weakness, they resolved, by complots and other desperate means, to rouse up the people. The affair of which we are about to speak was the result of one of these desperate resolves.

M. Gisquet relates that, when scarcely entered upon the discharge of his duties, he was informed of a complot, the signal of which was to be a conflagration of the towers of Notre Dame. By the light of the flames, which were to devour one of the wonders of Paris, some bands of conspirators were to spread themselves through the streets and arouse the people to a revolt. The incendiary was to be M. Couridère, who was to be assisted by six devils incarnate, youths of nineteen or twenty years of age. Among the chiefs who were to act in the streets were M. Pelvillain, well known since for his pot house conspiracies, and Napoleon Chancel, who pleaded contumacy at the trial of Bourges in 1849. The affair was fixed for the 2d of January. Although M. Gisquet could hardly credit such a savage project, yet, persuaded that scepticism is a bad policy in such matters, he examined into it and took his measures accordingly. On the day fixed, a vigilant watch was established, and every disposition made for seizing the culprits in the act; but nothing, however, occurred; the old cathedral slept as usual amidst its solemnity of ages, escaping the sinister aureole with which it had been threatened. The prefect concluded that the detestable project was either a simple rumor, or had been very much exaggerated. He knew well, that, in the lower stratum of the factions, there are always dreams of assassination and destruction, but which fortunately never reach beyond the dens where they have their birth. On the 3d the same tranquillity prevailed about the church; and then the police were convinced that the alarm had been false, and took no further concern about it. But lo! on the 4th, at about 3 o'clock in the morning, the bells of Notre Dame sent forth a hurried peal, awakening the neighborhood from their sleep; and immediately the police were informed that the complot which was to have come off on the 2d, having been adjourned for some cause unknown, had just broken out. The individual who brought this information was one of the conspiracy; and he added, that the conspirators had sixteen hundred republicans and six regiments.

The sixteen hundred republicans were one of those calculated falsehoods of which parties are always so lavish. The popular societies all together did not amount to that number; and it is very certain that all the republicans would not take a part in such a diabolical machination. As to the six regiments, the conspirators here also indulged in a figure of rhetoric, taking a part for the whole. We shall have an occasion to show more than once that the troops which were said to be gained over by the democrats, consisted of a few ignorant or drunken soldiers, who were indoctrinated by fine speeches or glasses of wine.

Detachments of the police hurried to the cathedral, where they learned from the guardian that a pistol had just been fired at him, and that the stairs were barricaded. The policemen, overthrowing the barricades, found themselves in the presence of persons who fired upon them and fled. These persons were pursued, and in the pursuit they were seen to throw handfuls of proclamations into the streets below. Six of their number were soon arrested; but the public force had arrived too late to prevent a commencement of the conflagration. Fire had been set to the wood work of one of the towers, and the flames were threatening a catastrophe; but, fortunately, prompt measures arrested the danger.

At this moment several bands were seen gliding along the alleys of the neighborhood, directing their course towards Notre Dame and repairing to the rendezvous. They were led by Messrs. Pelvillain and Chancel. Being discovered and pressed upon by the troops, they were apprehended before knowing what condition their abominable enterprise was in.

It was learned from the guardian that seven persons had entered the towers, and there still remained therefore one more to be found. This person proved to be M. Couridère, the most important of all. It took three hours to find him; and it was perceived that he had set fire to the place where he had taken refuge.

M. Couridère, the inventor and hero of this wretched affair, was at that time, like the rest of his accomplices, a young man of an insensate exaltation and unbridled energy. To the judge, who asked him his profession, he replied, "A mobber." On the pronouncement of the sentence, which condemned him to an imprisonment of five years, raising himself up with a savage air, he cried out to the President,

"Thou shalt have five years imprisonment, and the expenses to boot! I'll pay thee from the chest of Louis Philippe."

Such bravery as this the patriots called, valiantly maintaining a cause. We shall not comment upon this character of mobber which M. Couridère arrogated to himself; all that we can say is that he was not boasting; for Paris at that time contained men- whose only profession was to excite mobs.

By this affair an idea may be formed of some of the inferior leaders of the party. A few words now with regard to the doctors of the party. During the legal proceedings of the 10th, 11th, and 12th of January, 1832, the chiefs, whose names are as follows, Messrs. Raspail, Gervais de Caen, Blanqui, Antony Thouret, Hebert, Trélat, Bonnias, Rillieux, and Plagnol, were brought to the bar to give an account of divers publications that had emanated from the society. Extracts from these publications would be useless, since their character may be conceived by the defence which was set up by the accused. After M. Raspail had led off with a tirade of abuse against the king, then came M. Blanqui, who, full of his mad dreams and hatreds, delivered a speech designed with the view of stimulating the people to social subversion. "This," said he, "is war between the rich and the poor; the rich desire it, because they are the aggressors; the privileged few roll in wealth acquired by the sweat of the poor. The Chamber of Deputies is a pitiless machine, grinding to powder twenty-five millions of peasants and five millions of workingmen for extracting their substance, which is transfused into the veins of the privileged class. The taxes are plunder which is made by the idle upon the laboring classes."

There is no need of commenting upon the folly of such artificial phraseology as this, so zealously restored to honor in our days; for M. Blanqui, from whom the *reds* of the present day have plagiarized, was himself only a copyist of the levellers of '93.

M. Bonnias came next; he harangued against tyranny, the civil list, the pilferers of revolutions, the cudgellers, the spies, and all that sort of thing. Messrs. Gervais and Thouret joined in the chorus, and sustained, one by his bilious chicanery, and the other by pompous verbosity, the declamation of their comrade. It was a perfect flood of insults against the chiefs of the government, the court, the law, and the rules of common decency.

All the accused were acquitted on the chief counts of the indictments; because it could not be proved that they were the authors of the publications. But in consequence of their behavior before the court they were sentenced to various periods of imprisonment; Messrs. Raspail and Bonnias, for fifteen months, M. Blanqui for one year, and Gervais (de Caen) and Antony Thouret for six months. The latter, on withdrawing, gave an emphatic menace to the court in the following words—"We still have bullets in our cartridge boxes!"

This was an unnecessary piece of information to the authorities; for the audacity of the republicans had emboldened other parties, which, with the common object of overthrowing the government, were already requiring the most vigilant attention. Besides, a thousand circumstances, either fortuitous or premeditated, augmented, every day, the excitement and hopes of the republicans. The excitement of to-day, perhaps, would be some scandalous trial; that of to-morrow, a furious book; one day a mob in the provinces, and the next, anarchical speeches in the National Assembly, where the *Friends of the People* counted as members, or patrons, about a dozen deputies, such as Messrs. Cabet, de Ludre, Lafayette, Lamarque, Audry de Puyraveau, Laboissière, and Dupont (de l'Eure). In the month of November, the workingmen of Lyons, for a cause not political, and while professing submission to the king, took possession of the city, and forced the prefect to make improper concessions. In the month of March following, the ill-disposed part of the people of Grenoble succeeded, as the finale of a disgusting masquerade, in overcoming the feeble garrison of the place, and compelling the authorities to capitulate. The *Friends of the*

People, who had an affiliated society in Grenoble, contributed a great deal towards this success against the government.

In the midst of such excitements as these, and burning with impatience to out-distance their rivals (the Napoleonists and Legitimists) and to arrive at once at their object—it can be judged to what extent the republicans had taken fire, and how near they were to an explosion.

The serious minded men of the party saw clearly two things: first, that an insurrection could not succeed, because of its being opposed by the bourgeoisie; and second, that the insurrection, nevertheless, would inevitably take place. One of those moments had arrived in the conspiracies where the current of things rushed hurriedly to a solution. In order to make proselytes, the chiefs exaggerated the number of their army; magnified the spirit of insurrection, and infatuated the minds of their followers with the ideas of an approaching battle. The followers took every hint as a promise, and of which the chiefs were reminded, first gently, then with bitterness, and finally with threats, until at last the day arrived when the committee had to give the signal for the fight, or be considered as traitors. We shall see this condition of things occurring more than once.

Now, the persons who were really deserving of consideration in the society, the directors, inspirers or patrons, such as M. Cavaignac, General Lafayette, etc., found themselves in the situation which we have just described. Not that we ascribe to them the responsibility of false assertions or promises, but that lures of this character had been offered to the crowd, and that the crowd held their highest chiefs accountable for them. And as this higher order of chiefs were too prudent to flatter hopes which they could not entertain themselves, they had inevitably to lose influence and give way to chiefs of an inferior order, who had nothing to lose and everything to gain. Such was the state of things that took place during the first months of the year 1832. The men who from that time took the direction of the affairs of the conspiracy were leaders of secondary consideration, of mediocre talents, little influence, and without social position.

In case the reader should wish to know these men, we give a few of their characters.

M. Rittier, editor of the *Censor* of Lyons; one of the mildest and most credulous of the revolutionists—somewhat of the M. Dapoty stamp; full of fears and complaints, which the logicians of the streets translated into blows and hard knocks with the musket.

M. Toussaint Bravard, the type of the student who never studies; drinker, phrase-maker and fighter; ruler of the roast of the Latin quarter; firing at marks with the crossbow; squabbling with the police; great at billiards and *pot-house* dances; the first in every harum-scarum party, and the last in his course of studies, having spent seven or eight years in arriving, with much difficulty at that, at the position of health officer of Paris. At bottom a man of no reach of thought—a worthless fellow—an ex-member of the third house.

M. Cahaigne, a very good man, but who had labored for thirty years under the illusion that he had a talent for literature and politics, which he could make nobody else believe. Ex-editor, in short, of the *Commune* of M. Sobrier.

M. Felix Avril, Secretary of the *Friend of the People.* The eternal formula of—Felix Avril, Secretary, at the bottom of the publications of the society, had finally transformed into a person of distinction, a young man who was otherwise extremely insignificant. Until February, 1848, he remained one of the flies of the democratic coach; but, at that period, M. Louis Blanc took him from the baggage-office of the Rouen Railroad, and made him prefect of Calrados.

M. Bergeron, known for the pistol-shot fired upon the Pont-Royal; which affair made a great deal more noise than have the literary labors to which he abandoned himself in the *Siècle*, under the signature of Emile Pagès.

M. Charles Teste, a friend of Babœuf, whose doctrines he transfused into *carbonarism;* a conspirator, demi-secular, and not very noisy, brooding in the shade, with a select circle of friends, over savage convictions; but rather sincere on the whole—rather an honest and disinterested man.

M. Danton, having had, as it appears, no other merit than his relationship with the terrible orator of the Revolution.

M. Delescluze, an obscure libellist, and rather of an equivocal character. One of the men who has been well acquainted with him, M. Sobrier, for example, tells some anecdotes of him before the affair of February, which would hardly find place in our histories of instruction. His character as a writer was somewhat of a brutal pugilist, which has no name in literature.

M. Imbert, founder of the *Sovereign People* of Marseilles; a travelling wine merchant; commandant of the Tuileries; originator of the Risk-All; dealer in conspiracies; a very busy sort of body, and rather worthless.

There were, also, M. Adam, M. N. Lebon, M. Aubert-Roche, M. Plagnol, M. Madet, M. Fortoul, M. Caunes, M. Sugier, and M. Lebœuf, who were of not much account. Some of them had a great exaltation, others great presumption, and all a very great ambition.

The most of these men yielded to the inordinate pressure of the popular societies, and allowed themselves to be persuaded that the hour of battle had arrived. All that remained, then, for them to do, was to draw up their forces, and look for some favorable opportunity.

CHAPTER VIII.

The mob of the rag-pickers—The cholera, and the pretended poisoners—Credulity of the people—Odious machinations of the republicans—The legitimist party—Affair of the street of Prouvaires—A patriot writer.

In the beginning of April, 1832, the affair of the rag-pickers, and that of the pretended poisoners, excited a mob in Paris. The interests of one of the industrial classes, and the ignorance of all the lower order of people, were in a ferment; and what richer mine for working could possibly present itself? The republicans eagerly took advantage of their good luck.

A few words upon the cause of the disturbance.

The contract for cleaning the streets having expired, a new one was given out according to form, but with a provision that the contractor should have the right to carry off the grosser part of the rubbish during the night time, and thus abridge the work of the day. But this right deprived the rag-pickers of a very considerable part of their pickings; and hence they became highly exasperated. They came together in a mob; stopped the tumbrels of the new contractor; broke them to pieces and threw them into the water. Some of the cartmen, also, were thrown in together with their carts. Such was the beginning of the mob. The next day the affair became complicated with pretended attempts at poisoning, an idea which had originated in the cholera, and which the credulity of the people, driven by their fears, received without examination. The scenes that followed set back our civilization and struck Paris with dismay. The very idea of having over one's food a phial, a bottle, a vase, or what not, gave rise to suspicions which the merest trifle served to confirm as a fact. At the Place du Caire, an employé of the government was massacred for having put poison, it was said, into the jars of a wine merchant; in the quarter des Halles, another was torn in pieces; at the Place de Grève, a third was assassinated and thrown into the water, and M. Gisquet affirms that a fourth was taken from his post at the Hôtel de Ville by a man who was so enraged that he beat him to death, and then gave him to be eaten by his dog!

These things took place as late as 1832! and yet it will be remembered that after the affair of July, 1830, the extreme moderation and the extreme wisdom of the people were not less extolled than their extreme courage. Now, from two such facts as these what inference can be drawn? It is this —that the flatterers of the little and the flatterers of the great are precisely of the same stamp, bestowing their fulsome praises indiscriminately upon any one and every one from whom there is any object to be gained.

This hideous madness, that led people to believe that the epidemic was in fact a general attempt to poison them, had seized upon all the lower classes of Paris. It is true that the occurrence of some remarkable incidents—which in order to place the responsibility where it belongs we shall explain—might easily have excited alarm among the old women; but that the people of the suburbs should generally believe in an absurd and infamous machination for poisoning them, does not certainly give us a very high idea of popular wisdom. Let us not be mistaken as to our intentions: we do not intend to insult the people; but on the other hand we shall not extol their infirmities; we deplore them. To tell this people, as they are told every day, that they are perfect, is a criminal piece of stupidity. We repeat it, for it cannot be too well known, that this race of the lowest stratum of society, ignorant, brutal and savage, plays the principal part in all our revolutions; it forms the main body of the rank and file of the streets. And thus is France condemned to bow, with hat in hand as it were, to those governments which are created by such men as beat pretended poisoners to death, and give the corpses to their dogs.

The occasion of alarm with the old women was as follows:—and the reader will judge by it whether the credulity of the people tended nearer to imbecility than the patriotism of certain men did towards the extreme of villany. In the midst of the cholera, that strange and terrible disease, which is every way calculated to excite the fears, it was proved that the appearances of attempts at poisoning had actually taken place. In the suburb Saint-Antoine, a packet of drugs was thrown into a well by some persons who immediately fled into the midst of a crowd, where they were seen to change their dress and make their disappearance. Some wretched looking men were seen writhing in the streets, crying out that they had been poisoned. In one place colored sugar-plums were found; in another, some tobacco powdered over with a whitish matter; in another still, some bottles of wine covered with a reddish paste. But on examination, the reddish paste proved to be soap: the whitish matter, flour; and the colored sugar-plums, ordinary comfits. The men who said that they were poisoned, had either been taken with the cholera, or pretended to have convulsions. As to the well of the suburb of Saint-Antoine, its water, when carefully examined, proved to be perfectly salubrious.

But those men who declared that they had been poisoned, or who disseminated matters that were said to be poisonous, were no illusion; they at least had an actual existence, and were seen in a great many places. They were in fact the actors in a complot for creating the impression that there was a general attempt to poison the people; and as the people, from the fine ideas with which they had been inspired, could not well impute such a crime to any other source than the government; and as the result of this horrible accusation could profit only the revolutionists, it is evident that the revolutionists should be held responsible for it. And if there can be any doubt in the matter here are the proofs.

In a proclamation which was thrown into the midst of the mob, were read the following words: "Already now for two years the people have been a prey to the agonies of the most disgraceful misery; they have been attacked, imprisoned, assassinated. And this is not all; for under the pretext of a *pretended* epidemic, the people are poisoned in the hospitals, and assassinated in the prisons. Last Sunday, it is a well established fact, a crowd of spies forced their way into the prison of Sainte-Pélagie; and these rascals fired upon the patriots who were shut up within. O shame! O crime! how long, just Heaven, must thy decrees enchain our arms? What remedy is there for our ills? It is not patience, for patience is at an end; it is not insignificant mobs, which are so easily repressed; no, it is by means of arms that the people gain and maintain, at one and the same time, their liberty and their bread. Let the *torch*, then, the *pike* and the *hatchet* open to us a passage. There is no middle course, it is only by destroying the dens of all the brigands who conspire our ruin, and by purging society of the monsters by whom it is infected, that the people can come to breathe a pure and free air. To arms! To arms!"

This production which, it is evident, cannot be censured for hypocrisy, is the open avowal of conflagration, destruction, and carnage. Without dwelling too long upon all the ideas which are here set forth by the revolutionists, we may remark first, that they sustain the notion of attempts having been made at poisoning; and then, we may observe this important declaration, that the chiefs were no longer satisfied with mere mobs, but they must have a rising in mass, with torch, pike, and hatchet—a general slaughter of the Nero style, illuminated by a conflagration. Now this second idea, according to their way of reckoning, was to follow as a consequence of the first; they counted upon deceiving the credulity, and exasperating the ignorance of the people, and thus impelling them to one of those moments of passion in which governments are overthrown. The proclamation is not the only proof of this plan; these were concurrent facts; a commencement of execution of the plan had already taken place. On the 1st of April two hundred men of the sections had attacked Sainte-Pélagie from without, while the prisoners arose against their keepers within. Troops arrived and forced their way into the prison; but they experienced such a resistance that they were compelled to fire in order to suppress the mutiny. The attack on the outside was conducted by a chief of a savage character named Valot, who was sentenced to the galleys.

The newspapers took up the cause of the rag-pickers, and gave a great deal of credit to the stories of poisoning. As to the revolt of Sainte-Pélagie, they declared that it was a stroke of policy on the part of M. Gisquet, who was thus endeavoring to begin his campaigns of September over again. This imputation shows the extravagant hatred which was entertained against this courageous magistrate. And M. Gisquet was not the only one who drew such hatred upon himself. On the 14th of May, 1832, M. Casimir Perrier died of the cholera; and on the 17th, the following announcement appeared in the *Tribune:*—

"On the news of the death of the president of the council, the undersigned political prisoners, carlists and republicans, have unanimously resolved that a general illumination shall take place to-night in the interior of their *humid* cells.

"Signed: BARON DE SCHAUENBOURG, ROGER, TOUTAIN, LEMESLIE, HENRY FIFTHISTS, PELVILLAIN, CONSIDÈRE, DEGANNE, republicans."

This union of legitimists with republicans on the inside of their *humid* cells, must not surprise us, for it existed also on the outside; not, indeed, that the more serious portion of the legitimists had ever given countenance to such an unnatural monstrosity, but that there were certain members of the party who, either from impetuosity or impatience, allowed themselves to be hurried beyond the respect which they owed to their position.

In order to complete the picture of events of this period, we must revert briefly to the acts of the legitimist party from the days of July.

After every revolution there is among us such a noisy enthusiasm—such a perfect infatuation for the triumphant cause, that the one which has been vanquished seems to be lost sight of, and to become annihilated. This state of things continued with the legitimists until the middle of February, 1831. At that period a funeral ceremony which the legitimists caused to be celebrated for the repose of the soul of the Duke de Berry, gave rise to a manifestation on the part of the republicans which ended in the devastation of the church of Saint-Germain-l'Auxerrois and the sacking of the archbishop's palace. The ceremony was to have taken place in Saint-Roch's; but as the curate refused the use of his church, the curate of Saint-Germain-l'Auxerrois, judging that it did not belong to him to refuse the use of his church for the prayers that were to be offered up for a massacred prince, opened his doors for the occasion. A catafalque was set up and the services took place. But towards the close of the ceremony a young man advanced towards the catafalque and placed upon it an engraved likeness of the Duke of Bordeaux, together with a crown of everlastings. The women contended with each other for the flowers of which this crown was made up, while the men took off their decorations in order to place them beside the engraving. The authorities interposed and arrested the young man, together with several of the legitimists. And there, since the law had taken the matter in hand, the affair, one would suppose, ought to have stopped. But a crowd of republicans, informed by their emissaries of what was going on, rushed to the church in a rage, threw themselves into it, and never retired until it had been completely sacked and plundered. The next day, while still hot from this exploit, they assailed the residence of the archbishop; broke up objects of art, the furniture and wainscoting, and threw them all into the Seine, leaving the palace in a complete state of devastation. Scarcely the four walls remained standing.

Six months afterwards, the conspiracy known as the "affair of Prouvaires," broke out. A newspaper called the *Revolution*, edited by M. Antony Thouret, declared that this affair "was a simple repast among friends, during which an *improper* intervention on the part of the police had occasioned a quarrel." The reader will now have an opportunity of judging as to what that affair was, and will thus be able to appreciate the choice of words made use of by the republican editor.

There had been for some time an extensive plan in contemplation, for re-establishing the elder branch of the Bourbons upon the throne. The Duchess of Berry was the authoress and the heroine of it. It was arranged that this princess should disembark in the South of France, where her arrival was to be the signal for a rising prepared for the occasion; that from there she should repair to the west as the head-quarters of the legitimist army, and that these movements should be supported by a *coup de main* upon Paris. The principal agent of the duchess in the capital was the Marshal Duke de Bellune. He was in a direct correspondence with the august conspiratrice, and received from her the funds destined for the conspirators. Under the orders of the marshal there acted a committee of twelve persons, among whom were Messrs. the Count de Florac, the Baron de Maistre, the Duke de Rivière, the Count de Fourmont, the Count de Brulard, and Charbonnier de la Guesnerie. Each of these superior chiefs commanded an arrondissement, and had under his orders four chiefs of quarter; and these chiefs of quarter commanded detachments of ten men, who, in their turn, were each to form a group the union of which was to constitute the main army. The enlistments went on rapidly; a large number of soldiers of the guard, ancient employés, and the Swiss, lending themselves readily to a project which promised to restore them to their former positions. The workingmen were attracted by bounties for enlistment; and persons of all classes and characters took a part in the conspiracy, including the Bonapartist general M. Montholon.

M. Louis Blanc, in his desire to catch the police in a fault, pretends that the government was very badly informed upon that affair; giving as a reason that the agents who had been charged with watching it, had sold themselves to the legitimist chiefs, to whom they were very sincerely devoted. Such stories may do for children; but if M. Louis Blanc had been a prefect of the police for two weeks—a real, earnest prefect, he would have learned that the infidelity of an agent is not quite so easy as he imagines; and that, besides, a faithless agent only renders himself useless to the administration, without being of any use to others.

A powder manufactory, which had been established at Bellville, in the house of one Grenet, was seized, together with the paymaster of the establishment; and at the same time, in order to break up the threads of the conspiracy, about a score of the most active chiefs were arrested. M. Charbonnier de la Guesnerie, ex-captain of the Royal Guard, and Valerius, who was compromised in the affair of Saint-Germain-l'Auxerrois, were among the number. But the complot was not to be baffled by a few arrests; two weeks sufficed for filling up the vacancies, and restoring everything to its former condition.

The police soon perceived that the conspiracy was assuming the most formidable character. A manufacturer of arms gave information of a contract that was being made between himself and the conspirators, for furnishing muskets. The police had, moreover, learned that at a council of the chiefs, it had been resolved to commence action on the night between the 2d and 3d of February. On that night there was to be a great ball at the Tuileries. The royal family, the ministers of state, and the principal functionaries, were to be present; and the design was to take them all, and thus effect a radical abscission of the government.

On the day appointed, everything being in a state of readiness, and without a suspicion of treason, the conspirators began their work. At about ten o'clock at night, numerous groups began to put themselves in motion, converging from a great number of points, towards the four following rendezvous, viz: the canal Saint Martin, the barrier d'Enfer, the boulevard Montparnasse, and the street of Prouvaires. All these detachments carried concealed arms, and pursued lines of march which had been designated beforehand, and which led through the most unfrequented streets. Those who went to the street of Prouvaires were generally in carriages. The police, being preinformed of these movements, allowed them to be executed, intending to act simultaneously upon each column, when the groups should be finally united. A signal to the municipal guards was then given; and these, hastening, in strong platoons, to the three rendezvous of the suburbs, broke them up, bore off some of the conspirators, and dispersed the rest. A story is told that one of the groups, composed of citizens of the lower classes, in endeavoring to make their escape, requested a patrol to conduct them out of the city, so that they might avoid the municipal guards; but the patrol, understanding how the matter stood, and finding itself too weak to arrest these ingenuous conspirators, led them to a station of the troops of the line, where they were duly taken care of.

But there were among the scattered columns men of less timid character, who, believing that only a partial check had been given to the affair, hastened to the street of Prouvaires, the centre of operations, for the purpose of receiving orders, or, at least, of learning the news. As fast as they arrived, however, the police seized them in a sort of mouse-trap which it had drawn around the point of union.

A boot-maker, M. Poncelet, was the chief of the assemblage in the street of Prouvaires; and from the position that was intrusted to him, from the part which he had played in the preparations, and from that which he was to play in the execution, he might be considered as the commander-in-chief of the conspiracy. He was a man of uncommon intelligence and of extraordinary resolution.

The point of reunion was a restaurant, where a supper had been ordered for the night. The leading conspirators had been notified to repair thither in order to arm themselves and receive their last instructions. At about midnight the greater part of them were at the rendezvous. Soon afterwards a fiacre was seen to arrive laden with boxes of muskets, which were carried into the restaurant. Without the loss of a moment every one proceeded to arm himself; but while engaged in this operation, the police, having at their head the chief of the municipal police, M. Carlier, fell upon the midst of the conspirators like the falcon upon a quarry of sparrow-hawks. A musket was fired at the courageous functionary, but it fortunately missed its aim. Then a warm engagement ensued, in which furniture and dishes flew about on all sides. Several shots were fired, by which one of the policemen was killed; but the public force, commanded by a resolute chief sure of his arrangements, showed an energy of action which soon put the plotters to a complete rout. Two hundred persons were taken and immediately led to the prefecture of the police.

M. Poncelet, who was one of the number, was discovered in a chimney, having on his person a large sum in bank-notes and a key for opening the gates of the Tuileries.

By the trial, which followed, it was proved that from twelve to fifteen hundred conspirators were to have concentrated upon the Tuileries in four separate columns. The first, under the orders of M. Poncelet, was to enter the Tuileries through the picture gallery, and then rush suddenly into the midst of the ball, and take possession of, or make way with the royal family and the members of the government. One of the door-keepers of the Louvre who was in the plot, was to open the passage to the gallery. The second column was to make its attack by way of the garden, and the other two by way of the Carrousel. The simultaneousness of these movements; the numerous detailed measures by which they were supported; the audacity of the chiefs; the organization of the party in the capital, and the presence of the Duchess in La Vendée, taken all together, gave this enterprise a character which was certainly very formidable.

Sixty-six of the accused were brought before the Court of Assizes.

Against two who were contumacious, the sentence of death was passed. M. Poncelet and five others were sentenced to deportation. The same sentence was also passed against five of the principal conspirators who had fled; also against the Counts Fourmont and Brulard. Eighteen others received sentences less severe.

In declaring that this affair "was a simple repast among friends which had been disturbed by an improper interference on the part of the police," was M. Antony Thouret jesting with his readers, or was he making a fool of himself? The public will judge; in either case some idea can be formed of the veracity of our patriot writers.

CHAPTER IX.

Preparations for an insurrection—Order of battle of the secret societies—Political Refugees—An attempt at assassinating General Bem—Young Italy—M. Mazzini—A secret tribunal—A frightful drama.

The descent of the Duchess of Berry at Marseilles towards the close of April, 1832, and the ineffectual attempts at a rising in the West, proved that the hopes of the legitimists had survived the check which they had received in the street of Prouvaires. The police soon learned, in fact, that a new plot was being formed by the party; but as prompt measures were immediately taken to suppress it, the more prominent chiefs perceived the uselessness of their efforts and abandoned the undertaking. But the more exalted of the republican party, although professing a contempt for the legitimists, watched, nevertheless, their movements, with the view of making use of them to hasten an insurrection which a growing impatience had rendered inevitable. Among some of the sections of the popular societies there was exhibited all that ravenous fury which animates the pack when about to seize upon the quarry. It was impossible to restrain men to whom power had been held up as their assured prey. To prevent an explosion under such circumstances, would have required a veto sustained by all the energy of the principal chiefs. The revolutionary populace, when once engaged in their work, obey only a brutal instinct; but before becoming engaged, they wish to make sure of their commanders. And the reason is, because, before the affair begins, there is time for reflection, which convinces the old dogs of the streets of their incapacity for managing the affair by themselves; but when once in the midst of the fire, when intoxicated with powder, wine, and blood, all prudence disappears and leaves room only to the inspirations of violence.

As in the committee of the *Friends of the People* some of the members had already lost their senses and all were hurried away by the excitement of the hour, and as the secondary chiefs called loudly for the fight at all hazards, the insurrection became adopted in principle, and its execution fixed for the early part of May. The only remaining question, then, was to find some good pretence.

When things are in such a state that the chiefs of an army allow themselves to be led by their corporals, we may naturally expect all kinds of blunders; and it was one of these blunders, it appears to us, the choosing the 5th of May as the occasion for a republican insurrection: such, however, was the fact. The sections were directed to assemble at the place Vendome, with orders to bring crowns of everlasting and to hold themselves in readiness for the combat. The chiefs were to rendezvous at a cook shop where they were to recruit their strength, in a patriotic repast before giving the signal. The police, however, were on the watch; they took it upon themselves to countermand the orders for the banquet, and arrested the principal plotters; but that did not prevent the *manifestation*. Hence, there were the knock-downs, the hoarse clamors, and all that sort of thing, as usual in such cases; and one of the mobbers fired a pistol upon one of the police. But as it missed, the mobber than drew a sword from his cane and tried to strike the agent of authority. The policeman, however, out with his sword, and soon left his man upon the pavement. And of course, for this act of self-defence, he was called an assassin; but if, on the other hand, he had fallen instead of the other, his murderer would have been styled a hero.

Here, then, we have another mere affray, and which could not have been otherwise, considering that the impelling cause had come from what are called hot-heads, and that hot-heads are seldom characterized by much genius.

The committee of the *Friends of the People*, who trusted but little to Messrs. Casimir Perrier and Gisquet, had contented themselves for some time with a direction by means of pamphlets, avoiding meetings and such measures as were too compromising; but in view of the imperious movements which compelled the party to act, they decided to take the initiative openly. A meeting of the leading members was held on the 7th of May in the suburb Saint Martin; and the principle of insurrection, already admitted by the subordinate groups, was voted in an official manner.

It so happened that a few days afterwards an influential republican, M. Gallois, was killed in a duel; and it was resolved to make his funeral an occasion for taking arms. Besides that the funeral of a patriot was a very natural occasion for assembling the party, the juncture of affairs, moreover, was very favorable, for the attempts of the Duchess of Berry to excite a rebellion in Brittany would occupy the attention of the government in that quarter, and restrict its liberty of action in Paris, while the schemes of the legitimists in the capital might be made to contribute to the disturbance. To this train, then, the match was to be applied. But before arranging the final measures, a grand meeting was fixed for the first of June, to be held in the street of Saint André des Arts, at the house of a chief of section, named Desnuaud. The police, however, being informed of what was going on, and not exactly approving of an insurrectional council of war, placed their seals upon the premises. The conspirators, therefore, on their arrival, saw the signs of the law; but being altogether above such things, broke the seals, entered the house, and commenced proceedings. About thirty of their number were taken by the police, and the rest made their escape.

The affair, however, was not to be delayed on this account, and the next day, the day of the funeral, remained still as the day for action. But while the procession was on its way, the news was spread through the ranks by means of emissaries, that an adjournment had been ordered. It had just become known that General Lamarque was at the point of death; and the occasion which his funeral would offer, appeared to be much preferable to the one which had been chosen.

The general died that night; and the news that his burial would take place on the 5th, irrevocably fixed the insurrection for that day.

On the fourth of June, the committee of the *Friends of the People* drew together the chiefs of the societies and other various elements of the insurrection, in order to arrange the plan of battle. Having recapitulated the forces upon which they could rely, the points of rendezvous were assigned as follows: The *Friends of the People,* to the place of the Louvre; the *Political Convicts,* to the place of the Madeleine; the *Students,* to the place of the Odeon; the *Refugees,* to the street of Taranne; the *Parisian Artillery,* to the place of the Palais Royal. These were the forces which were more immediately under the control of the *Friends of the People.* The *Claimers of July,* under the orders of M. O'Reilly, and the

Gallic Society, commanded by M. Thielmans, had also their rendezvous; and also the few remaining fragments of the Societies of *Aid-thyself*, the *Union, Free and Gratuitous Education*, etc.

These forces, when all united, might have amounted to about two thousand men, of whom six or seven hundred were under the direction of the *Friends of the People*. The effective strength of the whole party, in the capital, did not exceed three thousand. It must be remembered that the people formed but a very small portion of the societies, and that the word Republic was almost unknown to them. The abettors of anarchy are almost always recruited from that class of the bourgeoisie which I have designated by the name of *Imbeciles*.

The minor details of the plan were immediately arranged. Arms and ammunition were distributed; certain places were pointed out where those who were not already provided with arms, could find everything that was wanting, and masses of pamphlets for exciting the people, including the usual proclamations, were prepared for the occasion. The list of a provisional government, too, was not forgotten; it was made up, according to established usage, of men whose opinions in the case had not been committed. These men, however, are always ready to accept if the affair succeeds; but if it miscarries, they disown the conspirators with indignation.

Upon this list shone the names of several deputies, who, after having assisted in giving birth to the new government, had immediately declared themselves its systematic adversaries, reproaching it for having deviated from its origin. Rather of a singular accusation, it will appear, when we come to examine into it; for, in fact, the origin of the royalty of July was a revolution; and would they wish, therefore, to set up a revolutionary form of government? There was no necessity for appointing a king for that. Would they wish to establish a progressive monarchy? But progression can only be secured in a state of order and tranquillity, and this state the new reign was sparing no efforts to restore. The fact is that the close, niggardly, and envious opposition which was displayed against the new government, foreshadowed the object of overthrowing that government from the very first days of July. As early as the month of May, 1832, this opposition had become sufficiently soured to array against the government that machine of war, which was called *pecuniary accountability*, a manifestation which, falling from on high, gave a forcible concussion to the lower basis of society, and inflamed, to a still higher degree, those anarchical hopes which broke forth on the 5th and 6th of June.

If experience is not a matter to be wholly disregarded by constitutional oppositions, these repeated instances of the *pecuniary accountability*, which aided to bring about the affair of June, 1832, and that of the *banquets*, which led immediately to the affair of February, 1848, should serve, one would suppose, as a lesson.

We have just said that a place had been assigned, in the insurrection of the 5th of June, for political refugees; and hence, before proceeding to an account of this insurrection, a few words upon the position and character of these men may not be inappropriate.

Since France has the misfortune to serve as a precedent for every revolt, it may follow that the defeated insurgents of other countries come among us, and demand, as it were, our hospitality. To succor the unfortunate, especially when they become so by our own fault, is a duty of honor which, in our country, can never be disregarded; but then it so happens that these refugees, in order to revolutionize Europe again, set ardently at work to get up a revolution among us; so that those men who have been granted shelter and security, reward their benefactors with perils and disorders. Far be it from us to wound, by a single unfriendly word, those true representatives of fallen nationalities, those sober men who have left their native soil in its subjection, and who base their hopes of enfranchisement upon other grounds than the ruin of their hosts; for such men deserve our sympathy and respect. But as to those who go about from country to country, making themselves busy in every disorder, colporteurs of engines against governments, Lucifers driven from their own country to conspire the ruin of the human race, those stage managers of revolutions, dealers in civil war and traffickers in public misfortunes—as for such men as these, the generosity which is shown them is, in our opinion, nothing short of the absurdest folly. For why should we be bound to receive among us the wolf which our neighbors have got rid of?

The Poles, in consequence of their ill success in 1831, came to France in great numbers. And almost immediately after their arrival they formed a committee, the members of which pretended to represent their country, and thus form a sort of government of Poland in Paris. They hurled a protest against the measures concerning the press, which had been taken in Germany; addressed an appeal to revolt to the Russians, and declared themselves ready to aid anybody in effecting a revolution. Such acts as these were all very well for men who had nothing to lose, but as France found herself responsible for them to other powers, she had some reason for interfering in this government of Poland; hence the committee was expelled.

But it soon became known that the Poles, not content with fomenting insurrection abroad, were becoming affiliated members of our secret societies. In consequence, the assistance which had been granted to them by the government was withheld from the most dangerous, and others were scattered among the depots of the interior. And this proceeding furnished an occasion to the *Tribune* and other papers of that character, to thunder against the despotism of the government. According to their accounts, all these refugees were serious, inoffensive men, who were entirely innocent of any revolutionary projects. But what did they know about it? And besides, if they had known anything about it, would they have told the truth? No! their wordy protestations in favor of the refugees, sprang either from ignorance or knavery. What member of government in France or anywhere else could be so cowardly as to persecute exiles for the mere love of the thing? or impose unnecessary restrictions upon unfortunate men who, in submitting to the law, demanded our protection?

Among the Poles of chief importance were reckoned Gens. Bem and Ramorino. These gentlemen, in endeavoring to be useful to themselves and their companions, proposed to form a corps for the service of Don Pedro. The plan was at first favorably received; but in a very short time, at the instigation of the revolutionists of Paris, those who had intended to go to Portugal began to cry out treason, and to pretend that the object was to get rid of them, or, at least, to compromise them in the service of tyranny. These declamations so embittered the minds of the hot-heads that one of their number lay in wait for General Bem, the chief of the expedition, and fired a pistol at him close to his breast. The general escaped death as by a miracle. From such an attempt as this some idea may be formed of this class of strangers.

As to the Italians who had alighted upon France after the failure of their revolutionary efforts, the city of Paris contained but a very few of them; they generally remained in the South, where they distinguished themselves by acts of a character still more detestable. An association existed among them which was called *Young Italy*, and it had for its chief a man whose demagogic antecedents, together with the recent events in Rome, have given him an unenviable reputation; I allude to M. Joseph Mazzini. Every member of the association was bound to provide himself with arms; to be at the discretion of his chiefs; to labor unceasingly for the extermination of kings, and to take an oath to assassinate whoever should be pointed out to him by the committee. And this oath was not one of those vain obligations which are so freely administered and taken in all secret societies; for persons were admitted only after a rigid examination which guaranteed fanatic devotion and ferocious determination. A single fact will exhibit these men at their work.

Four refugees, Messrs. Emiliani, Scuriatti, Lazzoreschi, and Andriani, who, though very ready to fight the *tyrants* of Italy, were not willing to become members of the Mazzinian society, had explained themselves openly to this effect;

and this constituted a crime of high treason, which had to be brought to the cognizance of a secret assizes. M. Mazzini came from Geneva expressly for the purpose of presiding at the trial, which was held at Marseilles agreeably to the forms decreed by the statutes. A man by the name of La Cécilia was the secretary, and several chiefs of the society took their seats as members of the gloomy tribunal. The free and accepted judges assembled at night at the house of one of their number; gravely constituted themselves a sovereign court of justice, and proceeded to examine indictments without the presence of either the accused or their defenders. At the order of Mazzini the secretary read the facts of the accusation. The accused were charged, 1st, with having propagated writings against the *holy* society; 2d, with being partisans of the infamous papal government; 3d, with seeking to paralyze the efforts of the association in favor of the sacred cause of liberty.

The proofs, consisting of various written evidence, were produced and discussed, and, in the absence of contradictory testimony, it was easy to come to an agreement as to their enormity. In consequence, the tribunal made an application of the statutes, and condemned Messrs. Emiliani and Scuriatti to suffer death. With respect to Lazzoreschi and Andriana, as the charges against them were less serious, they were sentenced only to be whipped with rods—"saving and excepting, that on their return to their country, a new sentence may send them to the galleys *ad vitam*, as notorious traitors and brigands."

A copy of this sentence was seized and is still in existence, signed: "Mazzini, President, and La Cécilia, Secretary." The condemned persons being domiciliated at Rhodez, the sentence bore the following addendum: "The president of Rhodez will make choice of four executioners of this sentence, who will be held to a strict account of its execution within a period of twenty days; and if any one refuses to execute it, he will incur the penalty of death *ipso facto.*"

Here, then, we have all that summary mode of proceeding, the ferocious penalties and the pitiless character that marked certain tribunals of barbarous times. This phantasmagoria has been often repeated for the purpose of frightening credulous conspirators; but in this case the drama was only too real. M. Mazzini, a perfect type of the cold, perfidious and sanguinary Italian, aspired from that time to the domination which he finally succeeded in imposing upon his country; and in his revolutionary Jesuitism he has made use of the same means for which he condemns his enemies—dark and gloomy punishments and terrors of the imagination.

A few days after the sentence had been rendered, while Emiliani was passing through the streets of Rhodez, he was attacked by six of his fellow countrymen, who stabbed him with their dirks, and fled. The victim, however, escaped with his life, and the assassins were arrested. The affair being examined into, was soon brought before the Court of Assizes, and the executioners of M. Mazzini were condemned to the cells for five years.

M. Emiliani, though still suffering from his wounds, accompanied by his wife, who bestowed upon him those cares which his condition required, was present at the trial. On leaving the court, finding himself fatigued, he entered a coffee house with his wife and his friend Lazzoreschi. Scarcely were they seated, when a man by the name of Gavioli made his appearance, went up to M. Emiliani, and, without uttering a word, plunged a dirk into his breast. At a second blow he struck down M. Lazzoreschi; and, as Madame Emiliani was hastening to the assistance of her husband, he twice stabbed her. He then fled, and was captured only after a desperate resistance which he offered to the young men by whom he was pursued.

The affright occasioned by the terrible tribunal was such that, two days afterwards, at the funerals of these victims, not a single Italian dared to make his appearance.

The assassin, being tried and condemned, suffered the penalty of his crime. As to M. Mazzini, returning to Switzerland, as the tiger returns to his den after a scene of carnage, he coolly resumed again his work at social destruction.

And such are some of the men who come to claim our

generosity! Such are the interesting exiles in whose favor the demagogic papers make such touching appeals!—Mazzinis, deriving an execrable influence from sanguinary mockeries, and brutes whom these Mazzinis make the instruments of their assassinations!

In the south, they imbrued their cowardly hands in the blood of their fellow countrymen; and at Paris, they labored with zeal to plunge us into a civil war. But was their conduct worse than that of their hypocritical defenders?

But we have arrived at length at that great conflict which every new government among us, it would appear, is destined to sustain; a terrible shock, in which the revolutionary spirit makes its last desperate struggle before acknowledging its impuissance, and a scene, it would seem, for which the month of June has received a sort of sinister consecration.

CHAPTER X.

The revolt of the 5th and 6th of June—A theory of insurrections—Why the plan of General Cavaignac is a bad one.

WHILE revolutions displace a crowd of existing things, they make vacancies for the incapacity and absurd pretensions of the whole hungry troop of aspiring men. Many of these men find at first very brilliant positions; but as these positions are much better for them than they for the positions, their good fortune is of but short duration. Every office that is bestowed makes implacable enemies against the new power. They who have not had the cunning or the luck to seize upon a morsel of the spoils, declare war against the new order of things. It is not on their own account that they complain; Oh no! God forbid! They are forced to raise their voice from a violent love for the people with which they have become seized, and especially just at that moment when all their little plans have miscarried. It is then that they cry out; then they groan, and then they set to work at conspiracies with a right good will. And inasmuch as the poorer class of people always suffer from the consequences of a change of government, readily persuading themselves therefore that the evil arises from the new administration; as there still remains after every commotion a germ of the fever which may easily cause a relapse; as they who get up the revolution are styled heroes, and hence conceive themselves authorized to show the same sort of heroism on every other occasion; as the laxness of authority permits the concerting of all kinds of conspiracies, it hence follows that soon after a successful revolt there is always a second revolt, terrible, obstinate, and bloody, the ostensible object of which is to perfect the first. Such a revolt, we have seen, took place after 1848, and we shall see the same thing occurring after 1830.

The events of the insurrection of 1832 are known; and as it is not our province to give them in detail, we shall mention only such as come within the plans of this work.

The general rendezvous of the insurrectionists was in the vicinity of the house of burials, of the street Saint Honoré. At about ten o'clock A. M., at which hour the funeral procession began to move, all the societies were at their post. Curiosity, stimulated by a thousand rumors and by an expectation of events generally foreseen, had drawn together an immense crowd, through the midst of which the manifestation moved on like a noisy flood. Excepting a few relations, friends, or disinterested admirers of the deceased, the procession was wholly composed of revolutionists. The *Friends of the People*, flanked by the students, the artillerists of the National Guard, and the refugees and political convicts, formed the main body of the army. The *Claimers of July* and the *Gallic Society* followed in separate corps; and then came a confused mass consisting of fractions disposed for the fight. Above their heads floated a large number of banners of various colors, and some with emblematic devices. M. O'Reilly, marching at the head of his band, displayed a red flag; and the refugees bore the colors of their respective countries.

The spirit that animated this throng began to manifest itself at the street de la Paix. Instead of pursuing its course along the boulevard, the procession, by order of the chiefs, turned down this street towards the column of the Place Vendome, with the pretence of rendering homage to the Emperor. But when arrived further on, at the boulevard Montmartre, an incident of quite a different character signalized the march: the procession had just saluted the *representative* of French dignity, and now, there was nothing better to be done than to degrade, as soon as possible, that dignity itself; the horses were detached from the hearse, and the patriots took their place; a happy conceit on the part of men who were groaning under the debasement of the human race.

All along the route, until arrived at the place of the Bastile, the passage of the procession was marked by scenes of disorder, which, though of little consequence in themselves, served to show the disposition of the throng. At one moment arose the cry of—"Hurrah for the Republic!" at another, a policeman was knocked over; and a little further on, an inoffensive citizen was stoned for not taking off his hat. They were thus getting their hands in for the decisive blow which was to be struck at the bridge of Austerlitz. It had been agreed that when the hearse should arrive at that point and begin to turn off toward the barrier in order to reach the birth-place of the deceased, the cry of—"To the Pantheon!" should be set up on all sides, and a feigned effort made as if the design was to force the corpse to that quarter. As the authorities would oppose this measure, the crowd were to insist upon it, and thus a quarrel would arise which was to be the signal for the attack.

This plan was known; and hence, when it came to be put in execution, the authorities were on their guard. A strong detachment of municipal guards had been put in charge of the hearse, under the orders of a resolute officer, Lieut. Colonel Dulac, who kept a vigilant lookout. When, therefore, the cry of war was raised, and the stones began to fly, the detachment made face to the assault, and stood firm to their ground. A party of armed republicans came up, and opened upon them a murderous fire, by which the Lieut. Colonel was wounded, one captain killed, and many of the guards killed or wounded. The detachment still held their ground, and while the main body delivered their fire, others placed the coffin upon a travelling carriage, which gained the barrier and disappeared from the view.

The first flash had thus burst forth, and the insurrectionary crowd that had amassed itself between the Bastile and the river, was already reverberating with the thunder of the storm. Presently a man made his appearance mounted upon a horse, forcing his way through the crowd, and shaking forth the folds of a large red flag, upon which were seen the words —"*Liberty or Death!*" This flag was borne by a ferocious demagogue, named Pieron; and immediately a classifying movement took place; for the curious, and all those who had come in good faith to pay their respects to the illustrious deceased, perceiving at a glance the sinister designs that were on foot, abandoned the place at once, leaving the ground free to the revolutionists.

A barricade had already been formed near the Granary of Abundance; and from this point, and also from the interior of the establishment, which was protected by a palisade, some shots were soon fired upon a squadron of dragoons. The dragoons made ready to return the fire; but some worthy men interposed to prevent it, and thus stopped, for a few moments, an inevitable conflict. The whole regiment was quartered near there, and, as they came out to the assistance of their comrades, they received a lively fire of musketry, which wounded the Colonel and Lieut.-Colonel, and decimated the corps. It was now time to act; and the dragoons charged in close order, but with calmness and composure. Without using either their fire-arms or lances, they drove back the crowd, and cleared the place.

The republicans being repulsed from this point, where, however, they had no design of making a stand, separated into a large number of small groups. These groups scattered themselves on all sides, each to a position which had been designated beforehand, and taking possession of these positions by surprise, they there established themselves. In this way they succeeded, in the space of two hours, in occupying more than half of the capital.

From this manner of proceeding on the part of the insurrectionists, spreading themselves with the rapidity of the torrent, we may rest convinced that the plan of General Cavaignac and every other system of temporization are radically bad. The scattering of the insurgents is the consequence of a general rule which arises from necessity and instinct; they separate for the better procuring of arms and provisions; and every one goes to some point with which he is familiar, where he will find comrades, and where he thinks he can make the best attack or defence. To wait until the insurrection has disclosed its plan of attack in order to oppose it by a regular plan of defence, is nothing less than to deliver up the ground to the enemy. The soldiers of the streets have their tactics, but not a system; and this tactics, which is the highest effort of their skill, consists in taking posts and barracks for the sake of getting arms, and, when the arms are got, in intrenching themselves in populous quarters difficult of access; they have no other plan. The course to be pursued, then, is very plain; it is to prevent the people getting arms and intrenching themselves at the corners; and by this means the insurrection may be taken by the throat as soon as it arises, and stifled before it can advance a step.

This plan, which is the only good one, and which would enable a government that has confidence in itself, and knows how to inspire it in others, to crush a revolt with ease, was not sufficiently observed in the affair of June, 1832. Though the government was then sure of making a good defence, and had taken excellent measures; though there were 24,000 men in Paris ready to act upon any point; though the municipal guards were with the procession with orders to act at the first sign of hostility—yet the insurrectionists succeeded in enveloping Paris in a very short space of time; by three o'clock in the afternoon their success was such that, though what we have said may explain it, yet nevertheless it will appear extraordinary. The arsenal, the mayoralty of the 8th arrondissement, the posts of the Place Saint Antoine, Galiote, Chateau d'Eau, and many others all along that line, were in the possession of the insurgents. A manufactory of arms in Popincourt Street was pillaged, and the barracks of the firemen in Culture Sainte Catherine Street were taken. From that point, and in approaching the centre, the republicans spread themselves with the same rapidity through the quarters of the Marais, Lombards, Arcis, Halles, Montorgueil, Cadran, Montmartre, etc. They even reached the post of the Bank, and took possession of it. They attempted that of Petits Pères, but the National Guard held its ground, and gave them their first check. Upon the left bank of the Seine there was the same promptness of movement, and almost everywhere the same success. The barracks of the veterans near the Garden of Plants, the Poudrière, many of the posts, and all the little streets of the Cité, fell into the hands of the insurgents.

On all sides the call to arms was raised, and barricades were thrown up. The malefactors began their work, some of the barriers were delivered to the flames, and edifices to devastation.

Thus was three-fourths of the capital invaded; and this surprising result, we must repeat it, was the work of but a few hours. And why? Merely because of an excessive confidence on the part of the government. The revolt, it was believed, would be suppressed under any circumstances, and the troops were held in reserve instead of being deployed at once.

Had the 24,000 men of the garrison been posted in the streets in the morning, a strong column stationed at the Bastile, where it was known the first explosion would take place, and vigorous instructions given to the officers, nothing more would have been necessary for cutting short the barricades, the disarmment of posts, the carrying off of arms and munitions, and, in short, in putting an end to the insurrection itself.

But experience in this respect is at last acquired, we should hope. If not, we may repeat, and re-repeat even to satiety, that our successful revolts are only the result of surprise, and that every government which will guard against being surprised, will have the advantage over the revolutionists. It is true that the concentration of troops, the measures of the police, the arrests in mass of demagogic chiefs, and especially the deployment of a considerable force at the first symptom of the revolt—all this would raise a great outcry, and give rise to a great deal of fine eloquence. But let it be so; the cries will be lost in the air; Paris will not have to wade in blood, and a band of reprobates could no longer have the liberty to plunge France periodically into a state of anarchy.

We shall be told that we are preaching despotism; but in fact we merely preach respect for that object which of all others in the world is the most deserving of it, viz: the legitimate personification of a people. That a government may have faults, and, indeed, numerous ones, is very evident; but that under the pretence of these faults which are often involuntary and almost always remediable, a handful of worthless men should suddenly rise up against the government, overthrow it, and establish one of their own in its place without forewarning or even consulting the country of which they form but an insignificant portion—that worthless men should be permitted to do this, is utterly intolerable, and ought to be stopped on every consideration. And it can be stopped by very simple means; all that is needed is a constant vigilance, a repressive force always at hand, and then a rapid and vigorous attack in mass upon the enemy the moment that he shows himself.

In this manner a government may maintain itself within national limits, pursue a course of moderation, without either haste or stubbornness, and thus escape one of those lamentable falls by which authority among us has become so grievously disparaged.

But to return. Paris, then, was invaded by the insurrectionists; and it really began to seem that the state of things was desperate; but there was a better point of view to the picture. An invasion of revolutionists in the capital proves nothing by itself; it is the general disposition of the public mind which is to be regarded as of the most importance. The movement, if favored by this disposition, may assume a broad development, and become a revolution; but unless so favored, the immediate result is a mere affray. Now it became evident to every practised eye, from an early hour on the 5th, that the revolt excited no sympathy among the people. From that moment, abandoned to its own resources, reduced to struggle alone against the government, its defeat was no longer doubtful.

At about four o'clock in the afternoon, Marshal Lobau, who had been invested with the command of the regular troops and National Guards, gave the order for a general attack upon all points. Those soldiers whom, it was said, had been gained over to the revolt because a few corporals had tippled at the barrier with the solicitors of anarchy, marched to the assault with their ordinary resolution. The National Guard, and especially that of the vicinity of the disturbances, were full of ardor, exposing their persons with the greatest intrepidity. At nine o'clock at night the left bank had been completely swept. At that hour the king entered Paris. He held a review by torch light upon the Carrousel, where the army gave the most striking evidences of their sincere devotion. In order to hem in the revolt as much as possible that day, the combat was continued until midnight. By that time the insurgents had been driven from all their minor positions, and were shut up within the space included between the middle of Montmartre Street and the market of the Innocents, extending by the way of Cadran and Montorgueil Streets, as far as the cloister of Saint Méry, where they were strongly intrenched. They remained masters besides of a few barricades at the entrance of the suburb Saint Antoine.

The republicans of any reflection, and all those who looked rather to their safety than to glory, had already abandoned the cause. The open hostility of the people destroyed their illusions and their courage.

All the information that arrived at the prefecture during the night, confirmed this discouragement and desertion. Those insurgents who still maintained their ground, were overcome with fatigue and drink, and could no longer oppose much resistance. At Saint Méry alone, a knot of men were running bullets, and making cartridges, with every appearance of being disposed for a desperate struggle.

To put an end to the affair as soon as possible, the attack was recommenced at four o'clock in the morning. The quarter Montmartre was carried; then the suburb Saint Antoine; then all the other positions excepting Saint Méry. The resistance at this point was obstinate and bloody, and yielded only to the fire of artillery.

At six o'clock in the evening, the revolt was at an end; all that remained of it was the blood of victims, ruin, disaster, and public indignation.

CHAPTER XI.

Shows that the advisers are not the payers—M. Jeanne—Decadence of the republican party—The affair of the bridge of Arcole—The good faith of the demagogues—The pistol-shot of the Pont Royal—The *Rights of Man* —A remarkable similitude—The necessity of putting a stop to anarchy.

From amidst the disturbances of June, the courage of the chiefs of secret societies and directors of propagandism does not stand forth in very bold relief. Though some of these chiefs had been arrested before the affair took place, yet of the many others who were still at liberty, hardly one of them distinguished himself with musket in hand. But this is a fact which should not surprise us much, since there are numerous other instances which show that the heroes of the clubs, the Attilas of the quill, lose a great deal of their audacity when they come to the pavement. It is true that a great many poor men are made to receive bullets in their places; they acquit themselves conscientiously of this part of their performance.

But, to be candid, we must confess the fact that the republicans of intelligence and character were opposed to the insurrection, and had taken no part in a disturbance which they had disapproved. It would have been something of a redeeming trait, however, if among all those second-rate chiefs who had shown so much ardor in fanning the flames of revolt, some few of them had clearly exhibited themselves in the midst of the fire, or, for the sake of disinterestedness, had even suffered themselves to get shot; they might have proved, in this way, at least, that they had no design of reserving all the advantages of the republic solely to themselves.

They had reckoned upon several persons of distinction for the fight, Messrs. Mauguin and General Clausel among others, who, however, had not made their appearance. To the first gentleman, several emissaries were sent; but they found him trembling with fear; he had no idea that such a terrible explosion would take place, and he could only see the most frightful results. Marshal Clausel, either from weakness or a desire for popularity, made promises to all parties, and complied with none. As for General Lafayette, his fondness for revolutionary adventures had become a perfect monomania. He was near the bridge of Austerlitz when the disturbance broke out, and some of the insurgents, by whom he was recognized, put him into a carriage, with the view of taking him to the Hôtel de Ville, where they intended to make a rallying point of him. He gave himself up to their manœuvres without the least objections. But, as this plan could not be realized, inasmuch as the hotel was not in their possession, the friends of the general conceived another plan, the originality of which was rather ferocious; they proposed to throw the good man into the river, and lay the charge of his death upon the police. Very fortunately, this patriotic idea was not carried into execution. At a later date, the general, in reverting to this circumstance, used to say, that the idea was not a bad one, but we have never learned whether he considered it so at the time of its occurrence.

It was known by papers which had been seized, that other personages had had a hand in the preparations. Of this number were Messrs. Laboissière, Garnier-Pagès, senior, and Cabet. They received the mandamus. The editors of the demagogic papers were also taken; and among these latter, one of them was found composing an article, the object of which was to prove that the police had provoked the revolt. This assertion was quite seriously maintained by one of the papers, which declared as a proof that Vidocq had been seen, on the 6th, leaving the prefecture with an armed band. Such was in fact the case; but this chief of the brigade of safety had gone to the vicinity of Notre Dame, in order to arrest one of the chiefs of the insurrection, M. Colombat, who was taken and condemned to deportation.

The state of siege had been declared, and the councils of war immediately entered upon their functions. One of the first of the accused who was tried, was that Pepin who was afterward guillotined with Fieschi. In the attack of the suburb Saint Antoine, a hot fire had been opened upon the National Guards and regular troops from Pepin's house; Pepin himself had been found armed with a pistol, which he endeavored to use against those by whom he was arrested, and on searching his house fourteen muskets were found that were still warm. But, notwithstanding all this, he stoutly denied all participation in the combat, and was acquitted. And it is true, too, that the National Guards did not take the execution of justice into their own hands when this insurgent returned to the suburb.

Pepin was an obstinate conspirator, who had a hand in every plot. He harangued little, but acted a great deal, although in the irregular mixture that made up his character, courage was not always the predominant element.

One single man, throughout this lamentable struggle, showed a real and well sustained bravery. Neither was he, any more than Pepin, a phrase-monger, or an ostentatious character at the clubs; he was one of those cool revolutionists who become chiefs because they expose their lives more freely than others. We allude to M. Jeanne, the commandant of the barricade of Saint Méry. He fought during two days, and finally cut his way out, sword in hand, not being taken till some time afterwards.

It will be remembered that, in consequence of a strange interpretation given to the state of siege, the Court of Cassation invalidated the proceedings of the councils of war, and sent all the accused before the Court of Assizes. From that time a multitude of trials took place, which occupied the jury during several months. Seven persons were sentenced to suffer death, viz: Messrs. Lepage, Cuny, Lacroix, Bainsse, Lecouvreur, Toupriant, and Forthoin; four others were sentenced to deportation, Messrs. Jeanne, Colombat, Saint Etienne, and O'Reilly, and others were condemned to hard labor. This last sentence was generally commuted. It ought to have been executed, however, in the cases of some of the patriots, Messrs. Léger and Didier, for instance, who had already commenced the practice of some of the extreme doctrines of socialism, and had become seriously involved with the penal code, section on theft.

Messrs. Thielmans and Marchand, chiefs of the *Gallic Society*, were sentenced to an imprisonment of seven years.

Hence, we perceive, there is hardly a trace to be found of the *Friends of the People*, who had labored so ardently in exciting the insurrection by means of writings, speeches, orders of the day, instructions, etc. Nevertheless, it is well known that there are but a very few among our great men of February, who are not willing that it should appear that they were heroes also of June, 1832; but we can tell these gentlemen that hardly any one of their class was seen at that time on top of the barricades, and we are certain that not one could be found beneath them. And this fact should be kept well in view; for the same men who, in June, 1832, were seen fanning the flames with particular care not to burn themselves, repeated this management again in February, an affair in which, though their prudence was equally great, their efforts met with better success. Undoubtedly a general aught not to expose himself too much; but then, a general in epaulettes has generally given proofs of his courage, which is not the case with many of the chiefs of the conspiracies; and moreover, this prudence of the general, especially when he has shown a great deal of ardor before the fight, is a matter which ought not to be carried too far. But if we look back through a period of eighteen years, we shall find that a crowd of poor devils have died in the streets, upon hospital litters, or in the cells of prisons, merely because they had listened to men who ought to have put themselves at their head in the hour of danger, but who have only put themselves at the head of the government on the day of success.

We might take this occasion to compare some of these chiefs of conspiracies, who are not to be found when their men are falling, with those chiefs of the government who appeared in Paris on horseback in the hottest of the fire. There was, for instance, the king, who, at mid-day on the 6th, when the cannon shot were crashing in upon Saint Méry, traversed the capital from the Champs Elysées to the suburb of Saint Antoine; and not without danger, it would appear, since a discharge of musketry whistled around his ears on the quay of Grève; and then M. Thiers, whom the patriots always assign a place in the hour of peril at the bottom of a cellar, but who on that day heard the music of the balls at a little less enchanting distance than very many of their number.

As a strange laxness still existed in certain branches of the government, and had even just exhibited itself by a new and striking example in annulling the consequences of the state of siege, the prudent instigators of revolt, the barkers of the republican press, opened again with their beautiful vociferations. Two sentences of death had just been passed against Messrs. Lepage and Cuny; they were the first sentences of the kind, and they were immediately commuted. This fact was known by Messrs. Marrast, Sarrut, Bascans and other writers of the faction, and yet they assumed the attitude of the bully, and dared the government to set up the scaffold. Impudence and cowardice! Impudence in thus seeking to exasperate the remnants of the sedition by a falsehood, and cowardice in tempting the wrath of the government, and in thus exposing unfortunate persons to the danger of a new butchery. For if the king and his advisers had not been governed by a sense of justice more calm and serious than theirs, might not this defiance have well thrown an obstacle in the way of indulgence? But that was, perhaps, what these honest men really wanted. They had conceived the idea of drowning General Lafayette at the beginning of the affair, and why may we not believe that after the defeat they endeavored to bring in play the knife of the guillotine in order to rekindle the flames of revolution?

The affair of June was an era for the faction, not only on account of the battle which it occasioned, but especially from the decadence which it began to experience from that period. It will be seen, in fact, that during the monarchy it never brought so large an army again into line.

The revolutionary fraction of the legitimist party had its Waterloo at Paris in the affair of the street of Prouvaires; and it soon met with the same fate in the provinces. It is but justice to repeat that the most important men of that cause never approved of the conspiracies of the capital, nor of the civil war in the West. Indeed, the heroism of the duchess and the impatience of a few gentlemen, led only to disturbances which injured rather than benefited the family of the elder Bourbons.

A few smouldering sparks of the explosion of June burst out again several weeks afterwards on the occasion of the second anniversary of July. Several hundreds of mobbers, overheated by the vapors of patriotism and wine, descended Saint Denis Street, singing the Republic, and crying out—"Down with Louis Philippe!" They continued on in this way to the market of the Innocents, where were some of the tombs of July, and from there proceeded to the Louvre, where other combatants had been buried, and they seemed to think that the best way to honor the dead was to insult the agents of authority. From the Louvre they repaired to the bridge of Arcole, the theatre of a prominent event of the Revolution, which they must also celebrate. All this took place at about eleven o'clock at night—rather an inappropriate hour, one would think. The police thought so too, and concluded that such a peculiar sort of pilgrimage could not be tolerated. Some of the policemen were therefore sent to put a stop to it. The disturbers of the peace were found upon the bridge of Arcole, singing and vociferating in the most beautiful style. As the policemen approached, they were received with the cry of—"Hurrah for the Republic!" and then assailed with clubs. The police had to draw their swords, and five of the patriots were wounded.

The next day it was related in the newspaper of M. Marrast that the extermination of the republicans upon the bridge had been perfectly complete, *all* had either been left for dead or thrown into the river; and as some few of the latter still gave signs of life, the policemen went down and ran them through while in the water [doubtlessly by swimming after them], and, in short, as a proof of the butchery, it was stated that in the nets below, at Saint Cloud, three corpses had been found—a part of the account as true as any of the rest. But such is the character of certain papers; they furnish their readers daily with such accounts as these, which would put one to sleep standing were it not for their detestable impudence.

The fight at the bridge of Arcole was the last act in the grand mob-drama which had continued since July; if the disorders of the streets were not to disappear entirely, they were at least to permit intervals of quiet in which Paris might breathe in peace. But no sooner was peace restored to the city from the weakness of the factions than another series of criminal acts was begun. Unable longer to contend openly, the factions found culprits within their bosoms who had recourse to assassination. In their fury they pursued the king for the space of sixteen years, either while engaged in his duties as head of the state, or as a father in the midst of his family. There is not, perhaps, in all the annals of savage life, a parallel instance of such diabolical madness.

The first attempt at assassinating the king is known by the name of the affair of the pistol-shot. On the 19th of November, 1832, the king, in going to open the session of the Assembly, had just left the Tuileries, surrounded by a retinue who were greeting him with numerous acclamations, when, at the end of the Pont Royal, a group of men was seen who made themselves particularly noticeable by a sort of affectation which seemed to pervade their noisy acclamations of—"Long live the king!" Presently a pistol was fired from the group, and the ball just grazed the person of the king. At the same time a great commotion took place among the group from which the shot had come; there was a pushing and crowding, an apparent rush upon the assassin, the end of all of which was, the said assassin was hustled out of sight without being recognized. A pistol was found upon the spot, and another a little further on.

A woman who was near by, a Miss Boury, seized with a sudden idea, hastened to the ministry of the interior, then to the Tuileries, and finally to the prefecture of the police, where M. Gisquet received the important declaration which she had come to make. According to her account, she happened to be standing beside the man when he fired, and she prevented the shot from taking effect by pushing the pistol to one side. She also gave marks by which the assassin, she said, could be recognized. But on being closely questioned by the prefect, the good woman hesitated in a way that was not very favorable to her veracity. In fact, in the course of a few days it was clearly proved that she had neither seen nor done anything in the matter; and that, in order to escape from an embarrassing situation, she had invented this story of being the protectress of the king. Abandoning then this false trail, the police took up another, which had been indicated by anterior information, and which promised to be much more certain. Several days previously it had been intimated by a report that a plot had been formed similar in character to the one which had just been exhibited. An attempt upon the life of the king had been premeditated by four republicans, viz: Messrs. Bergeron, Benoit, Girou, and Billard. M. Billard was to fire the shot from a short musket, which could be concealed under his dress; and his accomplices and other friends were to surround him in order to favor his escape. The last part of the plan was indeed put in execution; but Billard had not been able to have a hand in it, inasmuch as he had already been arrested and his short musket seized. The researches that were made pointed out his three companions, who were immediately arrested; but the proceedings against Messrs. Girou and Benoit were stopped, and M. Bergeron alone appeared at the bar. Besides the report which we have just mentioned, there was other weighty evidence against him; such, for instance, as the words uttered by one Planel, who, after having seen the accused some minutes before the affair, had said to another person: "Bergeron is a perfect madman, he absolutely means to kill the king." Another person had received from Planel a description of the pistols, which corresponded exactly with those of the accused. But notwithstanding this, M. Bergeron was acquitted.

So had Pepin been acquitted, too, though found with hands blackened with powder; and so were writers, of the most detestable character, daily let loose by the verdicts of—"Not guilty."

The first impressions of the affair of June had passed away. The government had armed itself with no new law against its enemies; and these enemies, therefore, lost no time in recommencing the war. Trials for political offences were of continual occurrence, it is true, but from the lofty bearing of the republicans at the bar, and the extraordinary character of the verdicts, by which the public conscience had become disconcerted, they seldom resulted in much advantage to the authority. The newspapers of the faction exhibited a violence and cynicism which might have been considered unparalleled, if the unbridled press among us had not always delivered itself up to the same orgies of falsehoods and fury. The *Tribune*, in its attacks upon men and things, spared no effort in the way of venomous irony, or the most savage ferocity. The *Charivari* and the *Caricature*, pretended to expose, either by the pen or pencil, the domestic life of the king and his family; showing them up in grotesque and hateful forms.

The propagandism, by means of pamphlets, was begun again, pouring its arsenic in upon the brains of the ignorant; and everything showed that the demon of revolution had taken breath, and was making preparations for a new campaign.

And amidst such throes and spasms as these, was brought forth the *Rights of Man*, that celebrated society which, by organization, numbers, influence, and audacity, was to grind royalty to powder at the first effort. But it only served to show, however, the radical imbecility of all secret societies, when brought to an issue by a vigilant and resolute power.

The *Rights of Man*, it will be seen, came to its end in the affair of April, 1834; an affray which might be considered ridiculous, when compared with the great noise which the conspiracy had made before breaking out; and which was, moreover, the very last spasm of the revolutionary monster.

Let us now pass over a period of fourteen years, and fix our attention upon the affair of 1848; and we shall discover a most astonishing similitude of events. In the first place, while the revolution of February was still in all its effervescence, there followed the bloody battle of June, which corresponds with that of June, 1832; then the demagogues, who attributed their defeat to the want of direction, immediately set to work in bringing the elements of the party together, and subjecting them to the severest discipline; and when this was done, or nearly done, the chiefs, being impelled by popular impatience, sounded the call to arms, which resulted in the affair of the 13th of June, 1849, a worthy pendant of the 4th of May, 1834. But from this moment the city began to breathe again more freely; partly because the fever of anarchy gradually subsided of itself, but especially because the government took care to place public order under the safeguard of severe laws, and to recognize thereafter, not only as a right, but as a duty, the necessity of striking demagogism to its heart.

Let us repeat it again—our revolutions are nothing but accidents—nothing but criminal coups-de-main, violent robberies of power. It is useless for the mass of the people, from credulity or timidity, to claim them as their own, for in so doing, they only yield to the law of the stronger, or give way to an unworthy surprise. From every consideration, then, these insurrections ought to be stopped. Undoubtedly, the best means to accomplish this end is to bring the government into an accordance with the general sentiments of the nation; for it is very wrong, among a people so irritable, and already so old in liberty as ours are, to pursue the system of the princes of the North, stifling public opinion, instead of adopting the English policy, which causes the government to yield to every reasonable exigency; but as this harmony of the government with public opinion among us has never prevented the revolutionist from plying his trade, and as, indeed, the greater this harmony is, the less is his influence, and the greater, therefore, his spite, it is indispensably essential, hereafter, that the government should show an energy to be surpassed only by its vigilance, and that the arsenal of the laws should always be kept furnished with all the means necessary for giving a victorious repulse to every unprincipled attack.

CHAPTER XII.

Formation of the Society of the *Rights of Man*—Names of the members of the committee—M. Millon, a publicist coachman—Orders of the day—The detached forts—A complot—Why it proved a failure—a trial —Violence of the accused, and especially of M. Vignerte.

ALREADY, in the times of the *Friends of the People*, there existed a revolutionary section, which was called the *Rights of Man*. The republicans of principal weight and character had taken refuge in this section, and it became the centre of a grand association, of which we are about to give the history.

About the close of the year 1832, the most substantial men of the party, with the view of escaping the controlling influence of second-rate conspirators, concluded to put themselves at the head of the *Rights of Man*, and draw together all the revolutionists. They elaborated a plan of organization, which was adopted on the following basis, viz: a committee composed of eleven members, called directors; under the directors, twelve commissaries, one for each arrondissement; and then, forty-eight commissaries of the quarters subordinate to the commissaries of the arrondissements. The commissaries of the quarters were charged with forming sections composed of one chief, one sub-chief, three quinturions, and twenty members at most; the number of members being fixed at twenty, in order to elude the law; and with the same object, every section was to have a different name. Rigidly speaking, these sections might be considered as so many separate societies, limiting their numbers to the prescriptions of the code.

A certain number of sections were immediately organized: these appointed their chiefs, and the chiefs were invited to elect the directors. The following persons received majorities of the votes, and were proclaimed members of the committee, viz: Messrs. Audry de Puyraveau, Voyer d'Argenson, deputies; Kersausic, G. Cavaignac, Guinard, N. Lebon, Berryer Fontaine, J. J. Vignerte, Desjardin, Titot, and Beaumont.

Under the direction of such men as these, some occupying high social positions, others possessed of a high order of talent, and all animated by zeal or activity, the association received a rapid development. On the part of the police at that time, there were two true men, Messrs. Gisquet and Carlier, who promptly unravelled the conspiracy and denounced it to the courts; but these officials were informed in reply that the courts could do nothing in the case, the sections being within the limits of the law, and the police were reduced, therefore, to a passive observance of the progress of the association.

It will be readily conceived that this toleration was taken advantage of; new sections were formed every day; and three months had not elapsed when the army of the *Rights of Man* was spoken of as something formidable. Its numbers were very greatly exaggerated; but the chiefs took good care not to undeceive the community on that point, knowing that there is no better allurement than large numbers for drawing persons into such enterprises. In other respects there was no trouble taken on the part of the members to conceal their characters as members of the *Rights of Man;* it was openly avowed, and the republican writers of the papers very composedly added this title to their signatures.

The system of orders of the day was soon adopted; these orders were printed and sent to every chief of section, who was charged with having them read. They appeared at regular intervals; and the meetings themselves were not long in assuming that character of periodicity which had been provided against by the law. Then, indeed, the courts began to take action; and it was certainly high time. These publications, read in a mysterious manner to ignorant or fanatical men, were dripping with the poison of communism; for, even at that time, the nauseating common place of the socialist—democracy—began to be lisped forth in such expressions as, "The preying of man upon man,"—"the vampires who suck the sweat of the people," etc. etc. In one of the first orders of the day that made its appearance, it was shown how the republic was to secure the happiness of all—"not excepting even those rascals who were swimming in opulence." It was by—"despoiling these rascals of their possessions, of those treasures which caused them so many cares, and which degraded them in the eyes of the true patriot, and by rendering to them, through poverty, the happiness and virtues of the community."

The courts finally decided to act with energy, and the police brought before them the first members of the sections who fell into their hands. They were a group consisting of Millon, the coachman, and Petit Jean, a lawyer, as chiefs, and several other patriots.

M. Millon, the coachman, was a genius whose patriotism shone a great deal more brilliantly than his language. He was the author of sundry beautiful productions which were read in the sections, and in which occurred such passages as this: "It is enough! The torch of liberty has exposed to view the dens of crime. Away with the king! the time has come when we are to have a settlement with those vile sluggards who have become fat upon the products of our labors; we are to share an equal half with them in the wealth of which they have robbed us." From this it will be seen that M. Millon was one of the predecessors of the celebrated president of the Bank of the People. In other respects, this publicist coachman was comparatively a very reasonable fellow; he only asked to share half and half, while the more modern socialists would hardly be guilty of such an inconsiderate piece of disinterestedness. The profound rascality, too, of the middle classes, who have the impudence to decide for order because merely in a state of order they find work and subsistence, had been discovered as early as the times of M. Millon; and hence, the coachman gave them a smart touch of his whip, as follows: "Every remnant of this small-fry aristocracy, which has grown up under the name of the bourgeoisie, must be pursued and extirpated even to its foundations."

M. Millon and his three companions were sentenced to pay a fine of 200 francs, not a very exorbitant sum; but by the same verdict the society of the *Rights of Man* was declared illegal, and dissolved. A satisfaction of this kind, given to public opinion after so many scandals, was not much to the liking of the *Tribune*, which cried out in the extreme of bitterness: "How thirsty these gentlemen are for civil war! But they may rest at ease on that score, for the day of insurrection will come, and a little too soon for their liking; a single hour will suffice to make them regret their impudent decision, and that hour will be struck!" The *red* editor was thus trying his hand at intimidation; but the authorities, in mass at least, very seldom trembled much at such menaces as these.

But why did Messrs. Marrast and Sarrut trouble themselves about the matter? Had not the republicans sufficient imagination and audacity to evade the law, and make a mockery of it, and especially when they knew that the magistracy were so generally circumspect? One thing is very certain, that the dissolution pronounced by the tribunals produced no effect, and that propagandism was not checked a single instant. The popular orators continued their declamations; pamphlets were distributed by cart-loads through Paris and the provinces, travelling agents continued their patriotic peregrinations, and, in short, demagogism pushed on its siege against society as actively as ever.

According to the plan of the association, every section took a different name; and perhaps these names had some relation with the work which the sections were to perform. In the list of designations we may remark the following: The *Robespierre* section, the *Montagnards, Death to Tyrants*, the *Twins, Marat*, the *Beggars, Babeuf*, the *Truants, Louvel*, the *Tocsin*, the *Phrygian Cap*, the *Abolition of ill-gotten Wealth, Couthon, Lebas, Saint Just*, the *Levellers*, the *Ca ira*, the *Insurrection of Lyons*, the *Twenty-first of January*, the *War upon Castles*, etc.

We have now arrived at the period of the 5th and 6th of June, an anniversary which the *Rights of Man* thought it proper to celebrate as the successors of the *Friends of the People*. To this end an order of the day was read in the sections. We give the principal part of this production, which, emanating from the committee of eleven, made known the tone, the views, and the hopes of the faction.

" Citizens: The anniversary of the 5th and 6th of June calls not for vain regrets; for the cypress of liberty must be watered with blood, and not with tears. Behold! how often during the last forty years have not a miscreant aristocracy clapped their hands at the fall of the most noble heads! How often has it not been announced that the genius of revolution was crushed, while we have seen it rising again stronger, and more powerful than ever. Not a brother of ours is killed, but there come to us ten, although the blood drenched pavements of the streets are reeking to the summer sun with insurrection and death! Recall to your minds those days which followed the combat of Saint Méry; we were dispersed then, and the government was threatening us with all the persecutions of its victorious cowardice; and what had we wherewith to defend ourselves? Nothing but our moral force and the holiness of our cause. Ah well! the government did not dare to act; it hesitated, and not from generosity but from cowardice."

Let us dwell a moment upon this latter point, where the word cowardice is lavished so freely. It may be well to see what kind of an acknowledgment the republicans made to the magistracy, who were so reserved with respect to them, and to the government which had taken no advantage of its victory. Although the republicans had been spared, and no demand made upon the Chambers for arming the authorities with new laws against them, yet the inference which they drew was, not that the government of July was governed by generosity and an excessive respect for liberty, but that, simply, it was actuated by cowardice. Ah! gentlemen, but what kind of courage must you have had yourselves, to be conquered by such a cowardly government?

But let us proceed: "Now, then, let come what may, the Republic has taken root in France, and not all the force of the aristocrats of low degree can suffice to shake it. A year ago it was vanquished, but to-day it is more powerful than before the combat; for it has acquired the force of unity and discipline which was then wanting. The only tendency of the government is to shut up and confine human beings within the limits which chance or the infamous organization of our social system may have assigned them; to some riches, and to others want; to some a pleasant idleness, to others hunger, cold, the hospital and death! Tears are not for us, they are for our enemies; for, after their death, there will remain no trace of them except the memory of a curse. The arm of a terrible sovereign shall soon fall upon their heads; and then, let them hope for neither pardon nor grace! When the people strike, they are neither timid nor generous; for they strike not for interest but for eternal morality; they know well, that no one has the right to show grace in their name. HEALTH AND FRATERNITY."

This production is quite different, both in force and importance, from the literary excrescences of M. Millon; it was conceived by a revolutionist who knew his trade, and written by a man who could wield the pen. Those who are familiar with the style of M. G. Cavaignac, say that the energy of touch and the gloomy fierceness are his; but the mode of life of this son of the conventional, at that time, was rather too disorderly to permit the belief that he was the author of this production. The ideas of absolute equality, and the bloody threats which gleam through it, though they might come to the end of his pen, could find no place in his heart. But it is of but little consequence who the author was; he was a chief of demagogues, speaking to his men a language which they understood and appreciated. And this language shows to what extent the head had become turned with the members of the sections during the six months which had elapsed since the creation of the society, and how difficult it would be to restrain such men, for any length of time, by the mere force of discipline. When excitements of this kind are practised, the chiefs must decide to lead their men into the streets, or their men will take to the streets without them.

Towards the month of July, 1833, the question of detached forts fell upon the world of the press like a rock upon a sheet of water, making a great splashing. Every journalist immediately became a consummate strategist, proving that the forts proposed were useless for interior defence, and that the only object which they could subserve was the ruin of Paris. The incredulous upon this subject were directed to suspend their opinion until the first popular movement, and then they would see what the detached forts were made for. We all know how these predictions have been fulfilled; since the erection of the forts two battles have taken place in the capital, and neither of the contending parties has had the remotest idea of making use of them.

But such are the pretences which are made use of by the opposition; the brave men who inflated their lungs to the point of bursting in cries against the forts, were only playing their usual part; they either knew nothing of what they were saying, or they said to the contrary of what they knew; and nine times out of ten this is the case with the newspaper writers of the opposition.

The question, however, made a great appeal to the passions, and the clamor became so general that the wire-pullers of the *Rights of Man*, who were in search of an occasion for a tumult, thought that they had found one to their purpose. The anniversary of the affair of July was near at hand; the king was to have a review; cries against the forts might be set up on all sides, from the ranks of the militia as well as from the crowd; a collision might take place, either naturally or by means of skilfully prepared combinations, and the sections, profiting by the disorder, might make an armed irruption upon the city. Such was the plan conceived, not exactly by the committee, the principal members of which were under the impression that the hour for action had not yet arrived, but by a knot of impatient men, at the head of whom were Messrs. Kersausie, Barbès, Sobrier, etc. The tail ran away with the head, as usual. The eleven, not daring openly to oppose the attempt, allowed the preparations to have a free course, hoping that reflection, or some lucky incident, might arrest the explosion. But if men who are respectable in some points of view will ally themselves with fools, they must expect to bear the responsibility of follies. This was the fate of M. G. Cavaignac all his life.

The leaders then betook themselves to the work. But as they were not positively certain of the anti-fortification sentiments of the National Guard, they conceived the idea of introducing a large number of republicans into the companies commanded by the patriots, with the view of rendering the cries imposing, at least at certain points. These clamors, thus organized, were to express with astounding effect the sentiments of the bourgeoisie. The students, great lovers of noise, promised, on their part, a collection of the most stentorian voices. All the other necessary measures usual in such cases were taken; the sections were assured that their brethren of the provinces had received the word, and were hastening to Paris; the propagandism of newspapers and other publications was in a perfect rage; care was taken to give the histories of patriots who had been tortured, knocked down, trampled upon, and left rotting upon the *humid straw;*

and, in short, none of the usual means were left untried for turning the heads of the simple minded and the ambitious.

At the same time, orders were given to have arms and ammunition in readiness. But notwithstanding this, the newspapers represented the manifestation as perfectly pacific. The fact is that many such manifestations *are* pacific, but it is owing wholly to the measures which have been taken by the government. In maintaining the perfect innocence of its friends, the *Tribune*, whose readers had the upper hand of the *Rights of Man*, lied with its accustomed impudence. As to the other mere ordinary papers of the opposition, they seemed to think that it was their duty to make solemn asseverations of what they knew nothing about; it is their habit.

In every emergency like the one which we are relating, the mob making Paris naturally turns her eyes towards her sister in disorders, the capital of the south. In response to this solicitude, the *Tribune* declared that the condition of Lyons was the *best possible*, that the workingmen were dying from hunger, and that they were ready to rise; everything there went on swimmingly.

On the 24th of July, the order of the day ran upon the subject of the manifestation. The language of the committee was full of confidence, not to say of revolutionary fatuity. It promised that after the victory, rigorous justice should be meted out to every one. These words, as well as others in a preceding order of the day, were not, as one may readily imagine, the language of mere ingenuousness and philanthropy; for the question of the abolition of capital punishment was not the topic of those days. No; we have here one of the most odious features in the tactics of the insurrectionary chiefs; they well know that certain vengeful sentiments, excited by envy, are very gratifying to the crowd, and no shame deters them from making an appeal to such detestable passions.

The order of the day of the 24th of July, prescribed a permanence of manœuvres during the three commemorative days, and the sections were notified to be at their place of battle, and to await the instructions of the committee. A paper was distributed at the same time among the troops, promising them the election of their officers, glory, honor, no more passes, no degrading countersign, all to be generals at twenty-one years of age, and a universal war!

The dispositions were complete; but two causes prevented them from taking effect. In the first place, the police knew very well where to find the sections, and how to forestall their attacks by carrying off all the members whom it could lay hands on; and in the second place, the occasion which had been anticipated, did not occur. The *manifestation* was to break forth at the moment that cries should be uttered against the forts by the National Guards; but it so happened that there were no cries. An immense majority of the Guards became so strongly suspected by the patriots that the brethren who had smuggled themselves into the ranks, dared not open their mouths. It was a pitiable failure; and all haste was made to divert the attention to other objects. An order of the day was scribbled off and thrown in haste among the republicans. It stated in substance that the committee had declared a permanence of action only with the view of testing the discipline of the patriots; that the result had corresponded fully with their hopes, and in consequence they offered their sincere congratulations to the members of the society.

The measures of the police, together with the good sense of the bourgeoisie, had caused the conspiracy to prove a failure; and the demagogic papers, especially the *Tribune*, which was deeply implicated in the affair, cried out with violence—such tyranny was intolerable; citizens were arrested without a cause; the police was above the law; Frenchmen were subjected to the sway of the Cossack, etc. etc. Poor police! whatever it might do, its censures were all marked out beforehand. If it prevented a plot, why, then the plot never existed. If it seized upon a plot in full execution, why, then the plot was one of its own contriving. The papers of the factions never deviated from one of these two conclusions, and the papers of intermediate color foolishly followed their lead. The conspirators who were caught in the act would swear by everything holy that they were perfectly innocent, and their friends of the press would repeat their assertions in the most flaring characters; it was the least that they could do, after having instigated the guilty. What interest could a reasonable opposition have had in giving currency to such impudent lamentations? A demagogue, an habitual disturber of the peace, a martyr to the penal code, is heard to cry out; the opposition knows nothing of the facts in the case; but between this man and the police, which is charged with a rigid and delicate duty, all sympathy is on the side of the man of anarchy! Verily, we are a people very much to be pitied. Instead of respecting authority in its great character of protection to all, we busy ourselves in constantly finding fault with it in its thankless task of repression, and in seeking to bind its arms and render it odious. The consequences are, that while other countries have their society, in France we have our socialism.

Upwards of a hundred members of the *Rights of Man* were compromised in the affair which we have mentioned. The principal ones were Messrs. Kersausie, Raspail, Noël Parfait, Latrade, Kaylus, Langlois, and Chavot. This last named person will be met with again in the course of this recital in an attempt at assassination.

The republicans, among their means of propagandism, have always placed legal prosecutions in the first rank. In the affair in question, the audacity of the accused, added to the aggressive character of the attorneys, promised an excellent contingent of scandal; and the expectations of the amateurs were not disappointed. M. Raspail took the word and denounced the abomination of the police. And from that epoch the monomania of that singular man became fully declared. He was convinced that the patriots were never to blame, and that every one accused of political offences was a victim to the machinations of M. Gisquet. Among the attorneys who, under the pretext of defending the accused, made the occasion one for outraging the government and attacking the laws, were Messrs. Michel (de

Bourges), Pinard, and Dupont. In return for their exemplary zeal, they received a double recompense; the republican party bestowing upon them its greatest honors, and the tribunal which they had insulted, suspending them from their functions. M. Dupont for one year, and Messrs. Pinard and Michel for six months.

The most characteristic incident, however, of the prosecutions of the epoch, was one which occurred in regard to the attorney-general. This magistrate, in a review of the doctrines of the accused, was proving that the tendency of these doctrines was to a division of property, when M. Vignerte, who was nothing but a witness in the case, sprang up upon a bench, shook his fist at the attorney-general, and exclaimed: "You are a d——d liar, sir!" This patriot was brought before the court for his politeness, which made short work in giving him an opportunity of practising his beautiful language for a period of three years in prison.

It is to be presumed that M. Vignerte had some queer sensation of the nerves, which he was determined to relieve at any cost; for, as to his wrath at the words of M. Delapalme, he was by no means justified in it, as will be seen. Some time previously a schism had taken place in the *Rights of Man*, which resulted in professions of faith that classified the members as Girondins and Montagnards. The Girondins, represented by the *National* of M. Carrel, endeavored to diplomatize with the bourgeoisie, and win it over gradually to an armed resistance, under cover of the charter. The Montagnards recognized neither law nor charter, and saw in the middle classes only a new species of aristocracy which it was necessary to intimidate. As to bastard alliances or compromising compromises, they would not listen to them for a moment. Not they! Their ideas went altogether beyond the narrow and contracted horizon of their brethren. In one of their productions were read the following words: "What we want is, an equal amount of well-being for all, the *levelment* of fortunes, the *levelment* of conditions." Here is an agrarian law for us, with a spicing of communism to boot; and what does M. Vignerte think of it?

These ideas emanated from the Montagnards, and M. Vignerte, God forbid! never had anything to do with the Girondins. Why, then, did he get in such a passion?

The reader will doubtlessly wish to know what became of the accused, the most of whom were chiefs of a formidable secret society, and the organizers of a revolt which miscarried from circumstances beyond their will—they were all declared not guilty, and sent back to renew their conspiracies.

CHAPTER XIII.

Robespierre's Declaration of the rights of man, published as the republican gospels—The Committee of Action—Its chief—Reviews of the sections—Morality of the conspirators—The law respecting associations—Battle is decided upon.

THE Committee of Eleven, with the view of rallying the dissenters and establishing a unity of principles, conceived it necessary to prescribe articles of faith. After due deliberation upon the subject, and perceiving that they could not get up anything better than Robespierre had already done, the *Declaration of Rights* of that very celebrated citizen was adopted as the creed of the society. The new editors, however, thought proper to add a commentary; and this commentary, incredible as it may appear, succeeded in excelling the radicalism of the text. It is well known that in the Declaration of Robespierre there are the following articles, viz:—

"Property is the right which every citizen has of enjoying, and making use of at his pleasure, that portion of wealth which is guaranteed to him by the law."

"Every institution which is not based upon the supposition that the people are good and the magistracy corrupt, is vicious."

These doctrines are high-flavored enough to do without any additional spicing.

But the *Declaration*, though flanked by a commentary, was far from attaining that fusion and unity which had been expected. It was openly rejected by M. Carrel, of the *National*, a cool and resolute man, whose ideas were altogether transcended by such extravagant doctrines as these. This gentleman and his associates professed anti-socialist principles which kept them aloof from the *Rights of Man*. They had never been on very intimate terms with the society, and from this moment the breach between them became the wider. An intercourse, however, was still kept up, and on more than one occasion M. Carrel exercised a controlling influence over the committee through the esteem in which he was held by Messrs. Cavaignac, Guinard, Voyer-d'Argenson, and other members of importance.

As to the mass of the society, composed of reckless and worthless men, the *Declaration* was received by them with enthusiasm, every one swearing to adhere to it as the true creed for the future. There was a perfect agreement of all parties as to what is called the idea of their operations; but though this appeared to be a principle of harmony, yet at bottom it proved to be nothing. There were other grounds, such as self-love and pretension, upon which union and harmony soon became shipwrecked. The second rate chiefs concealed their envy of the influence of the higher chiefs, under the name of exalted patriotism. The reflecting men of the committee were, according to their way of thinking, only timid men, demi-revolutionists, who dared not to speak of a battle, and even doubted of victory, which was but little short of treason. With the view of restoring order in this state of things, the impatient spirits resolved to form a sort of old guard in the *Rights of Man*, to be composed of well-tried patriots, and charged with the execution of decisive measures. It was thought that this corps would soon gain a preponderance of influence, and thus hurry the moderate members to extreme lengths. One of the members of the committee, Captain Kersausic, made himself the chief of this schism. He was a democratized gentleman of wealth, of an adventurous and inconsistent character, who was just the man for the hot-heads of the society. His principal partisans became his officers; they were Messrs. Sobrier, Barbès, and others of that stamp, who were never noted for much good sense. M. Kersausie declared that he wished to become the only chief; and that under this condition alone he would be responsible for the trustiness of the men and the success of the enterprise. This point having been conceded, he immediately sat to work at the formation of sections. His corps, called the *Society of Action,* was divided into *centuries, decuries,* and *quinturies.* The captain communicated solely with some of his principal officers, and these officers transmitted his orders in hierarchical succession down to the lowest members, who were called *rangers.*

On certain days the frequenters of the streets found the boulevards and other thoroughfares filled with crowds of silent promenaders, who had been drawn together for some unknown object. No one knew why such crowds had come together except the police, whose business it is to know everything. These crowds had assembled in order to be reviewed by the chief of the Society of Action. He would arrive, accompanied with one or two aids-de-camp, go to a chief of some one of the groups, to whom he would make himself known by a sign; cast a glance at the members of the section; receive the news; give his orders, and then pursue his way to go through the same ceremonies a little further on. The agents of the police, who were close upon his heels, would see him slipping through the crowd and playing his part as inspector-general with the most surprising facility. As soon as the review was over, he would disappear in a carriage ready at hand; go and knock at some house having two entrances, and there steal away to his lodgings and shut himself up for several days. He possessed three or four domiciles, and passed under several different names; his most trusty lieutenants alone gained admittance to him, and his servants and agents consisted only of well-tried men whose zeal he rewarded with liberality. He was one of those decided, mysterious, and picturesque conspirators who might figure to advantage in a romance.

The Committee of Eleven, of which Captain Kersausie still remained a member, called upon him for explanations; for it really seemed, in fact, that he designed to assume the dictatorship of the society, and dispossess his colleagues. He explained himself without concealment—the direction of the *Rights of Man* appeared to him too lax; many of the sections were not to be relied on; the police could see into the mechanism of the society, and it had appeared to him indispensable to remedy these three vices. It was not the design of the Society of Action to dissolve the *Rights of Man*, but to strengthen it.

The captain being powerful enough to act alone, and the members of the committee perceiving that to break with this man would deprive them of the most vigorous force of the party, a compromise was agreed upon by which he was recognized as chief of the corps of action, but under the condition of preserving an understanding with his colleagues of the committee, and of not taking arms except upon a decision of all the members.

Owing to this treaty, the two divisions of the army came to an understanding, or nearly so. To expect a perfect agreement between men of whom the least vain considered himself a Colbert, of whom the least aspiring would have left the poet Ennius out of sight, and of whom the least avaricious could not have been content with the seraglio and treasures of a king of the East, would have been altogether unreasonable.

Not long after this fusion took place, two of the principal members of the committee, Messrs. Voyer-d'Argenson and Audry de Puyraveau, resigned the honors of their position. The household of the *Rights of Man* was a little two disorderly for these honorable gentlemen, for they were no longer at an age when noise is loved for the mere sake of noise; and, besides, they perceived in the air a certain odor of insurrection, which did not seem to them very promising.

A change had already taken place in the committee several months before; Messrs. Desjardins and Titot had given place to M. Delente, a public crier, and to M. Recurt, a doctor.

The latter had been promoted to this eminent position from a chief of the section of the *Beggars*.

The promotion of M. Delente to a membership of the committee, was a reward to this sectionary for his services in the character of public crier, and at the same time a compliment to all his associates. It must be remembered that at this epoch, the public sale of pamphlets and prints had attained an expansion which has never been surpassed at the extremest rage of our revolutionary orgies. A single item alone will give an idea of it; six millions of demagogic impressions were thrown off to the public in the space of three months.

As to the courts, they seemed even to favor the vendors of this public poison. The law concerning the matter, it is true, only required a previous declaration, but then, by another law, it was declared that every political article should be subject to the stamp. The question was, then, whether the publications of republican propagandism should come under this law. The public criers said—"No;" but M. Gisquet said—"Yes;" and he seized upon their pamphlets. The administration, however, by a singular sort of disinterestedness, refused to apply the penalty. The consequence was, besides the detestable moral effect, this strange anomaly, that while newspapers were held responsible through their editors and printers, and subjected to the stamp, other publications offered no guarantee, and escaped all liabilities.

It can hardly be believed that pamphlets whose very titles were insulting to the authorities and to the constitution, were brought openly every day to the police to receive their stamp. The title of one of these pamphlets would be—"*To the Lampposts with the Policemen.*" That of another—"*The Declaration of Rights of Robespierre*," etc. etc. The commissary of police refused to give them his stamp; and, in consequence, a flood of abuse was poured forth from the republican press, redolent with insults against those very authorities which were compelled to witness the sale, directly before their eyes, of the infamous productions to which they had refused their signature. The criers, however, for once, were arrested, and it seemed as if justice began to perceive the respect which was due to the government; but no! the criers were acquitted, for if they had sold pamphlets without the stamp, it was merely because the stamp had been refused them. Hence, the pamphlet—"*To the Lamp-posts with the Policemen,*" ought, according to the jurisprudence of those days, to have received the approbation of the prefect of police, in order to give it currency among the patriots! Was ever pleasantry carried to greater lengths?

One day M. Delente presented himself at the prefecture with a republican pamphlet which was rejected: "Reject and be d——d," said he, "but I'm according to law; I have the law on my side. I'll sell; and if they attempt to arrest me, the arrest will be arbitrary, and I'll resist it."

He sold, and was arrested, notwithstanding his threats. Brought before the correctional police, he received a verdict of acquittal; but as he had had the patriotic idea of appearing before the tribunal in a red cap, he was kept in confinement.

The acquittal of M. Delente left the ground free to the criers; and they determined to celebrate their victory by an imposing manifestation. Three days after the trial, M. Rodde, editor of the *Good Sense,* gave out a solemn announcement that he would appear himself upon the place of the Exchange, and cry his own pamphlets. True to his word, he made his appearance, armed with two pistols, and followed by two porters, staggering under their loads of printed stuff. As the police had their hands tied, they could do nothing but look on, and M. Rodde was suffered to withdraw with all the honors of a triumph. But the subject of his conquest was not M. Gisquet, who had evaded a conflict—not exactly from fear of M. Rodde's pistols—he had conquered a principle of authority itself. Fortunately, however, the measure of scandal was full to overflowing, and the national representation began to interpose in the case. The complaints of the courageous magistrate were felt in the tribune, and gave rise to a bill which became enacted as a law against the criers. The substance of this law was contained in a very simple article: "The public vendors of writings and drawings, must have an authorization of the police."

The authorities from that time found themselves the masters of the pavement of Paris, which had thus been wrested from the most cynical exploitation.

Touching this race of street propagandists, who, owing to a latitude of the law, were recruited among the most suspicious characters, the opinion of a man every way competent to judge, may not be uninteresting. Louis Blanc, in his *History of Ten Years*, says: "The criers who were thrown upon the public places and into the streets by the enemies of the government, were often nothing less than the colporteurs of scandal, the heralds at arms of the mob. In the libels which they distributed, bad faith in attacks disputed the supremacy more than once with indecency of language, and a certain fulsomeness of demagogic praise. Now, to flatter the people is cowardly; to deceive them is a crime."

The law on the subject of the criers came in force on the 20th of February, 1834; and the occasion with the republicans was, as may readily be conjectured, a cause of disorder. We say *cause* this time, and not pretext, because the party had been struck in a vital point; and another similar blow, which was about to be dealt in the shape of a law against associations, was to put an end to their scandal and their rage.

The crier, M. Delente, it will be borne in mind, was a member of the committee; and almost all the criers were members of the sections; hence, by the new law, an immense and formidable means of propagandism was stopped off, a cause more than sufficient to throw the mob into a rage and bring it roaring into the streets.

An event occurred which increased the agitation. Lyons had resumed her old quarrel again concerning the tariff, and it became complicated this time with the bad elements which were introduced into it by politics. It was thought that by a simultaneousness of movement on the part of the two cities, matters might be carried far beyond a simple demonstration. The committee had not decided upon an attack, but it was known that the Society of Action could hurry it beyond the limits which it had prescribed to itself. Besides, even Captain Kersausie, in spite of his authority over his men, soon found himself elbowed to one side. The sections grew impatient, and imperiously demanded the fight.

On the day of the promulgation of the law, the vendors of the *Good Sense* and the *Pillory* made their appearance in the streets with an air of defiance; but they were seized at the first cry which they uttered. Several others followed their example, and were dealt with no better than the first. This put the finishing touch to public crying; and the whole band disappeared from the view. But though they made their exit as criers, they had still a part to play as mobbers; having thrown off their costume—their pamphlets—they returned again to the stage among the crowds of the factious.

During the space of several days the boulevard of Saint Denis, a classical place for sedition, was filled with crowds who shouted at the top of their voices—"Down with the censure! Hurrah for the Lyonnais!" A section of the *Rights of Man* was thus endeavoring to excite a mob among the people; but their efforts were fruitless; for the true people of Paris, longing ardently for peace after so many ruinous tumults, entertained for the disturbers only hatred and contempt.

However, with the assistance of Parisian clamor, matters began to assume a very serious aspect. On the 24th of February, two or three thousand persons assembled upon the place of the Exchange, armed mostly with dirks or canes, and assumed the most threatening attitude. An individual, mounted upon a corner stone, read an article of M. Cabet concerning some sixty thousand workingmen of Lyons whom tyranny, perhaps, was about to grind to the dust, because they were suffering from hunger. It was an indirect, but at the same time a very clear appeal to revolt. The arrest of the reader gave rise to a scuffle, in which an officer of the peace and several policemen were very seriously wounded. Troops were then brought up and the place cleared, but not without a very vigorous resistance. In several places the members of the sections threw themselves upon the troop with so much violence as to twist their bayonets. They fell upon the policemen with their canes; and as the policemen had no notion of taking a beating without returning the compliment, more than one of the mob received two blows for one. A member of the *Rights of Man* was killed in the affair, and others received some hard knocks when they were endeavoring to give them; and hence, it was evident, that on the next day the police would have to withstand a perfect hail-storm of accusations, of scoundrelism and assassination. But as hateful as these accusations are in such cases, they are almost always mingled with something ridiculous. One of the deputies, M. Salverte, collected the complaints of the demagogic papers and carried them into the tribune; and, among other pitiful stories, he was pleased to state that the *corpses* which were lying upon the pavement, had sprung up and fled on the approach of their barbarous assailants.

M. Gisquet, upon whom the epithet of chief of ruffians, and galley slaves was very graciously bestowed, could have had easy work in replying to the gentlemen of the *Rights of Man;* for though the composition of this illustrious corps was, according to its leading men, irreproachable; though a letter published by four members of the committee contained the following words:—

"Placed at the head of the society of *Rights*, we appreciate every day whatever offers on the part of morality; the lives of our members do not fear examination"—yet the police looked upon the morality of some of the conspirators in quite a different light. Several edifying stories were known of more than one of their number, such, for instance, as that of a chief of section named Stevenot, who, in his leisure moments, used to practice highway robbery in the vicinity of Paris.

The law upon the subject of the criers had come too late; their work had been accomplished. Millions of publications had been distributed, stirring up from the depths of ignorance and passion crowds of revolutionary characters who were caught in the *Rights of Man* as if in a net. In the beginning of 1834, the number of the members in Paris amounted to 3,500; besides which there were a large number of affiliated members in the provinces, and a few platoons of ambitious sergeants and undisciplined soldiers in the army. The moment had arrived when the high pressure of extravagance was at the point of an explosion; and under any circumstances this explosion was inevitable. In case of need, the very first pretext that offered would have been made use of; but, of course, a good occasion would be preferred. Such an occasion actually presented itself; and under conditions which ought to have satisfied the most exacting. The law upon the subject of associations, which was passed in the month of April, was a menace of death against the *Rights of Man;* the question with them was no longer one of attack, but of defence. The alternative presented to them was imperious; they must either submit, after all their efforts and bravados, to a shameful dissolution, or they must take to the musket in earnest.

There could be no hesitation on the part of the committee; they decided that the promulgation of the new code should be the signal for an insurrection.

That the law upon the subject of associations should have thrown the *Rights of Man* into a rage and impelled them to measures of desperation, is all natural enough, for their very existence was at stake; but that it was the indispensable right and duty of the government to arm itself with new legislation, is as clear as the sun in mid-heavens. The clamorous republic of the press, and all its train of gaping admirers will answer us now, as they did answer then, by vociferations: very well; but we would remind them that a man of socialistic democracy, a doctor of the party, whom we have already quoted once, is also the author of the following words: "If the law against the associations had not been passed, and in the shape that the government wished it, there would have been an end to constitutional monarchy; nothing is more certain."—LOUIS BLANC (*History of Ten Years*).

These lines are sufficient for us, and they ought to be sufficient for every man of good faith.

We may give a brief explanation of the law. A single article of the penal code, article 291, related to associations. It proscribed societies of over twenty persons, and that was all. The many cases where the court had thought proper to be governed by the strict letter of the law, had demonstrated only but too clearly the radical defectiveness of the law; and an irresistible fact rendered the demonstration complete. The society of the *Rights of Man*, notwithstanding the decree of dissolution which had been pronounced against them, claimed to be in conformity with the conditions of the law; and they succeeded in becoming recognized as such by the courts. By what means, we have already related—by limiting the sections to the number of twenty members, and giving to each section a different name. It was well known that these sections were connected with each other and directed by the same committee, and that they formed only one and the same large association; but this was a fact to be proved, which, however, it would appear was never done. When a sectionary was seized and brought to trial as a member of an illegal association, he would plead in defence that he was only a member of a society of twenty persons, called the *Ca ira*, the *Twins*, or the *Beggars*, etc. The plea would be admitted and the prisoner discharged. This might have been adhering to the letter of the code, but it was certainly not entering into its spirit. At all events, a legislation leading to such results, had need of a thorough remodelling. The new law declared guilty not only associations, but the fractions of associations. Article 291, of the old law, related exclusively to periodical meetings; held only the chiefs responsible, and brought cases of infraction before a jury. The new law declared that no regard would be paid as to whether the meetings were periodical or not; that all the members of an illegal association would be held liable to a prosecution, and that the correctional police would take the place of the jury in the cognizance of such matters.

10

These measures were hailed with sincere satisfaction by the members of the government and by all honorable men; that is to say, by an immense majority of the country.

CHAPTER XIV.

A great patriot—M. Cavaignac devoted to the dagger—Preparations for the insurrection.—The forces of the Republican party in 1834.

From a long course of impunity, the *Rights of Man* had attained to such a degree of audacity, that they believed themselves able to compel the government to recede. On the news of the discussion of the law, they informed the associations of the provinces that Paris would never submit to it, and that resistance must be proclaimed in every quarter. These instructions were duly observed; and the demagogic papers were filled with indignant editorials, the windings up of which were invariably threats of a revolt. The newspaper, called the *Patriot Franc Comtois*, lead off with a plea which did the very greatest honor to M. Miran, its editor. And who was this M. Miran? Listen to the sentiments of M. Garnier-Pagès, senior, expressed in honor of the editor of the *Franc Comtois* at a banquet: "If a long and painful voyage could have procured me no other advantage than the acquaintance of so honorable a citizen, I should never regret having undertaken it"—a recommendation, certainly; as satisfactory as could be desired. But on the other hand, this very honorable citizen, among other aliases, had the true one of Gilbert, and on the judicial records there were exhibited against him the following memoranda, viz:—

1813, accused of forgery; acquitted.

1817, accused of swindling; sentenced to six years hard labor; exposed and marked.

1828, sentenced to five years imprisonment for an outrage against public morals.

1834, prosecuted for forgery, and sent to the galleys for twenty years.

And besides these, three or four other sentences for political offences; making the docket, it will be perceived, quite complete.

The lead of the patriot Miran was followed by protests against the law from some thirty different places, all shaped upon the same model, and thus betraying the connection between the associations of the provinces and that of Paris. In the mean time, chiefs from each of the affiliated societies arrived in the capital in order to have an understanding upon a definitive resolution. This congress decided upon the following measures, which were published, viz: The maintenance of the existing associations; the creation of new ones; the organization of a refusal to pay taxes, and the bringing in play of every means suggested by patriotism and courage for getting the better of the government. In such measures as these we perceive the especial adeptness of those men who frequent manifestations and raise great outcries about violations of the constitution on the faith of the newspapers; but within the sections the language of these measures was translated to mean, open resistance with dirk, pistol, and musket.

The preparations were set about with zeal; powder and muskets were bought, balls run and cartridges made; the friends of the cause among the regular troops were feted and flattered with glowing promises, and in fine, orders were given for a general review of the forces. The recapitulation of these forces, however, did not answer expectations. In Paris there were 163 sections which, at twenty members per section, ought to have furnished 3,260 men; but this number was not attained by a considerable. The men of the first consideration in the party, moreover, such as Messrs. Lafayette, Voyer-d'Argenson, Garnier-Pagès, and Carrel, when the question came to be an issue at arms, began to withdraw, conceiving that the prospects of success were too unfavorable. In the committee, too, more than one member hesitated at the responsibility which he was about to assume; and

M. Cavaignac was of this number. Convinced as he was of the wretched moral force and comparatively insignificant numerical strength of his party, he felt himself possessed with a profound distrust which the loyalty of his character could not conceal. He by no means advised to recede, for he was not one of those who, after having incited the people to acts of violence, then make their disappearance from the scene; but in the foreshadowing of a defeat which would strike the Republic to the heart and a sacrifice of men whose blood would be partly at his doors, he dared not to decide. His scruples were very badly interpreted; and it was not long before accusations were made against him; that of moderatism was highly emphasized, while that of treason was uttered in low murmurs. The extravagance of the republicans gave to this latter accusation the importance of a fact, and some of the more furious members proposed nothing less than to make way with a leader who was the most loyal and intelligent man of the party. Here is a spectacle, and a severe lesson, one would suppose, for those men who aim at the domination of the mass, but who must inevitably end in becoming either its instrument or its victim.

Neither the formal disapprobation of some nor the incertitude of others could prevent an outbreak; and it was decided that a recourse to arms should be had on the day that the law should come in force. On that day, viz: the 11th of April, the news which arrived from the interior fell upon the sections like a spark of fire upon powder; the news was that the provinces had risen in all quarters, and that Lyons had fought for two days. The agitation was intense; the cabarets were filled with crowds of stirring men; sinister looking figures hurriedly traversed the streets, and the air seemed to smell of powder and blood. On the 12th of April, the *Tribune* informed us that "the people of Lyons had remained masters of the ground; the troops were nearly discouraged, and a truce of several hours had been asked for by the general"—a statement which contained almost as many falsehoods as words; but such impudence as this had become too common for a comment. The next day the same paper gave accounts of all the victorious insurrections that had recently taken place, and of which it had either received bulletins or had made them up for the occasion. Chalons, Beaune, Dijon—all were in the hands of the patriots, and the authorities were in prison; ten thousand inhabitants of Saint Etienne had gone to the assistance of Lyons; the whole line between this latter city and Paris was in commotion, and finally, a regiment, the 52d, in garrison at Béfort, had mutinied at the cry of—"Hurrah for the Republic!" To this news, which appealed merely to enthusiasm, an addition was made which was to excite to frenzy. General Bugeaud, exclaimed the *Tribune*, has made the following speech to his officers—" The government knows how much it is indebted to you, and if the republicans move, remember that every one is to be put to the bayonet; no prisoners, and no quarters." The red paper added: "There is no kind of provocation which these men leave untried." This latter phrase might pass under the circumstances; but no one was deceived by it; every one knew that it emanated from the usual effrontery of the party.

The battle was decided upon for the next day, the 13th of April; and on such an occasion Captain Kersausie, as chief of the Society of Action, was to have the influence to himself. It was by him and his fiery lieutenants, rather than by the committee, that the attack was decided upon. Besides, this committee, it will be seen, was no longer in a condition to direct the insurrection.

The forces which the republican party was about to bring into line, were not composed solely of the army of the *Rights of Man;* other revolutionary societies existed at that time, the concurrence of which became inevitable in every democratic movement. These societies either moved like satellites around the *Rights of Man* as a centre, or were indiscriminately intermingled among its members.

The two most important of these societies were the *Society for the Defence of the Press* and the *Commission of Propagandism.* The object of the first was to extend assistance to those writers who were condemned for political offences; and it included in its committee the greater part of the more important democrats, such as—Messrs. G. Cavaignac, Carrel, Cormenin, Lafayette, Kersausie, Marrast, Raspail, Charles Teste, Voyer-d'Argenson, Etienne Arago, de Briqueville, Cabet, Dupont de l'Eure, Garnier-Pagès, etc. Almost all these names are met with again in the general staff of the *Rights of Man*, which shows that this *Society for the defence of the Press* was only an accessory of the greater association. M. Marchais was the secretary of the committee, and he had quite as much as he could do to satisfy the demands of the unfortunate writers, great and small, who harassed him with their claims. Among the papers that were seized upon in his house there were found some very curious lists of democratic claimants who called for patriotic aid. Of these claimants, Messrs. Marrast, Dupoty, Trélat, Antony Thouret, Philippon and Noël Parfait, established their right to assistance in the most touching manner.

The *Commission of Propagandism* busied itself with nothing more nor less than the fomenting of coalitions among the workingmen, a monstrous task, which occupied the indefatigable labors of a committee of twenty-two members. Among these members were Messrs. Recurt, Dufraisse, N. Lebon, Vignerte, and Berryer-Fontaine, who were also coryphœuses of the *Rights of Man*, another evidence that this *commission*, too, was in fact a mere mob-making machine, which received its impulsion from the Committee of Eleven. One can hardly withhold a feeling of indignation against men who, under the pretence of studying the interests of the workingmen, labored to excite discords between these men and their employers, impelling them to strikes as a preparatory step towards leading them to revolt. Perhaps it might be thought that such efforts would remain fruitless on account of their infamy; but alas no! for are not the poor and honest fatally condemned to the influence of those charlatans who offer them their panaceas? The exciters of coalitions succeeded so well that, by the end of the year 1833, almost every trade in Paris had struck. The typographers, mechanicians, stone-cutters, rope-makers, hackney coachmen, ceilers, gloviers, timber sawyers, bonnet-makers, locksmiths, ornamental paper-makers—all had left off work. Among the strikers there were reckoned 8,000 tailors, 6,000 shoemakers, 5,000 carpenters, 4,000 jewellers, and 3,000 bakers. What a picture of empty larders, children in tears and mothers in despair, does not this present! And let him who can, refrain from a feeling of detestation against those men who thus base their schemes upon the hunger of the people! But one day, while the committee were assembled at the houses of Messrs. Vignerte and Lebon, the police, being informed of it, repaired thither and captured almost all of them; and immediately the strikes ceased. All that the honest workingmen wanted in order to resume work, was to get rid of the tyranny of the bad. In the legal proceedings which grew out of this affair, Messrs. Lebon, Mathé, and Lemonnier were sentenced to imprisonment for five years, Vignerte for two years, and Recurt and Dufraisse for one year.

Good people of Paris, do you rejoice at having seen at the head of the government, men who have been condemned by justice for having made it their profession to famish you?

Besides these two societies, there were, 1st. *The Society of Father Andrew*, the object of which was the publication, colportage and sale of demagogic writings. Its members, who were numerous, were also connected with the rights of man. Its directors were Messrs. Roux, Hadot-Desages, and Rion.

2d. The *Society for the Assistance of Political Prisoners*. The object of this society was to aid all kinds of democrats; differing in this respect from the *Society for the Defence of the Liberty of the Press*, which occupied itself only with writers.

3d. The *Society for the free and gratuitous Education of the People*. This society took its members from whatever quarter it thought fit, and never troubled itself about general rules. It was originated by an honorable man, and had been tolerated by the ministry; but afterwards, on the withdrawal of its founder, the schools which it had established became so many centres of republicanism. The pretended instruction of these schools was for the benefit of the working people; and all the pupils, or at least those who had beards upon their chin, were more or less directly implicated in the machinations of the *Rights of Man.*

4th. The *Masonic Lodges;* among which were organized several corps of action, with a revolutionary object instead of a philanthropic one.

5th. The *Society of Aid Thyself*—a fragment of the old liberal association of the same name of the period of the restoration; but renewed, transformed, and redyed with the red of republicanism.

6th. *Carbonarism*—another meagre and dislocated fragment in which the ancient reputation of Messrs. Charles Testes and Buonarotti still preserved, with much difficulty, a trace of existence.

There were, besides, several other assemblages with various different objects, but all making an open profession of anarchy, among which may be mentioned the historical society of M. Laponneraye, established for the especial glorification of those immortal citizens Robespierre, Marat, Couthon, etc.

All these assemblages, some of which depended wholly upon the *Rights of Man,* and all of which acknowledged its ruling influence, were to furnish their effective quotas for the great battle of the 13th of April.

CHAPTER XV.

The effective strength for war of the *Rights of Man*—The forces of the government—Preparations for the conflict—Review of the *Society of Action*—Arrest of Captain Kersausie—Insurrection of the 13th and 14th of April—Why the rout of the republicans proved complete.

HAVING exhibited the resources of the insurrectionists, we may now give their effective strength. As nearly as can be ascertained, it consisted of the Society of Action 1,000 men, of the sections subject to the control of the Committee of Eleven 2,000, and of sundry isolated revolutionary associations 1,000, making in all 4,000 men. And this was, at the very highest estimate, the number of the republicans who were then in Paris—or at least, of those who, in speaking of the Republic, knew what they meant.

As to the resources of the government, on the other hand, they consisted of, besides the troops of the army, two elements of force which are equal to hundreds of others, viz: experience and confidence. The manner in which the insurgents in the affair of June had simultaneously scattered themselves through all quarters of the town, alarming the people and embarrassing the defence, had made due impression upon the government, and its measures were taken accordingly. There was a conviction of the necessity of attending to three principal points: 1st. The arrival upon the ground before the enemy: 2d. To attack them as soon as they should make their appearance, and 3d. To prevent them from making use of the pavements, those materials for the breastworks of civil warfare.

Forty thousand men of the regular troops were held in readiness in Paris and its vicinity. The National Guards had been warned at their houses, and were ready to assemble at the first signal. The artillery was pointed upon the exposed points, and numerous detachments were in possession of strategic positions. Marshal Lobau, who was charged with the general command, had planned his measures in concert with his lieutenants, among whom figured General Bugeaud.

The vigilance and zeal of the police were redoubled. From a change in the ministry, which had taken place since the first appearance of the storm, M. Gisquet found in M. Thiers a superior of promptness and decision. A large number of the chiefs of the sections had already been taken in preceding mobs; Messrs. Delente, Dufraisse, Eugène L'Heritier Vignerte, Guignot, Herbulet, Pornin, Chilman, Schirman, Petitjean, and Landolphe, were all under lock and key. This last named person, to whose house a domiciliary visit had been made, without result, published a letter in which the prefect of police was charged with ignominious baseness, for having violated, *without cause,* the domicil of a citizen. M. Gisquet had not the time to reply to these civilities in words, but he made his response by a conclusive fact; he had M. Landolphe seized, six days afterwards, while in the possession of a good supply of cartridges.

All uncertainty as to the designs of the republicans being at an end, the furious appeals of the *Tribune* and chiefs of the *Rights of Man* having heated the members of the sections to the explosive point, and the reports received at the police all agreeing upon the 13th as the day fixed for the attack, the prefect resolved to give the association a decisive blow. A foray, resolutely planned and executed, resulted in the capture of the principal chiefs, with the exception of Messrs. G. Cavaignac and Kersausie. A muzzle was put upon the *Tribune*, that fiend of anarchy, and the license of its printer, M. Mie, confiscated; and by this means the appearance of a placard was prevented, which had been prepared by one of the chiefs still at liberty, calling the people to arms.

These essential dispositions, and many other especial measures had been taken, when the sun of the 13th of April was to usher in either the Austerlitz or the Waterloo of the republic.

As the main army of the insurrection consisted only of the *Rights of Man*, and as this army, distracted by dissensions, had been deprived of its principal strength by the capture of its officers, the cause of the republic was as good as lost before the battle commenced. Among the most extravagant, those who still preserved some glimmerings of reason, were aware of this fact, and were only prevented from receding by self-love; but then there were a great many others in the association, reckless men, infatuated with foolish hopes, whom nothing could undeceive. Their chiefs we already know; first of all Captain Kersausie, and then a troop of demagogues, among whom shone Messrs. Barbès, Sobrier, Blanqui, etc.

Captain Kersausie, who had escaped capture, arranged measures for the fight. He had appointed a rendezvous for the *Society of Action*, at 4 o'clock P. M., upon the boulevards. The other sections also, as far as their state of disorganization would permit, were to be assembled. But as neither M. G. Cavaignac, who foresaw the failure of the attempt, nor any other member of the committee, had given any positive orders, this very considerable portion of the main army found itself reduced to its own impulsion. Some few isolated groups came together, but without concert of action; others disbanded, and roamed at large, wherever their instincts led them, and many had not been notified at all.

At the hour appointed, the Society of Action was upon the ground, spread along the boulevards and lateral streets, from the chassée d'Antin as far as the Bastile: and there it awaited the arrival of Captain Kersausie, in order to pass inspection. The captain made his appearance, escorted by four trusty friends, bearers, like himself, of concealed weapons, and began his review. As he passed along by each section, he took its number of men, pointed out the posts of attack, recommended promptness and energy, and moved on, promising that night a triumph for the Republic.

But in the vicinity of the gate of Saint Denis, an event occurred, which put an end to both his review and his hopes. A few minutes before his arrival at that point, an officer of the peace, M. Tranchard, had posted himself there with a section which, though of a very different character from that of the captain, was not the less inured to the coups-de-main of the streets. The officer of the peace, surrounded at a distance by his men, and keeping a searching glance upon the crowd in the boulevard of Poissonnière, saw at last among the thousands of heads there, one which his practised eye detected as soon as it made its appearance. Making a sign to his men, they followed close upon his steps, and he rushed forward to meet the expected man. The captain had not time to perceive the danger that threatened him before he was seized around the arms by the courageous functionary, raised from the ground, and borne off out of the group by which he was guarded. He endeavored to fire his pistol and make an appeal to his friends, but it was all in vain. Wrested from the midst of his troops, who were kept at sword's length by the agents of authority, he was carried to the mayoralty of the seventh arrondissement.

The sectionaries had not dared to attempt a deliverance of their chief; but to be revenged, they immediately gave the signal for the fight. The cry—"To arms!" resounded through the neighboring groups, and in the quarters of Saint Denis and Saint Martin, the sedition burst out into a blaze.

The mobbers who had taken their positions in narrow streets could not be pursued with sufficient rapidity to prevent their recovering from their surprise. They succeeded in barricading themselves in a sort of intrenched camp, embraced between Temple and Saint Martin Streets on the one hand, and Gravilliers and Saint Méry's on the other—an old and favorite ground of the insurrectionists. At a later moment Sainte Hyacinthe and D'Enfer Streets were intersected by barricades thrown up by the students and other sectionaries of that quarter. With the exception of these two points, which, from the suddenness of the attack—not expected till night—the troops had not time to cover, all Paris was secure from the insurrectionists. Several bands showed themselves in Montmartre, Saint Honoré, Montorgueil, and Saint Eustache Streets, but on being driven out at the point of the bayonet they dared neither to pull up a paving stone nor make face to the troop.

The barricades of the left bank of the Seine being attacked at once by a detachment of the National Guards, were overthrown without much resistance. A single incident marked the defeat of the republicans at that point; it was a cowardly assassination. Major Bailliot, of the general staff, on arriving in Sainte Hyacinthe Street with orders from Marshal Lobau, was shot through the body with eight musket-balls, fired upon him at a short distance.

While this odious crime was being perpetrated by some of the sections, others were at the coffee-house of Neuf-Billards, Mathurius Street, in deliberation over their glasses. The police forced their way into the doors, which had been barricaded, and carried off sixty persons, together with an arsenal of arms and ammunition

Upon the right bank the insurgents posted up, at about six o'clock in the evening, the following proclamation:—

"The too long chain of humiliating tyrannies, infamous perfidies, and criminal treasons, is at last broken. Our brothers of Lyons have shown us how ephemeral is the brutal force of tyrants when arranged against republican patriotism. The work which the Mutualists have commenced with so much success, will the conquerors of July hesitate to accomplish? Will they allow to escape such a beautiful occasion for reconquering that cherished liberty for which French blood has been so often shed? Citizens, so many generous sacrifices will not be rendered nugatory by an unworthy cowardice. To arms! republicans, to arms!"

The sterility of imagination and the flabby furor of this morceau produced the least possible effect. The few copies of it which had been posted up were immediately torn down by the agents of the police.

Without a chief of importance, without orders, and abandoned to their own low impulses, the sectionaries exhibited a hesitation which presaged a prompt defeat! Some of the leaders, in endeavoring to inspire them with courage, decided upon forming a new committee of directors; and with this view they repaired to Saint Germain-l'Auxerrois Street— to the house of a washerwoman who was honored with the friendship of one of the conspirators. But the police were on the ground almost as soon as they were; and all the members of the conventicle were arrested, the new committee being destroyed before it had been fairly organized.

The regular troops and National Guards had lost no time in clearing the central quarters of the town. The barricades of Saint Martin Street were first carried, and then those of Poirier, Saint Méry, Transnonain, Chapon and Geoffroy-Langevin Streets. At night, when the general-in-chief ordered a cessation of fire for the purpose of allowing the troops some repose, the sedition had been hemmed into a small corner of the Beaubourg quarter, and was no longer a cause of inquietude. The governmental troops bivouacked throughout Paris; their communications were open, and they could not doubt of the sympathies of an immense majority of the population.

During the night, M. Thiers, in company with General Bugeaud, made a reconnoissance of the camp of the insurgents; and they were fired upon from different points. An auditor of the council of state, a captain of the line and three soldiers fell dead at their side.

At five o'clock in the morning four columns, commanded by Generals Bugeaud, Lascours, Bourgon and Colonel Boutarel, rushed upon the cluster of houses that still remained in the possession of the insurgents. After the first resistance, which was rather spirited, the barricades were overthrown, the insurgents dispersed, and their positions carried. It was in this attack that an event occurred which requires—not excuses, but explanations. The 35th regiment had met with a severe loss; two of its captains had just been mortally wounded, one of whom was hit in a cowardly and doubly criminal manner by a ball fired from a loophole. A moment afterwards a soldier was killed by a discharge from the house No. 12, Transnonian Street. Such attacks as these on the part of enemies who were concealed and inaccessible to the brave soldiers who were fighting openly in the streets, were enough, certainly, to fill these soldiers with rage. A company rushed into a house from which they had been fired on, and as the guilty one, as usual, could not be found, they did justice upon every one whom they met with. It is in vain for the republicans to continue their unending imprecations on this subject, for they will receive no attention from honest men. That innocent blood has been shed is certain, but let it fall upon those who are the cause of it, upon the bandits who, in the dark and through holes, fire upon the brave men who attack them openly.

At about six o'clock of the evening, the Dukes of Orleans and Nemours, while passing over the scene of conflict on horseback, were repeatedly fired upon; but fortunately the shots were badly directed. This was the epilogue of the drama; and Paris had nothing further to do than to wash the blood from her pavements.

The regular troops and National Guards had eleven men killed and fourteen wounded. On the part of the insurrectionists, there were reckoned fourteen killed and about a dozen wounded.

Such was the work of the republican party under the auspices of the *Rights of Man.* That famous society which was to have swallowed up Paris, was completely crushed, and less by the employment of force than by its own impuissance and public indignation.

CHAPTER XVI.

The *Rights of Man* and the *Mutualists* of Lyons—Insurrection—The theatrical part of M. Lagrange—Eclipse of the principal chiefs.

As it was at the signal of Lyons that Paris had arisen, we may now relate how the second city of 'the kingdom and many cities of the east and south had been delivered up to civil war.

In the year 1828 there was formed at Lyons, under the name of *Mutualists,* a society of weavers, which soon became very numerous. The civil authorities and the clergy became the patrons of this society, a circumstance which was viewed with great pleasure by the workingmen who were at that time exclusively occupied with the philanthropic object of the institution. From the high order of influence that then animated the society and the wisdom of its founders, who had interdicted all political and religious discussion, the members lived in peace and prosperity. How many recent attempts at the incorporation of workingmen might have attained success if the first chapter of their association had established the wise principle of the *Mutualists!* How many worthy artisans, led astray by heartless sophists, might, instead of finding misery in their Utopias, have attained to well-being in all its reality! The palace of fortune is closed to the laboring man, it is said; and it is true that the entrance to this palace is not open to all; but are there not hundreds of thousands of workingmen who have become employers, and are ready to testify that the door is opened by intelligence and labor?

The society of *Mutualists* was divided into lodges of less than twenty members; and a certain number of these lodges were co-ordinate, each one appointing two delegates who formed a central lodge. The committee was composed of all the presidents of these central lodges. The power of this committee had made itself felt very often in the industrial quarrels of the city, and especially in 1831, but no political or socialist motives had ever entered into the disputes. By *Socialist* we mean the modern acceptation of the word; it is very true, indeed, that the workingmen in the difficulties with their employers sought an amelioration of their condition, but they never dreamed of such social chaos as is proposed at the present day.

About the middle of the year 1833, the *Rights of Man* of Paris, in busying itself with establishing affiliated societies in the provinces, did not forget the good city of Lyons, which had always been so faithful to the standard of revolution. In order to give a proof of the esteem in which she was held, the principal member of the Parisian committee, M. G. Cavaignac, went himself to preside at the organization of an affiliated society in Lyons. A meeting of influential republicans was held at the office of the *Precursor*, and resulted in the nomination of a committee which was composed of the following persons, viz: Messrs. Jules Favre, Baune, Charassin, Rivière, Perrier, Poujol, Lortet, Jules Seguin, Berthollon, and A. Martin. As a leading resolution, it was decided to stimulate by every means possible the republicanization of the working classes, and to draw them into the *Rights of Man;* and the *Mutualists*, especially, were to be worked upon with unremitted ardor, and freed from their anti-revolutionary prejudices. The committee took the name of the *Invisible Committee* · a title which could be easily realized, inasmuch as it was a general staff without soldiers. When by means of propagandism some recruits had been made, a change took place in the personality of the committee; the more timid members, among whom was M. Jules Favre, withdrew, and the committee remained definitely composed of Messrs. Baune, Berthollon, A. Martin, Albert, Court, Poujol, and Hugon. The recruiting then went on with great activity, and the most distinguished part of the patriots were enrolled within the space of a few months. One of the groups, though professing the same principles as the others, produced a schism, and persisted in conspiring under the old masonic form; but a division soon arose among its members which led to its dissolution. M. Lagrange, who was one of this sect, reassembled its fragments and reorganized them under the name of the *Society of Progress*.

It was this *Society of Progress* that, together with the *Rights of Man*, undertook the conversion of the *Mutualists;* and they succeeded only too well. The consequence was, a considerable accession to the strength of the revolutionists, and an immediate discord and anarchy among the weavers. The wedge of politics once entered, a spirit of disorder, strife, contention and coalition soon followed. The first event which showed this change in the spirit of the *Mutualists* was the disorganization of the committee. The old members of the committee were broken, and their places supplied by a general election. Scarcely was the new power installed, when, having to decide upon the question of pay, it yielded to the spirit of disorder with which it had been inspired, and dictated to the master manufacturers a threatening ultimatum. The employers showed opposition; by order of the committee a strike was declared, and two days afterwards all the manufactories of silk were deserted.

In this terrible game of strikes, where the workingman stakes the bread of his family more from anger than from the hope of advantage, the tyranny of a few leaders generally controls the greater number; and this was the case in the present instance. The peacefully disposed weavers, revolting against the instigators of the strike, showed a desire to return to their work; but they were opposed and fought against by their patriotic brethren.

Among the Lyonnais members of the *Rights of Man*, as well as those of Paris, there was a knot of furious men who, dreaming only upon destruction, thought that the discords among the laboring classes offered a good pretext for resorting to the musket; but the committee was not of their opinion. This committee showed at that time a degree of prudence which might perhaps be called by a different name. It had not been sparing, thus far, of bravados and excitations, but finding itself at length at that delicate point which is termed the foot of the wall, it exhibited a degree of reserve which was not exactly heroic.

Not knowing how to extricate itself from a difficult compromise between the weavers who persisted in the strike on the one hand, and the sectionaries who were determined to set fire to the powder on the other, the committee decided upon calling for assistance from Paris. An agent was dispatched thither with the mission of bringing back with him some mediator of influence. On the representation of this agent, two men, who were governed by very different intentions, but both of whom wished to avoid an issue, Messrs. G. Cavaignac and Carrel, decided upon setting out. But just as they were about to start, the news of the cessation of the strike arrived; and as the difficulty was removed, the journey was not performed.

But immediately afterwards, on the announcement of the bill against associations, the fire burst out again in great fury. The *Mutualists*, who by that time had almost all entered the *Rights of Man*, took up the matter in a revolutionary fashion. Their organ, the *Echo of Manufactures*, published a protest which was nothing short of an act of revolt; it declared that the law would not be obeyed.

The government perceived that it was time to take measures of defence. An experiment had been made in Lyons in 1831; on which occasion the workingmen had been treated with, and concessions had been granted from generosity, which the mob mistook for weakness; and, emboldened by this, they had taken possession of the city and forced the authorities to a capitulation. But on the present occasion the authorities pursued a different course. In order to show at once that the law against associations was a serious matter, six of the principal instigators of the strike among the *Mutualists* were arrested. This was but so much oil added to the fire; but nevertheless, an energetic act of the kind had to be done. On the news of the arrest, the suburbs fairly leaped with rage. Many of the *Mutualists* went directly to the magistrates and declared that they were decided to share the lot of their comrades; and some of them, listening only to the dictates of their wrath, exclaimed that it was time to take arms and have done with the affair. It was with difficulty that they could be restrained by their chiefs, who promised them a general movement, of which the measures were about to be arranged. A sort of council of war, then, was held, at which the various trades of the city, conjointly with the secret societies, were present. There were in the assembly the chiefs of the *Mutualists*, and the *Rights of Man* united, those of the *Society of Progress*, the *Independents*, the *Association for the Liberty of the Press*, the *Freemen*, the *Freemasons*, the *Unionists*, *Concordists*, *Ferrandiniers*, etc. All these societies, whose existence was threatened by the new law, and which pursued a course in opposition to their own statutes, were ready to deluge the city with blood. A general committee was formed in view of action. The trial of the arrested *Mutualists* had been set for the 5th of April, but was put off till the 9th; and that was the day fixed upon for taking to the streets; the resolution was formally decreed.

The general committee, however, which was under the control of the members of the *Rights of Man*, fine speakers and great boasters, did not dare to declare openly for an attack; and it contented itself, therefore, with proclaiming resistance to aggression. But as it had been agreed upon that all the societies should be present at the court on the day of the trial, this amounted to about the same thing, with this difference, that the responsibility of the attack would be thereby very much diminished.

Such precautions on the part of the chiefs will not astonish those who have much experience in these matters. The moment of action with the committees of secret societies and all other conspiracies whatever, is that moment which is triflingly called the quarter hour of Rabelais; the leaders having succeeded in inspiring their men with a blind confidence which they do not share themselves, find when the current of things sweeps on to an inevitable conflict, that they must indeed give the signal, but they contrive to do it with especial care for their own safety. Some few of them have the courage and self-love to march on to the sacrifice; but the greater part become eclipsed, and never again make their appearance. It is only the conspirator who has become fanatic by incessant excitements, who is full of faith in the success which has been pointed out to him as certain, who has confidence in his chiefs, while they on their part are trembling in despair; it is only the conspirator like this who marches resolutely up to the attack. And this fact is so invariably true that, on the occasion in question, several examples of it were witnessed at the same time. Thus, Lyons sought shelter under the right of self-defence, and Paris intrenched herself behind the initiative of Lyons. At Lyons they waited for the government to make the attack; and at Paris, they waited the movements of Lyons; the hesitation of the leaders in both cases was the same. And the reason is that the time for fine words in the clubs had passed, and the shock of arms in the streets was to bring quite other consequences with it.

As is always the case, the revolutionists of Lyons counted, or affected to count, upon the regular troops, who were to pass over to the revolt, and thus render the victory easy. Such is one of the illusions of which the conspirators will never be cured in proportion as experience points out its puerility. We have already said, and may repeat it to satiety, that our soldiers, with their rigid system of discipline, will, when well commanded, be always found opposed to revolt.

Notwithstanding the resolution of fighting on the 9th, the committee remained in a state of uncertainty which manifested itself in a variety of ways. Although the powers of the committee had received all the regularity possible, yet this committee demanded a new election. We may suppose, and perhaps without being too insolent, that more than one of their number hoped that he would not be re-elected; but the hope proved fallacious, for they were all confirmed in their functions. An indecision, moreover, existed in other quarters besides among the chiefs of the *Rights of Man;* M. Lagrange, the principal director of the *Society of Progress*, also experienced a state of tergiversation; his last word being that the affair was a bad one, but that he would support it since it had been undertaken.

On the 9th of April, the sections having been convoked, and having for the watch-word *Association, Courage, Resistance*, assembled in a mass in the vicinity of the palace of justice. Several members of the committee were seen circulating among the groups, and among others M. E. Baune. Seeing his men full of the highest spirits, he thanked them emphatically in the name of the democracy, which was about to triumph. This done, M. Baune fell sick, and, returning to his house, did not again make his appearance.

Soon after the mass of the insurrectionary forces had assembled, the cry—"To arms!" arose, and without any other preliminaries, all hands set to work at the barricades. A few minutes afterwards the first reports of fire-arms were heard. Three or four members of the committee were in a neighboring house in the act of deliberation, in which they found great difficulty in coming to a resolution. Some one arrived to tell them that the affair had commenced. "Be it so!" said they; "go and announce that the signal for the fight has been given." They would have ordered a retreat if the affair had not broken out of itself. The people, in such cases, take their parts in a little more serious-earnest than their chiefs.

The regular troops allowed but a short time of suspense as to what their intentions were. Led on to the attack by energetic officers, they did their duty without hesitation. They were soon supported by a cannonade; for the importance of an expeditious repression was well understood. Things were managed in such a manner that the invasion from the suburbs was driven back in all quarters, so that by nightfall the insurgents retained only one position in the city, that of the church of the Cordeliers.

This day's work was a warm one; all the courage and skill of the Generals Aymar, Fleury, and Buchet, and the twenty thousand men whom they commanded, were put to the test. The old means made use of by seditions were put in practice by the revolutionists; a placard posted up in profusion, announced the proclamation of the Republic in Paris; the flight of the king; the rising of the principal cities; the desertion of the troops; the arrival of twenty thousand Dauphinois, etc. Such impudent falsehoods as these are always made use of on similar occasions, and always with the same effect. Another odious species of tactics was also brought in play; some women, who were animated by the ferocious fanaticism which such contests are calculated to excite, formed breastworks of their persons at the cross-streets, from behind which their husbands fired upon and decimated the troops. Though the soldiers were trembling with rage, they respected the extravagance of these misguided women. It became necessary to enter the houses and leave detachments there and also at the barricades; for every point which the troops abandoned was immediately taken possession of by the insurrectionists. Neither chiefs nor direction and concert of action was perceived; nothing but sinister animosity and desperate courage.

Driven from the city, the revolt returned to the suburbs, which it aroused to the fight, and where it maintained for three days more a second contest, which was as obstinate as the first. Two cannons, of which it had taken possession, were discharged from the heights of Fourvières upon the quays of the Saône and the place of Bellecour. The intrepidity of the troops checked and repelled at every point the savage energy of the assailants. On the 12th, the troops carried the several positions of the suburbs and the church of the Cordeliers, the last formidable intrenchment of the revolt.

It was at the Cordeliers that M. Lagrange figured; and by his costume, his attitude and his speeches, he produced an effect the tendency of which was, especially, to render conspicuous the superior part which he himself played. The truth is that he gave a great many orders and threw himself into a great agitation; but his companions found that his air was too much that of a conspirator of the stage, and paid but little attention to him. One of the real commandants of the position was M. Callès, a manufacturer of silk cord; he had nothing majestic in his manner; but he directed the defence with a sombre sang froid and with a conscientiousness that the troops will long remember. He remained at his post till the last; and, when the cannon had broken in the doors of the church, taking refuge in the corners with a small band of men as mad as himself, he still poured a shower of balls upon his assailants.

Many other chiefs were remarked, who remained at the head of their men during the combat; such as M. Reverchon, at Vaise; M. Despinasse, at the Guillotière, and Messrs. Carrier and Gauthier at the Red Cross. As to Messrs. Sylvain Court, Antide Martin, Albert, Hugon, and E. Baune, the committee men on the part of the *Rights of Man*, and who may be considered as the organizers of the revolt, not a trace was seen of them wherever musket balls were to be given or received.

CHAPTER XVII.

The conspiracies of Luneville, Saint Etienne, Chalons, Clermont, Grenoble, Vienne, and Marseilles—The trials of April—The accused—Their defenders—The escape from Sainte Pelagie—Verdict—M. Marrast in prison—An odious illumination—The revolt of the cells—An attempt to assassinate M. Carrel.

A HUNDRED and thirty-one soldiers, including one colonel and twelve other officers, were killed in the revolt of Lyons, and one hundred and ninety-two were wounded. On the part of the insurgents one hundred and seventy were killed, the number of wounded remaining unknown. Such was the funeral trophy of the *Rights of Man* in the second city of the kingdom.

The number of arrests amounted to four hundred, several of whom were legitimists; among others, M. Saint Genest and the Abbey Noix, who were brought before the Court of Peers.

The propagandism of the too famous society had extended to many cities which had their sections and committees and received their orders from Paris. Among the princpial affiliated societies we may mention those of Saint Etienne, led by the Caussidière family; that of Perpignan, directed by the Aragos; those of Arbois and Epinal, organized by Messrs. Desperey and Mathieu; that of Dijon, commanded by M. James de Montry and Lieutenant Demay; those of Clermont, Marseilles, Grenoble, and Metz, of which Messrs. Trelat, Imbert, Saint Romme, and Dornez were the chiefs; and, in fine, those of Luneville and Nancy, which had their nucleus in four regiments of Cuirassiers, who garrisoned the department of the Meurthe and the Vosges.

This latter conspiracy presented a particularly serious aspect on account of the military element which entered it

M. de Ludre, a deputy, had gone to Nancy to hurry on the affair with the quarter-masters Clement Thomas, Tricotel, Bernard, and Regnier; but the law against associations intervening, a council was held, the result of which was that the four regiments should be carried away by the sergeants, and marched to the assistance of the insurrection in Paris, raising up the people as they went along. The quarter-masters having courted popularity with their inferiors, fancied that they had only to say the word in order to determine the squadrons to a revolt; but, unfortunately for them, their projects were known and their proceedings closely watched. General Gusler sent for M. Thomas, and was satisfied with merely addressing him a severe admonition; but this was an indulgence that the ambitious sergeant showed himself incapable of appreciating. Several days afterwards, on the 16th of April, a false report having been spread of a revolt of the garrison of Béfort, M. Thomas and his colleagues decided upon the immediate execution of their plan. M. Tricotel repaired to Nancy at a gallop to give the signal, while his three accomplices went through the quarters, haranguing the men, making the fine promises usual in such cases, and never doubting that the whole would follow them. They then assembled the quarter-masters, leading them out of the city into a desert place, and made known to them their plan, the means for carrying it into execution, and the magnificent advantage to be derived from its success. The sergeants of the 10th regiment flatly refused to have anything to do with it; others listened to it coldly, without disclosing their opinions, and it was received favorably only by a few. The leaders returned to the barracks, followed by their colleagues, and prepared to mount their horses in order to take off the regiments; but this audacious attempt had already been carried far enough. The chiefs of the corps, knowing what was going on, had taken their measures; and the places of resort of the soldiers were filled with men who were on the look out for the conspirators, and whom they seized at the first order given by their officers. Instead of the triumphal procession which the rebels were expecting from their comrades, they received an escort by which they were conducted to prison.

At Saint Etienne the reverberation of the movement of Lyons was felt on the 11th and 12th of April. On the first day, there were seen to defile before the Hôtel de Ville, to the music of republican songs, various assemblages, amounting to four thousand persons. They were miners and ribbon weavers, who had become brigaded in the *Rights of Man* of the place, and were thus responding to a general call. M. Caussidière the elder, his two sons, and one of his daughters, had organized the association; but M. Marc Caussidière having been arrested in February on account of serious disorders, had taken no part in the affair; it was his father who applied the match to the train, and his brother lost his life by it. There was nothing heroic in this mob; a few isolated soldiers were knocked over; an attack was made upon a manufactory of arms; a few barricades were thrown up, and this was all, except the pillaging of a few gunsmiths' shops, and the breaking open the doors of a church. Not that the crowd of poor workingmen, incited to disorder by the demagogues, were not disposed to commit greater excesses, but that order was restored by a few vigorous charges of cavalry. On the 12th a few evidences of fermentation still existed, but they were easily suppressed.

Chalons-sur-Saône had, too, its *Rights of Man*, and must also have a scene in the insurrectional drama. The sectionaries barricaded the bridge of the Saône, and set to work ringing the bells. At the same time the cry "To arms!" was raised through the city, and the Hôtel-Dieu was taken possession of. A single company of Voltigeurs launched against the mobbers, put them to rout, and delivered the city. But the society had its ramifications in the vicinity; the communes arose at the sound of the bells; the mails were stopped, and a detachment of soldiers were pressed upon, and their standard wrested from them and thrown into the fire—a noble act! Emissaries were dispatched into the environs, announcing the triumph of the Lyonnais, and proclaiming the republic to the country. Such proceedings as these continued until the 14th, when the fall of Lyons being officially known, the chiefs of the *Rights of Man* took to flight, leaving their men to the cares of Providence.

At Clermont-Ferrand, there was great agitation, great speech making at the coffee-houses, and a great desire to do something; but nothing was done. A single insensate act exhibited the only evidence of democratic life in Auvergne, and that act was committed by a drunken officer. Drawing his sabre as the guard was filing by, he brandished it over his head, and shouted—"Hurrah for the Republic!"

There were also faint attempts at sedition in Grenoble, Vienne, and other cities in the environs of Lyons. The cries of—"Hurrah for the Republic! To arms! Let us fly to the rescue of our brothers!" and other similar well-known clamors were heard; and to the cries succeeded the pillaging of a few shops, acts of violence against the agents of authority, several discharges of fire-arms, and, in short, the usual details of every mob.

M. Imbert, the principal chief of the *Rights of Man*, of Marseilles, and the commandant of the *Cougourde*, a society of scapegraces recruited from the dens of the city, showed no disposition to be behindhand in attempts at disorder. The committee of the *Rights* had published the following declaration—"The Society of Marseilles binds itself, upon its honor, to listen only to its conscience, and resist the law." On the 14th, the *Sovereign People*, directed by M. Imbert, gave forth one of those impudent bulletins which almost every one knows by heart—"The king was besieged in the Tuileries; the queen and princesses had fled, and the troops were passing over to the revolt." But all this was not enough to move the people, and the patriots threw their last desperate effort into a feeble appeal to arms, which fell without an echo.

Since it was quite evident that all these movements were of one and the same conspiracy, the machinery of which lay in the *Rights of Man*, of Paris, the government decided to unite all the cases in one single trial, and to bring them before the Court of Peers. A detailed account of this formidable affair does not lie within the plan of our work, but we give a simple historical sketch of it, because of the persons who figure in it, and whom we must follow in their route up to the days of February.

The accused were not expecting, by any means, to limit themselves to a mere ordinary defence; on the contrary, they intended to make a solemn and triumphant exposition of their doctrines. With this view, they called to their aid, not as advocates, but as assistants in their confession, all the republicans of any notoriety. They came together from all the four quarters of France; and the truth might permit us to say that a great number of them ought to have come before the High Tribunal in any other character than that of advocates. Among the quota furnished by Paris to this army of pretended defenders, we may distinguish the following persons—Messrs. Barbès, Blanqui, Flocon, Bergeron, Vignerte, Martin Bernard, Buonarotti, Marc Dufraisse, Raspail, Charles Teste, Grouvelle, Laponneraye, Latrade, Carrel, Dussard, Hyppolite Fortoul, Charles Ledru, Ledru-Rollin, Pierre Leroux, Jean Reynaud, Voyer-d'Argenson, Carnot, Auguste Comte, Dupont, Garnier-Pagès, F. Gérard, Lamennais, Landrin, L'Heritier, Marie, Moulin, Ploque, Virmaître, Vervoort, Thomas, and Lebreton.

From the provinces, we find Messrs. Jules Favre, Degeorge, Dornès, James de Montry, Michel (de Bourges), Trélat, Saint Romme, Joly, Coppens, Coralli, Demay, Senard, Antony Thouret, and Voirhaye.

A committee of direction was formed in each of these two categories; that of Paris consisting of Messrs. Chilmann, G. Cavaignac, Granger, Lebon, Marrast, Pichonnier, Guinard, Vignerte, and Landolphe; and that of Lyons, of Messrs. Tiphaine, Caussidière, Martin, Taillefer, Baune, and Lagrange.

The design was to enlighten the court with an encyclopedic exposition of democracy; and, in order that the questions might be treated *ex professo*, a part was assigned to each. To one was assigned the question of administration; to another, problems in political economy; to another, philosophy; and to another, the politics of foreign relations. These gentlemen deigned even to comprise the fine arts in their programme; and one of the accused was to give up his lofty lucubrations on barricades and infernal machines, and take to teaching the true principles of literature, science, and art.

This beautiful plan, the object of which was to show the great superiority of the republican party in everything, extended into a region which lay altogether beyond the jurisdiction of the High Court—it entered the regions of the ridiculous; but a matter which came nearer home to the court, was the solemnly declared intention, on the part of the accused, to prosecute the judges themselves. The Court of Peers, however, would not submit to this inversion of parts; it decidedly declined acting on the defensive in the case, and proceeded to assign attorneys to the accused. It was well understood, moreover, that every member of the bar might lend his assistance; the main object of the Peers being to check the very first effort that should be made, under a pretence of sacred right, to outrage the law and glorify revolt. Complaints, clamors, and protestations, burst out on all sides at the announcement of this decision; both counsel and accused declaring that they would not offer any defence. This resolution, however, was not generally followed; for several of the accused wished to make a figure before the court; and some of the advocates, who hoped to produce an effect, urged warmly that there should be both defence and defenders. Of this number was M. Lagrange, a man who has always conceived his political part in a picturesque point of view, and also M. Jules Favre, who has never allowed an occasion to pass without giving one of those peculiarly bilious speeches, for the concocting of which he seems to have the special recipe.

By permission, the accused and their counsel held a large meeting at Sainte Pélagie, at which it was decided that the Republic must not yield, and that the court must be forced to admit the defence, as proposed by the republicans. M. Ledru-Rollin, who at that time was but little known, opposed this decision, and M. Michel (de Bourges), whose reputation was already made, sustained it. M. Jules Favre having declared himself, with his usual benevolence, for the minority, the advocate of Bourges, who was not a whit behind him in amenity of manner, replied in such terms that the two black gowns came very near tearing each other to pieces.

In the midst of such proceedings as these the trial commenced. The colossal proportions of the affair had required an examination of thirteen months, and the accused were not called to the bar until the 5th of May, 1835. The various names upon the docket amounted to a hundred and twenty one; the principal of which were as follows: Messrs. Cavaignac, Marrast, Guinard, Recurt, Kersausie, Clément Thomas, Berryer-Fontaine, de Ludre, Lagrange, Baune, Reverchon, Caussidière, N. Lebon, Vignerte, Landolphe, Maillefer, Mathé, Imbert, Delente, Villain, Mathieu (d'Epinal), Crevat, Beaumont, Pornin, Chilmann, and Chancel.

The Parisians refused to respond; but those from Lyons joined issue; and dramatic protestations and scenes of violence occurred which are too well known to be repeated. In order to maintain the dignity of justice, the court was obliged to disunite the cases; and the accused from Lyons were sentenced first. During this time the Parisians, who were imprisoned in Sainte Pélagie, were making preparations for an escape, the success of which delivered them from their embarrassment; and there are reasons for believing that the government was not inconsolable for their loss.

With respect to this escape we may give a characteristic fact. Before the arrival of the Lyonnais in Paris, two of their number, finding the watch over them not very strict, took advantage of the occasion and ran away. The severe republicans of Paris published a proclamation against this disloyalty, in which they said that "it was unworthy republicans, to shun the discussion of the trial." This production was signed: Marrast, Guinard, Cavaignac, Berryer-Fontaine, N. Lebon, Landolphe, Vignerte, Delente, Lecomte, Pichonnier, Crevat, Delaquis, and Caillet. Now all these gentlemen were of the number who afterwards made their escape from Sainte Pélagie; and on leaving their prison they published an article in which were the following words: "It is time that men of heart should render oppression vain and ridiculous by evading its pursuit." Explain, who can, how the same men considered it on one day disloyal to shun discussion, and on the next, pretended that one should render oppression ridiculous by escaping it.

The general verdict which was rendered on the 13th of August, against the contumacious, as well as against those present, sentenced to deportation Messrs. Cavaignac, Guinard, Marrast, de Ludre, Kersausic, Berryer-Fontaine, C. Thomas, N. Lebon, Vignerte, Delente, Beaumont, Baune, Reverchon, Antide, Martin, Albert, and Hugon; to imprisonment for twenty years, Messrs. Lagrange and Bernard; to imprisonment for ten years, Messrs. Caussidière, Landolphe, Mathé, Stiller, and Tricotel, and others, to penalties less severe.

The insurrection and the trial of April, together, had dispersed the famous society of the *Rights of Man;* but before expiring, the fragments of the serpent were to writhe in a few desperate convulsions.

During the examination of the cases, privileges of all kinds had been granted to the prisoners of Sainte Pélagie; they were permitted the free access of wives, parents, and friends; they were suffered to go at large upon their parole, and even festivities were tolerated, by which the republicans of Lacedemon would have been somewhat scandalized. Their prison had something of the appearance of a hotel. Everybody there *rotted*, if they rotted at all, upon very good beds instead of *the humid straw*, and from morning till night they feasted with their friends, who brought them loads of provisions. M. Marrast, especially, managed to support the afflictions of his captivity by a nourishment highly flavored with truffes, and moistened with champagne; a circumstance which the brothers who were less delicately fed viewed with a sinister eye, and a terribly envious mouth. But as the illustrious editor of the *Tribune* troubled himself very little about these little men, and gormandized with an insolent air under their very eyes, he came at length to be hated by them so cordially, that they promised him a good lamp-post in the future republic. It is from this circumstance that may be dated that implacable hatred which the patriots have since vowed against this personage; a hatred which isolated him in exile, which has followed him to the *National*, and which has certainly not abated since the days of February.

The prisoners of Sainte Pélagie, then, accused of having organized and attempted the subversion of France; of having commanded the fratricidal contest of Paris, and originated that of Lyons, crimes the most heinous of all others, ought, one would suppose, to have shown some acknowledgment to the government for the consideration with which they were treated; but not at all; on the contrary, too little was done for them; they must have the delicate attentions due to unfortunate princes. Such are the habitual pretensions of conspirators; the greater the crimes which they commit, the greater is the regard which they expect to have shown them. And some of the men at the head of the departments of government appear to humor these pretensions. It is true that the outcries of the demagogic journals are calculated to frighten functionaries of a timid nature; but then, there should be no reasonable objection against applying to the anarchists those principles of equality of which they say themselves they are so very fond, and regarding, whatever may be the person concerned, a crime as a crime, and a criminal as a criminal. Besides, partiality in such cases as these generally springs from an unworthy sentiment. It is said that no one can tell, in such tempestuous times, when he himself may not be pursued in his turn and given up to reprisals. And it is thus that individual character becomes lost; cowardly circumspection and distrust of one's rights and strength constitute the main force of the enemy, and render revolutions eternal.

We have just given an idea of the indulgence which was shown towards the chiefs of the *Rights of Man;* and it will now be seen in what appreciation this indulgence was held by them, and by what noble conduct they relieved themselves of their sufferings during their captivity.

On the 20th of May, during the examination of the causes, General Lafayette died, and the republicans, in accordance with the precedent established in the case of M. Casimir Perrier, illuminated their cells! One of the newspapers having maintained that this indignity had called forth a protest from some of the prisoners, M. Vignerte indignantly declared this assertion to be false, and maintained that the manifestation was an honorable act, in which all the prisoners gloried at having taken a part. But M. Vignerte, however, was boasting of a falsehood; for there were men of heart among his comrades whom he volunteered to gratify with an act of cowardice; but such was the feverish excitement of the times that no one paid any attention to it.

Some time afterwards, the prisoners made one of those often repeated requests which had the appearance of shameless effrontery. No reply was made to it, and immediately these gentlemen proceeded to revolt; they shut themselves up in the corridors, broke up their furniture, and set the fragments on fire. The agents of the public force arrived and ordered the disturbers of the peace to be quiet; but they were answered with bravados and insults. But such madmen as these had to be reduced to submission, and the Municipal Guards received orders to load their arms. This brought the patriots to their senses, and they became quiet, with the reservation of amply revenging themselves through the columns of the newspapers. The *Tribune*, that fury which had been silenced only for a moment, and which had just begun its vociferations again, exhausted a whole vocabulary of outrages against M. Gisquet for the guilt of not having abandoned Sainte Pelagie to revolt. A man who has since been called to the prefectureship of police, but who has shown no evidence of an ability to comprehend its duties, M. Gervais (de Caen), a mediocre and venomous busy-body, declares, in a speech full of absurdities, that the police had provoked the prisoners, and had formed the infernal scheme of renewing upon them the massacres of September.

Manifestations by means of candles had become all the vogue. On the 21st of January, 1835, the prisoners decided to celebrate the death of *Capet* by a general illumination. M. Carrel, who had been recently condemned for contempt of court, and who was confined among the prisoners of April, refused to take any part in such a cynical display. The epithets of coxcomb, yellow-glove, and aristocrat, were lavished upon him by the *Purists;* and not content with insults, they rushed to his chamber swearing that they would hang him, and had not the keepers arrived, they would have assassinated a man of heart, whose crime consisted in having brought a blush to the cheeks of wretches who were a disgrace to his party.

CHAPTER XVIII.

Still another mob—M. Raspail and M. Gisquet—The complot of Neuilly—The Chaveau family—The attempt of Fieschi—M. Recurt and Pepin—The part played by the *Rights of Man.*

THE scene of the drama presented by the *Rights of Man* in prison has been exhibited. Those who had escaped justice were to display the last agonies of the association, with still more violent contortions.

The arrest or flight of the chiefs had brought a complete disorganization upon the sections; only a few groups, which had scarcely been able to reform themselves, preserved their hopes and sought a new occasion for revolt. It was one of these fractions that during the trial had excited a mob in the boulevards of Saint Denis and Saint Martin. During a space of four days, there were assemblages of persons who, growing bolder by degrees, finally proceeded to the throwing up of barricades. A grand cordon was drawn by the authorities around the sectionaries, and three hundred of their number were taken at one swoop—a species of sweepstakes that disgusted the others and restored peace to the quarter.

As usual, the mob was attributed to the police. A newspaper had been established some time previously with the name of *The Reformer*, of which M. Raspail was the editor in chief. This man has always had a monomania on the subject of the police; he saw spies everywhere; and even the honest M. Dupoty, his fellow collaborator, was more than once the object of his suspicions. One day, finding something suspicious in a person who entered his office, he seized him by the shoulders and brutally ejected him from the door; but the person in question happened to be a worthy man, who had merely come to pay his subscription. M. Raspail labored assiduously through the columns of his paper to prove the excessive ignorance of his confederates on the subject of chemistry, and to denounce the perpetual provocations which were given by the police. Did two drunken men fight in the streets, or some old woman announce a new scandal, the *Reformer* immediately saw a machination of the police in it. True to his system, M. Raspail peremptorily declared, and offered to prove, that the disorders of the boulevards had been the work of the prefect of police. M. Gisquet took him at his word, and gave him an opportunity of exhibiting his proofs at the correctional police; but the great man could not, it would appear, furnish his proofs as peremptorily as he had his assertions; for he was sentenced to a three months' imprisonment and a fine of three thousand francs.

The disturbances occasioned by the trial of April were a mere ordinary mob. The old style of agitation which had been so often resorted to since the days of July, was henceforth to lose its attractiveness; and we shall see hereafter only faint traces of its recurrence. But in the place of grand attacks, made in open day and in battle array, we shall see attempts at regicide which, in their turn also, became periodical. The *Rights of Man*, before finally making its disappearance, added to its other lofty exploits two of these abominable attempts.

Among the sections which had escaped the rout of April, there was a group of reckless men who had for their chiefs Messrs. Charles and Gabriel Chaveau, the latter of whom had already been implicated in the disorders of July, 1833.

These two wretches drew together several meetings in which the assassination of the king, after mature deliberation, was decided to be a holy and necessary act, and one to which they ought to devote their efforts. The two brothers Chaveau, one of whom was nineteen and the other seventeen years of age, had for their accomplices Messrs. Huillerie, Huber, Husson, Leroy, Leglantine, Delont, Combes, Dulac, Duval, and Boireau, whose ages were about as respectable as those of their chiefs, and all whom were poor workingmen who had received their political education from the *Tribune* and other publications at two cents a piece. To these must be added Madam Chaveau the mother, the Cornelia of the suburbs, who was proud of the schemes of her sons, in which she became an abettor. Such were the characters of the persons who pretended to the right of changing the destinies of France by the perpetration of an execrable crime. It would be puerile, perhaps, to discover in a scheme like this, conceived by such men, any other motive than that infernal thirst for celebrity which has nailed the name of Erostratus to the pillory of history; but whatever the detestable motive may have been, it is certain that the plan was seriously contemplated.

It was agreed that the assassins should take up a position upon the road to Neuilly, and that when the king should pass, they were to rush upon the carriage, cut the traces, and then massacre the royal family with the pistol and dagger.

On the day appointed for the deed, every one was at his post. They had informed themselves of the hour at which the king would go out, of the road which he habitually followed, and they were waiting for him, armed to the teeth. But an emissary was sent to inform them that the king had taken another route. Hence, all they had to do was to return to Paris, which they did, with a bravado air, like men who had compelled the enemy to give way, and who were confident of better success the next time. In order not to be disappointed in the second attempt, they resolved to lie in wait for the carriage upon the Place de la Concorde, and to attack it at the moment when about to enter upon one of the three roads leading into the Champs Elysées.

On the day and hour fixed, the assassins were again at the rendezvous. Whilst they were taking up their positions, the king, on his part, though informed of everything, but unwilling to believe in such bloody designs from a band of boys, or perhaps being determined to face the danger, entered his carriage in spite of the supplications of his family and his officers. The queen, having tried in vain to conquer his resolution, resolved at least to share his danger, and placed herself by his side. M. Thiers, who as minister of the interior was the first guardian of the public safety, having endeavored to dissuade the august couple from a serious imprudence, solicited the honor of accompanying them.

The carriage took its departure with the ordinary escort, the only difference being that the horsemen by whom it was surrounded were prepared to give the assailants a warm reception. One of the assailants seeing the approach of the carriage, made a sign to the others to show that the decisive moment had come. Some of them rapidly advanced, others were more slow, and others still appeared to pretend that they had not seen the signal. They who were nearest turned back towards the others in order to hasten their arrival; and these did the same towards those who were behind them; they waited reciprocally for each other; they called upon each other in the hardest of terms, and, in short, gave time to allow the carriage to pass by.

This miserable result of such a proudly conceived plan was not calculated to soothe the exacerbation of the conspirators. The design was still maintained, and a few days afterwards, in a new meeting at the house of Dame Chaveau, another plan of regicide was brought upon the carpet. The police had finally been able to penetrate the mysteries of this complot; it got wind of the conventicle and sent its agents there. They found the doors barred, and had to force their way in. They found in the lodgings Messrs. Huber, Husson, Leroy, Huillerie and the Dame Chaveau, whom they thought it their duty to take away. In the mean time, M. Charles Chaveau had made his appearance, and he was seized and placed among his companions, whom he assailed with bitter invectives, reproaching them for having allowed themselves to be taken like a set of cowards. The truth is, these gentlemen had the means of defending themselves; for there were found not long after, under a bed, a dozen of loaded pistols, together with daggers, muskets, and ammunition. The reproaches of M. Charles having stirred up his companions, the whole band, Madame Chaveau included, raised a clamor of patriotic vociferations, interlarded with couplets of the *song of the departure*, and hurrahs for the Republic!—a deplorable spectacle, which caused the agents of the police to hurry off the furious fools as soon as possible.

M. Gabriel Chaveau, who remained at liberty, and who wished to show that if he were arrested it would not be without a cause, continued his preparations, and made the acquisition of a little barrel of powder, which he was to throw into the carriage of the king. Mister Gabriel and his barrel were taken and snugly stowed away in a safe place.

Five of these wretches were condemned to severe and well-merited punishment.

But of all the lofty achievements of the *Rights of Man*, the one which we are about to give caps the climax.

It will be remembered that in the affairs of June, 1832, there was a merchant of the suburb Saint Antoine, by the name of Pepin, who had made his house a place of arms for the insurrection. This man had never ceased his conspiracies from that time, and although a timid and irresolute character, he had always mingled with the most violent of the revolutionists. He belonged to the Society of Action of M. Kersausie, and owed his escape to the insignificance of the position which he occupied in the conspiracy; he was not, however, a mere common member; for a group of some importance obeyed his orders. Finding the association destroyed and the patriots demoralized, and perceiving that the time for open attacks had passed, he concluded that some extraordinary event was alone capable of re-awaking the party, and restoring the fortune of the Republic. And of all extraordinary events, the assassination of the king appeared to him the most admirable. This idea had taken root in his mind, and was germinating there, when one of his comrades, a sectionary like himself, came to see him one day, and disclosed a plan of regicide which seemed safe and infallible. The safety of the plan was a consideration of importance; for though Pepin was an approved patriot, yet his courage had its moments of relapse, and this fact his friend knew very well. This friend was no less a person than Morey, the harness-maker—a mere fragment of a man, used up by age and infirmity, but in which there survived an organization of iron animated by a fanatic devotion to the work of destruction. Fieschi, a rascal by profession, had addressed himself to this old man a few days previously, and offered to place at his disposal a bloody machine, of which he was the inventor. Fieschi confessed that, having lost his honor, and being without resources, he was ready to sacrifice his life in any great political enterprise; all that he asked, he said, was to be provided with the means of action and money enough for his subsistence until the moment of execution. There was no doubt, indeed, of his willingness to hazard his life, but still, he exhibited certain evidences of a leaning towards safety, and even of ambition, which did not escape the eye of old Morey, but which the old man resolved, in his own mind, should not haunt the party after the deed was done.

As soon as Pepin was informed of the plan, he consented to it without hesitation. The old Corsican, whose plan they accepted, was sent for, and the oath, under pain of death, was taken by the three conspirators. An occasion soon offered itself: the king was to hold a review on the 29th of July, the anniversary of the Three Days, and it was decided that the crime should be committed during the ceremony.

Pepin immediately took his measures for forewarning the revolutionists. He set out for the departments; visited the principal chiefs of the association, and, without disclosing the complot, gave them to understand that an important event was about to take place, which would render their concurrence necessary. On returning to Paris, he took into his confidence several eminent chiefs of the *Rights of Man*, and among others his particular friend, M. Recurt, with whom he often shared his table. The whole plan, as well as the names of the accomplices, was known by this ex-minister of the provisional government; the confessions of Pepin, made at an hour when there is no longer a motive for lying, attest the fact. It was at night, after the first glass of wine, that the execrable machination was confided to M. Recurt, with the offer of a part in it; but finding the game a little too rude for his liking, he declined. In so doing, he followed the rules of prudence; but what a terrible reckoning have not social probity and the cause of humanity to demand of M. Recurt for not having denounced the assassins? What! he look on and see the match of Fieschi lighting in the dark, and make no effort to arrest the wretch who, at the time and place appointed, piled his heap of corpses upon the pavement! M. Recurt has not been called to the bar of justice, it is true, but men of heart and of loyalty remember him. This republican, who has been one of the chiefs of government, and expects to become so again, authorizes the destruction of his enemies by means of assassination.

Some of the fragments of the *Rights of Man* formed, at this period, a new association, which took the name of the *Society of the Families*. Of this society, Messrs. Blanqui and Barbès were the principal chiefs. Pepin became connected with these conspirators, to whom also he imparted his secret. It will be easily credited that Messrs. Blanqui and Barbès had not the scruples of the physician of the suburb Saint Antoine, and that they, therefore, went much further than the mere omission of denouncing the assassins. In anticipation of the success of the plan, they had even prepared a proclamation, which was subsequently found at the house of M. Barbès, and which was in his handwriting. It was a monstrous specimen of demagogism, in which occurred, by way of a summary, the following atrocious phrase—"People, bare your arms, and thrust them up to the shoulder into the entrails of your executioners!" Fieschi, it was evident, was dealing with men who understood him.

Others still were admitted into the complot; and it is believed that M. Godefroy Cavaignac was of the number.

It was to him, at least, that Pepin was directed for getting the principal parts of the machine. The plan was, it will be remembered, to adjust twenty-five musket barrels upon a frame in such a manner that they could all be discharged at once by a train of powder. M. Cavaignac, whom Pepin went to see in Sainte Pelagie, had still several depots of arms under his control, which had been collected for the use of the *Rights of Man*. He gave an evasive answer at first, but finally decided not to furnish the muskets.

Whether the knowledge of the intended crime came from M. Cavaignac, who might have been informed of it, or from whatever other source, it is certain that the prisoners of the *Rights of Man*, who were in Saint Pelagie, were advised, generally, of an expected catastrophe, which might possibly change their destiny. It is not improbable that this information had as much to do with their escape as the desire of eluding justice; at all events, it had something to do with the delay which the fugitives made in leaving France. This delay could not be sufficiently explained by the difficulties in the way of flight; and what other cause could it have than the hope of profiting by an expected event? This opinion is strengthened by a simple comparison of dates; it was the 11th of July that the prisoners made their escape, and it was the 28th that the attempt at assassination took place.

As Pepin had not been able to get the musket barrels from M. Cavaignac, he gave money to Fieschi to buy them; he then provided himself with the wood necessary for the frame, and had the whole carried to the garret of the house No. 50, boulevard of the Temple, where Fieschi had taken lodgings, under the name of Girard. Fieschi set to work in putting up his instrument of carnage, and while thus employed, he was visited by the old harness-maker, who looked on with a stoical regard, making now and then some malignant remark calculated to stimulate the Corsican in his diabolical resolution. The musket barrels were soon incased in solid pieces of wood, and fixed in the window, ready to execute their terrible office. The train of powder was tried, and all that remained was to fix the aim. For this purpose, Pepin decided upon admitting a fourth accomplice, and M. Boireau, who was then being prosecuted for the affair of Neuilly, rode along the boulevard of the Temple on horseback, so as to give Fieschi an opportunity for pointing his machine. This was done on the 27th. On the evening of that day—the eve of the day supreme, Morey went to the house No. 50, and passed the night in loading the musket barrels. He showed himself very skilful at this business, and endeavored to accomplish it in such a way as not to be deceived in his expectations. These were double; first and above all he wished to exterminate the royal family, and then, from the loftiest considerations of prudence, he had thought proper to involve the Corsican in the same massacre. This supplement of victims was to be effected by a certain irregularity, which he had calculated in loading the barrels. This old Morey was not one of your mere fanciful conspirators; he plied his trade with reflection and conscience; and hence, we are not to be astonished at the homage which has been paid by the patriots to that precious head of his, which dropped so piteously into the willow basket. One of the great citizens of the republic of those days, M. Marc Dufraisse, now a representative of the people, declared on the day following the execution, that the patriot press had been guilty of the most decided cowardice, in not highly extolling the butchery of the 28th of July, and the heroism of the assassins who executed it, especially of Morey—"that heroic old man, so sublime in the act which he premeditated, so sublime at the bar; that old man, so *brave*, so *good*, so *generous*, who died without the stupid crowd deigning him a single word of admiration!"

Limited to four accomplices and a few chiefs of the *Rights of Man*, the complot did not reach the ears of the police until the morning of the 28th; it was then partly divulged by an indiscretion of M. Boireau. But notwithstanding the most careful and vigilant investigations, no discoveries were made; and as the indications that had been given were of the vaguest kind, it was judged unnecessary to countermand the review. The report which had been received on the evening previous referred to the boulevard Saint Martin as the place where the crime was to be committed; and the researches were confined to a minute examination of that quarter.

The king, surrounded by his sons, set out for the review, and began the inspection of the National Guards. When arrived at the boulevard Saint Martin, there was a suspense of the heart throughout the cortége, and a redoubled vigilance on the part of the police; but nothing noticeable occurred, and everything passed off well. When, therefore, the cortége had reached the summit of the slight ascent in the boulevard of the Temple, every one began to breathe more freely. But all of a sudden, from a window that had just been unmasked, there poured forth a volume of smoke, accompanied with a discharge of fire-arms that crackled like a platoon of musketry, and at the same moment there was a fall of corpses all around the king, who, with his sons, had miraculously escaped.

The masterpiece of demagogism had thus been accomplished. The society of the *Rights of Man* had given this time a clear and unmistakable expression of its sentiments; its true, ultimate, practical tendency was at length attained, viz: assassination, destruction in mass, indiscriminate butchery!— a terrible species of logic, but just the kind which must inevitably be made use of by those men, who, led on from error to error, finally come to believe that society belongs to them, and that they have the right to get possession of it by any and every means that lie in their way.

Whilst that old demon Morey was fastening himself upon Fieschi till the very last moment, surrounding him with his baneful fascination, and nailing him, as it were, to his machine, four of the barrels of which had been loaded for the especial benefit of Fieschi himself, Pepin was hurrying through the suburbs of Saint Antoine and Saint Marceau, assembling the sectionaries and preparing them to rush into the streets at the news of success, and to raise the cry of revolt over the corpse of the king. But the crowd which had scattered itself through the thousand avenues of the capital, soon spread the report of the safety of the royal family, and the conspirator, seized with fear, abandoned his men and ran to hide himself in some retreat which he had prepared for the emergency.

The rest is well known; the three principal accomplices were guillotined, and the fourth condemned to an imprisonment of twenty years.

But what may not be so generally known, is that the day after this republican massacre, which indiscriminately cut off a marshal of France, one general, several superior officers of the National Guards, an old man, a young girl of 15 years, a poor laborer, etc.—one of the demagogic papers, one of those hideous things which ought to be destroyed, like so many vipers or wolves, published in a cheery vein the unqualifiable lines which run as follows: "It is a beautiful evening; and everybody, divided between perfect indifference or idle curiosity as to the accident of yesterday, is out enjoying its attractions."

But notwithstanding this indifference or curiosity, there were *sensible* patriots to be found, who were ready the next day, if not on that very beautiful evening itself, to charge the government with cannibalism, should it refuse to set at liberty the friends and colleagues of the assassins of General de Bréa.

The *Rights of Man* gave up the ghost in this sea of blood which it had caused to flow in the boulevard of the Temple. Two months previously, the *Tribune* had succumbed under a repetition of prosecutions which had been accumulating for a period of twenty years. It is our opinion that every regular system of government ought always to have the right of destroying at once such papers as those which were issued by Messrs. Marrast, Sarrut and company; for when a mad dog makes his appearance in the streets, he is killed without mercy; but hydrophobial papers are much worse than mad dogs, since they are biting every day, and extending their madness to thousands of people.

CHAPTER XIX.

The laws of September—Their necessity—Bad newspapers do more harm than good ones do good—It is not true that the shutting up of the clubs induces secret societies—The folly of unrestricted liberty.

The establishment and the proceedings of the *Rights of Man* having been carried on in open day, the law against associations, which had been passed for the express object of preventing this scandal, had driven the sections into the streets, and thus effected their dissolution, as is always the case after a resort to arms in which the chiefs are either seized or dispersed. Hence, rigorously speaking, the famous association could not be called a *secret* one. Although many of its acts bore the character of conspiracies, yet it was found that the law, or its interpreters at least, authorized these acts and permitted men who were organized and armed for the purpose of revolt, to style themselves simply men of opposition; an intolerable mockery which ought never again to be repeated. In consequence of the recent legislation, the conspirators were forced to adopt the forms of strict secrecy. Henceforward we shall see no more well-known chiefs stalking across the stage, no newspapers which become the *Monitors* of conspiracy, no special pamphlets for the benefit of the sectionaries, no noisy propagandism, no initiations without examination; but everything is to become severe, mysterious, and surrounded with precautions. And to such a degree of perfection was this mystery carried, that four years afterwards, in May, 1839, when the *Seasons* made their irruption upon Paris, the *National*, a republican newspaper, was wholly ignorant of the existence of this republican conspiracy, and taken perfectly by surprise by it.

The new phase which was about to be assumed by the

new societies will be especially observable in the absolute circumspection which was to be imposed upon the members, a circumspection which was never to be omitted even in presence of the neophytes; and also in the ceremonies which were to be observed in the act of initiation. A difference will also be remarked with respect to orders of the day and other printed communications which are to be prohibited. In other respects, as to the personality of the societies, that must remain the same for some time to come, that is to say, it must be drawn chiefly from the ambitious and turbulent youth of the middle classes. It is a remarkable fact that the conspirators who have been occupied since 1830 in remodeling France in the name of the working classes, had never derived their support or soldiery from those classes. Among the *Friends of the People* there was not a single blouse; and in the *Rights of Man*, with the exception of those who were recruited from among the *Mutualists* of Lyons, there were but a very few. And this fact may serve both to explain the total routs which the republican faction has so often met with, and illustrate the good faith of those pretended benefactors who presume to speak on behalf of men by whom they are not recognized.

We must not forget, before resuming our narrative, to refer to a political event of importance, which naturally followed the exploit of Fieschi; we allude to the vote upon those laws which are called the laws of September. Three bills were brought in by M. Persil, one of them authorizing the ministry, in matters of crime against the state, to establish as many tribunals as might be judged necessary, and permitting the procurors-general to abridge the formalities in bringing cases to a decision. It also authorized the presiding judges of these tribunals to send away by force all such accused persons as should disturb the proceedings, and proceed against them in their absence. Another of the bills provided that the vote in future should be secret, and that the number of votes necessary to a sentence should be reduced from eight to seven. The third bill declared punishable with imprisonment and a fine from 10,000 to

50,000 francs, every attack, by means of publications, against the king and the basis of the government. It prohibited every one from styling himself a republican, from mingling the name of the king in political discussions, from publishing the names of the jurors otherwise than as given in the reports of the proceedings, from disclosing the deliberations of the jury, from getting up subscriptions in favor of condemned newspapers, from giving signatures in blank on the part of the managers of these papers, from exposing, publishing or offering for sale drawings, emblems, engravings, and lithographs, and from exhibiting theatrical representations without the sanction of the authorities. To these bills the chambers added some amendments with regard to attacks upon property and want of respect for the laws, and then passed them without hesitation. It was moreover decided that the bail, in future, for a daily paper of Paris, should be increased from 48,000 to 100,000 francs, and that the manager should be a bona fide owner of one-third of the bail.

The tempest which this legislation excited is still in the memory of everybody; the republicans were seized with an indignation beyond all limits. It was no puerile comedy or preconceived farce with them this time, but the real agonized shrieks of the beast smitten with death. It is of but little consequence to us to know whether the laws of September were or were not more or less Draconian, as the republicans were pleased to term them; we are satisfied with the conviction that the republicans had rendered them necessary. There is not a robber who does not also find the penal code Draconian; but no one, therefore, is obliged to rob. Every one of these laws had for its object to prevent the renewal of some great scandal, either legal, moral, or political. But the feature of the law which caused the greatest outcry —(and the race particularly attacked by it is clamorous above all others)—was the increasing of the bail for the newspapers; it was considered exorbitant! Perhaps it was exorbitant, but why had the newspapers become so extravagant? In the affairs of state there is but one rule for measures of repression or prevention; and that is determined by the facts of the case. The political laws of England and the United States, it is said, are a hundred times milder than ours are; but it is because the public mind of those countries is a hundred times more peaceable than it is with us. There are logicians who will maintain that the raising of the bail too high would defeat the object aimed at, since it would destroy the good journals as well as the bad. But this objection is not well founded, since the good journals do but little good, while the bad ones do an enormous amount of harm. It is very certain that all the subscribers to the *Debats* would be men of law and order without the instrumentality of that paper; while a great number of persons would never have become demagogues at all were it not for the red republican sheets which they read. The readers of moderate journals generally have their opinions made up, while those who are influenced by the detestable opinions of the anarchical papers are poor devils, who, if it were not for these papers, would be at work gaining an honest livelihood.

If our papers are really so detestable, some socialists may ask, how happens it, then, that they have such a circulation? It happens in this way: these papers have to do with passionate and ignorant men whom they continually spur on with falsehoods and excitements, speaking to them of a thousand chimerical rights, but never of their duties; bestowing upon them a thousand fulsome flatteries, but never inculcating a single truth; imperturbably affirming that they are on the road to happiness, but never showing where this happiness lies, unless, indeed, when arrived at the end of the road, as after February, when they are obliged to come out and show their hand—why, then, this happiness consists in calumniating the adversaries who have opposed their extravagances! The conductors of these papers are charlatans who gain credence, like all other charlatans, by lying with impudence, by making a great bluster, and suborning confederates who fall into ecstasies over their panaceas. They assume the mask of generosity, of patriotism, and loyalty, and smile winningly upon the enthusiastic crowd who never suspect them of being the trifling, heartless, and faithless sepulchres that they are. They infect simple-minded men with fanaticism, and take good care to destroy the influence of men of sense by defaming them. Their course is to level down and degrade by the instrumentality of the libel; for this pleases the mass. They affect grossness and brutality; for the crowd considers this as homage done to their habits. They preach up destruction; for this is agreeable to the instincts of the poorer classes, who are fond of revolutions because they think that they are to be the gainers by them; and then, it is very pleasant to men who have nothing to lose to see everything at sixes and sevens; and besides, it is very flattering to the crowd to hear itself styled the *Great People*, the *Popular Lion*. etc. This is the way that bad papers get a circulation; and the conductors of them know it very well, rubbing their hands over it in great glee.

The effect of the new laws was immediate and decisive; a score or more of demagogic prints fell dead upon the spot— a result of some importance. By referring to the period immediately following the year 1834, we shall see that the republican party had not the ability to resuscitate a single daily paper. Society remained in a state of peace until 1843, its repose hardly broken by the bayings of the *National*. At that period the *Reform* alone succeeded in struggling into existence, but only to vegetate until the revolution with something less than two thousand subscribers.

But we are aware that still another objection lies in our way; we are told that by stifling democracy upon the pavement and in the press we have only driven it into secret societies, where it has dug the mine which has blown up our throne. "Yes, verily, this thing is repeated as a fact, that secret societies have made the revolution; but this is one of those mythological notions which, together with many others, it is our especial task to eradicate."

Let us see what must be the inevitable consequences of a vigorous system of legislation against societies, clubs, and the press. The factions at first resort to complots, and their leaders seek to lead their men into them, with all the ardor of violent rage; but the mass who go readily to meetings of a legal character which are attended with no danger or constraint, cannot easily accustom themselves to secret proceedings, which impose constraint and are accompanied with dangers; the difference between this dull and unexciting régime and that of public assemblies full of variety and emotion, is too great to be pleasing. The least zealous soon give up their attendance; others gradually become discouraged, until finally a disbandment takes place where, if the meetings had been public, the orator in his tribune would have proved a sufficient bond of union, and as to the chiefs themselves, that great enthusiasm by which they were inspired when acting their part before the public, stimulated by impassioned audiences, soon becomes lost in the incognito of secret societies; and the greater part of them abandon the cause, and by insensible degrees return to ordinary life, where the fierceness of their opinions is lost. Agitation is kept up and extended by agitation; by stopping the noise the echo is prevented—two truths which are incontestable. It is our opinion, and we speak from experience, that if a public club were transformed into a secret society, not one-fifth of its members would remain at the end of six months; and even those, lost in the shades of their mysteries, would have no demoralizing influence. If, then, we are told by orators and writers, that a free scope must be left to parties, for otherwise they will conspire, we may reply to them boldly that their conspiracies are mere child's play, which can always be managed by the police, while on the other hand the preachings of clubs, of writings and public societies, are spots of rancid oil that strike in to the very heart of society, and which can be taken out only by the ordeal of fire.

There is another class of doctors who preach unlimited liberty, affirming that evil is cured by evil, and that licentiousness may be left to destroy itself. This doctrine may indeed be true in the long run; but we believe that if our demagogues were to be left to themselves, they would, long before coming to blush at their extravagances, have time to upset France over and over again, if not all Europe.

We have no confidence in such romantic measures for the prevention of wrong; there is a way pointed out which is as old as the world itself, and which consists in protecting the good and punishing the bad; and let us hold to that.

CHAPTER XX.

The *Revolutionary Legions*—Political assassination—Alibaud—M. Sobrier—M. Recurt—M. Flocon—M. Barbès—M. Martin-Bernard.

THE secret societies which had collected together the principal fragments of the *Rights of Man* and succeeded to it, was the society of the *Families;* but there was formed, at the same time, under the name of *Revolutionary Legions*, another association to which we must devote a few words.

The government of July gained daily in strength, and the impuissance of the republicans against it became momentarily more evident until the reckless men of the party came at length to dream upon the destruction of this government by means the most extravagant and ferocious. A fever for the enterprise seized upon many; it was no longer upon a few madmen that the genius of regicide shook the fury from his wings; it was upon whole crowds at once. The *Revolutionary Legions* were nothing less than so many legions of assassins. The following extract from one of their orders of the day will leave no doubt upon the matter:—

"Under our title, be it well understood, you will not form merely a regicide society, but above all an exterminating corps, by which, after the victory, there must be annihilated those underhand measures of the new exploiters who will not fail to present themselves."

Nothing could be more clear or explicit: the king was to be killed first, the royal family, and then all the new exploiters; that is to say, all the men who are opposed to the autocracy of bare arms, which would amount to massacring about nineteen-twentieths of France.

A plan of organization was drawn up, according to which the number of members of the society was to amount to twenty-five thousand; a number which could not have failed to be very alarming; but these redoubtable legions were never drawn up, except upon paper. M. Gisquet was informed of this savage project; he captured the chiefs and threw them into prison, and that put a stop to it.

And this is not the only case where organized attempts have been made at assassination; for when the strength of the revolutionary monster is exhausted, his instincts drive him to wilful murder and assassination. After June, 1848, the police had to deal with bands of rascals who sought to establish their principles at the point of the dagger; and it may be that more than one of us is now elbowed, without suspecting it, by some of these minions of the modern old man of the mountain. The plans for destruction in mass are too easily laid open ever to arrive at their execution; but from these ferocious bands there comes forth now and then some individual fanatic, who undertakes by himself the accomplishment of the work of blood. It was thus that in the month of June 1836, when the nucleus of the revolutionary legions had already become merged in the society of the *Families*, a laborer by the name of Alibaud went to post himself at a back gate of the Tuileries, where, at the distance of four paces, he discharged a fire-arm upon the king. An interposition of providence again saved the head of the State. Alibaud declared that he had acted solely by himself, and had not confided his scheme to any one, which proved to be the case. He showed but one single regret, and that was the failure of his attempt. The madman was turned over to the executioner. On leaving the Court of Peers, he met with a person who bestowed upon him the word of admiration which M. Dufraisse regretted so much had not been called forth in behalf of the sublime Morey. This person was a woman, Miss Laura Grouvelle, a demagogue in petticoats, who, in her turn, was condemned the year following for a similar attempt. She afterwards became deranged.

The idea of the creation of the *Families* is due to Messrs.

Blanqui and Barbès. This latter person was at that time a student. M. Blanqui appears never to have had any other profession than that of conspirator.

The whole race of revolutionists who had kept the country in a constant state of agitation ever since 1830, made their disappearance at this period; some had been condemned; others had fled, and a considerable number, giving up the cause of the Republic as lost, had withdrawn. It is a great mistake to imagine that all those political mushrooms which sprung up in February had always been nurtured in conspiracy; for after the affair of April many of those men who remained at large conceived either a disgust for their colleagues or despair of success, and abandoned their secret enterprises. Of this number was M. Sobrier, one of those light-headed young men whom the imprudence of parents allows to remain their own masters in Paris, where they fall a prey to exploiters of all kinds, political as well as others. M. Sobrier took leave of secret societies and never returned to them again; but not because he had got rid of his wrong notions and reformed his character. This poor young man, who has always had greater need of physicians than of judges, is afflicted with one of those perverse natures which is never found to be in a normal condition. His whole life has been only an exaggeration; he is either foaming or in a state of utter prostration; when he speaks he either drawls out his words lazily, or hurries into violent extravagances. By the year 1846 he had fallen into an acrid misanthropy which he endeavored to deaden as well as he could amidst the smoke and domino parties of an *estaminet* in the street of Notre-Dame-des-Victoires. His opinions, confected as it were in bile, exhaled a most repulsive odor; his policy being, in politics, to guillotine everybody, and in socialism to burn everything up. But this was all talk with him; for at bottom M. Sobrier has no more viciousness than a child. He is the very counterfeit of a moral man; his education has been detestable, and he fancies that the evidence of deep conviction consists in appearing to have the fits accompanied with ferocious words. In other respects, his material position contributed to render him intolerable. Embroiled with his family, he had adopted for a livelihood one of those bastard professions which are found in Paris alone; he became a placer of assurances. It is certain that his abilities were far above such a profession as this, and the necessity of exercising it contributed to thicken his humors. Finally, being able to endure it no longer, he left it and abandoned himself to Providence. The conductor of an establishment in Notre-Dame-des-Victoires street provided for his principal necessities. While there, the inheritance of one of his parents came to find him, rendering him the possessor of ten thousand francs a year; and if his party does not succeed in abolishing property he will ultimately have twice as much—a handsome fortune, which would render almost any other person happy; but as for him, his life was henceforth a nullity. Shutting himself up in a remote corner of the town, he was visited only by a few pretended friends, who, in exploiting him, increased his hypochondria. Unfortunate in his temper, unfortunate in his relations, he was seized up by the tempest of February, and, after being whirled about for awhile amidst its stormy whirlwinds, was thrown at last, mangled and half deranged, into a horrible abyss.

Messrs. Recurt, Flocon, Raspail, Trélat, etc. were others of the conspirators who returned to ordinary life, at this period. M. Recurt, a sort of refined peasant, a finesser, a politician of the school of the *National*, which consists in being always ready, not to fight, but to profit by the battle, perceived clearly that conspiracies were not to his purpose. He had already dexterously withdrawn his stakes from the game in retiring from the committee of the *Rights of Man* at the moment when the law against associations was passed; and he judged that it would be wise henceforth to wage his war against power quietly and perseveringly, but legally. By his profession of physician he could render himself popular; and he went to establish himself in the suburb of Saint Antoine, where, in return for services rendered to poor men, he required them only to share his hatred against the government of July. He was, until the revolution, the evil genius, politically speaking, of that quarter.

M. Flocon is a man who takes great pains with his personal appearance, not seeming to know that the usual evidence of able men is to appear otherwise. M. Flocon pretends to be a statesman, but has shown himself a greater bungler in this way than even the men of the *National* themselves, which is saying a great deal. M. Flocon has the certainty of being considered one of the great writers of Paris; for those who pretend to be knowing in such matters place him on a level with Messrs. Durrieu and Bareste; but that is a height which ought not to make one's head giddy. The transitory fortune of M. Flocon might appear inexplicable were it not known that the *Reform* has been, and still is considered as the machine of the Revolution, and that M. Flocon was the editor-in-chief of the *Reform*. In fact, to a small modicum of merit, which is allowed him, he adds a most complete unpopularity with his party. His various pretensions to finesse, political science, and literary art are not only displayed on every occasion, but are imposed upon you with the air of the dictator. As his gestures are of the epic style, his conversation coldly cutting, his eye somewhat inclined to the Olympian cast, and as, after having spoken, he stops awhile, as much as to say—reply to that now, if you can—he is taken at once as a very *strong* man, and the public gave him the reputation of it after July. He showed himself not altogether unworthy of it at first; he was at the head of the crowd which undertook to throw the deputies out of the windows on the 4th of August; he afterwards took an active part in the proceedings of the *Friends of the People;* and he is pleased to claim the honor of having been one of the famous defenders of the barricade of Saint Méry, on the 6th of June. It is possible that he was; but we have already said that the patriots who pretended to have taken a part in that warm affair are reckoned by thousands, while the actual number of men which M. Jeanne had with him did not exceed a hundred. On the fall of the *Friends of the People*, M. Flocon followed his companions into the *Rights of Man;*

but as his character and pretensions were by this time well known, very little attention was paid to a man so exceedingly disagreeable. Hence, the part which he played in the new association was comparatively an obscure one, and had but little influence in the events of April. When the *Families* succeeded to the *Rights of Man*, very good care was taken on the part of the members not to make him any advances. Chilled by this disdainful neglect, he abandoned to their wretched fate the men who were so blind as not to discover and make use of his extraordinary capacities. It was not till 1843 that he returned for awhile to the secret societies; and in this long interval of nine years he was forced to listen to, and reproduce as a stenographer, the speeches of such miserable statesmen as Messrs. Guizot and Thiers—the sad consequences of our social organization! When M. Flocon flattered himself in the Constituent Assembly that he had conspired all his life, his fellow members were right in telling him that that was but a miserable sort of glory; and we, on our part, can tell him that even that glory he did not merit; for he has not conspired all his life by a very great deal—he was boasting.

Of M. Trélat we have already said a few words; he was very suitable for that epoch when the republic was maintained chiefly by fine speeches. Of a weak and feeble nature, and led into revolutionary practices rather from instinct than by courage, the societies which received a military organization and aimed at carrying out their designs by violence, offered no place for him.

M. Raspail could no longer see among the men who had escaped the disasters of April any one of sufficient importance to rub against him; and besides, it was his firm conviction that where men of his calibre had failed, it was useless to try any farther. He declared that, in future, every member of a secret society ought to be considered as little better than a disturber of the peace. He shared, with M. Flocon, the reputation of being dogmatical; and while draping himself in his own importance, the world passed on.

Many of the secondary order of members of the *Rights of*

Man also abandoned their secret practices; such as Messrs. Cahaigne, Bonnais, Avril, etc. The car of the Republic having become stalled in a deep mud, these men perceived their inability to set it agoing again; and the more so as they had an innate consciousness of never having been anything else than a fifth wheel to it.

The two most important revolutionary characters of the period on which we are about to enter were Messrs. Blanqui and Barbès—the first, an untamed wolf, cautious, pursuing his prey in the dark; the other, a sombre lion, bold and audacious, delighting in shaking his mane to the run: dangerous, both, to the highest degree; Barbès by his indomitable energy, and Blanqui from his Machiavelic spirit, and both by their revolutionary frenzy. They were, in fact, the two most perfect types of the conspirator which were presented during the last form of government. M. G. Cavaignac was much more popular than they were, but he never had such a decisive influence over the masses as they possessed—for the reason that he was prevented by his character from making use of certain means which those, his successors, under the sublime jesuitical principle proclaimed by M. Barbès, of *The sovereignty of the end*, had recourse to without scruple. These two men had wholly confounded their personal identity with the end which they performed; and their union formed a type of terror. M. Blanqui was not brave among flying bullets; M. Barbès was possessed of only an ordinary degree of intelligence; but the two characters united, made up a being capable of conceiving and executing the most terrible designs.

The personal appearance of these men is a description of their characters. M. Blanqui is a small thin figure, of a ruddy complexion, with restless, suspicious eyes, over which impends a heavy pair of brows, and with closed lips, which are always playing under some bitter smile. One perceives at a glance that this weak but calmly nervous frame is animated at least as much by hatred as by ambition. M. Barbès, on the contrary, has a tall, upright figure, with an eye frankly open, and an austerity of repose that comes from conviction.

Stronger at heart than his companion, he is obliged to yield to him the superiority of head. Impelled by his nature to undertake great things, he is hurried away, in spite of himself, into the most detestable excesses. He is a Doctor Faust, ambitious to seize upon the secret of God, and listening, for this purpose, only to the Devil.

The head of another conspirator comes up through a trap-door of the political stage at this moment; it is that of M. Martin Bernard. It takes its place intermediately between those of MM. Blanqui and Barbès. It is a less marked head than theirs, but seems expressly designed for constituting, together with the two others, a harmonious triumvirate, consisting of a man of conception, a man of execution, and a man of organization. This last character was to be personated by M. Martin Bernard; and he accomplished in it prodigies of activity, zeal, and prudence. Being a simple printer by trade, he might be seen, when his day's work was done, or in the intervals of his meals, scudding indefatigably through the streets, and never losing a moment from the precious work of propagandism. In the new enterprise on foot he represented the truly popular element, which, thus far, had hardly made its appearance in the associations. But a gradual change in this respect is now to take place in the *Families*, to be finally consummated in the *Seasons*. M. Blanqui swayed the most violent elements of the *Rights of Man;* M. Barbès, the students—two nuclei composed of either the unclassified or most turbulent bourgeoisie. M. Martin Bernard drew his followers from the heart of the working population, of which he was a member. This trinity, the power of which became formidable from the various qualities of its members, might, at certain moments of oscillation in the government, have succeeded in overthrowing it; but as it was, it arrived upon the ground too late; its efforts were hardly felt by the government of July.

CHAPTER XXI.

Organization of the *Society of the Families*—The form of reception—Despotism of the chiefs—Secret details.

THE *Society of the Families* was organized at the close of the year 1834. Around Messrs. Blanqui and Barbès, its founders, there grouped themselves, first, M. Martin Bernard, who soon took a part in the direction, and then, as principal lieutenants, Messrs. Hubin de Guer, Dubosc, Beaufour, Raisant, Nettré, Troncin, Lebeuf, Dussoubs, Lisbonne, Guignot, Lamieussens, Seigneurgens, Schirmann, and Spirat, almost all of the middle class of society—students, clerks, men living upon their rents, etc.—having already been conspirators among the ranks of the *Rights of Man*.

The act of reception which had been accompanied with no form in the preceding societies, consisting merely of a promise of adhesion to the statutes, became a matter of importance in the *Families*, and was surrounded with mysterious solemnity.

The candidate for admission was subjected to a preliminary examination upon his course of life and his opinions, and if the result proved favorable to him, he was notified to hold himself in readiness for the initiation. The member of the society by whom he was to be introduced, went for him, took him into an unknown place and bandaged his eyes. There, without knowing whom he had to deal with, or what was going on, he remained in waiting. A board of examiners, consisting of a president, an assessor, and the introducer, then examined him. The president taking the word, pronounced the following formula :—

"In the name of the executive committee, the proceedings are now open. Citizen assessor, why are we assembled?

To labor for the deliverance of the people and the human race. What are the virtues of a true republican? Sobriety, courage, force, and devotion. What penalty do traitors deserve? Death. And who should inflict it? Every member of the society who receives orders to do so from his chiefs."

This was the prologue of the piece; a scene designed for making an impression upon the imagination of the candidate. The part to be played by the candidate was to commence only after this formula had been gone through with.

The president addressed him in these terms:—

"Citizen, what is thy name? thy surname? thy profession, and the place of thy birth? But before proceeding farther, take this oath: I swear to observe the strictest silence upon what is to take place in these precincts. Thou must know that before admitting thee into our ranks, we have taken note of thy conduct, and of thy morality; the reports addressed to the committee are favorable to thee. We now address thee the necessary questions:—

"Is it thy labor or thy family that supports thee?

"Hast thou ever been a member of any political society?

"What thinkest thou of the government?

"In what interest is it occupied?

"Who are, at the present day, aristocrats?

"What is the right in virtue of which the government rules?

"What is the predominant vice of society?

"What takes the place of honor, probity and virtue?

"Who is the man that is esteemed in the world?

"Who is despised, persecuted, and outlawed?

"What thinkest thou of city tolls, and taxes upon salt and drinks?

"Who are the people?

"How are they treated by the laws?

"What is the lot of poor people under the government of the rich?

"What ought to be the basis of a regular system of society?

"What ought to be the rights of the citizen in a well-regulated country?

"What are his duties?

"Must a political revolution be made, or a social one?"

One may guess the answers of the candidate to these questions: the government was traitorous to the people and the country; it labored for the interest of a small number of privileged persons; the aristocrats were men of money, bankers, exchange brokers, monopolists, great proprietors, and in fine all those who are termed in modern parlance the exploiters of man by man. The right of the government consisted only in force; the predominant vice of society was egotism; what held the place of honor, probity, and virtue, was money; esteem was granted only to the rich and powerful; contempt and persecution were the lot of the poor and the weak. City tolls and taxes upon salt and drink were to be looked upon only as an odious means of increasing the riches of the rich at the expense of the poor. The people were the aggregate of the working classes, and their condition was slavery; the lot of the poor man was that of the serf and the negro. The basis of a regular system of society was equality. The rights of the citizen were summed up as follows: assurance of existence, gratuitous instruction, and participation in the government; and the duties of the patriot were devotion to society, and fraternity towards fellow-citizens. As to the kind of revolution which was to be made, that must be a social one.

The president continued in these terms:—

"Has the citizen who made overtures to thee, spoken to thee of our object? Thou oughtest to have some idea of it from the character of my questions; but I am going to explain it to thee still more clearly. The oppressors of our country endeavor to keep the people in ignorance and isolation; our object is to disseminate instruction and form a fasces of the forces of the people. Our tyrants have proscribed associations and the press, and our duty is to associate ourselves with renewed perseverance, and to supply the place of the press by a propagandism of *viva voce;* for thou knowest well that the arms which our oppressors have forbidden us to use are those which they fear the most. Every member is bound to spread republican doctrines and to prosecute an active and indefatigable propagandism.

"Ultimately, when the horn shall sound, we must take arms for overthrowing a government which is traitorous to the country. . . . Wilt thou be with us on that day? Reflect well. It is a perilous enterprise; our enemies are powerful; they have an army, and treasury, and the support of foreign kings; they reign by terror. But we, on the contrary, poor working folk, have nothing but our courage and our good right. Hast thou the resolution to brave these dangers?

"When the signal for the fight shall be given, wilt thou be ready to die, arms in hand, for the cause of humanity?"

The candidate having replied in the affirmative to this last question, the president requested him to arise, and then continued as follows:—

"Citizen, here is the oath which thou must take: I swear never to disclose to any person, not even to my nearest relations, anything that is said or done among us. I swear to be obedient to the laws of the association; to pursue with my hatred or my vengeance the traitors who may insinuate themselves among us; to love and serve my brothers, and sacrifice my liberty and my life."

The neophyte having pronounced the oath, was proclaimed a member of the association. The president then requested him to be seated, and proceeded thus:—

"Hast thou arms and ammunition? Every one on becoming one of our number must have a quantity of powder, a quarter of a pound, at least; and he must procure two pounds more for his own use. There is nothing done in writing in the association; thou wilt be known only by the new name which thou art to adopt. In case of being arrested thou must never make any answers to the examining judge. The committee is unknown; but the moment that the fight is given, it is obliged to make its appearance. It is expressly forbidden to take to the streets, unless the committee puts itself at the head of the association. During the fight, the members must obey their chiefs with all the rigor of military discipline.

"If thou art acquainted with citizens who are sufficiently discreet to be admitted among us, thou must present them; every citizen of discretion and good will, deserves to enter our ranks, whatever may be his degree of instruction; the society will complete his education."

At these words the bandage was removed from the eyes of the candidate, and nothing remained to complete the ceremony except his announcement of the new name which he wished to bear.

The reader will have observed in this formula that the overthrow of society is pointed out as the end to be attained by a revolution. This was a means for captivating the masses; but with the exception of equality of condition and a few vague principles, M. Blanqui took good care not to enter into the details of a new social system, well knowing that by so doing he would open a field for discussion to the conspirators, which would have destroyed the conspiracy by destroying discipline. In this respect he showed a superiority of revolutionary tact, and at the same time the leading instinct of the heroes of the streets, *i. e.* dictatorship. How is it to be expected that these chiefs, knowing the ignorance and inordinate passions of their bands, should attempt to control them except by a rod of iron? Did not the committee of public safety establish its power upon a most frightful despotism? It is thought that clubs and popular manifestations are a fixed principle among the conductors of revolutions; but not at all, they are only the temporary means made use of by these conductors, who, as soon as the end is attained, hasten to destroy them lest they should be directed against themselves. Those who have studied the revolutionary *art* are not ignorant that its *beau ideal* consists in inspiring an exclusive devotion to a few vague dogmas and an absolute submission to command. Many persons, on seeing the terrible efforts made by M. Blanqui after February, to arouse the secret societies, naturally inquired where this lava of demagogism would have stopped in case the socialist republic had triumphed;—it would have stopped at the same orders by which it had been brought to a state of ebullition. Had M. Blanqui become dictator by the grace of the clubs, he would then have shut up the clubs, and much sooner even than the dictator of the *National.* Our Catilines know their men; and no old Marquis, mummified in his castle, ever dared to dream of a right-divine so absolute as that which these men claim in the name of the sovereignty of the people.

This point being established, then, that the members of the society of the *Families* were to labor for an equality of condition by a remodelling of society, they were bound to abstain from all controversy and discussion upon the relative merit of systems, and confined thmselves to the implicit obedience of the soldier.

The revolution accomplished and the ground once cleared, they were told, the doctors of the party would set to work to give form to the new science, and nothing would be more easily done. But we have seen that it was not quite so easily done as they pretended—the confusion of Babel might be considered luminous in comparison with that of the constructors of socialism.

The neophyte having been admitted, was duly impressed with regard to his duties by his sponsor, who generally became his immediate chief. The first of these duties was to furnish powder and munitions; the second, to be in readiness to obey the orders which should be given him; the third, to observe absolute discreetness, and the fourth, to labor at propagandism. He was also informed that he would be called on now and then to take a part in the meetings of the particular *Family* of which he was a member. These meetings were the only bonds by which the society was held together; the reviews, orders of the day, and frequent assemblies being suppressed.

In these meetings of the *Families* the chief called for an account of the proceedings of his men, as well concerning their supplies of munitions as their efforts at propagandism; received information of requests for admittance, and fixed the day for receptions. When the group became too numerous, one of its members was designated for forming a new one.

The number of men in each *Family* was not to exceed a dozen. It was expressly prohibited to assemble in public places, coffee-houses, wine-shops, etc. Some member of the *Family* was to lend his house for the meetings. The affairs of the association having been examined into, the chief made a short address and the meeting was dismissed.

A certain number of *Families* received directions from a chief called the chief of section; the chiefs of section were under the orders of commandants of quarters, and these latter were under revolutionary agents who were to communicate with the committee. But this committee was nothing less than the revolutionary agents themselves; that is to say Messrs. Blanqui, Barbès, and Martin Bernard. The committee was to remain wholly unknown until the day of battle, when it was to make its appearance and lead the members to the onset.

This association was very simple; but from its very simplicity, its discipline and measures of prudence, it seemed likely to become a force of very serious importance. The care which M. Blanqui had taken to isolate, as it were, his soldiers, excluding them from a knowledge of important acts, secured him against treachery. A single member knew only the names of those who belonged to his *Family;* and hence, the secret which he might tell was limited to a matter of trifling consequence. As to the commandants of quarters, they were chosen from among old patriots whose fidelity, it was thought, could be depended on; but alas! among the most ancient democrats, even such as have *rotted* in prison, there is often found a sly dog who puts on the skin of the wolf for the purpose of better strangling the wolf. In spite of the thousand precautions on the part of M. Blanqui, his mysterious proceedings were scented out and delivered over to the police.

CHAPTER XXII.

A clandestine manufactory—The powder affair—Complot of the Arc de Triomphe—Project against the Tuileries—M. Gisquet retires—The affair of Strasbourg.

The *Families* having found numerous and ready prepared elements in the debris of the *Rights of Man*, soon attained to a considerable number. In the early part of 1836 the committee estimated their strength at a thousand men. And until the days of February we shall see that the total of the secret societies seldom varied much from this number. Thanks to the salutary effects of the new laws, the four thousand sectionaries of the *Rights of Man* are not to be met with again.

The committee soon perceived that under the severe organization of the society an attack could not be long deferred without disgusting their men. Already, in the month of August, 1836, symptoms of impatience had been discovered; the occasion was the funeral procession of one who died from the effects of an amputation in June; but the police were on the look-out, and they soon restored order to the feeble attempts which were made, by arresting one of the leaders, M. Leprestre Dubocage, at whose house a dozen of the members were found together with a large quantity of munitions. The chiefs then endeavored to hasten the preparations. They had promised arms and ammunition for the day of combat, and it was to this matter that their attention was now turned. The difficulty and danger of establishing depots of arms was perceived, and hence the places where they might be found were merely pointed out; as to ammunition, it was thought that a mass ought to be collected which should prove sufficient for every emergency. Some of the members frequented the barriers, and by means of libations or money, succeeded in getting the soldiers to give them their cartridges. They thus led these soldiers to an abuse of confidence and an infraction of military discipline; but what are such considerations as these in comparison with the sublime principle of M. Barbès, the sovereignty of the end? These means, however, did not produce the desired result; a few packets of ammunition taken from a soldier here and there were not enough for supplying the arsenal of an insurrection; and hence it was decided to establish a manufactory of powder. Messrs. Blanqui, Martin Bernard and Beaufour, the latter a broken-down merchant, took charge of the operation. Hiring an isolated house, No. 113 Oursine Street, they set up a dryer there, procured the necessary utensils and materials, and set to work. M. Beaufour conducted the labors, and had under his orders three or four trusty members of the society. The process of manufacture was furnished by M. Blanqui, who daily stole into the laboratory in order to inspect the works. Between eleven and twelve o'clock at night, M. Martin Bernard, after having made a turn in the suburbs, might be seen to arrive at the mysterious house, and, instead of knocking, make known his presence by a handful of sand thrown against the window-panes. Through a door swung half a-jar he would then make his disappearance in a dark corridor. After a while a window would be thrown open, at which a man would be seen with a light carefully examining the premises. This done, and the ground seeming to be clear, M. Martin Bernard would make his appearance again, bearing a supply of powder, with which he would nimbly tread the streets, traverse the Latin quarter, and stop in Dauphine Street at a house numbered 22 and 24. It was there that the general depot had been established, and it was there that balls and cartridges were made and sent to the chiefs of quarter for supplying their men.

These nocturnal visits to the house of Oursine Street; the solitary noises heard within; the suspicious looking persons who were seen in the vicinity, and the hints given by treachcrous brothers, all this put M. Gisquet upon the trace of the plot and the plotters. Agents of the police were posted around the house No. 113, and when it was certain that the conspirators were within, a detachment closed in upon the place, and an officer of the police, accompanied with a strong escort, made his entrance. M. Beaufour was found at work in the midst of his worthy apprentices, who proved to be three students, Messrs. Robier, Canard and Daviot, and a workingman who, as it appeared, had made the framework of the machine of Fieschi. They were secured; and a visit was then made to the rooms, which resulted in the discovery of all the things appertaining to the manufactory, consisting of powder already made, the apparatus and implements for making it, and a considerable quantity of raw material.

The same operation was practised at the depot of Dauphine Street. Some young men were found, in blouses, their hands all blackened, some around a furnace casting balls, and others making cartridges upon a table. M. Cabet, nephew of the ex-deputy, and Messrs. Guillemain, Grooters and Genin were taken into custody, together with 15,000 balls and an enormous quantity of powder—it is affirmed that there was enough for 200,000 cartridges.

During this foray against the laboratories of ammunition, another expedition was on foot for capturing the principal chiefs, of whom the police had an exact list. As M. Barbès was found at his own house in company with M. Martin Bernard, two of the birds were thus killed with one stone. M. Blanqui, according to the reports which had been received at the police, usually carried with him a list of the members of the society, and he was asked for his portfolio; or rather, in anticipation of a refusal, it was snatched from him and given to a commissary; but it had hardly come into the commissary's hands, when the conspirator, by a sudden spring, snatched it back and succeeded, in spite of the efforts to the contrary, in extracting some of the papers, which he swallowed. But, unfortunately, the famous list remained in the portfolio, and that was recovered. M. Barbès had in his lodgings cartridges and bullet-moulds, and some papers which were in every way in keeping with these articles. Among others was the proclamation which had been prepared in view of the attempt of Fieschi, and which had doubtlessly been preserved for some other similar occasion. It was in this proclamation that occurred the passage which we have already given, but which, nevertheless, will bear repetition: "Now, people, no longer any pity; lay bare your arms, and thrust them up to the shoulders into the entrails of your executioners."

Together with these principal chiefs were arrested Messrs. Martin Bernard, Nettré, Dubosc, Guignot, Lamieussens, Dussoubs, Raisan, Lebeuf, Troncin, Hubin de Guer, Robert, Spirat, Lisbonne, Hertfort, Payet, Legeret, Grivel, Venant, Dupuis, Villedieu, the brothers Seigneurgens, Schirman, Léon, Quétin, Houtan, Lacombe, Molly, senior, Voiturier, Geoffroy, Rousset, Palanchon, Deligny, Halot, Gay, Gallien; all chiefs of *section*, or *quarter*, or *family*. At the houses of the most of them were found arms and ammunition.

These arrests took place in the month of March, 1836; and the accused, amounting to forty-three, were brought to trial in the August following. Messrs. Blanqui, Beaufour, Lisbonne, Robert, Rabier and Genin were sent to prison for two years; Barbès, Hertfort, and Lamieussens for one year; Palanchon, Canard, Villedieu, Grivel, Gay, and Venant for ten months; Dupuis for eight months.

During the period of such trials as these, a vapor of revolution, as it were, of the intensest kind, seems to fill the air; the companions of the accused become extravagantly excited, and, before disbanding or entering into some new association, they endeavor to signalize their end by some brilliant achievement. The attempt of Fieschi was the death-rattle of the *Rights of Man;* and the *Families,* too, dreamed of sinking, since sink they must, amidst the wreck of a public calamity.

Several weeks before the trials took place, a grand ceremony had been announced for the inauguration of the Arc de Triomphe de l'Etoile; and the king had chosen this occasion for another review of the National Guards. In spite of the repeated attempts which had been made upon his life, his nature revolted against a seclusion which was recommended by his advisers. To live behind walls or a hedge of bayonets, like another Louis XI., was contrary to every habit of his life. The series of attempts at assassination made upon this prince, whose tyranny existed neither in shadow nor in substance, who abstained from shedding the blood of those enemies who opposed him openly to his face, and who abandoned his throne rather than fire a single shot upon the National Guard, that is to say, upon the bourgeoisie by whom he had been elected, must be regarded by future history as one of the peculiar monstrosities of this age.

Whether imprudent or not, the king determined to hold the review; and those chiefs of the *Families* who were still at large, resolved, on their part, to take advantage of the occasion for a new attempt to assassinate him. With this view they designed to form several platoons of National Guards from among the members of the association, who should present themselves at the review with their arms loaded, and, on filing by, fire upon the king. The monarch was informed of this from the police; but he still persisted in his design, prescribing, however, certain measures for warding off the danger. It was decided that the Arc de Triomphe should be surrounded by a cordon of tribunes forming an exterior wall of sufficient height and solidity to prevent an attack; the king was to take his place in the centre of this inclosure, and the National Guard were to file past upon the open spaces on both sides of the Arc. Each company, moreover, before passing the prince, was to have its arms carefully inspected. These precautions seemed sufficient; and the greater confidence was reposed in them, inasmuch as the chiefs of the complot, and all the members of the *Families* known for their extravagance, had been arrested. But before the ceremony took place, new perils were discovered; it was learned that the conspirators were to enter the tribunes by means of counterfeit cards, and, at a given signal, throw themselves upon the king armed with pistols and daggers. The character of this design is such that the republicans have some chance to be believed when they treat it as a calumny; but we can tell them that as extravagantly audacious as it may appear, it was, nevertheless, rigorously true. The ministers succeeded in prevailing upon the king to give up the review.

We now enter upon a period marked by a series of secret machinations, the greater part of which have come only to the knowledge of the police. Although justice has not been able to fix the true character of these machinations, and although they are not of public notoriety, yet we have no hesitation in affirming that they have nevertheless taken place.

If the pigeon-holes of the street of Jerusalem were open to the examination of those ingenuous men who take as current money the modesty, true or pretended, of the enterprising men of anarchy, they would see masses of complots and schemes of blood and devastation, which they had never heard of before, but which are supported upon such concurrent and detailed proofs that there cannot be the least doubt of their occurrence.

Thus, not long before the last plot mentioned, another plan for killing the king had been conceived, discussed and decided upon. It was to be effected by an attack upon the Tuileries made by the *Families* in concert with a number of sergeants of the army. The sergeants were to seize upon their officers, carry off the troops, and move against the palace in several columns. The *Families* were to come up to their assistance, and the palace being taken by surprise and pressed upon from all quarters, was to succumb and give up its inmates to the fury of the assailants. The blow was to be struck at four o'clock in the morning. The workingmen who go to their labor at that hour would be hurried into the conspiracy; the government would not have time to assemble its forces, and success would be certain—everything gave flattering promises of it—everything except the good sense of the public and that hundred eyed man of Jerusalem Street, who smiled in pity over such dreams as these, which were hardly less ridiculous than they were odious.

The sergeants were removed from Paris and sent to conspire in Africa; and in consequence, the bitter groans of the republican press were painfully distressing: the brethren of the army were treated like Cossacks; their generous instincts were tyrannized over; they were sent away to be killed by the barbarians—poor men! It is a sad thing, without doubt, that these brave men of the sword could not be permitted to massacre the royal family and upset the state, although there are countries where such attempts would have cost them their lives. But, everything considered, the *brave* sergeants had not a great deal to complain of.

The ministry retired from office at this period, and M. Gisquet, who had shared their labors, thought it his duty to share in their retreat. And this was an occasion, indeed, which the republicans might celebrate by an illumination; for they were freed of their rudest adversary. M. Carlier, his lieutenant, had already left the prefecture, much to the satisfaction of the patriots; and the police was thus deprived of two men who had delved into the machinations of demagogism with unabated activity and perseverance. The reader has seen what a frightful series of mobs, insurrections and complots were continued against the government from 1831 to 1836; and also with what persistence, secret machinations have been pursued, and by what fulminating energy seditions have been crushed. This result was due to two forces, which became one in a simultaneity of resolution: the force of direction represented by Messrs. Casimir Perrier, Guizot, and Thiers, and the force of supervision incarnate in the person of M. Gisquet.

Like the majority of magistrates who have the courage to pursue an undeviating course of duty, M. Gisquet had none of that ferocity which was attributed to him. He is a man of ardent and susceptible temperament, but without animosity; and all the patriots who have passed through his hands are well aware of this fact. He was the very first to ask pardon for the men in whom he discovered that the head was more at fault than the heart, and in rendering them this service he never troubled himself to know whether they had ever imprudently attacked him or not. In the early days of the revolution, the frankness of his advice saved many a young man from ruin who has since become an honorable citizen, but who otherwise might at this moment be a minion of socialist democracy. They who know what it is to suppress a revolution, and whose ideas have never become denaturalized by unworthy passions, will ever hold in esteem not only the services, but also the person of the ex-prefect of the police. The great crimes with which he has been reproached, when fully investigated, are reduced to the impulse of an inconsiderate generosity; and it can be boldly affirmed that the manner in which he was treated on his leaving office, was marked both by misunderstanding and ingratitude.

But enough of this. M. Gisquet has given one of those proofs of his convictions which no one has the right to dispute, and which is the highest eulogy that the statesman can merit—he still continued to respect the government and serve it with fidelity when that government was endeavoring to dishonor him.

At the time when the *Families*, having been dispersed by the powder affair, were reforming themselves under another name, the conspiracy of Strasbourg broke out. This affair had been planned in Switzerland by the Prince Louis Napoleon, Messrs. de Querelles, Gricourt, Madam Gordon and others. Its ramifications extended to Paris, among the old officers of the empire and a certain class of republicans, who wished to make the prince their instrument; but the principal means of action lay at Strasbourg, among three regiments of artillery and a battalion of pontoniers who formed a part of the garrison of the place. M. Vaudrey, the colonel of one of these regiments, had been gained over, and was to deliver up the keys of the arsenal, of which he held possession. The pontoniers lent an implicit obedience to M. Laity, their lieutenant; and it was thought that the neutrality, at least, of the major-general commanding, M. Voirol, might be reckoned upon.

The movement broke out on the 30th of October, 1836. The regiments which had promised their concurrence, remained true to their word; the magic name of Napoleon thrown among their ranks educed an impulse of enthusiasm. General Voirol, whose views had been mistaken, was arrested, as were also the prefect and other functionaries. There was nothing wanting to take possession of the city and move upon Paris according to the plan, except the gaining over of a regiment of infantry, which also formed a part of the garrison. The infantry, on seeing the artillery salute the prince with loud acclamations, were ready to do the same thing; but a rumor was spread that it was all a joke, and that the pretended relation of the emperor was merely a son of Colonel Vaudrey. This was the beginning of a rout. An officer sprang forth to seize upon the prince. The prince, by a discharge of his pistol, might still have retrieved his fortune; but though other conspirators might not have hesitated, he had the prudence to abstain, and all was lost.

The king, Louis Philippe, had him embarked for America; his companions were acquitted by the jury of Alsace.

The prince, since that period, and while in prison for a second attempt of this kind, has made a noble and touching confession, which absolves him from the rashness of youth. It is his fortune, moreover, to have been the instrument for the re-establishment of order on the 10th of December. The duty of every good citizen is to encourage and follow him in his new career, without a useless recurrence to the things of the past.

CHAPTER XXIII.

Organization of the *Seasons*—A new personality of conspirators—Reviews—Prudential measures—M. Martin Bernard—Regicides—An amnesty—Its effect—Recrudescence of propagandism—A new formula of reception—Hatred against the bourgeoisie.

THE Bonapartist conspiracy, although concurring in some respects with the views of democratic adventurers, was wholly an affair of dynasty, having nothing to do with the republican party, and least of all with secret associations, whose designs are not only a change of persons but an overthrow of society. These associations consisted at that time of the fragments of the *Families*; but the groups were soon drawn together again and reconstituted under the name of the *Seasons*.

The organization remained pretty nearly the same; six members under the orders of a seventh called *Sunday*, formed a *Week*; four weeks commanded by a *July* constituted a *Month*; three *Months* obeyed a chief of *Season* called *Spring*—four *Seasons* to one *Revolutionary Agent*; it was the calendar applied to a conspiracy. The strength of a battalion consisted of 336 men. The *Revolutionary Agents*, who were considered as the immediate lieutenants of the committee, were, as they had been in the *Families*, the committee itself. The same mystery enveloped the acts of the association; but in other respects there were many important changes. The system of isolation which had been practised in the *Families* was to give way to meetings of some kind or another, either of the *Weeks*, *Months*, or *Seasons*. The meetings were visited by the chiefs of various grades, who gave their orders and kept excitement alive by energetic addresses. A course like this could not be pursued in public places, and as the lodgings of the patriots were not sufficiently capacious, recourse was had to the halls of wine merchants. It was at this period that conspiracy installed itself in drinking shops; and there it remained until the revolution.

The want of a convenient place for meeting was not the only cause of this modification; for at this time the secret societies were made up of an almost entirely new set of characters; recruiting went on exclusively among the very lowest classes of society, where, it is well known, a conspiracy is not retarded by being prosecuted with glass in hand.

It was a remarkable period in the career of secret societies when they were entirely abandoned by the bourgeoisie; it was the confession of a radical impotence on the part of those ambitious men by whom the country had been torn and harassed during a space of six years. And as to the societies themselves, it was a moment of their existence really in accord with their name; they indeed became secret, without noise, external evidences or agitation; but seeming, therefore, from their concentration and mystery, to become more seriously threatening than ever.

M. Martin Bernard, having been acquitted of the powder affair, immediately renewed his illegal proceedings, and became the director of the *Seasons*. Finding that the old knot of conspirators were tired and worn out by their fruitless efforts, he perceived that there lay among the lower classes excellent resources of credulity and discipline, which had not yet been exploited. The decree, therefore, went forth, and propagandism was thereafter addressed to the suburbs. The tactics of M. Blanqui, consisting in alluring simple minded men by vague principles, and forbidding all discussion, was to be practised with great assiduity. The ardent and disorderly men of the masses who are swayed by self-love and the hopes of chimerical advantages, and who moreover had nothing to lose by an upheaval of society, promised to be much more submissive instruments than brawling students, ambitious clerks, avaricious advocates, and all that crew of busy bourgeois with whom nothing successful had thus far been accomplished.

Besides the partial meetings of the *Seasons*, there were more general assemblages, called reviews, which were held by the revolutionary agents. The manner of proceeding at one of these reviews was as follows: some long street with numerous lateral ones, such, for instance, as Sainte Honoré, was chosen, and the men were scattered along the lateral streets, while the chiefs alone took their stand at the corners upon the principal street, awaiting the arrival of the dignitary, by whom they were to be reviewed. This dignitary then began his inspection; visiting the chiefs and receiving from them a report of the effective strength of their commands, and the number who were absent. As the formula of reception enjoined upon every member to be always in a state of readiness, informing him that he might be called to the combat without previous notice, the *Seasons* might believe, at every review, that they were possibly called together for the purpose of taking arms; and hence, by the promptness with which they responded to the call, the chiefs might judge of the number of men which they could bring into line.

The question of arms and ammunition, when maturely examined, received a different solution from that which had been arrived at by the *Families*. It was considered prudent not to amass provisions of war until a short time before the fight, and to distribute them only upon the field of battle. By this means the society would elude the pursuits of the police, and prevent that imprudence or treachery, in consequence of which the *Families* had become broken up and disorganized.

Every chief and member, moreover, was rigorously prohibited from writing or preserving a single line with regard to the association; and it was declared that the infringers of this regulation should be considered, and dealt with as traitors.

These combinations, which show a skill derived from a long course of experience, were the work of the old chiefs of the *Families*, who were the reorganizers of the new society. M. Martin Bernard found means, either personally, or through the instrumentality of trusty agents, to communicate frequently with M. Blanqui; concerting with him upon the measures to be taken, and rendering him accounts of what progress had already been made. Their united efforts gave motion to a machine whose dark and invisible operations were to end in a bloody and unexpected explosion.

Owing to a sense of lassitude among the revolutionists, and the character of the new recruits, the *Seasons*, at first, made rather a slow progress. The workingmen felt but little inclined, after their day's toil, to resort to political exercises, the dangers of which were evident, and the advantages rather doubtful. After many months of active propagandism, M. Martin Bernard and his lieutenants had succeeded in drawing together only four hundred individuals—young, heedless men for the most part, who were ambitious of playing a part in a conspiracy.

The most rigid secrecy was observed. There was nothing which could lead the public to suspect the new mine which was being dug under Paris. The very existence of the society was not known, even by a certain class of the republicans themselves. And even if they had known it, the majority of the party would have censured the new attempt. Secret societies had become discredited. The army of the *Rights of Man*, perceiving the folly of armed attacks, had retired in mass, leaving their cause to the favor of a democratic Providence.

The abandonment of the Republic on the part of the intelligent men of the party, was calculated to drive the more violent characters to a state of desperation. To become confounded broadcast among the ranks of the *Seasons*, under chiefs of no distinction, was a part altogether too inconsiderable for certain members of the party; and hence, some of the more reckless ones were not long in coming to ruminate upon new plans of regicide. A mechanician by the name of Champion was seized at the moment in which he was about to execute one of these attempts. Profiting by the negligence of his keepers, he strangled himself in prison, and it is not known whether he had any accomplices or not.

Some time afterwards another of these hateful attempts upon the life of the king, made by Meunier, also miscarried. The king condescended to pardon this wretch, who went to die a miserable death in America. Meunier had belonged to the *Families;* his name was found upon the lists of M. Blanqui.

There were other symptoms at this period which went to prove that the impotence of the party was disclosing itself by an access of rage. At one time placards would be exhibited containing cynical calumnies against the royal family, or bloody threats against the members of the government; and at another, schemes were on foot for the destruction in mass of persons and property; in all of which could be seen the dreams of furious men who were held in check by the police, and who were arrested the moment that a tangible fact gave room for an action at law.

The men who were versed in revolutionary matters perceived clearly that such convulsions as these were but the death-rattle of the republic militant. Indeed, after the formidable efforts which the government had defeated, the mere complots of isolated demagogues and the mysterious manœuvres of the battalion of the *Seasons*, might be considered as vain and powerless.

At the moment, however, when anarchical proceedings seemed to be at an end, a political act occurred which inspired them with a new life; and this act was not, as might be supposed, one of rigor on the part of power; it was simply a measure of clemency.

The democrats have always been warmly in favor of amnesties; for, what it called an amnesty among us, consists in duping the government. To give pardon to repentant men who show themselves worthy of it, is to do well; but to set at large a crew of madmen who will abuse their liberty as soon as they get it, is perfect folly. If we remember rightly, there has been shown no little excitement against certain governments because of their requiring that a request should be made in favor of persons whom they were expected to pardon; but for our part, we do not consider even a request as sufficient. No one should trust a man who when imprisoned for an attack against the government, would not bind himself in writing to refrain from such attacks in future. Why should we release one whom we have in our power, if he is always to be our enemy? Are we obliged to have less regard for our own safety than for that of others? Humanity, clemency, and many other fine things have nothing to do in a case of this kind. True humanity consists in the preservation of the greatest number, and true clemency in pardoning him who repents.

The amnesty took place on the 8th of May, on the accession of the Molé ministry. The doors of the prison were thrown open to several classes of prisoners, and among others to Messrs. Barbès and Blanqui of the powder affair. The next day Messrs. Barbès and Blanqui went to find M. Martin Bernard, their ancient accomplice, and resumed in the *Seasons* the same rank which they had held in the *Families*. Is there any man in his senses who could approve of a generosity so strange as this, which resulted merely in changing so many prisoners into conspirators? The republicans could not certainly have expected it, for they have never concealed their hostility. The fault lay in an error of the government; in order to please the journalists, or those who are called philanthropists, it set at large individuals who immediately became obstinate aggressors.

The three chiefs being united, and the body of officers very materially reinforced in consequence of the royal clemency, the association received an impulsion of sudden development. Propagandism, under practised agents and a multifarious direction, penetrated the obscurest retreats. The workshop, especially, was beset with emissaries; for the principle of M. Martin Bernard was recognized as excellent—it was in the laboring classes, credulous and easily impressionable, that the insurrectionary army would find its best soldiers. In order to reduce these soldiers to the necessary severity of discipline, it was decided to give more form to the doctrines of the society, and to the ceremony of reception. The mind of the member must be struck by a forcible impression; a sentiment of revolutionary duty must become fanaticism, and political hostility a frenzy.

The formula of the *Families* which we have given, served as a basis to that of the *Seasons;* but it will be seen that the latter is marked by a much greater severity of language, and by a solemnity calculated to make a much deeper impression upon weak minds. The text, together with the responses which the candidate was to make, being prompted by his sponsor in case of embarrassment, was as follows :—

The candidate was first introduced with his eyes bandaged.

The president then demanded his name of the introducer, and said :—

"Citizen (the name), what is thy age? thy profession? thy

birthplace? thy domicile? What are thy means of livelihood? Hast thou reflected upon the step which thou art taking? upon the obligation which thou hast just taken? Knowest thou that traitors are smitten with death?

"Swear then to disclose to no one the things that shall take place here.

"What thinkest thou of royalty and of kings?"

"That it is execrable; that kings are as fatal to the human species as tigers are to other animals."

"Who, at the present day, are the aristocrats?"

"The aristocracy of birth was destroyed in July 1830; the aristocrats now are the rich, who constitute an aristocracy as devouring as the first."

"Is it enough merely to overthrow royalty?"

"All aristocrats whosoever must be destroyed, and all privileges whatever; for otherwise nothing would be accomplished."

"What must we put in their place?"

"The government of the people by the people; that is to say, the Republic."

"Those who have rights without fulfilling any duties, such for instance as the aristocrats—are they a part of the people?"

"They ought not to be considered a part of them; they are to the body politic what the cancer is to the human body. The first condition of the restoration of the body to health is the extraction of the cancer. The first condition of a restoration of the body politic to a proper state is the annihilation of the aristocracy."

"Can the people govern itself immediately after a revolution?"

"The body politic being gangrened, heroic remedies are necessary for bringing it to a healthy state. The people would still have need, for some time, of a revolutionary power."

"What then, in short, are thy principles?"

"To exterminate royalty and all the aristocrats; to substitute in their stead the Republic, that is to say, the government of equality, and for the attainment of this government, to employ a revolutionary power which is to prepare the people for an exercise of their rights."

"Citizen, the principles which thou hast just announced are the only just ones, and the only ones which can direct the march of humanity towards its manifest destiny; but their realization is not easy; our enemies are numerous and powerful; they have at their disposal all the forces of society; as for us, republicans, our very name is proscribed; we have nothing but our courage and our good right. Reflect, for there is still time, upon the danger to which thou art exposed in entering our ranks: the sacrifice of fortune, the loss of liberty—death, itself, perhaps—art thou decided to brave them all?

"Thy answer is the proof of thy energy—arise citizen, and take the following oath:—

"In the name of the Republic I swear eternal hatred against all kings, all aristocrats, and all the oppressors of humanity. I swear an absolute devotion to the people, and fraternity to all men except aristocrats; I swear to punish traitors; I promise to give my life and to mount even upon the scaffold should this sacrifice be necessary for the reign of the sovereignty of the people and of equality."

The president then put a dagger in his hand.

"May I be punished with the death of the traitor, may I be stabbed with this dagger, if I violate this oath. I consent to be dealt with as a traitor if I disclose the least thing to any individual whatever, even though my nearest relation, unless he is a member of this association."

After the neophyte had taken this oath, the president resumed:—

"Citizen, be seated; the society receives thy oath; thou art now one of the association; labor with us for the enfranchisement of the people.

"Citizen, thy name will not be uttered among us; here is thy number in this workshop—. Thou art to provide thyself with arms and ammunition. The committee by which the society is directed will remain unknown until the moment of taking arms.—Citizen, one of thy duties is to spread the doctrines of the association. If thou knowest devoted and discreet citizens, it is thy duty to present them to us."

At these words the candidate was restored to the light.

This production speaks for itself. We see that the author, in laying down as a doctrine several general formulas, had in reality as a main object that of infuriating the hatred of the lower classes against the middle classes. But what, indeed, is the actual position of these middle classes in modern society? It is evidently this: They represent the tradition of labor, of morality, and order, all of which are the elements of power in every state. Can it be said that there is a barrier between the laborer and the middle classes which these classes seek to strengthen with jealous pride, as was formerly done by the nobility? Every one knows to the contrary. The laboring man now who receives, soon becomes the laborer who pays; and there is no other difference; the employer has a task to perform not less severe, and more burdened with cares than the simple laborer. If, then, the chiefs of demagogism are bent upon the destruction of this peaceful and laborious part of the community—a class without pride or intolerance, and which incontestably includes within itself the wisdom and power of the country, what other motive can they have than a jealous hatred against men whose sterling qualities cause *them* to blush for their pretentious nullity? What object can they have but to wrest the power from its just and rightful possessors? But this matter is too clear to need elucidation, and the people themselves would be the first to see it were they once clear of the fog of false doctrines by which they have become enveloped.

CHAPTER XXIV.

The *Republican Monitor*—The *Free Man*—M. Joigneaux—Siezure of powder—Skill of the committee of the *Seasons*—Preliminaries of the 12th of May—M. Barbès hesitates—How he is decided by M. Blanqui—Counter order of the battle—The choice of ground.

At the close of the year 1837, M. Huber, whom we have already met with in the complot of Neuilly, lost a portfolio in which was found the plan of a new infernal machine against the king. His two principal accomplices were M. Steuble and Miss Laura Grouvelle. M. Huber was condemned to deportation, and the two others to five years' imprisonment. It is well known what has since become of M. Huber; M. Steuble cut his throat, and M. Laura Grouvelle, the admirer of Alibaud, went mad.

The trial of conspirators usually gives a new stimulus to conspiracies; but the *Seasons* had no need of anything of the kind; for the subjects of the amnesty were to recompense the government by laboring conscientiously to effect its ruin; The propagandism of the suburbs, prosecuted to the extremity of zeal, was producing its fruit, and the revolutionary tide arose to the highest mark.

There were, however, several undisciplined spirits in the society who could not submit to have their importance buried beneath a passive silence, and who must needs play a more conspicuous part. Some of these joined together and formed the plan of a clandestine journal, by which they could give a louder and more commanding exposition of their revolutionary ideas. The chiefs could not approve of this derogation of the regulations; but no attention was paid to their wishes. The dissenters procured, by various means, theft among others, a set of types, got a printer, and brought forth, by way of experimental effort, several pieces of verse, of which the following are specimens:—

> To morrow the regicide goes to his place,
> Amidst the pantheon of gods.
> * * * * * *
> Though thieving and murder his soul may stain,
> It is rendered all white and pure again,
> When washed in the blood of a king.

Such poetry as this was the perfect admiration of the demagogic masses, and the flattered authors resolved to undertake a publication in consecutive numbers. They issued the *Republican Monitor*, a work of darkness which, without name of either editor or printer, came from some unknown laboratory at irregular periods and circulated, under the blouse, through the lodgings of the democrats. It was not bold discussion or violent conviction that marked this piece of gray paper, printed, it would seem, upon a form made up of heads of nails—it was nervous folly, a spasm of the nervous system, a sort of revolutionary erethismus. The editorial of the first number, dated Frimaire 3, year XLVI. (November, 1837), ran thus:—

"The journal is to appear without any of the fiscal fetters which were imposed upon the liberty of thought by the renegades of '89 and 1830. We shall speak against royalty; we shall attack the government both in principle and form; shall protest against the ridiculous respect paid to the charter, and to those laws which are set up against the people by bigoted tri-colored gentlemen; we shall make the apology of political acts which are qualified as crimes and transgressions by the people of the king; we shall strive by every means, and without scruple, to effect the destruction of the government and the aristocrats. And in a word shall do all that is prohibited to be done under the penalty of fine, imprisonment, and the guillotine by the salutary laws of September."

The second number made its appearance in December, and was addressed to young men; and its sly insinuations were well calculated to lead them to the bagnio or the scaffold. The following is a specimen:—

"Every one of you is upon an immense theatre where it depends solely upon one's-self to play a great part—a theatre where many a Brutus and Alibaud have, by immolating or seeking to immolate tryanny, transmitted their names to every age of the world."

The *Republican Monitor* ought, in fact, to have been called the *Monitor of Regicide,* for it harped upon the assassination of the king as if that were the only political capital of the editors. The sixth number was especially devoted to this subject, and contained at its head the following sentences:—

" A king is not judged, but killed."—BILLAUD-VARENNES.

" One cannot govern innocently."—SAINT-JUST.

" Regicide is the right of every man who cannot obtain justice except by his own hands."—ALIBAUD.

The seventh number was occupied with the trial of Huber, who was condemned—" by the testimony of men vomited forth from the bagnio, and blocking together for the support of agonized monarchy.

The *Republican Monitor* died a natural death at the eighth number. Several hundred copies of it had been published and thrust under the doors of houses and into workshops; but it was especially read and devoured among the groups of the *Seasons.* The unfortunate men who composed that society, fancying that the best patriotism was that which made the greatest noise, applauded the *Monitor* with enthusiasm. The committee were not altogether displeased at this result, although the publication interfered somewhat with their plans. It was perceived that a paper of such sentiments could not be very well received by the public; and that the establishment of a republic, such as proposed, would be favored only by a few. This the directors of the famous sheet were finally made to understand, and the publication was abandoned, or rather transformed into a new one. It took the title of the ancient journal of Babeuf—the *Free Man.* The editors remained the same, and the principles advocated received little or no modification; but the forms of expression were somewhat softened. This change showed itself in the first number, wherein it was stated, that " even on behalf of principles, too rude a shock of stupid prejudices would be avoided." But although the *Free Man* proved to be more sparing of bloody extravagances than the *Monitor*, it was filled to overflowing with a sort of provocations which were not less detestable; instead of stimulating to assassination, it incited to theft and devastation. The fourth number contained this apostrophe: "War to the knife between you who enjoy an insolent idleness and us who have suffered for so long a time! The time is nigh when the people will demand, with arms in their hands, that their property shall be restored to them; the possessions of the rich are often nothing but the fruit of rapine."

The police, after numerous researches, finally succeeded in discovering the locality from which this incendiary sheet emanated; it was a porter's lodge, the proprietor of which, M. Fomberteaux, senior, assisted in the publication. The principal editor was M. Fomberteaux, jr., a shoemaker by trade, and to assist him he had four coadjutors, viz: M. Joigneaux, now representative of the people, M. Minor-Lecomte, since married to the widow of Pepin, and Messrs. Guillemin and Houdin. These five writers for the public were condemned each to imprisonment for five years, and to a five years' supervision of the high police.

Inflamed by the indefatigable zeal of its chiefs, heated to a white heat by the journal of Messrs. Fomberteaux, Joigneaux, etc., the society of *Seasons* arrived, at length, about the middle of the year 1838, at that state of super-excitement which compelled the committee to prepare for an explosion. We have said that the affiliated members of the society were not to occupy themselves with forming depôts of arms or ammunition, that each was to limit his attention to his own personal supply, and that the committee had assumed the care of providing for all at the moment of the fight. But notwithstanding this regulation, some of the over zealous members resorted to the old method, and collected supplies of powder and balls—thus furnishing a new prey for the police. One morning, M. Rouyon, a secondary chief of the society, was visited by a commissary, who sent him to the prefecture with eleven hundred cartridges, which were seized in his lodgings; and not long afterwards, M. Danguy was also called thither, to give an account of a supply of powder found at his house. At about the same time it was learned that an engraver of the Palais-Royal, M. Raban, had transformed his house into a perfect arsenal; and a detachment being sent there, took possession of ten thousand balls and a large quantity of powder and cartridges. While this seizure was being made, Messrs. Dubosc and Lardon arrived with another quantity of ammunition, and men, powder, balls, and all were taken into custody.

But the trials resulting from these seizures served only to increase the exaltation of the members of the society. The committee felt that the pressure was becoming intense, and that to check the growing impatience, a positive promise had become necessary. However, as it was near the close of 1838, the committee urged the advanced state of the season as unfavorable to an insurrection, and that, besides, several months were still indispensable for the preparations; but that by spring everything should be arranged for giving battle. With this decision the exalted were appeased. Propagandism was pushed on with renewed zeal; the affiliations went on increasing; frequent reviews accustomed the men to discipline, and redoubled activity animated the association.

True to their promise, the committee, early in 1839, occupied themselves with preparations for the combat. As the fabrication of powder had become too dangerous, it was decided to procure it by purchase from the merchants. Orders were given among the groups that it should be bought by such members as were pretty well off in their circumstances, in small quantities, and from different shops, in order not to excite suspicion. By this means, a very considerable quantity was procured; but as the greater part of the members were poor working men, the supply was still insufficient. M. Barbès, M. Dubosc, of the *Journal of the People*, and others, therefore, clubbed together and formed a fund, which was given to trusty men, for the purpose of continuing the purchases. A sufficient quantity being thus procured, and sent to the revolutionary agents, was given out, and well tried men were chosen for making it into cartridges.

As to arms, the committee having engaged to supply them at the hour of the fight, they took measures for fulfiling their promise; but to avoid a surprise, they took care not to collect them beforehand. There existed in the association several *Weeks*, composed of young men of the schools and of the press, a remnant of the bourgeoisie, who had strayed into this army of the men of the suburbs, whose dress and bearing enabled them to execute certain missions which would have rendered their brethren of the blouse suspected, and to this general staff of the army was intrusted the care of ascertaining where muskets might be found. For this purpose they visited the different armorers' shops, and under pretence of making purchases, took notes of the contents of the shops, of the condition of the arms, and the locality of the premises.

Although this was done with *sangfroid* and adroitness, the police got wind of it; knew that powder was being bought, and that armorers' shops were being inspected; but no one could be taken in the act. Glimpses of the insurrection were seen, and an approaching outbreak was conjectured; but the secret remained with the three chiefs, who communicated it to no one, and who, moreover, if they really had fixed upon the season for the movement, had not yet decided upon the day, and were awaiting for some favorable circumstance.

This conspiracy of the *Seasons*, together with that of General Mallet, is, perhaps, the most astonishing one of this country. It is the only one, since 1830, which has taken the government by surprise. Its secret was kept until the last, and although vaguely known, it fixed the day, and made the irruption without the police being informed of it.

Its disastrous defeat proves what we have already said, to wit, that popular conspiracies, though even the most skilfully combined, can never attain their object, nor effect a revolution. The *Friends of the People* and the *Rights of Man* conspired openly, and their anticipated explosions found the power upon a terrible defensive. The *Seasons* prepared their mine in secrecy, and sprung it upon the public like a thunderbolt; but if the government was astonished, the people were not less so; the majority of the republicans themselves were stupefied by it; and hence, the consequence was that it nowhere found sympathy or support, and fell stillborn, amidst the indifference of some and the indignation of others.

M. Barbès being a proprietor in Aude, had gone there to reside upon his estate, when in the month of March, 1839, a letter from M. Blanqui recalled him to Paris. This letter informed him of a favorable circumstance and of a determination for immediate action. M. Barbès set out, saying that he was going to make a tour in the provinces, where he had been called by a friend, and proceeded to Narbonne; but when arrived there, he faced about and went directly to Paris.

M. Blanqui gave him a detailed account of affairs; the men had been promised a movement in the spring; they were reckoning upon it as a settled matter, and murmurs of impatience were already heard. The society was in the finest state of discipline and full of confidence in its chiefs; but a period of three years had elapsed since its organization, and a longer delay might, at any moment, lead to a disbandment. The preparations were finished; there were cartridges for the men in abundance, and as to arms, it was known where they could be found. In order to surprise the government, it was necessary to avoid the old method of proceeding, not to make use of some marked occasion, such as a festival or a solemnity, but merely to assume a position in the midst of advantageous circumstances. A favorable conjuncture presented itself in a ministerial crisis, which, prolonged beyond all expectation, was powerfully agitating the public mind and disturbing the action of the government. The only question, then, to decide, was the day for the battle.

M. Barbès had arrived in Paris in the expectation of an approaching conflict; the precautions which he had taken with respect to his return, prove it; but, braver than either of his colleagues, Messrs. Blanqui and Martin Bernard, he wanted time for reflection before becoming engaged in the affair; for, having once taken his part, he was not a man to back out. He did not, therefore, exhibit such zeal as his friends had expected; and he even raised objections, which showed no great confidence in success. The society presented a total of about twelve hundred members; but the recent reviews showed that not more than two thirds of this number could be relied on; and was that enough to undertake the affair? Yes, certainly, for merely undertaking it; but was it enough to insure the victory? No. What was the state of mind of the people of Paris? what assistance might be expected from them? That was the question.

He was answered that the people would rise; that everything authorized such a conclusion. But M. Barbès regarded this as an assertion without proof. M. Blanqui, however, savage with impatience, and burning to come to an issue with a government which he deigned to regard as his personal enemy, knew how to overcome the scruples of his colleague:—

"But there is one consideration, said he, which thou hast forgotten; our honor as chiefs is implicated; if we delay the combat, that honor is lost; we shall be regarded as cowards and traitors, and our men will disperse."

To this M. Barbès said not a word; his assent was given.

This took place about the middle of April. The three members of the committee, under their title of revolutionary agents, held a general review of the sections. Each *Month*, assembled by its *July* at the house of a wine merchant, was closely inspected by the superior chief. Many of these assemblages took place at the house of M. Charles, Grenelle Saint Honoré Street, who held the rank of *Spring;* and it was then that the *Seasons* were inspected by M. Barbès. He repaired thither; took an account of the men present, and then made a short address, in which he excited expectation, but without making known his designs.

"You know, said he, that when called together by the committee, the design may be to commence action; it is therefore your duty to be always ready at a moment's notice. The responsibility of the committee is very great; they will meet it; but at the same time every member has a responsibility which he must acquit himself of towards the chiefs; let every one do his duty when called upon, and the committee will do theirs."

The result of this review appeared satisfactory. The effective strength being numerous and every group full of revolution, M. Barbès conceived new hopes. He had seen a thousand rough but disciplined men who had promised him to march at the signal, and he expected to find them all upon the ground. His two confederates, pushed on to the contest by their hatred and impotence, did not share in his illusions. They well knew that many of these wretches, induced either by diplomacy or self-love to enter upon a terrible enterprise, would not make their appearance at the decisive moment, and would leave the weight of the affair to fall upon a small and determined troop; but this was enough for them. They counted upon a favorable effect which the surprise might produce among the people and upon the taking possession of some prominent point where they might await the current of events. And besides, the stakes were down and the game must be played.

The ministerial crisis still continuing, and M. Blanqui conceiving that a republican explosion would find the government in a state of disorganization, induced his colleagues to hasten the day of combat. As it was desirable to take the city by surprise, it was considered that Sunday, a period when many of the citizens leave Paris, would be the most favorable day. There was still another reason for choosing a day of festivity; for the plan of M. Blanqui consisted in moving directly upon a central position, throwing up strong intrenchments, and making it the head-quarters of the insurrection; and as this central position was to be the prefecture of police, it was calculated that on Sunday, from the absence of the employees and the solitude of the place, a surprise would be rendered comparatively easy. Hence, the movement was decided upon for Sunday, the 5th of May.

The revolutionary agents gave orders to the *Springs* to assemble the *Seasons* for another and a rigorous review, informing them that the greatest promptness would be expected at the rendezvous. Several of the *Springs*, Messrs. Meillard, Nettré, Charles, and Dubosc, of the *Journal of the People*, had the confidence of the chiefs, and might have conjectured their plans; but these plans were not, however, divulged; for the three members of the committee had sworn to keep their secret until the end.

The groups were to assemble at mid-day, at a great number of points and await for further orders. Every one was promptly at his post; the *Sunday* at the head of his *Week* awaited orders from *July*, and July awaited them from *Spring*. At about one o'clock it was made known that the committee were satisfied with the zeal of the revolutionary army, and that another meeting would soon be called at which it was hoped the same alacrity would be shown. For that day there was no further communication.

This, it was understood, was a counter-order. It was occasioned by a change of regiments, which was announced for the following week. The wars of the streets, like all other wars, require a knowledge of the ground. It was a practical knowledge of the revolutionary field of battle which rendered the old municipal guard so terrible. New troops just arrived in the city, it was thought, would be embarrassed in their movements, and thus give an advantage to the insurrectionists.

Towards the middle of the week the assemblages of the *Seasons* recommenced. These repeated meetings showed clearly that something was taking place; but the reserve of the chiefs remained unbroken, and the groups were reduced to mere conjecture.

The committee had caused cartridges to be made, half for fowling pieces and half for muskets, and dividing them among themselves, took measures for placing them near the point of attack. This point, as usual, was in the heart of Paris, in a populous and frequented quarter. From the visits made to the armorers' shops, it had been ascertained that the store of Lepage, Bourg-l'Abbé Street, contained arms enough for the whole association. The store, besides being very conveniently situated, was chosen as the general place of meeting; and all the chiefs caused their arsenals to be conveyed to its vicinity.

Before making these dispositions, the committee took care to rally all the men and enforce the attendance of the absentees. Among these latter was a young man, at that time a resident of Angers, to whom one of his friends wrote a letter, of which the following is an extract: "I learn that thou art at last turning thy regards towards the rising sun, towards that star of the world of which I have the honor to be, for the moment, a sublime ray of light. Hasten, then, if thou dost not wish to see it descend without being present at the feast, for everything gives the assurance that a day of jubilee and hot work is preparing here, in which we may intoxicate ourselves with the perfumes of powder and fire." Pitiable bombast, characteristic of the order of ideas by which these wretched men were animated. It may be seen that the person to whom this letter was addressed, a boy named Maréchal, had just been dragged into the ranks of the conspirators. He responded to the call, and was one of the first victims of the sedition. How much ought not his family to be indebted to those who thus lured him on to this abominable murder.

CHAPTER XXV.

The chiefs of the *Seasons* and their general staff—The inspection by M. Blanqui—Everything in readiness—Call to arms—The store of Lepage—The committee called for—Perplexity of M. Blanqui—M. Barbès—The post of the Palace of Justice—Proclamation—Mialon, the galley-slave—M. Tisserant—Suspected courage of some of the chiefs.

On Sunday, the 12th of May, towards mid day, the groups reassembled at the wine-merchant's, or private lodgings in the vicinity of the quarters of Saint Denis and Saint Martin. The object of the meeting remained unknown. At one o'clock the *Springs* passed the word of the committee to amass the men in the streets of Bourg l'Abbe and New

Bourg l'Abbe; no other instructions, nothing to make known the intentions of the chiefs.

At the hour in which this command was being communicated to the groups, one of those *Weeks* which we have already mentioned, consisting of young men of a superior condition, were also awaiting instructions in a coffee-house at the corner of Mandar and Montorgueil Streets, among whom were M. Napoleon Gallois, editor of the *Journal of the People*, M. Noyer, a proprietor, M. Dupouy, a man of letters, and many others. Messrs. Barbès, Blanqui, Martin Bernard, Guignot, Meillard and Nettré soon arrived, and M. Blanqui, addressing himself to the young men, and looking them full in the face, said:—

"You know what is to be done; we are going to unrip."

But as these words were not well understood, he added: "Yes, we shall soon have a fight."

This was perfectly intelligible. He was answered that they were obliged to obey, and that they were ready. The committee, the *Springs* and the group, after having talked for a moment, went out with a tranquil air, and separating into three parties, repaired to the coffee-house upon the corner of the arcade of Bourg l'Abbe and the street of that name. They were still a hundred paces or more from the store of Lepage and the place of assembly. M. Blanqui then left, in order to make a last inspection. His two confederates and their companions ordered beer to be brought, and entered into a conversation upon things in general, endeavoring to show a degree of stoicism. Every one chatted with an air of gayety which easily betrayed his affectation. The conversation of M. Barbès alone was marked by a natural manner; he neither feigned an ill-timed gayety nor discovered any signs of fear, but showed the serenity of a man of courage.

At about half past two o'clock M. Blanqui returned.

"Everything goes on well," said he; "not a cat suspects the move."

He had just visited the vicinity of the prefecture of police, where reigned an air of calm and security. M. Delessert was at that time at the races of the Champ de Mars.

The three chiefs and their lieutenants issued from the coffee-house, and entered among a crowd which was rapidly increasing in size; groups were approaching from six different avenues, of which this point was the centre. The hour fixed for the meeting had already passed, and all who were to come were already present. One accustomed to estimate the number of persons in a crowd might have given the number of sectionaries on the ground at from five to six hundred; and this was about the aggregate of the republican army which was on the point of entering into a conflict with the government.

Every one knew by this time what was to be done; some had been informed of it while on the way to the rendezvous, and others upon the spot. Pensive and restless looking persons might be seen amongst them, but the greater number bore themselves with spirit and energy.

And now was the time, according to the promise which had been given, for the chiefs to come forward and make themselves known; but they were not ignorant of the general impression which prevailed, that these chiefs were to be men of distinction; and as a deception at such a moment might jeopardize the undertaking, they endeavored to extricate themselves from the difficulty by hastening the attack; the usual course of proceeding of men who keep up a loud talk of loyalty in order to conceal their works of duplicity.

Amidst the expectant crowd whose restless looks showed the fever of the soul, M. Martin Bernard forced himself to raise his arms into the air and cried out in a loud voice, *To Arms!* His two colleagues and the small band that followed them repeated the cry and rushed upon the store of Lepage, which was right before them. The door of the interior court being open, they entered without resistance; but in the absence of the armorer, a domestic who held the keys of the store refused to give them up; and it became necessary to force open the doors in order to get at the arms. Messrs. Barbès and Blanqui directed this operation, and made short work of it. Once entered among the arms, the windows overlooking the streets were thrown open, and the distribution commenced. During this time M. Martin Bernard, with whom the members of the society were the most intimately acquainted, was called upon by them to give the names of the chiefs. Perceiving that there was no longer room for hesitation, he ran to join his colleagues, crying out—

"We are the committee! and we are at your head, as we have promised to be. There are other members whose names will be made known in a proclamation."

This was not exactly what had been expected; more than one disappointed conspirator held himself in reserve in order to see what turn the affair would take before proceeding any farther. Of the five or six hundred members who appeared upon the ground, three hundred at farthest took arms. The remainder gradually drew off, extricated themselves from the crowd, and made their disappearance.

On the morning of that day, the 12th, M. Meillard, who had been intrusted with the ammunition for the troop of M. Martin Bernard, had sent to Bourg l'Abbé Street, to the house of one of his friends named Bonnet, a large trunk filled with cartridges; and as soon as the cry of war arose, the trunk was brought forth and its contents distributed, every one helping himself. At the same time a *July*, M. Brocard, a journeyman packer by trade, came upon the ground with a box under his arm, and a ring was formed around him, believing that there was to be another distribution of cartridges; but what was the stupefying astonishment of his comrades on seeing their *July* gravely draw forth from his box the fancy dress and armor of the stage and proceed to put it on!

The fire-arms during this time were handed down or rather thrown into the street from the windows of Lepage's store. There was a great scramble for them, and more than once the possession of a gun was obstinately disputed.

After an hour of violence and confusion, during which the chiefs, in order to beguile the impatience of the groups, struck up the *song of the Departure*, the store was finally emptied; and then the three members of the committee made their reappearance in the street in search of their men. But many of these men had vanished from the view—careful patriots, some of them, who prudently remembered to carry off some of Lepage's valuable guns and pistols, for which a very good price could be got.

M. Barbès, surrounded by men who were in want of cartridges, put himself at their head and hastened to the house of Dame Roux, Quincampoix Street, where he had deposited the cartridges of his *Year*. This dame, ignorant alike of the character and the object of the deposit, was not at home. Her door was forced open, and the contents of a box furnished the band with an ample supply. M. Barbès immediately returned to Bourg-l'Abbé Street to communicate with his colleagues. There he found M. Blanqui alone, breathless, overwhelmed, but contending against a crowd who were crying out treason, declaring that there was neither any plan or committee, and that the patriots were only led on to be butchered. M. Barbès looked on for a moment with a heavy heart, contemplating a scene which seemed to open before him like an abyss; then, resolving upon his course, he called out to the men of courage to follow him, and set out at the head of a small band towards the prefecture of police. Going by the way of the bridge of Notre-Dame, he halted at the flower market in order that his men might load. This done, he pushed directly for the Palace of Justice, which was but a few paces in advance. A physician, M. Levraud, had informed the guard of that point that the insurgents were coming upon them, and that they ought to take measures for defence; but the insurrection, the rumor of which had already began to spread, appeared to be so very strange that it could hardly be believed; so that the chief of the post, notwithstanding the information which he had just received, did not even take care to have the arms of his detachment loaded.

M. Barbès, addressing himself to the men who were hurrying out to oppose him, summoned them to surrender and to deliver up their arms; the officer, M. Drouincau, made a reply in accordance with his duty. A short parley ensued, and then, all of a sudden, the muskets of the insurgents were brought down to an aim, their report rang upon the ear, and the chief of the post, with half of his men, fell dead upon the spot. The remainder were immediately surrounded and disarmed.

M. Barbès has been accused of the assassination of the unfortunate Drouineau, and he has denied it. We believe, from what we know of M. Barbès, that his word ought to possess some weight; but if the mortal shot was not aimed by himself, it certainly came from one of his men, and even that is no small responsibility. It must be borne in mind, moreover, that in a proclamation which we shall give, this chief lent his hand to a falsehood; it was before the danger, however, and in a case which was not personal. Perhaps it is true that in the hour of danger, and when he has no one to defend but himself, M. Barbès does not lie—such is the character of the man. He possesses all the pride and fanatical energy of certain chiefs of the savage tribes which figure in the works of Cooper. It is not improbable, indeed, that he may have been instigated by their examples. When brought before the Court of Peers and called on for his defence, he replied that the conquered savage offered his head to the scalping knife, but never gave an excuse. The attorney-general might well say that in comparing himself to a savage he did himself no more than justice.

The guards having thus been assassinated and disarmed, the next move was made upon the prefecture of the police; but the alarm had been given, and the few disposable men there had prepared for a defence, which secured the place from a *coup-de-main*. A small band of the insurgents fired a few shots in Jerusalem Street, and that was all; a formal attack was not attempted.

M. Barbès rallied his men and directed his course upon the Hôtel de Ville, the post of which had been left by the National Guards who had charge of it. The people of Paris in general were still unaware of the revolt. Several officers and the sentinel on post finding themselves opposed to a band of insurgents, deemed that a defence would not be possible, and surrendered their arms. The republican chief immediately mounted upon the steps of the hotel, and to an audience composed of the assailants and a few groups of idle persons, read the following proclamation.

"To arms, citizens!

"The fatal hour for our oppressors has struck.

"The cowardly tyrant of the Tuileries laughs at the hunger which is tearing the bowels of the people; but the measure of his crimes is full; they are now to receive the punishment which is their due.

"Betrayed France and the blood of our butchered brothers cry out to you and call for vengeance; and let it be terrible, for it has been too long delayed; perish exploitation, and let equality rise triumphant amidst the wreck and ruin of royalty and aristocracy! The provisional government has chosen military chiefs for the direction of the combat; these chiefs come from your ranks; follow them, then, and they will lead you to victory."

"Augustus Blanqui is commander in chief, and Barbès, Martin Bernard, Guignot, Meillard and Nettré, are major-generals of the republican army.

"People, arouse, and your enemies will disappear like dust before the hurricane. Strike with pitiless extermination the vile satellites, the willing accomplices of tyranny; but extend the hand of friendship to those soldiers who have sprung from your bosoms, and who will never contend against you with parricidal arms.

"Forward! Hurrah for the Republic!

"Barbès, Voyer-d'Argenson, Aug. Blanqui, Lamennais, Martin Bernard, Dubosc, Laponneraye."

This production is shaped upon the same old model as usual, and gives rise to reflections which naturally occur to every one. It usurped the names of several persons who thus became seriously implicated, and impudently trifled with the good faith of the members of the society and the people. Three of the names upon the list, those of Messrs. Lamennais, Voyer-d'Argenson, and Laponneraye, it is well known, were forged; for although these citizens might have desired the success of the insurrection, they were not consulted as to the use of their signatures. The choice of these names instead of others, which seemed naturally to offer themselves, is explained as follows: M. Voyer-d'Argenson, as a large proprietor, was to give confidence to the wealthy classes; M. Lamennais, as priest, to the country people; and as to M. Laponneraye, ex-apologist of the heroes of the reign of terror, and at that time editor of a communist paper called the *Intelligence*—he was taken as a representative of the radical press; as was also M. Dubosc, editor of the *Journal of the People*. Another prominent feature of the proclamation is, the ever recurring falsehood with regard to the coming over of the troops—a snakishly perfidious affectation of monkeyism. These troops were not to turn their *parricidal arms* against the demagogues—oh no! but were to deliver up their arms to the demagogues, in order to sack and pillage society with! "*Extend the hand of friendship to those soldiers who have come from thy bosom.*" Oh, yes! certainly, if these soldiers would first disgrace themselves by yielding to the insurgents; but if not, if they should do their duty, why, then massacre them, as at the Palace of Justice, or, as we shall see by and by, at the market of St. John.

The insurgents, led by M. Barbès, were not in sufficient strength to hold the Hôtel-de-Ville, and he decided, therefore, to hasten to every mayoralty, to disarm the guards stationed there, and by thus executing a series of surprises, to at length astonish and arouse the people.

At the place of St. John was a post which he wished to carry on his way. An insurgent, M. Nouguès, stepped forward, and, addressing the soldiers, urged them not to make a useless resistance. Receiving an energetic reply, the band rushed forward and endeavored to throw themselves upon the bayonets, but, furious at finding themselves repulsed, they delivered a fire by which seven of the soldiers fell. An old galley slave, named Mialon, one of the most ferocious among the assailants, rushed upon the fallen victims, and, while uttering the most hideous curses, gave a finishing stroke to the work of death. This Mialon, an old man of bloody instincts, killed on the same day, and in cool blood, a quartermaster of the municipal guard—one way, certainly, of extending the hand of friendship to the brethren of the army! The brave soldiers who might have legally taken the offensive and destroyed a band of insurgents, showed merely a passive resistance, and their generosity was taken advantage of for butchering them in the most infamous manner.

After other attacks in various quarters of the town, the band of M. Barbès turned into Saint Martin Street, and mingled in a combat going on in Greneta Street, which was defended by a strong barricade. There the insurgents had to deal with a man of heroic valor, who attacked them, not at long musket-shot distance, and from behind intrenchments, but openly, face to face, at sword's point; we refer to Lieutenant Tisserant, of the municipal guard, now a commandant in that chosen corps. The troops of the army had not yet been brought out, although it was nearly five o'clock in the evening, and the only force that had been sent against the insurgents consisted of detachments of the municipal guard. One of these detachments, commanded by Lieut. Tisserant, had orders to oppose the insurrectionists in the quarter of Saint Martin, where they apparently designed to concentrate. While on the way the officer was stopped and told that he would certainly be crushed, that it was folly to engage with such a small command as he had; but the advice was not attended to, inasmuch as it might have been given in favor of the insurgents, and was addressed to a man not very sensible to danger. M. Tisserant arrived at the barricade of Greneta Street and immediately opened a fire upon it. This fire was returned by a terrible fusillade. Sheltered by their solid rampart, the insurgents calculated, as usual, to shoot down their brave assailants with ease and security; but such was not the case. The chief of the detachment, addressing a few words to his men, rushed at a charging pace towards the barricade, and was the first to scale it. One of the insurgents, M. Austen, fired at him; but his musket hung fire, and the lieutenant cut him down with his sword. He then leaped within the barricade and cut down another of the insurgents who was aiming at him;

but the latter in falling, caught him by the leg, which caused him to stumble. Immediately recovering, however, he pressed upon his enemy and thrust his sword into his breast. The guards followed close upon their chief; and in a furious hand to hand conflict they knocked down every one who came in their way. The insurgents then abandoned the first barricade, and took refuge behind a second, which had been thrown up a short distance farther on in the same street. The municipal guards followed them too closely to allow them to recover themselves, and the insurgents fell back successively, behind three other intrenchments, from which they were dislodged as vigorously as they had been from the first.

It was towards the close of these several conflicts, directed by subordinate chiefs, that M. Barbès arrived and joined with the insurgents; but his courage in no way changed the result; repeatedly wounded, he at last fell from a blow on the head, covered with blood. He managed with difficulty to crawl to a door-way, where he was captured.

The last remaining position of the insurgents, that of Saint Méry, was also carried by the command of M. Tisserant; the few subsequent efforts made by the revolt were isolated and insignificant, ending of themselves.

Such is the military aspect of the affair which occurred on the 12th of May. A single courageous man, with a handful of old soldiers, put an end to the affair at once. The bearing of M. Barbès was all that had been expected of him; but as to that of Messrs. Blanqui and Martin Bernard, it was quite another thing. One of the accused, M. Nouguès, believing that M. Martin Bernard had been killed, declared at first that he had seen him at the head of every attack; the object of his assertion being to throw the blame of the affair upon a man who was no longer responsible; but when he learned that the said Martin Bernard was safe and sound, he changed his tune, and said that he had not seen him anywhere. His last version was much truer than the first. There is considerable evidence to show that this chief was among the murderers of the place of St. John; which we shall neither affirm nor deny; but at any rate, there are no traces of him to be found upon the field of battle. With respect to M. Blanqui, if he really did take a glorious part in the fight, it is only known to himself.

M. Martin Bernard was concealed by one of his *Julys*, M. Charles, at the house of a man named Ardiot, Mouffetard Street, where he was arrested six weeks afterwards. His papers showed that he was already occupied in getting up another association; the blood which had been shed had not yet been washed away when he was meditating schemes for shedding it anew. It is certain that his own blood had not yet been exhausted.

M. Blanqui was not arrested till several months later; not till the moment when entering a carriage to leave France.

Severe sentences were passed by the Court of Peers, against the chiefs of the revolt. M. Barbès, found guilty of the assassination of Lieutenant Drouineau, was condemned to suffer death. Messrs. Martin Bernard and Blanqui were subsequently sentenced to deportation; Mialon, to perpetual hard labor; Delsade and Austen to fifteen years' detention; Charles, to eight years; Nouguès and Philippet, to six years; and Rondil, Guilbert and Lemière, to five years' imprisonment.

After the condemnation of M. Barbès, the remnants of the *Seasons*, under the orders of Messrs. Dubosc, N. Gallois, and Noyer, formed a scheme for his delivery. It became a fixed plan at the office of the *Journal of the People*, of which the first two were editors; but a pardon from the king rendered any further attempts unnecessary.

BOOK II.

Some of the events recorded in the first book of this work, are to some extent already known; but I am now about to enter upon a series of facts which are wholly unknown to the public, in which I myself have played a part, and which I shall expose with perfect candor. The several revelations made in my pamphlet—*The birth of the Republic,* have not yet been confuted by any one. The only republican who attempted to crush me beneath a terrible confutation, the Representative Miot, has done nothing more than confirm many of my assertions, remaining silent upon others, and replying successfully to none. I have purposely abstained from answering this excellent man's book, since he could not have done me a greater favor if he had been my most intimate friend.

The scrupulous correctness which characterizes that accessory work will be observed in the new details which I am about to make known. The dates and names of persons will be given in connection with every event, so that my opponents will have a fair field for refutation if I misrepresent the truth.

I have but a few words to say with regard to myself; I am sincerely devoted to liberty, but have a thorough detestation of those men who traffic in revolutionary ideas and speculate upon public calamities. I have had a close view of these men; I have examined the wretched life which they lead, their equivocal morality, their doubtful capacities, their schemes tending to the ruin of the moral and material interests of the country, and I have become convinced that it would be an act, if not of moral correctness, at least of true civism, to unmask these men and seize upon their influence in order to destroy it. Such alone was my object in the part which I have played, as the sequel of this work will show.

CHAPTER I.

Reorganization of the *Seasons*—The provisional committee—The four *Revolutionary Agents*—Orders of the day again brought in use—My course of proceeding with the patriots.

IMMEDIATELY after the catastrophe of May, M. Martin Bernard busied himself with reorganizing the *Seasons;* but his obstinate zeal was finally checked by his being tried and sent to Doullens. Then Messrs. Napoleon Gallois, Noyer and Dubosc seized upon the threads of the association, and endeavored to restore them to their original state; but none of them had the ambition to become a leader of the new society. M. Gallois, an obscure writer, was seeking a place in the democratic press. He was a young man, twenty years of age, a democrat by family inheritance, but of too trivial a character to devote himself seriously to the work of conspiracy. M. Noyer, a little dried up man, nervous and energetic, had not the disposition for intrigue necessary for secret manœuvres, and besides, notwithstanding his southern temperament, he was of a peaceful turn of mind, and found no pleasure in discord and fracas. M. Dubosc had had an ample opportunity of judging how very disagreeable it is to a man who can afford to live upon his rents, to pass his days within the four walls of a prison; he was willing to aid in collecting together the remnants of the *Seasons*, but had no desire to become implicated in a way that the courts might get hold of him.

But this provisional committee infused a certain degree of activity into their work. We have already said that after every insurrectionary movement a sentiment of spite and self-love seems to prevail, which stimulates the conspirators to contend against the consequences of their defeat, and to establish, as soon as possible, the work which has been destroyed; and this sentiment exhibited itself on the present occasion. The majority of the members of the *Seasons*, a wilful and imbecile crew, were ready to bend their necks to the yoke of the new chiefs—to become rounds in the ladder for the new exploiters.

There was a society in existence as early as the 12th of May, which, however, could not take a part in the revolt because of not having been perfectly organized, and because, moreover, it was not thought proper to claim its concurrence—this society was called the *Montagnards*. One of its chiefs was one Louis Gueret, called the Great Louis, a man of some influence, who became, together with three members of the *Seasons* and a considerable number of *Weeks*, the pivot of a new undertaking. The chiefs took the name of *Revolutionary Agents*. We have just mentioned one of them; the others were Messrs. Boivin, Dutertre, and Chaubard: M. Boivin was merely a man of action, exercising the profession of a copper turner; M. Dutertre, a gilder of porcelain, had a good personal appearance, and was not wanting in cunning; M. Chaubard, son of a hotel keeper of Toulouse, embroiled with his family and hence reduced to the condition of cook, was in no way distinguished from the ordinary run of conspirators. Louis Guerret was the most remarkable man of the four; although a simple worker in ebony, he had read a great deal, spoke fluently, and added to these advantages a fine figure and more distinguished manners than those of his companions. M. Boivin, the most ignorant of these companions, was, at the same time, the most sincere; he had conspired ever since 1830, without knowing exactly why, but playing his part nevertheless, conscientiously; M. Dutertre had a private object in view, which we shall see in the course of this work; M. Chaubard yielded to the necessity of action—to his southern temperament, and the Great Louis to the desire of playing a part.

Subject to these four superior chiefs were subaltern commandants, among whom we may mention Messrs. Albert, ex-member of the provisional government, David, Rozier, Marchand, Vellicus, Dorgale, etc.

The point in question was a new organization for the society; for it was also the tact of the trade to adopt, after every defeat, new appellations and new modes of recruiting.

Some few attempts at reorganization were made, but as the committee did not show the necessary zeal, everything remained in *statu quo*, that is to say, the drawing together of the ancient members of the society went on quietly, but the course to be pursued was left to future consideration. The four principal chiefs preserved for the time the title of *Revolutionary Agents;* their lieutenants took the name of chiefs of groups, and the members were designated under the generic name of—The Men.

When the principal pieces of the serpent had been joined together again, when the first flames of propagandism had sprung forth and the society was about ready to become reconstituted, the total of its forces might amount to five or six hundred men.

The ancient members of the society were naturally admitted into the new organization; the new members were subjected to the old formalities of reception; but for well-known patriots this formality was very much simplified.

The orders of the day, abandoned by the *Families* and the *Seasons*, was resumed. The necessity of this energetic mode of proceeding was felt to be imposed by a defective organization. Besides the direct effect of these communications, the success of which had been so great in the *Rights of Man*, they were known to inspire confidence in the members by leading them to believe that the committee consisted of men of learning and importance. The mob-going folk, notwithstanding their jealousy against the upper classes, are very well aware that they have to take their leaders from these classes; and it has ever been remarked that their chief care is to know whether their commanders are men of an elevated position. The dress and manners of a man are not viewed with so evil an eye by the conspirators as might be imagined ; at least, if the dress is worn by a patriot, and the manners are not marked by haughtiness. So long as the question is the organization of an insurrection, the bourgeoisie, or, in the parlance of the suburbs, the aristocrats, are very well received and their orders followed with implicit submission; but when the fight is once commenced, and the fumes of powder intoxicate the brain, then farewell to the bourgeoisie. But we have already mentioned this trait of the insurrectionists, and will not refer to it again.

As the effect of orders of the day become greater by being printed, care was taken to set up a clandestine printing establishment. There existed a press somewhere among the groups, and it was sought for and found. It was simply a mahogany box containing the means for setting up a page in quarto. Negotiations for its removal were entered into with the man in whose possession it was found, and who was glad to get rid of it for fear that it might bring him into difficulty. But the question was how to remove this dangerous object without risk and inconvenience; it was settled in the following manner:—

A day was fixed, and several members of the society were posted about the house containing the press. The premises having been thoroughly explored, M. Noyer, enveloped in a large cloak, arrived in a coach, entered the house, and immediately returned with the box under his cloak, and so perfectly concealed that there seemed to be no change in his appearance. The coachman dashed off at a round pace, according to the orders which he had received.

The sentinels followed the coach by way of an escort for some time; but as they were not able to keep up with it, and as nothing had occurred to disturb the operation, they soon slackened their pace, and the coach became lost in the mazes of Paris. But, as it appears, this did not satisfy the views of one of the men of the party; for, suddenly pretending some excuse, he left his companions, took a street which would lead him towards the coach, and, when out of sight, set to running at the top of his speed. After a run of a full quarter of an hour, he stopped, streaming with perspiration, and throwing back his head like a man who had given up the object of his chase in despair.

But the box was not lost to all the world; for at the moment in which that man seemed to despair at having missed his object, it arrived in Notre Dame des Victoires Street, at a place where it was just as safe as if it had been at the prefecture of the police; it was at my own house.

I knew the reorganizers of the society, and enjoyed their unlimited confidence. This confidence I had acquired by the following method: Always declaring myself a republican, I censured the temerity of the party and their secret proceedings; I showed myself ready to assist the serious-minded men among them, but never to become associated in rash undertakings; I refused to take a part in the new conspiracy, but offered my services. My combinations were, to appear exceedingly circumspect, and careful of the interests of the cause; for I was sure that this course would gain me the intimate confidence of the chiefs, and gradually render me indispensable. In order the better to preserve the influence which I desired, I was obliged to acquire it by insensible degrees, and without seeming to seek it. Such a man as M. Miot thinks that one must be constantly rolling up his eyes, making furious gestures and spouting forth Montagnard phrases in order to pipe up the patriots to the dance; but every one to his taste—that was not mine.

The orders of the day were issued every month. They were edited either by M. Gallois or M. Dubosc. The copy was sent by M. Noyer to a sectionary, a printer by trade, who came to my house to set it up. Some score of copies were struck off and distributed among the principal chiefs of groups, who were charged with having them read.

It might be said that, in order to escape all censure, I ought to have destroyed the box at once, and caused editors, printer, and propagators of these culpable publications to be arrested. Certainly not; for a course like this to-day would have to be done over again to-morrow. A few pounds of type are easy to be got by the chiefs of a conspiracy, and especially when they have type-setters among their men, who can furnish them at the expense of their employers. By checking acts like these every time they occur, the police would soon become limited to a too complicated system of supervision; the country would be kept subject to that agitation which results from a discovered plot, and above all, a certain class of men would be kept informed that conspiracies were still going on. In a country of hot heads and extravagant ambition, it is exceedingly essential to keep up the appearances of public tranquillity; for an excitement in one place is often enough to give rise to it in a dozen others. That foolish absurdity which has been repeated a thousand times, that the police traffics in political disorders, gives a shrug of the shoulders to men who are versed in these matters. To play thus with the fire may seem to be a very easy trade to the good readers of newspapers, and even to their very knowing editors; but the men who have been called to this difficult service of the French government, are perfectly well satisfied with the natural obstacles in their way, without the useless creation of new ones. Besides, it has already been said, that a too open repression of a conspiracy would tend to establish a belief in the strength of the cause, which would not otherwise be entertained, even by its adherents themselves, and to convert into heroes a set of poor devils whose example others would thus be stimulated to follow. It is excellent tactics, in times of tranquillity, to avoid giving a cause the advantage of publicity, and the prestige of persecution; for it is thus almost inevitably reduced to a stage of consumption. This tactics the government and the prefect of police of that period well understood. M. Delessert was animated by a spirit of conciliation and mildness which was admirably well adapted to the peaceful state of the times of which we are speaking. The remaining elements of anarchical extravagance had been banished to a small corner, where, by means of a quiet supervision, they could be narrowed down and hemmed in until their limiting circle should be reduced to nothing. Humanity as well as a sound policy pointed out a course of proceeding like this; and it was put in practice and attained its end, as will be seen.

CHAPTER II.

Two adventures—M. Dourille—He becomes chief of the *New Seasons*—The Journal of the People—M. Dupoty—His portrait.

The orders of the day being sent to the four revolutionary agents, these chiefs assembled their men in some of the drinking shops, divided them into fractions of fifteen or twenty persons, and, at an hour fixed upon in the evening, went to attend to the reading. Some of the wine sellers were recognized as good patriots, and were in the secret, and others were considered to know nothing; but they did know, however, quite as much as their fellows, for the bearing of such kind of customers was not easily mistakable. In other respects the measures of prudence were not neglected. One man was posted outside of the shop, in order to keep an eye upon the street, and another at the outer door of the hall to give notice of the arrival of persons of the house, and recognize the affiliated. Wine was called for by the quart; cards were brought, and in case of an alarm, every one took to playing, or commenced a noisy and idle conversation. When the meeting was full, the revolutionary agent enjoined silence; drew out his paper and placing it within a newspaper, read it as if reading an ordinary editorial of the day. A few brief explanations followed, and then the chief withdrew. Discussion and controversy were forbidden; for a Cossack system of this kind was necessary to discipline.

But, notwithstanding these precautions, an alarm was often given to the conventicles. One night the man on post outside of the shop suddenly entered and said that suspicious movements were taking place in the vicinity; and almost at the same time one of those cool, penetrating looking men, of whom conspirators are instinctively shy, made his appearance, followed by two others, whose looks, also, were not very consoling. As soon as they were seen, every body exclaimed at once: A commissary and two agents! The order of the day was immediately thrust into the flames of the candle, but as it was slow in burning, and as fear was gaining rapidly upon the nerves of the one who was trying to burn it, he threw it upon the floor; stamped out the flame with his foot, and then endeavored to chew it up. At this moment one of the three men went out, and not a doubt was entertained but that he had gone for a reinforcement. The sectionaries were seized with a panic. In spite of the recommendation to keep cool, the idea of imminent peril and the insecurity usually felt in such cases when shut up in an obscure room without any convenient outlet, prevailed over every other consideration, and, rushing together in a crowd to the door of the hall, they upset the two men in their way, trampled them under foot, and got clear from the house under the firm conviction that they had escaped a serious danger.

The next day, however, when one of them went to the wine-seller's to learn the news, he was told that the men who had been taken for a commissary and two agents were an architect and two laborers, who had come to have an understanding with regard to some repairs that were to be done to the house.

On another occasion a group had assembled in a cookshop at the barrier; and the order of the day was to be read in a shed, at the bottom of the court where the game of Siam was played. At the hour of the rendezvous two mechanics made their appearance in search of one of their comrades by the name of Joseph. As it so happened that one of the principal chiefs of the groups was of that name, they were allowed to enter without any farther concern. Entering among the crowd in search of their comrade, and not being able to find him, but seeing a game of Siam going on, they became lookers on like the rest. Suddenly the game was stopped, and the mechanics were astonished to see distrustful looks directed towards the doors, while a man drew forth a piece of paper and imposed silence. Not knowing what to think of this, one of them said to the other: "Hollo! What's going on here?" This remark was overheard by one near them, and he thought it rather singular; however, as the reading had commenced he allowed it to go on, not knowing whether the remark was of any consequence or not, but resolving at any rate to find out what it meant. The reading being finished he went to see Joseph, the chief, and informed him of what he had just heard; but Joseph knew nothing of the two men. A great excitement ensued, which was concealed as carefully as possible from those who were the cause of it, and it was resolved to find out who the intruders were and what was their object.

They were followed, their residence discovered, and a watch set upon their movements. It was soon reported by the watch that one of them had been seen to enter the prefecture of police. There was no doubt, therefore, that they had to do with spies. Information of the fact was given to a revolutionary agent, who laid it before the committee. The committee recommended to the chiefs of groups to describe the mechanics clearly to the men in order that they might be avoided, and declared at the same time that measures would be taken against spies. But this was not satisfactory to some of the patriots, and they decided to inflict an exemplary punishment upon the traitors. A day was fixed for lying in wait for them in an unfrequented street, which they usually followed on leaving their workshop, and six men placed themselves in ambush with iron-bound clubs, fully determined to leave their intended victims upon the pavement; but unluckily for these officious judges of the highway, the mechanics were informed of their danger, and on the eve of the intended execution had left their workshops and the capital.

The truth of all this is, that the presence of the mechanics at the game of Siam was a mere accident, and the visit of one of them to the prefecture of the police was not for the purpose of giving information. The only part played by the police in this affair consisted in preventing a crime by sending away two men whose lives it knew to be threatened.

It may readily be conceived how useless it would be to send agents in quest of conspirators who had so little experience as to make such an observation as was made by one of the mechanics. It is not from men exterior to the affiliation that information is received at the prefecture. Three or four of the chiefs of the society sent the orders of the day there themselves, and that was enough.

We have said that the three men who reorganized the society had assumed the direction only provisionally, without intending to retain it. In the mean time a bookseller of Dauphiné, in quest of fortune, M. Dourille, arrived in the capital, and was presented to Messrs. Gallois and Noyer. He was a man about thirty years of age, of a dry and nervous complexion, full of vivacity, eloquent, versatile, and withal somewhat perpendicular. At a first glance he would be taken as a well-known type of southern character; but on coming to examine his little blue eyes, which were always in motion, there was something there which claimed the attention. From the midst of a dishevelled beard, his pointed face, thin nose, and restless looks, peered forth like the head of a fox from a bramble-bush. He was not wanting in intelligence, nor in a certain degree of information. He was particularly remarkable for his powers of locomotion. His tensely formed leg, his elastic body, and in short his whole appearance was that of a determined walker. His radical opinions were disclosed at the first words which he uttered. Having his memory stuffed with the events of the first revolution, he referred to them on every occasion and with perfect enthusiasm; the men and things of that period danced through his head and kept his ambition in a constant state of excitement and fever.

Zealous radicalism, activity of mind and body, and an impetuous ambition, were certainly suitable qualities for a chief of conspiracies. The provisional committee were not long in having a talk with him. A part was offered him in the direction, and he accepted without hesitation. The zeal which he exhibited showed that his functions were much to his liking; but it was soon discovered, however, that this zeal was greater than his capacity; for he was wanting in the very first quality of a conspirator, viz: discretion. While constantly preaching up prudence, he was as constantly violating his own precepts. A candid effusion of his political sentiments was a necessity to him; he aimed at passing himself off as a revolutionary artist, and, in order to have his combinations appreciated, he exposed them to everybody.

During the first few months, he was so infatuated with his part that he hardly had time to perceive that his wife and little daughter were dying from want, and that he himself was living only at the expense of his comrades. He had come to see me at the suggestion of M. Gallois, and at various times I had to give him the means for a dinner. His usual company consisted of students; among whom figured M. André, since become a socialist democrat of the deepest dye, and M. Bordellet, who subsequently turned his attention to more serious matters. They had been affiliated by the chief, and were employed as his staff. The revolutionary business on hand being dispatched, he used to go with them to the grog-shops, where he passed around the bottle like any mere mortal—it being well understood that his companions footed the bill. It never seemed to occur to this poor man that he was thus leading a life of idleness and sponging, opposed to every principle of morality, whether republican or any other. Not till some offensive remarks had opened his eyes could he perceive the necessity of providing means of subsistence. Addressing himself to the *Journal of the People*, he was accepted, partly as collaborator and partly as solicitor of advertisements. M. Dupoty, during his trial by the Court of Peers, thought proper to degrade him to the simple part of an *employée* of the press; but M. Dourille was more than that; for he had written for the paper a series of articles under the title of *Revolutionary Chronicles*. The editor in chief might appear on this occasion to have been governed by aristocratic disdain, but such was not his design; M. Dupoty was afraid, and hence this act of injustice towards one of his colleagues—a mediocre writer, it is very possible; but who had his equal in this respect in more than one of his fellow collaborators.

M. Dupoty, a republican in good faith, but rather timid, declared that he would leave the success of his party to the force of principles alone; but in the mean time the character of his journal was dangerous in the highest degree. Good naturedness of tone, accompanied with a triviality of style, took easily with his readers; and a measured prudence in forms of expression only served to give greater effect to his doctrines. The *Journal of the People* was by far the greatest element of disorganization of the period; operating in a period of profound peace, it seemed to conform to the reserve of the public mind, and thus gave currency to its doctrines, which were of the most anarchical and obstinate kind. Without advocating any one of the ideas of communism, the spirit of the journal encouraged them all; without directly appealing to insurrection, it heated up all the instincts of revolution; it was the propagandism of disorder under the guise of wisdom at play—of logic in a good humor. But in all this, the chief editor candidly showed that he was playing off a piece of transcendental tactics; giving to his paper the simple expressions of nature, he made it a monstrously cynical amalgam of peaceable qualities and violent opinions. At a sight of the man one could form some idea of this measured character of his phraseology when compared with the incandescence of the subjects upon which he treated; he was spruce, beaming with smiles, and so coquettish that his colleagues could not help laughing at him. Always nicely shaved, and with his hair symmetrically dressed, well gloved, and wearing ruffles, gewgaws and trinkets, he represented at the age of forty five years one of those superannuated dandies whose costume is always exceedingly correct if not highly elegant. His mind and manners were in keeping with this tinselled exterior; he loved jokes, jovialities, conundrums, the pleasures of the night, followed after grisettes, and ogled the actresses at the little theatres. But in this respect he was really a good man—kneaded with a degree of epicurean clay that had nothing terrible in it; and it must be confessed that, at bottom, he was no worse a man, as a politician; for he entertained none of the savage ideas of his confederates, and had a sincere aversion for measures of blood. By his trial, which made so much noise, his friends were at least as much astonished as rendered indignant. One thing is certain, that M. Dupoty openly manifested his repugnance to conspiracies, and this repugnance was no affectation. He was not opposed to conspiracies from principle, but his temperament was such that he refused to have any part in them. But still, it is nevertheless true that the company which he habitually kept was not only almost wholly made up of conspirators, such, for instance, as Messrs. Gallois, Dubosc, and Dourille, but the tendencies of his paper led directly to popular anarchy. This fact may explain the persecutions of which he has been the object.

In fine, it has been seen that, since the days of February, M. Dupoty has taken no part in the scenes of revolutionary orgies. For a long time he had made no figure in politics. The patriots of action, who had begun by laughing at his dress, finally came to make sport of his pacific ideas; and some time before the events of February, this man, who had been reckoned a saint in the democratic calendar, became an object of insulting disdain among his own party. At the *Reform* they went so far as to spread the report that he had gone mad —*sic transit gloria.*

CHAPTER III.

M. Cabet and communism—The banquet of Chatillon—The republicans show signs of life—The banquet of Belleville in reply to that of Chatillon.

It was about the year 1840, that Paris became seriously infected with communism. Ideas tending more or less to this doctrine had been disseminated by Messrs. Godefroy

Cavaignac, Raspail and others, in the days of the *Rights of Man*. The *Families* and *Seasons* had also laid down conclusive formulas upon this subject, and from that time it was declared that property was to be—not destroyed, but very materially modified; or, in plain language, was to change hands. This was the way for arriving at the true principle, which was, to place all the possessions of the country in the hands of the government, and then turn the government over to the keeping of popular chiefs. By popular chiefs we do not mean such men as M. Ledru Rollin and other newspaper writers, who talk so confidently every day in the name of the people; we allude to a class of cool and malignant revolutionists, whose sphere of action lies beyond that of the more prominent leaders of the people, and who make use of word-dealers and pamphlet-mongers only as so many avant-couriers whose business it is to prepare for their reception. This class of men, indeed, understand the power of eloquence and the libel, and have recourse to it for establishing their domination; but as this power might subsequently be turned against themselves, they intend to destroy it immediately after having made use of it. Besides, as they themselves say, talent itself is a species of aristocracy, and all kinds of aristocracy ought to be made way with. Their beau ideal of government is a power purely popular, the laws being enacted by general acclamation, and the authority residing in a few hands which are completely enfeoffed to the people; it being understood that by people is meant the populace of Paris, that is to say, some fifteen thousands of persons, of whom a fourth part are in good faith, and the remainder being made up of such worthies as had a hand in the assassination of General Bréa.

The ideas upon the subject of communism, represented principally by M. Blanqui, were sufficient at first for the most exacting; but as they formed, after all, only a mere programme, there arose a set of cavillers who rendered necessary a complete plan of social revolution. The system of Babeuf, it is true, was still extant; had been re-edited, and was always resolutely adhered to by Messrs. Buonarroti and

Charles Teste; but these two old chiefs intermixed their doctrine with so many religious precepts, that it seemed ridiculous to the neophytes of the new faith. Besides, there were men among them who, fancying themselves the stuff of which heads of schools were made, undertook to get up a new gospel. Messrs. Laponneraye and Lahautière, in a paper called the *Intelligence*, which made its appearance in the times of the *Seasons*, commenced the communist movement; but not, however, with that boldness, and those external evidences of profound conviction which take with the masses. It was not till the throes consequent upon the 12th of May, not till the legal proceedings wherein the accused emphatically and flatly laid down their principles of absolute equality, that the monstrosity of communism first had its birth. New Messiahs from unknown regions were then seen to come forth, boldly preaching the subversion of everything which had thus far been approved of by human reason and experience. On the one hand were the initiators, teaching by the pen and the word, such as Messrs. Pillot, ex-priest of the French Church; Savary, journeyman shoemaker; Desamy, a literary pirate, sprung from no one knows where; J. J. May, Charassin and Pelletier; and on the other hand were the propagators, preaching their doctrine in drinking shops and other such places, such as Messrs. Rozier, Vellicus, and Lionne, who abandoned, one his bench, another his needle, and the third his comb, for the purpose of taking the apostleship.

The most distinguished transaction of these men was the banquet of Belleville. The republic of those days, in order to show some signs of life, had got up at Chatillon, near Paris, a banquet, the guests of which were reckoned by thousands, and the communists resolved to reply to it by another banquet at Belleville, at which the numbers present were about equal. The police thought that this anti-social festivity might be tolerated with safety, believing that the ideas emitted there would annihilate each other; a conclusion which was not altogether ill founded; for at that time the follies of pride and covetousness fell before the general good sense of the people. Hence, men who were well known for their radicalism, such as Doctor Lessere, for instance, were seen to withdraw from the cause, and repudiate emphatically the doctrines of the banquet. However, it is not safe to permit charlatans to sell their medicine, even in the times of the very best of health.

The rhapsodies of Babeuf, augmented and improved by the addition of many others, were revised by M. Desamy and published under the title of *The Code of Commonalty*, and the poor man might have added, *for the Savages*. Although M. Desamy was in favor of commonalty rigorously construed, mathematically adjusted and immediately carried out, he declared, nevertheless, that after the revolution he intended to go to the house of M. Rothschild, fill his pockets, and walk off. Walk off where? and fill his pockets for what? Was he not to share again with others? It is painful even to refer to such deformities; but hideous as they are, they were surpassed in ugliness by the physical deformities of M. Desamy. It were impossible to conceive anything more revolting than that physiognomy of his. A retreating forehead, a small eye unequally timid, a venomous mouth, and a skin smelling like a corpse, the whole animated by brutal avidity and cowardly pride, caused one to turn away from him in disgust.

He had collected together all the rags and fritters of his Utopian predecessors; and not long afterwards, still another Messiah, M. Jean Joseph May, made his appearance, announcing in the prospectus of a paper called the *Humanitarian*, a programme which ran as follows:—

"1st. We are to tell the whole truth.

"2d. The principles to be advocated by this paper are materialist.

"3d. We demand the abolition of families.

"4th. We demand the abolition of marriage.

"5th. We adopt the arts, not as a diversion, but as a duty.

"6th. We proscribe luxury.

"7th. We desire the abolition of capital, or centres of direction.

"8th. We desire the distribution of trades among the commonalties according to the circumstances of place and necessity.

"9th. We desire the development of travels."

As a beau ideal of communism this is certainly not wanting in vigor; and even the most fastidious of amateurs might be satisfied with it. But Mr. John Joseph May, who is since dead—may the genius of commonalty keep his soul!—was no mere common man; for M. Proudhon himself has deigned to borrow from him. The famous system of anarchical government, that is to say, a government without either governors or governed, is nothing, more or less, than the property of the late Mr. May.

One fine day, when all these splendid ideas, well digested and redigested, seemed on the point of becoming lost to the world, M. Cabet stepped in, and with a genius for invention which had certainly never yet turned one of his hairs gray, undertook to found a speculation upon communism. Taking quiet possession of the labors of his friends as the groundwork of his system, he wrought out a romance called *A Voyage in Icaria*, which he considered as the ultimatum of the question. Fearing that his book might be seized, like a pettifogger well versed in the expedients of chicanery, he administered it to the public only by gentle doses, giving it no publicity, and issuing but a small number of copies. As the work, from all appearances, would soon become lost in the shades of oblivion, the authorities took good care not to give it a chance for life by a prosecution at law. But the authorities were duped; for when the legal term of seizure had expired, the edition was drawn from the shop, announced by handbills, and distributed in profusion.

Rather a low and tricky part, one would suppose, to be played by a benefactor of humanity—in fact the gross monkeyisms of the sorcerers of the middle ages can hardly give any idea of his manœuvres. Shrewd, cunning, and with a mouth habituated to all kinds of subtleties, he pretended to frankness, and talked roundly in terms of candor and honesty. Knowing well what influence experience has over simple minded men when concealed under the exterior of good nature, he set his snare, baited with all sorts of the most delicious incitements, and took care to place it only in the way of the unsuspecting and the innocent. His book was the prospectus of a vast association which it was designed to establish, and which he partly succeeded in organizing by the following means.

His first adherents, fascinated by the austere fanaticism of his language, had to become absorbed in the will and glorification of their master. To spread the doctrine by every possible means and extol the man through every note in the gamut—such was the order of the day. A multitude of pamphlets, trivial in character but marked by a singular exaggeration of logic and eulogy, were sent to the faithful with orders to sell them. All of them came from the hands of the master; and if the eye of a man of sense should happen to alight upon them, he could not refrain a shrug of the shoulders at the absurdity, bad faith, and interested avidity of homage which they exhibited. They were nothing but the portrayals of an impossible state of happiness, given in terms of serious buffoonery—mere testimonials of veneration addressed to the apostle in the form of letters. The energy of these missives signed either by unknown or fictitious names, was enough to disconcert a face of brass; M. Cabet reprinted them with all the composure of the stoic.

The first moneys received from the sale of pamphlets furnished the means of dispatching agents into the provinces for the purpose of organizing the propagandism. These agents carried bundles of pamphlets with them, the sale of which was confided to their patriotism; it being understood that the sales were to be for money down. A point which M. Cabet regarded as by no means of the least consideration. In one of his pamphlets, published about the year 1843, called *The Masks torn off*, he showed who were to be considered as bad patriots. And who of them, according to his way of thinking, were the most criminal, and the most unworthy? Why they, to be sure, who injured in any way the sale of pamphlets. Such a one had undertaken the sale of Icarian commodities and had abandoned it; he was a doubtful democrat. Another had taken credit, by which the chest had suffered a loss; he was a suspicious character. Still another had openly cried down the merchandise; *he* was evidently a traitor. The pamphlet, in short, was a perfect monument of impudence.

The director of Icarian affairs, knowing how the ground lay, never strayed off into refractory localities, but addressed himself solely to the centres of the working population. Through the assistance of his agents he established nuclei of communists at Lyons, Toulouse, Limoges, Marseilles, Mulhouse, Saint Quentin, etc. The personality of these nuclei was always the same, the leaders consisting of ambitious men and fanatics of low degree, and the rank and file of poor wretches seduced by flattering visions of happiness and equality.

If the reader is curious enough to know the doctrine itself, it can be explained in a few words. It amounted to but little short of taking society and shutting it up in barracks; but the men, women and children, instead of going to drill, were to go to their work of some kind, under the command of a corporal. Bed and board were to be in common. As names would become useless, persons were to be designated by numbers. Family relations were to be licensed; that is to say, one might take a newly born child and adopt him as a son if he chose, or make to himself any other relation, accordingly as might be agreed upon by the society. With respect to religion there was free opinion; should any one wish to occupy himself with such trifles he would be free to do so; the social direction had nothing to say upon that point. The abolition of property followed as a matter of course; personality being abolished, everything pertaining to it disappeared together with it. The principles of justice for the government of Icarian life were very fine. The old men were to occupy the first story, as being the most comfortable; married men the second story, and as for young and active men, they were to perch in the garret, etc. As for a political organization in such a state of things, it would be useless to think of it; for as the whole world was to become Icarianized, states and empires would disappear of course, and together with them all national interests and differences. None of the influences now in operation were to exist in the new state of things. If you were an artist, a painter, an orator—you might exercise your talent if you pleased, but at a fixed hour, under certain conditions, and by the word of command given by your corporal; you might belong to a different section from the planter of cabbages, your neighbor, but still you would be only a mere number, like him; and when called to dinner, you must eat soup out of the same wooden bowl with him, enjoy perforce his gracious company, and have no taste or habit of a higher order than his; for that would be aristocracy, and destructive of the beautiful level upon which the whole institution is based.

It is no easy matter to conceive how such follies as these, the first consequence of which is the destruction of all liberty, could have found either preachers or disciples. Nor did there ever exist, we venture to say, one single Icarian among enlightened men, of good faith, or who pretended to any principle whatever. It is only by referring to that instinct which leads the lower order of men to level down to their own height everything around them, and by considering what great inducements an assured existence without the trouble of a family offers to certain unfortunate men whose life has been always precarious, that one can come to comprehend the existence of a public under such doctrines.

Icarianism, then, made its proselytes; but heresies, however, soon disturbed the unanimity of the church. M. Cabet, whose doctrine tended to the complete overthrow of society, pretended that his views were pacific; that his disciples were the agents of an idea of peace and fraternity; that the excellence of this idea would prevail of itself, and that all that was necessary was to let it shine before the world. Whether the apostle had the simplicity to believe all this, is doubtful; but it is very certain that the principle of propagandism by exclusively moral means, was inscribed at the head of the Icarian code, and that the true faithful conformed to it. It can be readily understood, however, that men of greater boldness or frankness could not reconcile themselves to such a pacific course; and hence dissensions and sects arose, orthodox pretty nearly as to faith, but disagreeing upon the manner of establishing the system. The majority wished to proceed by revolutionary means; and they were certainly not at fault in their logic; for, to undertake the destruction of the instincts, the tastes, and the interests of society simply by the force of argument, is a pretension which would hardly be considered practicable.

Communism, then, became divided into little schools consisting of resolute men, the majority of whom were ancient conspirators. M. Cabet, whose supremacy was no longer recognized, excommunicated them in his pamphlets; but it was labor thrown away; for these men were seriously bent on practical results, and they had no hesitation in saying that the inventor of Icaria was a knave.

These groups were joined by some of the sections of the ancient secret society. But the discipline which the laws of September had rendered necessary, and which the committees of the *Families* and *Seasons* had succeeded in establishing, was felt to be too constraining by the sectionaries: passive obedience and the interdiction of all discussion in the official meetings, gave no room for the exercise of pride and vanity. As this want of discussion checked propagandism and led to desertions, some of the chiefs set the example to their men of opposing it; but the majority, however, remained firm, and the society existed in that state of demi-organization in which we have exhibited it. The communist sects remained isolated among themselves, a prey to the jealousies of contending cliques, and emulating each other in exaltation and extravagance.

CHAPTER IV.

A strike—Revolutionary petulance—The communists of action—Messrs. Rozier, Lionne and Vellicus—M. Dourille parades his troops—An harangue upon the boulevards—The equipment of M. Rozier—Arrests.

ENLISTMENTS for the new *Seasons* still went on. M. Dourille, from a state of obscurity the year before, had run, seen, and talked so much that he had revolutionary Paris at his fingers' ends. There was but one other man, perhaps, who knew better than he all the names of the conspirators; that man was M. Martin Bernard; but there was still another man who could ferret them out sooner from the depths of their dens, viz: the prefect of police.

Not all the friends of M. Dourille, however, enrolled themselves in the secret society; the old patriots had burnt their fingers and dreaded the fire. Enlistments were hardly possible, except among a class of crotchety fellows and in the workshops; it was in the workshop alone that implicit submission and respect for old forms were still found. A group of students which the indefatigable propagandist discovered in the Latin quarter, and who were affiliated as representatives of the *Youth of the Schools*, did not do quite as much honor to the association as had been anticipated; they were very glad to have the title of conspirators, something which is very flattering to young men when about to leave college; but they preferred playing billiards to making proselytes, and as to discipline, it may readily be imagined that they never carried its practice to the extreme of abuse.

Notwithstanding all difficulties, however, M. Dourille succeeded in the formation of an imposing army. But by the word imposing it must not be understood that he had drawn together such masses as made up the *Rights of Man;* for since the enactment of the law against associations and the code of September, secret societies of four thousand sectionaries were no longer possible. The *Seasons* had never counted more than twelve hundred members; M. Dourille, with their organized debris and his new recruits, had arrived at a total of about fifteen hundred men. Of these, eight or nine hundred were disciplined, and the rest ready to take arms whenever the affair should be undertaken.

In the hands of any other chief this force would have been formidable; the Blanqui committee had attacked the government with a much smaller one; but M. Dourille had neither the head nor the audacity of his predecessors. Between himself and his recruits, with the exception of the sections commanded by the four revolutionary agents, there was no reliable bond of union; a fortuitous circumstance, the imprisonment or retreat of the chief, might at any time reduce the association to four grand disciplined battalions.

Besides, though M. Dourille knew how to group together, he had no skill at organization; he was a man of extreme zeal, but of no method. In confiding his plans to many of the old patriots, which he did out of pure vanity, since he knew that they were disgusted with secret proceedings, he rendered the existence of the conspiracy publicly notorious, and thus deprived it of its prestige, and at the same time prepared the way for his own ruin. This result, to which I was then involuntarily instrumental, is the one which I pursued, and which, subsequently, I partly realized.

At this period a very serious event occurred. We allude to the strike which, it will be remembered, took place in Paris, in 1840. Thirty thousand working men, deserting their workshops, spread themselves over the quays, the public places, and the environs of the city; laid siege, as it were, to industry, and excited those alarms which are occasioned by popular commotions. Divers leaders among the trades came to an understanding with each other, and got up a sort of congress for maintaining the workingmen in their course. This habit of resorting to strikes, the honor of which France has all to herself—a sad honor, which impels to the sacrifice of a real interest for the chance of gaining a chimerical advantage, had never presented an aspect more truly alarming and deplorable. But circumstances were very unfavorable for the factions; for the indignation against the attempt of the 12th of May was still warm, and the miserable failure of that affair was not calculated to inspire hope. If, however, the revolutionists were compelled to renounce an outbreak on political grounds, they had, at least, what is called the social question on their side; there, at least, were the means for excitement. To audacious men of a popular character, an occasion was presented for producing the greatest mischief. It is one of the merits of M. Dourille, that he found himself unequal to the task of giving this crowd the signal of eruption. He went to the heights of Saint Chaumont, where for two days the industrial army lay encamped, and where Paris with all her riches lay spread out at their feet, tempting them, no doubt, more than once, with the reflection that they had only to will it to become its possessors; but wisdom and prudence prevailed; and besides, the chiefs who might have been able to launch this mass against society, were wanting. M. Dourille, the only representative of an organized popular force, felt himself stifled in the midst of the honest prejudices of these men, who believed that they were justly pleading for the bread of their families. He confined himself to interviews with the leaders in which his democratic old stories were not listened to, and nothing that he could say was appropriate to the occasion.

They who saw this army suspended over the capital like an avalanche, but which dissolved of itself without leaving a trace behind, can fully perceive how serious the real workingmen are when left to their own judgment, and what value they put upon the vain hopes which are sought to be instilled into them in the place of their true interests. In view of this instinct of right reason which lies at the bottom of their heart, we can only pity them, sincerely, when they go astray; but we must detest the men who make it a profession to deceive them.

Hence, from the directorship of M. Dourille, may be dated

the decadence of secret societies. On the one hand, the heedless zeal of the chief deprived the association of its power of mystery, and on the other, the discussion of the communists introduced an element of discord. Other causes, among which may be mentioned the discovery of treacheries, and especially the uncertainty in which the men were kept as to the time of the revolt, contributed to a general debilitation.

It may be conceived, that among so many avaricious or credulous characters, who regarded the overthrow of the government as the object of their ambition, or the end of their ills, a lively impatience must have been felt; but even supposing that the day for the revolt had been fixed upon, according to their wishes, it would have been improper to make it known to the crowd. They understood this at first very well; but when whole years began to pass away without the revolt being attempted, lassitude and indifference began to be predominant. In his orders of the day, as well as in his conversation, M. Dourille indulged freely in empty words and brilliant promises; but the positive language which the conspirators wished to hear, was never uttered. The chief well knew the terrible importance of formal declarations; the example of M. Barbès, who had been hurried by his colleagues into a catastrophe which he had foreseen, was a lesson that had not been lost upon him.

In order to pacify his men, he endeavored to amuse them with plans of strategy and numerous other fine inventions of which he was the author, but which, however, proved quite insufficient. The old mobbists, confused more and more by explanations which they could not comprehend, came at length to take their chief for what he really was, viz: a very ordinary sort of a man.

Spurred on by self-love, and wishing at least to exhibit his forces, M. Dourille had been seeking for some time an occasion for a parade, when a favorable one seemed to offer itself, by the death of M. Garnier-Pagès. The funeral procession of this radical deputy would furnish the pretext for one of those manifestations, which were becoming too rare to be neglected by the republicans. The *National*, therefore, the chief organ at that time of the democracy, convoked its partisans, including a number of students, who were held in leash by the leaders. The *Montagnards* also passed the word to their men, although these were very much scattered, and pretty well recovered from their former audacity. Then came the society of M. Dourille, republican in opinion, but tending to socialism; and finally, the communists of both colors, those in favor of peace following the Icarian banner, and the revolutionists, under the orders of Messrs. Rozier, Lionne, and Vellicus. Of these three Luthers of the suburbs, who, in their impiety, had dared to assail the Icarian Rome, we may say a few words. M. Vellicus, a journeyman tailor, had at first marched forth boldly under the banners of his chief; but finally becoming cooled off, M. Cabet, with all the awful vindictiveness of an offended deity, visited the rebellious apostle with annihilating fulmination. Knowing that M. Vellicus had been imprisoned in London, for an attempt against good morals, he made the fact, in all its minutest ugliness, the subject of a pamphlet. Hence, the tailor very naturally passed over to the enemy, and became a revolutionary communist. M. Rozier was a little young man, horribly nervous and violent, who had deserted the society of M. Dourille, because that chief did not even know his first syllables in the science of communism, and had had the impudence to prevent discussion upon that important subject. He was considered, and not without reason, as the most active dissolvant, both of the secret society and the Cabetist sect. M. Lionne, as he declares himself, follows the profession of artist in perruquery; he is a dull, mild mannered, light complexioned man, who is in no way distinguished from other poor working men who set themselves up as prophets.

Conventicles were held on the eve of the funeral, both in the camp of M. Dourille and in that of the revolutionary communists. The latter, when carefully summed up, might possibly have numbered one hundred and fifty men; but as they had all Paris on their side—such is the usual pretension of these miserable wretches—M. Rozier had no hesitation in voting for the insurrection; and, in fact, he declared that he would fight all alone by himself, rather than not fight at all. M. Dourille and his lieutenants were not quite so determined. However, orders were given to the groups to hold themselves in readiness in case that some favorable event might call for the signal of attack. But in reality there was no intention of coming to an issue, and no one anticipated it.

The procession was a solemn one, and numerously attended. All the opposition of the left, deputies and citizens, were present in mass. They formed, together with the idle persons who usually mingle in such ceremonies, the main body of the procession. The republicans claimed the whole as a part of their effective strength. The truth is, there might have been counted, altogether, about three or four thousand men, a number which had varied but very little during the whole reign of Louis Philippe. The friends of the deceased, or in other words, the men of the *National*, might have been recognized by their self-sufficient air and parliamentary bearing; the *Montagnards* and the bands of Flocon, Raspail, and other fragments of former conspiracies, by their unpolished exterior and dogged looks, and the popular fractions, by their blouses and other corresponding signs. At the head of these latter appeared the troop of M. Dourille, machinery in good order and with all the evidences of an organized corps. They went arm in arm, divided into sections, which were headed by chiefs, who were easily recognized, and who moved from point to point, preserving the symmetry of the march, and transmitting to their subordinates the orders which they received from the chief supreme. But there was nothing in all this which seemed to be very dangerous. The little troop of conspirators, and especially their chief, seemed much more desirous of making a display than of fighting a battle. It can be understood, however, that the police, being aware of this band of revolutionists, took its precautions. Annoyed by such manœuvres on the part of the chiefs, and knowing that there had been signs of action manifested on the day preceding, it narrowly watched this suspected corps and surrounded it with a hedge of mounted men of the municipal guards. One of the guards accidentally caused some annoyance to the ranks, and was assailed with invectives; and thus a disturbance ensued which gave M. Dourille an opportunity of showing his authority. He mounted upon a corner-stone, ordered a halt, and delivered an harangue, the object of which was to appease the excitement. He was listened to not only by his own men but by those of the police. They could not understand such pacific language on the part of a chief of conspirators. Many of the patriots, also, and especially those of the *National*, could hardly believe their ears; they found the acts of this new Catiline a little too transparent.

In the mean time a small group of revolutionary communists under the orders of M. Rozier had assembled at a wine seller's on the borders of the canal. M. Rozier, armed with a pistol, burst out into violent discourses, accompanied with epileptic gesticulations. He wanted to fire his pistol at some one of the municipal guards, no matter which, and thus give the signal for the fight. His companions held him by the collar and endeavored to make him listen to reason; but in vain, for the little man becoming more and more excited, finally jerked himself loose from his keepers, rushed out of the shop, and fired at random into the crowd. Fortunately no one was hurt by it; and the police coming up took him into custody.

This was the only incident of any note that occurred during the ceremony.

For several days afterwards the band of men of the people, with its chiefs and discipline, which had made its appearance in the procession, was the topic of general conversation; and the least observant had detected in it a secret association. As the notoriety of the fact occasioned some uneasiness, the police thought it their duty to restore quiet by taking measures which would show their knowledge of the affair; and M. Dourille, together with many of his lieutenants, was arrested.

CHAPTER V.

The attempt of Darmès—Abominable instigations—A pistol fired at the princes—New free and accepted judges—Sentence of death—Its consequences.

At this period, and separated by about the interval of a year, two attempts at assassination were made upon the royal family. On the 15th of October, at the close of day, a man stationed himself upon the *Place de la Concorde* with the view of waylaying the carriage of the king, who was going that evening to Saint Cloud. As the king approached, this man drew out a carbine from under his vestments, took aim, and fired. The contents of the charge lodged in the panels of the coach. Arrested upon the spot, there was found on his person a work of M. Dourille, entitled: *The Conspiracy of General Mallet.* His name, as was soon ascertained, was Darius Darmès. On being asked what his profession was, he replied —a conspirator. Like Alibaud, he had but one regret, that of not having killed the king, whom he regarded as the greatest of tyrants.

This wretch was an emanation from the secret societies. He had belonged to the communist groups, together with two of his friends, the too famous Considère and a coachman by the name of Duclos, both of whom were arrested. Darmès had listened to the preachings of the republican apostles, had studied the apologist of political crimes, and had finally come to dream only upon one thing, viz: to carry out the doctrines which he had been taught. Since the chiefs, M. Dourille among others, were more ready to preach the destruction of the government than to execute it, the disciple, a man of ferocious energy of character, took it upon himself to push their principles to their natural consequences. He withdrew from the societies; shut himself up in infected lodgings, and there, a prey to wretchedness and delivered up to habits of idleness and debauchery, he gnashed his teeth in fiendish rumination over his execrable projects. In the rage of his fever he seized the pen and composed patibulary verses. Some of these verses were found, in which he glorified Alibaud and his admirer, Laura Grouvelle, and declared that the race of regicides was not yet extinct. At last, lashed up by demagogic maxims to the highest pitch of frenzy, he went and bought a carbine, and coolly consummated his attempt at assassination.

He was condemned to death and guillotined. His friends, Considère and Duclos, were acquitted.

Several months afterwards, a timber sawyer by the name of Quènisset happened to be confined in Sainte Pelagie in consequence of a quarrel. He was a worthy man, seeking to gain a livelihood without making any pretensions to reform the state; but a weak minded man withal, and with a head easily excited by wine. Some of the communists who shared in his captivity got around him, and finding him a courageous man, resolved to make him their tool. By the time that they left prison they had worked upon him with such success that the poor man was entirely at their disposal. But in order to keep him more effectually under their control, they affiliated him as a member of the *Equalitarian Society*, one of those communist fractions of which I have spoken, the tendency of which was to realize the doctrines of Charassin, May, Desamy, etc.—a second edition, in short, of the *Revolutionary Communists*. Between the principles of these two small groups there was but very little difference; numerous divisions were necessary for making places for all the chiefs.

Quénisset and one of his friends named Boucheron were taken to a wine-seller's shop, and there introduced, with their eyes bandaged, into a room where eight members of the *Equalitarians*, Brazier, Mallet, Dufour, Launois, Jarasse, N. Bazin, Boggio and Petit, were present, charged with their initiation. Petit being the president, he explained the object of the *Equalitarians,* which was the destruction of the throne; the establishment of *National Workshops;* a commonalty of life, wives, and property, and in fine, the realization of all the principles of pure communism. He then put a few questions, such as we have already mentioned in the formulas of the *Families,* and *Seasons,* and finally concluded by administering the oath, which, in order to frighten the candidates, he rendered terrible. Quénisset had given proofs of an impressionable nature, and they wished to make the most of it. "Raise thy hand," said the president to him, "and swear upon thy head that thou wilt divest thyself of thy property and thy fortune, that thou wilt leave wife and children, that thou wilt obey the first signal for the battle and fight unto death, however great may be the number of thy enemies! Think well; this oath is sacred; and if thou violatest it, not only thou thyself, but thy wife, thy children, and thy family—all shall be massacred! Swear, then, upon this dagger, which I hold in my hand, and which is designed for thee if thou betrayest thy word."

Seized with terror, but not daring to recede, the unfortunate man took the oath. His eyes were then unbandaged, and they gave him liquor in order to stimulate his courage. For some time he was hardly allowed to be out of their sight; they dragged him from one lodge to another, where he heard of nothing but pillage and murder, the demons who beset him thus familiarizing him with a crime which they dared not commit themselves.

On the morning of the 13th of September, Brazier took him into his room, and presenting him two pistols, said:—

"The moment of execution has arrived: Louis Philippe keeps himself close, and we cannot reach him; but three of the tyrant's sons are going to pass through the suburb of Saint Antoine with the 17th regiment which is returning from Africa, and the committee have agreed to sacrifice them. Here are pistols, and thou wilt fire when the signal shall be given thee; if thou failest to fire, thou knowest what to expect; we shall keep our word."

Frightened by this threat, Quénisset took the pistols and

set out. At the entrance of Traversière Street he found the whole band of his accomplices—his comrade Boucheron, Boggio, Mallet, Jarasse, Petit, and Brazier himself, who had joined them. From there they went to Montreuil Street, where they met the regiment coming in from the suburb. The Duke d'Aumale, its colonel, was at its head, accompanied by the Dukes d'Orléans and Nemours, who had gone out to escort their brother in. Brazier, who stuck to Quènisset like a tiger to his prey, waited until the princes were within pistol-shot, and then pointing them out in a group of officers said :—

"Now is your time, fire !"

The poor man raised his pistol at random and pulled trigger.

His companions, who were to have followed his example, seeing that none of the princes fell, got rid of their weapons and took to flight.

Quènisset, struck with horror at the idea of his crime and of the abominable machination of which he had been the victim, immediately made a full confession. He asked protection for his wife and child against the wrath of his enemies; but as for himself he submitted to the rigors of justice.

He was condemned to death by the Court of Peers, and the king pardoned him.

About the same time there took place in the *Seasons* a drama of another kind.

One evening, about 9 o'clock, the revolutionary agents convoked their chiefs of groups and repaired, each separately at the head of his little group, to a cook-shop in Couronnes Street, where they formed themselves all together. This general rendezvous was known only to the four lieutenants of the committee. The chiefs of groups did not know whether they had been called together in a simple assembly of sections or in one of the corps; nor did any one know the object of the meeting. M. Dourille had merely said that there was a matter of importance on hand.

For some time past I had been considered as the chief of a group in the society, and I was present at this meeting.

We ascended to a hall in the second story, from which the public were excluded; and the master of the house, who was known by the chiefs, was requested not to allow servants or any other persons to enter, as it was necessary that the meeting should not be disturbed.

A sort of presentiment, amounting in some cases to a positive annoyance, began to take possession of the assembly. The serious air of the chief, usually so open and loquacious; the mystery enveloping the object of the meeting; the vague expressions uttered by the revolutionary agents who seemed to be in the secret—all these indications gave rise to suspicions which increased the anxiety. Some extraordinary communication was expected.

M. Dourille, in a solemn voice which excited emotion, at length broke silence. He referred to the object of the society, which was the destruction of tyrants and the enfranchisement of the people; expatiated upon the sacredness of this object and the honor to be derived from its pursuit; and then, coming to the duties of the members and the oaths which they had taken, he asked what ought to be thought of a man who had abandoned the holy mission which he had thus taken upon himself to perform.

Some one answered that he ought to be considered a coward.

"And what if that man," continued M. Dourille, "not satisfied with deserting his post, should pass over to the enemy?"

"He would be a traitor."

"And if when having given up the secrets of his brothers he should turn against them?"

"He would be a wretch."

Every one remained struck with astonishment and indignation; some of them looked around restlessly with suspicion; but the majority maintained an anxious reserve, fearing to look at their brethren lest they might discover in them evidences of guilt. The object of the meeting was thus made known to all; but although nothing had yet transpired to show that the guilty man was present, yet every one feared that he was.

M. Dourille resumed:—

"When a man has behaved in this manner—when betraying the confidence of the chiefs he has come to occupy a grade in the society and has made arrangements for divulging its important secrets—what fate does he merit, according to our rules of justice?"

I arose and replied:—

"He deserves death."

I was near the door, standing up, with one hand upon the latch and the other in a pocket of my overcoat, where I carried a pistol; and I was decided, in case of an attack, to make my way out by the use of my weapon. However, I had no positive apprehension of danger, inasmuch as I knew that four of the members of the meeting were of the police.

Silence ensued, after which M. Dourille, calling upon the four revolutionary agents, two influential chiefs of groups and myself, requested us to pass into an adjoining room in order to examine the proofs of the accusation. The rest of the assembly had orders not to leave their place, and not to go out of the room on any pretext whatever.

The treason had but one proof; it consisted of a letter without signature, which called for explanations of certain facts with regard to the society. From the wording of this letter it appeared pretty plainly that between the police and the person to whom it was addressed there existed a regular correspondence. The letter had been accidentally sent to a man of the same name as that of the person to whom addressed; it had been opened, given to a patriot, and by him was turned over to M. Dourille. It remained to be proved that the letter was authentic. The accused would not fail to pretend that it was a machination designed to ruin him; that the letter, fabricated by the police, had been designedly missent, and that instead of being an agent, he was on the contrary a victim, of the authorities. To these anticipated objections it might be replied that the paper was recognized as that used in the offices of the prefecture, and particularly by M. Pinel, Secretary-General; that the writing was also of that functionary, for the two had been compared. And even supposing that the police had designed to ruin one of the chiefs of the association, is it probable that they would have chosen one of little note when they might just as well have aimed at one of more importance?

The seven members having the proof of guilt before their eyes, and weighing the observations of their chief, declared that there could be no doubt as to the treason.

Being agreed upon this, M. Dourille and his council returned to the room where they had left the chiefs of groups.

It can be imagined that the anxiety there had not diminished. Among some fifteen men there was one who was going to meet with a fulminating condemnation, and, beyond a doubt, with some terrible punishment; yet no one could imagine who the guilty one was to be; they were all alike in a state of agitation, and how, in the midst of a general paleness of complexion or shrinking of manner could it be told which arose from indignation and which from fear?

As for myself, I was out of the question; but there were still three men over whom the result of the deliberation hung suspended like the sword of Damocles. These three men were wholly unaware of the part played by each other, and each of them, therefore, might expect the blow to fall upon himself.

M. Dourille announced the name of the man who had just been found guilty by a first tribunal, and produced the evidence of the conviction, in order that every member might examine it for himself. He then demanded of the accused what he had to say.

Overwhelmed by the evidence brought against him, the man at first could only stammer out a vague denial, but soon recovering his *sang-froid*, he exposed as well as he could the system of defence which had already been foreseen by M. Dourille. He came at length by degrees to assume a tone which was not wanting in firmness nor unaccompanied with some pretty natural displays of indignation.

He was a man of little education, though rather intelligent, of a dark complexion and strongly defined features, who had thus far always borne the reputation of a very excellent patriot.

When he had made his defence, which gave rise to some doubts in his favor, M. Dourille resumed, and declared that the reasons which he had advanced had all been anticipated and replied to beforehand in the secret deliberation which had just been held: and that what had been said in that deliberation he would repeat, in order to leave no doubt upon the subject.

He then repeated his arguments one after another, and bore with stress upon the improbability and uselessness of explanations in face of the facts furnished by the letter. But as these arguments did not produce their due effect, the accused immediately replied to them with warmth, and, acquiring assurance in proportion as his cause appeared to be less bad, he finally succeeded in increasing the doubts which already existed.

But the majority, losing patience at a firmness which they considered as impudence, arose with a threatening air, and made known that they had heard enough, and were satisfied.

"The matter is understood," said one of the revolutionary agents, "and there is a sentence to be rendered. Silence!"

M. Dourille, in a solemn tone, then pronounced these words:—

"Citizens, swear to observe the sentence which I am about to pronounce."

The majority of the members swore.

"I declare," replied the chief, "that the accused is convicted of the crime of treason, and that, according to our rules, he merits the penalty of death. . . . ."

A threatening murmur interrupted these words, and it could be seen that sanguinary thoughts were beginning to occupy the minds of the crowd.

M. Dourille continued:—

"You have sworn to execute the sentence; but you are prohibited, be it understood, from exercising any violence here; the hour of execution will come, and justice will be done, but under conditions and at the time fixed upon by the committee. In virtue of your oath, I order you to dissolve, and leave the condemned man to his remorse; at a later day he will be smitten by your wrath."

The conspirators grumbled out their dissatisfaction, but offered no resistance. Soon afterwards the meeting broke up, and the members dispersed in different directions. The man who had thus been sentenced, escorted by two or three friends who remained faithful to him, slipped noiselessly and speedily along the houses, and was soon lost in the dark.

While descending the staircase of the cook-shop, some of the chiefs of groups, who had shown a sinister disposition, had opened their knives, with the design of rushing upon him; but, fortunately, the responsibility of a murder not being to the liking of all, the assailants were held in check, and prevented from the commission of a crime.

CHAPTER VI.

The revolutionary congress at Lyons—The wife of a conspirator—M. Callès—M. Bonnardel—M. Jailloux—A session of the conspirators.

ONE of the four revolutionary agents, M. Chaubard, having retired, the chief of the association offered me his place. I refused at first; but finally, after much affected reluctance, accepted it. Scarcely had I entered upon its functions, when an affair of great importance occurred, in which I became mixed up in the following manner: About the month of June, 1842, a letter came from Lyons to M. Dourille, which immediately occasioned a meeting of the four lieutenants of the society. The letter was read, and its contents were seen to be of the very first importance. The committee of Lyons had formed a plan of insurrection, which they considered decisive, and were making arrangements for its execution; but, before coming to the issue, they wished to have the approbation of the principal cities, in order to generalize the movement. With this object, a congress had been called at Lyons, to which delegates from the revolutionary centres were invited. Paris, especially was expected to send a delegate, in order that he might judge of the state of affairs, and give his opinion, which would have great weight.

The letter had been written by a manufacturer of silk cord, by the name of Callès; and, as a sign of recognition, he had sent the half of a billet, which was to be presented by the delegate as his credentials on his arrival in Lyons. The reader will remember that this M. Callès has already been mentioned in connection with the insurrection of 1834.

It was immediately decided that the call should be responded to, and all that remained was to determine who should be charged with the mission. M. Dourille having declared that his pecuniary circumstances would not enable him to meet the expenses of the journey, the choice was to be made from among the four revolutionary agents; and as among these there was only one who could afford to go, they, of course, fixed upon him. That person was myself.

Furnished with the sign of recognition, I set out for Lyons, where I soon arrived. Repairing at once to the place pointed out by the billet, I found a house with broken windows, and bearing all the external evidences of being uninhabited. Surprised at this, I began to examine the premises, and, finding the handle of a bell-cord, I pulled it at a venture. After a long time had elapsed, a noise began to be heard, and there made his appearance an old sort of a doorkeeper, who seemed to be living there in the midst of ruins. I inquired for a certain dame to whom I had orders to present myself, and asked if she was to be seen. The good man replied that she did not live there, but that he knew her residence, and would point it out; which he did.

The dame resided in a retired alley, which I discovered only after much difficulty. She proved to be a woman pretty well advanced in age, of masculine features, and dressed in a manner that showed her to be a member of the working classes in easy circumstances. Showing her the sign of recognition, I asked her if she knew what it meant. She perceived its import at a glance; and drawing out another piece of paper she compared it with the one which I had presented.

"Yes," said she, "it is indeed here that you were to come; you are the *Brother* whom we were expecting from Paris—you are welcome."

She offered me civilities; served wine; entered into a conversation upon politics; inquired after the patriots of the capital, and expatiated upon the events of the day with a loquacity and warmth which showed a very highly cultivated state of democratic education. More and more astonished, I was beginning to consider whether this woman could be the person to whom I had been accredited, and if it was expected of me that I should have to do with a conspiracy in petticoats, when an end was put to my quandary by the entrance of a man whom the virago addressed as follows:—

"I introduce to you our brother from Paris; he has given me his passport and it is all right—here are the two halves of the billet."

This man was M. Callès, the manufacturer of silk-cord from whom the letter had come to M. Dourille. Saluting me in a reserved manner, he took the pieces of paper; examined them attentively, and then came and took my hand.

"We were only waiting for *Paris*," said he, "and since you have come we will commence our work to-morrow. If you please to follow me I will introduce you at once to the other delegates."

He led the way, hurried on at a rapid rate, and conducted me to a hotel in Bât-d'Argent Street, where the majority of the members of the Congress had taken lodgings.

At the first sight of this man one could see that he was the type of a conspirator in earnest. He was small, lean, and nervous, with a broad forehead and a Roman beard; and upon his tight skin the swelled veins stood out, filled with vigorous blood. From the manner in which he verified the sign of recognition, some idea may be formed of his *sang-froid*, and his whole appearance gave evidences of a composure amounting to severity. Thin lips, a wrinkled brow, a short quick smile and a furtive glance of the eye, all showed a man of intelligent energy and a suspicious disposition.

At the hotel we met with three other delegates, one of whom had also but just arrived and been installed. This was M. Imbert, formerly a director of the *Sovereign People* of Marseilles, but at that time a travelling wine agent. He had come expressly all the way from the north to represent Lille, Valenciennes, and other places. A veteran in conspiracies, maintaining a regular intercourse with extravagant men in every quarter of France, he mingled more or less in every manœuvre of the Revolutionary cause, but without ever having directly under his orders a single organized corps. Neither at Lille or Valenciennes was there a secret society, properly speaking; a nucleus of patriots, held together by a community of hatred against the existing order of things, constituted the whole contingent of the republic in those places. M. Imbert had had an interview with them before setting out, and had agreed to inform them of the result of the conference at Lyons; and such was his true position in the congress. But over and above this restricted part, he might be called on to act in a more extended sphere; for in case an attack should be given, his numerous acquaintances in the departments would enable him to communicate orders at a great many places, and thus prepare these places for responsive outbreaks to the principal movement.

The two other delegates had come to represent, one Toulouse and Carcassonne, and the other Marseilles. The latter, a man of the lower classes, of little education, but a resolute character, was chief of the street porters of Marseilles. He held under his orders, in virtue of the double influence of his social and political position, an exceedingly energetic corporation.

The delegate from Toulouse and Carcassonne could not claim such a decided influence. The places which he represented had become infected with communism; and in consequence the party had separated into two intrenched camps, one consisting of pure revolutionists, and the other of idealists who were more or less pacific. The powers of this delegate had come from the latter; but as the objects of the congress were to be accomplished by force of arms and violent means, he found himself in a very embarrassing position.

Besides these representatives, the congress was expecting another from Grenoble, a man of little consequence, a glove-maker by trade; but whose patriotic antecedents had secured him the honors of the delegation.

Hence, the members of the conference, excepting those of Lyons, amounted to five. Many of the cities had excused themselves from sending delegates, on the ground of a want of disposable men; and others had declared that they would be bound by whatever resolutions might be taken.

M. Callès having introduced me to my colleagues, said that he had some business to attend to, and withdrew, appointing a rendezvous at ten o'clock that evening.

We soon issued from the hotel, and, conducted by M. Imbert, went to a coffee-house, *Place des Terreaux*, where another member of the conspiracy was expecting us.

To judge by M. Callès, the revolutionists of Lyons were engaged in no child's play; and this opinion was confirmed by the appearance of the man whom we found in the coffee-house. His name was Bonnardel, by profession a banker's clerk. He was a young man, of delicate features, who made a very pleasant impression by his open countenance and deliberate manners. The reception which he gave us was cordial, and without the least affectation. He showed no signs of self-importance from the prominent part that he was playing. Many of his friends, who were scattered about the room, were not aware of his secret position. Far from affecting mysterious airs in order to give rise to suspicions in favor of his vanity, he chatted gayly, going from one person to another, and finally passed off in the most natural way in the world, as a jovial good fellow who had got through with his day's work.

After a few manœuvres of this kind very well played off, he proposed to take a walk; and while still talking in a lively tone, he led us to another coffee-house of an uninviting appearance, at the further end of which was a private room which he had hired, and where we found ourselves alone.

As soon as the doors were closed, his whole aspect became changed. This little man, who had been so lively, became very serious; and the subject which he was about to broach might justify the change.

"Gentlemen," said he, "you have come from various quarters in order to examine a plan of insurrection which is very well conceived, and above all very audacious, but I must make known to you at once that I do not approve of it; and why? —the reasons I shall give you this evening in presence of my colleagues. However, I should not conceal from you that my opinion is in the minority; and I will add that, whatever may take place, I shall do nothing to oppose the operation of the plan. Our committee is composed of three members—Callès, Jailloux, and myself; my colleagues being agreed upon action, we have appealed to the most influential members of our association, and they have decided against me. A large majority having decided to go on, I am silent; but since you have been called in to give an imperative opinion in the case, I reserve the right of making known to you the motives of my disapprobation, and I hope that you will appreciate them. Be not deceived as to my intentions; my design is not so much to influence you as it is to avoid surprise at the opposition between me and my colleagues, and to prevent the impression of there being a division in our army. As to a division, there is none, since the men are agreed upon action, and have an entire confidence in my colleagues. By these few explanations you will be enabled to understand our relative positions in the discussion of this evening. I have nothing further to say at present, ... and now, if you find it agreeable, while waiting for the hour of the rendezvous, we will go and breathe the air of the Rhone —I have some good cigars to offer you."

We repaired to one of those avenues of trees which shade the quays of the Rhone, and there commenced a conversation upon things in general, enlivened by the fumes of tobacco and the starlight of a beautiful evening.

At ten o'clock M. Bonnardel led us to the place of meeting—a large room, which served M. Callès as a workshop, and which contained neither chairs nor furniture. A plank placed upon two stools supplied us with seats. An oil-lamp lighted up a part of the room, dimly disclosing amidst the obscurity a few machines for spinning silk, the blackened rafters of the roof, and the four dingy walls—a fit and impressive scene for the machinations of a band of conspirators.

The third member of the committee, M. Jailloux, was present. A clerk, like M. Bonnardel, he had given up his place several days since in order to devote himself wholly to the preparations for the enterprise; and this fact may give some idea of his character. With him, as well as with M. Callès, the plan of the insurrection had become wholly absorbing. For the space of three months they had prosecuted it through difficulties and with a perseverance that bordered on fanaticism. Although the equal of his colleague as a conspirator, and superior to him by education, he nevertheless yielded him the precedence; but a perfect harmony reigned between them, and that was the main point with the ex-clerk. His person, like that of his confederates, was small and thin, and to judge of these three men merely by their frail appearance, one would have smiled at the idea of their attempting to carry by assault the second city of the kingdom. In matters of this kind, however, it is not safe to scoff at anything; for the revolutionary vertigo never shrinks from the wildest attempt, and every attempt may be followed by torrents of blood.

M. Callès arose and stated the business of the meeting. Now this M. Callès was a very cautious man, and exceedingly methodical in everything he did.

"We shall submit for discussion this evening," he said, "the general idea of the enterprise; to-morrow we shall furnish the citizen delegates with the circumstantial details of our plan and its means of execution; day after to-morrow we shall examine localities and indicate the points of attack, and then we will put our deliberations to the vote. And finally, we have proposed to give the citizen delegates a review of our men, to conclude with a fraternal banquet, at which the citizen delegates will doubtlessly please to be present. For the present we may proceed to exhibit the state of our affairs. . . . . If citizen Bonnardel would like to speak first, he has the floor."

These latter words were uttered in a tone that evidently displayed a degree of acrimony; in short, it was the tone and manner of a Robespierre when provoking explanations from a man whom he had already marked out for the guillotine. The Lyonnais chief, indeed, was animated by a thirst for domination not less excessive than that displayed by the tyrant of the convention. His means of despotic rule were the same—puritanical pretensions, a cold enthusiasm, and the management of the masses through their worst instincts. A resemblance might also be traced between M. Bonnardel, his adversary, and some of those open characters who dared to oppose the terrible frown of Robespierre; the name of Camille Desmoulins occurred to the memory when the young man, with his good looks and fine manners, arose to address the language of reason and sentiment to a malignant fanatic.

M. Bonnardel commenced his explanations at once. He gave several details concerning the secret society; then came to speak of the plan, and finally entered into a long discussion which we need not repeat. It is sufficient to say that the plan was as follows: During the festivities of the Three Days of July, while the authorities should be at the cathedral attending the mass commemorative of the victims of those days, to seize upon all the forts by a *coup-de-main;* take two cannons from the fort of Fourvières; fill them with grapeshot; point them upon the door of the church, and then, when the authorities, civil and military, were coming out, to fire away and cut them in pieces. This butchery was to be the signal for the insurrection.

The abominable absurdity of this plan was seen at a glance. M. Bonnardel, in his endeavors to demonstrate it, sought to avoid giving offence to his colleagues; but his reasons were well set forth, and appeared conclusive to the delegates. M.

Callès bit his lips in a rage, but restrained himself till the conclusion of the speech. Then rising to reply, he declared that the arguments which had just been heard were very good in one point of view—that of fear; but for his part, that was not the point of view in which he should look upon matters. In the remarks which he made, however, he showed no want of confidence in his adversary, but rather a domineering impatience of opposition. His idea was, that in conspiracies the best course is the one which presents the most difficulties, and that the nearer the plan approached the impossible, the easier would be its execution; for all foresight and precaution on the part of the authorities would thus be transcended. In fact, according to M. Callès, the plan ought to succeed precisely because of its inconceivable rashness. M. Jailloux adopted this opinion, and shared fully in the astonishing confidence of his colleague. In the presence of such resolute men the delegates hardly knew what to say; they feared being considered as timid; but still, they could not help regarding the plan as rather fantastic.

In fine, M. Callès did not rest solely upon the force of his arguments. Satisfied for the present with having counterbalanced the opinions of his rival, he pretended that the hour was too far advanced for further discussion, and concluded by appointing a rendezvous for the next day. He knew that the occupations of M. Bonnardel would prevent him from being present, and expected, in his absence, to become master of the ground, and in order to be more certain of evading his dangerous adversary, he forgot to designate the place while in his presence, making it known only to the delegates themselves.

CHAPTER VII.

Details of the plan—Examination of localities—A nocturnal conventicle—Repast of the conspirators—Decision—Why the conspiracy proved a failure—Reflections.

According to the prescribed order of business, the second session was to be devoted to an examination of the details of the plan and its means of execution. For this purpose the delegates were led to a dram-shop, in a retired place out of the city, where tipplers usually repaired only by night. Having first breakfasted heartily and to the no small scandal of the two puritans of the committee, they then addressed themselves to their work. M. Callès drew forth from a case several carefully preserved plans of the forts of the city; spread them out upon the table; explained the general system of defence, and then marked such points as he conceived should be the points of attack.

A consideration of importance, and one upon which he laid great stress, was, that the works were hardly finished, contained neither armament nor garrison, and were guarded only by detachments of the police. Some of them were to be carried by means of ladders descending into the ditches, from which the main body of the works could be taken by surprise; others by a direct attack, and main force, the police being shot down at arms' length and the conspirators passing over their dead bodies. In order to facilitate this plan, fire-arms of a particular model had already been ordered, and were to be furnished to the conspirators—short copper blunderbusses, of a large calibre, which might be concealed either under the blouse or overcoat, and thus enable the bearers to approach the police without exciting suspicion.

All this was explained with so much minuteness and assurance that the delegates began to regard the plan as practicable. It is true, the enterprise required a terrible degree of resolution and a perfect precision of execution; but still, after all, it was not impossible. The question which remained to be examined, and by far the most delicate one, was whether the persons to be employed would prove capable of the execution, and above all, if it would be possible, while waiting the appointed time, to prevent betrayal by some indiscretion or treason. This point had not been forgotten by M. Callès.

According to his way of reckoning, success would be rendered certain in proportion to the fewest possible numbers engaged, and that sixty men would be enough. Ten conspirators to each fort, with their blunderbusses charged to the muzzle with slugs, could force their way in and take possession; and the proper men were on hand ready for the work. The secret society counted about six hundred members, and the advance guard had been chosen from among them with great care. Neither the day nor the means of action had been communicated to this chosen corps; but every one of its members had been taken individually and informed of the plan which had been meditated for a long time, and had given his oath to hold himself in readiness to obey the orders of the committee at any moment and with implicit submission. No explanations were to be given them until a day or two before the attack; and even then, the men would be merely warned to perform their oaths without receiving any positive information as to what they were to do. Not till the day of the affair, and but a few minutes before the execution, would they be minutely instructed; and the ten men appointed for each attack should swear not to quit each other for a single moment, but to keep up a mutual watch upon each other, in order to render all treachery impossible.

Such were the explanations of M. Callès with regard to the manner of carrying out the plan and the persons by whom it was to be executed. As to the generalization of the movement, that was to be effected in the old way, by the usual common-place means in such cases—the posting up of notices announcing insurrections, and the proclamation of the Republic in Paris, Lille, Toulouse, and Marseilles; sending trusty persons to spread reports in the popular quarters that the insurrectionists were in possession of the forts; that there were arms enough for the people, etc. etc. The working classes being once armed, the chiefs of the association would immediately form them into corps, by the combined operations of which the whole city would become enveloped. The working people, on learning the capture of the forts and the destruction of the authorities, which would be half the victory, would not fail to declare for the insurrection.

As feasible as the plan appeared, however, it could never have been entertained by men of reflection; for in fact a single accident interfering with the combinations might cause the whole to prove a failure. But the delegates were very willing to be convinced; and as the demonstration of the ferocious Lyonnais had been rigorously exact, they finally yielded by admitting his arguments. M. Imbert was the first to yield; and the deputies from Marseilles and Grenoble followed his example. From the want of the proper powers to stipulate positively for his constituents, the communist delegate did not express his opinion. As for myself, being deeply interested to know what would be the end of this abominable folly, I appeared to coincide with the opinion of the majority.

On the following day the manufacturer of cord came, agreeably to his programme, to take us to see the forts and give us a tangible view of the points of attack as indicated in the plan. He had said that he should come at an early hour; and by five o'clock in the morning he was at our hotel, Bât-d'Argent Street. He was accompanied by his aid-de-camp, M. Jailloux; M. Bonnardel was absent that day, as he had been the day previous.

The first fort to be examined was at Fourvières, and to that point we bent our steps. M. Callès was perfectly familiar with the topography of it; he gave us several details of its interior, and then led us around the outer circumference in order to show us how negligently it was guarded. Around a very considerable extent of fortifications there were but two or three sentinels, between whom it would be very easy to slip into the fort. This fact established, the Lyonnais, all the while walking on in order not to excite suspicion, requested two of the delegates to follow him to a place where the ground declined, and where the approach was facilitated by a sort of ravine.

"Here is the road," said he, "to be followed by my ten men. Now come to the edge of the ditch, and I will show you how easy it will be for us to enter the place. I say us, for I reserve the command of this attack to myself; it is the most important one, since upon its success depends the possession of the cannons for the destruction of the authorities."

Arrived at the edge of the ditch, we saw directly below us and against the wall on which we stood, a flight of stone steps which, ascending from the bottom of the ditch, stopped at about two-thirds the height of the wall, at a door leading to a subterranean vault.

"Now a ladder," continued M. Callès, "thrown from this point to the head of that staircase, is a very simple matter, and once in the ditch, we go to that little door which you see yonder, and which communicates with the interior; it is closed only by a latch, I am certain of that, and we enter the fort. Without troubling ourselves with the small garrison, a part of which will be at the review, we rush at once upon the station of the police, take possession of it, and then open the gates to a platoon of our men in the vicinity, who will enter, and arm themselves. In case of resistance, our blunderbusses will open us a passage; fired at so short a distance, the charge of slugs ought to kill four or five men at a shot. As soon as the fort is taken, the men will drag the cannons out, and follow the road which I will show you."

Rejoining the rest of the group, he led us to the front of the main gate of the fort, and from there, following a road wide enough for a train of artillery, we soon arrived at the site of the Observatory, from which point the city of Lyons lies spread out below like a map.

"This," continued he, "is our most important position. You have seen that there is no difficulty in bringing the cannon here; and what a place it is for a plunging fire upon the door of the Cathedral, and a part of the *Place Bellecour!* We have old artillerists for pointing the guns; and the matter will be properly attended to, you may rest assured of that."

The inspection of Fourvières through with, M. Callès led us to the fort of Guillotière; then to those of the Croix-Rousse, and finally to that of Montessuy, which commands the two quays of the Rhone. At every point, the same careful measures had been taken, and every plan of attack had been conceived in the same spirit of audacity.

From their long exploration, begun at six o'clock in the morning, and ending only at nightfall, the delegates returned to their hotel, worn out and exhausted. But the two members of the committee, whose fanaticism seemed to give them muscles of iron, continued their work, by attending the meeting of one of the sections in the suburb of Vaise.

The next day M. Bonnardel came to see the members of the congress, and found them completely won over to the opinions of his adversary. Their enthusiasm was not equal to that of M. Callès, but it had been proved to them that the plan was a feasible one, and self-love, co-operating with conviction, had determined them to support it. The young man was rather vexed than surprised; for he knew what effect the dogged obstinacy of his colleagues was capable of producing. Seeing his cause lost, he declared that in view of an inevitable catastrophe, his conscience forbade him from going any further, and that he should withdraw.

During the day, a council was held, at which the delegates were invited to give their official opinions. Those from the North, Marseilles and Grenoble, voted unreservedly for the insurrection; the one from Toulouse and Carcassonne pledged himself under conditions, and I gave my vote also with the understanding that it would have need of ratification.

A meeting had been appointed that night, for the principal members of the society, and M. Callès, as he had said, intended to introduce them to the delegates. This interview was marked by the same prudence and mystery which characterized all the other proceedings of the conspiracy. At ten o'clock, the two members of the committee led the delegates through devious streets, to a point beyond the city limits, and from there, their route lay through narrow paths, along hedges, and over pastures and cultivated fields. At eleven o'clock the party arrived upon a newly-mown meadow, where their attention was attracted by black masses covering the ground. The committee directed their steps towards these objects, which, to all appearances, were flocks of sheep in repose; but on our approach, the heads of men began to be distinguished, and we could soon perceive some twenty-five or thirty men of the laboring classes, whose forms, seen amidst the darkness, seemed to be endowed with a strange impress of energy. These men were the principal members of the association. The delegates seated themselves in their midst, and made such remarks as were called for by the occasion. They divulged nothing of the plan, but spoke of hopes about to be accomplished, of a glorious conflict, and a certain triumph; of everything, in fine, which went to the mark; that is to say, which kept alive excitement, without giving any information. The interview was prolonged until one o'clock in the morning. A very simple precaution rendered a surprise impossible; the group formed a circle around the speakers, each one facing outwards, so that nobody could approach without being seen.

At a dinner given the next evening, in the suburb of Vaise, the delegates met again, with the principal persons of the nocturnal meeting. M. Callès directed the model arms, which had been ordered for the insurrection, to be brought, and submitted them to the inspection of the delegates. They consisted, as I have already said, of short copper blunderbusses, capable of being concealed under the blouse, and of containing a handful of slugs, which, by the flaring of the muzzle, would be scattered over a considerable space. These huge pistols might also contain a large charge of grape-shot. Either by accident or design, two of these instruments of death were laid upon the table; and thus remained there during the whole repast, to which they seemed to impart a peculiar tone and character. The dinner, in fact, was a sort of patriotic debauch, pervaded by a sombre joy, and unenlivened by one single trait of natural gayety. The guests separated only at five o'clock in the morning. A good many heads, by that time, had become lost amidst the fumes of wine; but the two members of the committee had not drunk —their thoughts were elsewhere.

A last session was held, at which the previous resolutions were repeated and confirmed; and then the congress declared its labors finished, and broke up, appointing another meeting at Lyons on the 26th of July. It was agreed that each of the represented cities should send a new delegate at the moment of the insurrection.

Such was the plan; and I have thought it necessary to give it in detail. On returning to Paris, and reporting to M. Dourille what I had seen, I found that he was much more surprised than delighted; the incredible temerity of the scheme astonished his irresolute spirit. However, things had gone so far, that he feared the possible consequences of refusing to take a part in it; and it was decided that Paris should hold herself in readiness, and await the result of the Lyonnais explosion.

All this took place in the month of June, 1842. Three weeks afterwards, a horse took the bits in his teeth, ran away, and broke the head of the heir apparent against a stone. France was struck to the heart with mourning and grief, and an emotion of kindness drew the country still nearer to a family, and to institutions which were regarded as the palladium of national safety. The most obstinate perceived that, in such a moment, the effect of a conspiracy would be to group the whole nation around the royal family. M. Callès himself, penetrated by this conviction, gave up the execution of his scheme. He wrote to Paris that the enterprise was adjourned; and a thousand causes, in such cases tend to render an adjournment definitive.

And now, a few reflections:—

If the government had exposed this savage scheme, and delivered up to public indignation and the rigors of the law those men who designed to prelude social chaos by an infamous slaughter—would the journalists of the radical party have failed to say, and their good readers to believe, that it was all another machination of the police? But the proofs of the conspiracy exist, nevertheless, and the actors in it cannot deny a word that I have said. It is not wholly useless, perhaps, to enlighten the public upon the declarations made by a certain class of newspapers, with regard to secret proceedings. I venture to affirm, and I have some knowledge of what I am saying, that with the single exception of the *Reform*—and that has not known all by any means—there is not a newspaper which has had any knowledge, during the last ten years, of one in a thousand of the revolutionary schemes which have approached, more or less, the point of execution. The opposition newspapers may declare *à priori*, flatly, and by force of argument, that a complot is imaginary; but they know nothing about it, for the plotters certainly do not go to inform them. In fact, the newspapers, as viewed by conspirators, are mere old fogyisms, which, under the pretence of prudence, recommend only resignation and servility. How is it possible, indeed, that there can be any relation between conspiracies and the press? The press seeks for distinction, and expresses its thoughts openly; while a conspiracy is safe only when enveloped in silence and darkness. The press is based upon an industrial speculation which is obliged to observe all kinds of respect for the law; while conspiracies exist only beyond the pale of that law, which they labor to destroy. The writers for the press, excepting those who conspire (and such never have the direction of newspapers), are ignorant of the first syllables of what is going on in the subterranean regions of demagogism. There is one institution, however, which is considered as knowing something of the business, whose duty it is to penetrate these misty regions; and if from this institution, there comes a cry of alarm, putting society upon its guard, it is only after having watched the course of anarchy for a long time, and finally sees it about ready to spring for the possession of power, like the tiger upon his prey. It may happen, it is true, that when about ready to burst forth, it may be checked by some cause or another, by fear or prudence, but supervision and precautionary measures are not, therefore, the less necessary. At all events, between passionate men, who flatly deny things which they know nothing about on the one hand, and serious men, who affirm facts which they ought to know, and have the means of knowing on the other, can there be any room for hesitation on the part of an impartial public? It were useless to repeat to me the eternal old babble, that complots are means made use of by the government; for are there not quite too many real conspiracies among us, to give any occasion for getting up pretended ones? In a country of wolves, does the shepherd make use of mock wolves to frighten his sheep with?

CHAPTER VIII.

M. Flocon becomes a conspirator again—A meeting at the coffee-house of Saint Agnès—A Revolutionary decision—Fear of the laws of September—Nomination of a committee—A failure.

WHILE the death of the Duke of Orleans occasioned new disquietudes among the monarchical party, it reanimated the hopes of the republicans. The conspirators of any note, with the exception of the three heroes of May, had not given any signs of life since the passage of the laws of September. A great many of them, it is true, had been, until the amnesty, either shut up in prison, or dispersed in exile; but still, an important fraction of them had remained at large in the streets of Paris—and was it from the want of inclination that they had ceased to trouble the country? I cannot say that it was; but it is nevertheless true, that until 1842, they never budged an inch.

Among those who composed this fraction, may be mentioned Messrs. Recurt, Flocon, Felix Avril, N. Gallois, Fayolle, Sobrier, Bonnias, Cahaigne, etc. At the period of the dynastic catastrophe, these men had already been joined by a part of the general staff of the *Rights of Man*. Messrs. Godefroy Cavaignac, Guinard and Marrast, had returned from England and Belgium; but the latter was called to the direction of the *National*, and had no design to conspire *materially*. As the fortune of M. Guinard permitted him to wait, he chose to follow the course of events; and as to M. Godefroy Cavaignac, not only were there no longer elements of conspiracy equal to his capacities, but the offensive annoyance which he had suffered in connection with the affair of April, had sunk deep into his heart. The Lyonnais party, represented by Messrs. Lagrange, Banne, Caussidière, Tiphaine, etc., was then in the provinces, bound over to keep the peace, and had little or nothing to do with the affairs of Paris.

This nucleus of action which we have just mentioned, had no chiefs. Among the members, M. Flocon pretended to have the greatest influence, although in reality it was possessed by M. Recurt.

The obscure profession of stenographer began to weigh heavily upon M. Flocon. Determined to leave this miserable position, he sought to take charge of some newspaper, by which he might preach democracy as he understood it. The radicalism of the *National*, the only anti-monarchical paper of that time, was far from realizing his beau ideal; for he flattered himself that he alone was possessed of all the oraculism of democracy—this oraculism consisting, in fact, in a strict application of the measures of '93 to the society of the present day—something quite impossible.

Failing in his efforts to become editor, and thus play a part in the world of the press, he resolved to get up a party of adherents among the men of action, and organize a secret battalion. The occasion offered by the death of the Duke of Orleans was a favorable one; for this unfortunate event had aroused the old revolutionary instincts; and the idea of a regency was peculiarly flattering to the republicans, since its establishment, or the embarrassments that it must meet with, gave them great hopes of a triumph.

M. Flocon set to work. He called together at the coffee-house of Saint Agnès, Jean-Jacques Rousseau Street, an assemblage of republicans, chosen from among the most trusty persons of his acquaintance. About forty patriots, almost all of them ancient conspirators of the times of the *Rights of Man*, responded to the call. The small troop whose names I have given, made their appearance there in the first rank. All these gentlemen pretended to the exercise of liberal professions, although some of them never had any professions at all, and were what might be called the bourgeoise democracy. The *popular* democracy was represented by M. Dourille and his principal lieutenants. After several precautionary measures, M. Flocon opened the meeting as follows:—

"The members of the meeting will be pleased to remember that, against certain contingencies, our object at present is, to establish a newspaper, or in other words, an industrial enterprise which will have a right to the protection of the laws. . . . . . This point being admitted, nothing will prevent us, either from prescribing the course to be followed by the paper, or from an immediate inquiry, for example, as to what is best to be done under existing circumstances. A terrible blow has just been dealt against the present dynasty. The important act of transmitting the throne, which certain qualities of the Duke of Orleans might have rendered easy, is now subjected to the difficulties of a provisional government, called a regency, and to the obstacles presented by an unpopular prince. You will conclude, perhaps, that the occasion calls for the consideration of the patriots. I propose then, to submit for your discussion the course which the republican party might be called on to pursue in the case of certain contingencies, such, for example, as the death of the king."

The establishment of a paper was one of those malicious pretences which M. Flocon has repeated on numerous similar occasions until they have become monotonous; however, it was as good a trick as any other, and had but little to do with the main point of the meeting.

The first orator was decidedly in favor of an attack.

"The death of the king," said he, "is a precious occasion; there will be trouble in the government, disturbance among the authorities, and excitement in the streets; and besides, it will be a natural signal given to everybody; let us decide that on that day all the citizens shall resort to arms."

This opinion was very much relished; first one orator sustained it, and then another, and so on. It met with but one single opponent—some one who was foolish enough to entertain moderate notions and advance reasonable arguments. He observed that the time fixed upon for the attack was precisely that in which the government would be most upon its guard. It is certain that every possible measure would be taken for a safe transmission of the throne; a formidable force would be held in readiness, sustained by the moral force of the republican party, which would be united to a man to meet the test. Would it not be wiser to wait until the distractions of the regency should offer some better occasion? By pursuing a decisive course of action under circumstances which might prove unfavorable, the party might become compromised and its success indefinitely postponed.

Such arguments as these might certainly have been adopted without incurring the penalty of treason; but he who is versed in revolutionary matters would naturally expect, nevertheless, to see them rejected; for the patriots of whom such meetings are made up, are more like sheep, in one respect, than any other people in the world, following their leader, who is generally the most violent, under all circumstances, thinking that this is the only way in which they can show the greatness of their patriotism.

As M. Flocon contented himself with presiding over the meeting, without giving his opinion, but showed at length that he agreed with the majority, the assembly concluded that a longer discussion was unnecessary, and the question of an attack, on the death of the king, was put and carried.

One of the republicans of those days did not make his appearance at the meeting of the coffee-house of Saint Agnès. It is his habit never to be forward; he prefers to know something of the question, and be assured of his men, before taking part in an affair. Conspiracy is a fire which he has no desire to play with; not that he condemns it, by any means, for while abstaining from it himself, he is very willing to see it engaged in by others, and even encourages them in it, reflecting, and very wisely, that it may be made to serve his turn in some way or another. M. Recurt possesses all the ability which is pretended to by M. Flocon, but without any of that fidgety bitterness which is constantly neutralizing M. Flocon's efforts at finesse.

The meeting at Saint Agnès coffee-house, then, had decided that on the death of the king the patriots should resort to arms. This rule of conduct being once adopted rendered it necessary to prepare for the consequences; and this matter was attended to at another meeting, held, some time afterwards, at the barrier of Saint Jacques. The same men, with a few exceptions, were again present. M. Flocon declared that the object of the meeting was to prepare forces for the anticipated event; but as many of the patriots, even among the hottest of them, were very much afraid of having anything to do with secret societies, it became necessary to disguise things by means of words, and especially to let them understand that they would incur no danger.

This evidence of fear, inspired by the idea of resorting to illegal associations, is a remarkable fact, which shows the salutary effect of the political laws of that time. The patriots have managed to retort upon these laws that they were the mere instruments of dynasty; but since France is at last in a position to decide clearly upon the matter, she sees that the admonitions of this pretended barbarous code were designed for men who were even then scheming for a real barbarous code, not only in politics, but in every civil and religious institution of the country.

In order to quiet the fears of the patriots, M. Flocon proposed as follows: That those present should form the general staff of a revolutionary, initiative corps for the day of action; no rule nor hierarchic chain of connection should be imposed, no lists of members, no orders of the day, no periodic meetings, nothing, in fine, which should constitute them a secret society, and bring them within the purview of the law. The only thing to be done by the members would be to hold themselves in readiness, and make proselytes. The process of affiliation would be performed by a simple promise of devotion to the objects of the society.

Certainly, this was not a conspiracy; but an enterprise thus hemmed in with restrictions, and depending upon an uncertain date, which might be far removed, could not evidently accomplish much; hence, when M. Flocon urged the necessity of reorganizing a corps of direction and attack, something which, as *he* said, was no longer in existence, M. Dourille and his friends gave the orator to understand, with a smile, that he did appear to be very well posted up in the demagogic affairs of Paris. M. Flocon, in fact, considering himself as the centre of the republican world, had taken no part in conspiracies since the days of the *Rights of Man*, and hardly knew that there were any conspiracies in existence. This fact may serve to show both the isolation of M. Flocon in his own small church, and the change that had taken place in revolutionary plotting; it had been driven to the darkest caverns of the capital.

M. Dourille arose, and made several remarks, which appeared rather surprising to those present; however, he abstained from details, divulging neither the condition of the secret society, nor the grade which he held in it.

As M. Flocon wished to preserve the initiative, and as the assembly had no relish for becoming merged in the association, which had been hinted to them, the words of M. Dourille produced but little effect. The organization, as proposed, was accepted. It then remained to take a final measure, which, though accompanied with some of the perils that the meeting wished to avoid, was, nevertheless, indispensable; I refer to a commission for the direction of proceedings. It was decided that this power should be secret, should watch the course of things, decide upon the course to be followed in case of extraordinary events, or call a meeting for the purpose, and, in fine, make all material preparations possible for the day of the insurrection. The members of the commission were limited to four. A vote by secret ballot took place, and then the meeting broke up. One of the persons present had been appointed to count the votes; and he alone was to know the result, and communicate it to those who were elected, and as it was seen that he himself would be one of the four chosen, the commission might thus remain the sole possessors of their secret.

Messrs. Flocon, Gallois, Grand Louis, one of the revolutionary agents of M. Dourille, and a fourth member composed the committee.

It may well be imagined that this semblance of a secret society proved fruitless of results. In such cases, if the danger lies in organization, it is there also that lies the force. It was very natural that the members, after the lapse of some time, having no stimulus to maintain them in their first zeal, nor any reasonable expectations of the immediate death of the king, should gradually forget their mission and cease to make proselytes; and hence, the association found itself, at length, reduced to something quite vague and impalpable; or in plain terms, it proved a perfect abortion.

CHAPTER IX.

Retirement of M. Dourille—The new committee—A few words upon secret agents—New orders of the day—Honorable proceedings of M. Delessert—The communists of Toulouse—A delegate sent to Paris—Simplicity of the *Icarians*—M. Flocon becomes a committee-man of the *New Seasons*—Review of the groups.

By the close of the year 1842 M. Dourille had relapsed very much from his former zeal. He perceived that the men of note in the party held him in but very mediocre esteem.

He was reproached for the harangue made at the funeral procession of Garnier-Pagès; for permitting the seizure of a list of members with comments thereon, and for other imprudences not less real. He might well have received some consideration for his obstinate propagandism, for his lost time, for leaving his wife and children without bread and without resources; but if gratitude is not a virtue of kings, it is not that of republicans either. The party shows about the same respect for a used-up patriot that is usually paid to a worn-out hack horse. Deeply mortified, and tired, moreover, of his miserable life, he thought of retiring.

At this period Messrs. Gallois and Noyer had entered into a partnership for the establishment of a bookstore; and having need of an employee, and knowing the position of M. Dourille, they offered him the place, which he very gladly accepted. They were among those who considered him wholly unfit for the trade of conspirator, and they obliged him to renounce it entirely. It was very hard to leave a work which had cost him so much labor; but when he came to think of the annoyances which he had suffered, of the necessities of his household, and, above all, of the remote hopes of the republic, which were becoming every day more vague and uncertain, he silenced his grief and gave up.

The four revolutionary agents were assembled and informed of the resolution of their chief; and from that moment the direction of the society was given into their hands. M. Dourille explained that as his withdrawal was occasioned by domestic considerations, it should produce no change in the state of things. He requested his particular friends to rally around the committee; the orders of the day would be issued by De la Hodde; and in other respects there could be no difficulty, since the men were already under their command.

Each of us deeming it proper to fulfil our new functions, the combination was accepted, and we assumed the sovereign power. By this arrangement I found myself nearly in the position which I desired. Besides the advantages of education and social condition which I possessed over my colleagues, I had the reputation among the groups of being a man of prudence and good counsel. Being by nature neither high nor low, my manners were not unpleasant to the suburbans. I spoke their language pretty fluently, and we were not at all ill at ease together. Hence, I had the necessary influence for the new part which I wished to play in the association.

In times of revolutionary fever, the secret police is necessarily restricted to a certain course of conduct which is not exactly that of provocation, as it is called, but which consists in a connivance of words, and acts with the leaders of the parties. Generally speaking, it is very certain that for inspiring confidence and getting at the secret of important measures, a man of the police would do very wrong to show opposition or moderation. He is to follow the current and mingle with it; such is his part, and such are his instructions. A thousand times the cry has been raised against provocative agents, and a thousand times the accusers have been put in condition to furnish the proofs, and have failed to do so. The police of M. Gisquet has been particularly charged with these manœuvres; but has it ever once been caught in the fact? and as to the administration of his successor, that cannot be reached by such attacks; for the high morality and loyalty of character of M. Delessert are above a certain order of calumnies. But that an agent may assume the mark of those whom it is his business to watch, and imitate them, not only in the violence of their words, but in their acts—nothing is more certain; it is the very alphabet of the trade; it has been practised ever since the police had an existence, and always will be practised so long as political supervision shall be considered necessary. Such a course, it is true, does not exactly quadrate with perfect morality; but since it is the principal means for accomplishing the end, if the end is to be attained the means must be admitted.*

* It is needless to say, perhaps, that such an argument as this would hardly pass current in the United States. It is the Jesuitical doctrine that the end sanctifies the means; and in France and Southern Europe it is often practised by those who censure it in their adversaries. The politicians of our own country do pretty much the same thing in excusing their own faults by pleading those of their opponents.—TRANSLATOR.

However, there is still a better means—there is still a better course to be followed than that of insinuating one's self among the underminings of conspiracies for the purpose of checking them at the moment of explosion; it is to take up such a position that the whole field of operations may be visible at once, and, instead of allowing them to go on in order the better to stop them, to arrest and destroy them from the moment that they are commenced. For the accomplishment of this end nothing more is needed than simply this: to get the direction of revolutionary proceedings, and inspire sufficient confidence and have sufficient skill to lull men of habitual violence into a state of perfect inaction.

And such was the task that, agreeably to my own views and the orders of the prefect of police, I considered myself capable of undertaking.

During the direction of M. Dourille, the orders of the day had made their appearance regularly. The style of these productions had varied but very little since the days of their invention; those of M. Dourille, however, had their peculiar stamp, they were pretty good copies of the Robespierrian originals which he tried to imitate—sharp, dry, and fanatical. In substance they never varied from these three points—propagandism, energy, and approaching hopes. In order not to disappoint my public, I preserved the harshness and asperity of form, but managed to centre my declamation upon these two words—prudence and patience. I intended by this means, constantly preached and practised, first to enervate and then annihilate the secret society.

And it was indeed time to restore some order amidst the furious mania of the undertakers of conspiracy. Could there be anything more detestable than the part played by these men, luring on poor wretches by impracticable hopes to rush headlong into the streets at the first diabolic impulse given them, and only to be massacred? Witness the affair of June, 1842, that of Lyons in 1841, and again in 1844, and that of May, 1849—it is always the same thing; two or three chiefs distinguish themselves, the rest sink into insignificance, and the people leave their corpses by scores upon the pavement.

These men talk of provocation! could there be a more impious provocation than this, practised by themselves—setting a murderous snare for peaceful men whom they find happy at their work, and drawing them forth to incur misery, imprisonment, or the grape-shot of the streets.

The police of M. Delessert had not only the honor of having preserved the tranquillity of the streets since 1839, but of having accomplished it in the most honorable way. But it is true that the state of things permitted the employment of a system of mildness and conciliation, I will not say of fraternity, because that is a term which has been rendered ridiculous. The immense majority of the country, attached to the government which had the rare merit of securing peace, and founding public prosperity, gave up the idea of political squabbles, and was realizing in serenity that well-being which had been lost in the great noise of the revolution. The political franchise was too restricted; agreed, but besides that the abuse of certain liberties had become only too common, it cannot be denied, after all, that the government rested upon its true basis, *i. e.*, upon the middle classes, and that the entrance to these classes was open to all. Nothing then prevented the government from pursuing a lenient and humane course, even with respect to its most inveterate enemies, or from acting upon anarchy only by means of gentle dissolvents. We shall see that, dating from this moment until the days of February, the unfortunate army of conspirators raised by Messrs. Barbès, Blanqui, and Martin Bernard, which had left so many victims either upon the pavement or in the prisons, had no longer an occasion for regretting the loss either of the life or liberty of any one of its members.

Some time after this little revolution in the committee of Paris, the following events took place in the provinces:—

The doctrine of M. Cabet, propagated by the *People's Journal*, by cart loads of pamphlets and by crowds of traveling agents, had made proselytes in the departments of the Haute-Garonne, Aude, and Dordogne. At Toulouse, especially, there was a church of exemplary fervor, too exemplary, perhaps, since it deviated from the dogmas in contemplating an appeal to the musket in aid of precept. There was no spirit of revolt shown against the master; but quite to the contrary, a very natural impatience for the triumph of the cause, and the endowment of France and the world with the felicities of *Icaria*. The chief of these rather eager communists was a painter by the name of Gouhenans, a fine speaker, ardent and extravagant, a type of the enthusiast of the South. He had been led beyond the rules by an intimacy with M. Laponneraye, who had arrived from Paris saying that he was authorized to give new instructions. *The Intelligence*, a poor sheet which had withered away under public indifference, had finally died out; and as the ex-editor was thus left without any political enterprise on hand, he went to Toulouse to gain a livelihood in some way or another. An idea struck him; he took it into his head to upset the *Icarian* altar, and put one of his own in its place. The worship which he wished to establish, was exclusively that of his pamphlets, his books, and collections from his defunct journal. He gave himself out as one of the marshals of the equalitarian republic of Paris; declared that he had under his orders the twelve suburbs without including the vicinity, and that he was in a position to give the *brothers* the very gist of the matter. He admitted that beyond all doubt Icaria was a sublimity; but then the citizens of Toulouse ought not to be ignorant that pacific Cabetism was altogether out-distanced by the communism of action, which, sure of its fact, because possessed of the double force of principle and tradition, was going to resort to arms, and could not fail to triumph. The Toulousians had to look to it if they intended to remain inactive while their brothers were marching to the conquest of the future. By such pathos as this, it was meant, simply, that the revolutionary communists were in a majority in Paris, and that it was necessary to rally around M. Laponneraye their representative, and abandon M. Cabet, who was nothing less than an old fogy.

This communication was considered of immense importance; for a fundamental principle of the doctrine was at stake, and if it should be abandoned, would it not prove to be the destruction of one of the columns in such a magnificently constructed edifice? On the other hand, to be too late at the feast, and have only a bone to gnaw, that was a matter deserving of consideration. It was decided to remain faithful to *Icaria*, but at the same time to enter into relations with the partisans of propagandism by force; it being well understood that a deviation from an article of the *credo* would be made only with the object of arriving more promptly at the establishment of the true church.

A new prophet had thus arisen to scatter firebrands among the faithful and attempt a ravishment of infallibility from M. Cabet—a matter of no small importance certainly, but what was of still more importance, he designed to get all the fruits of the worship? And all this was taking place far away from the high priest, and without his knowing a word of it; for, from a sentiment of delicacy, his disciples in the very interest of the doctrine itself repugned the idea of informing him of the course which they had adopted.

Several months thus passed away, during which remorse assailed more than one conscience. M. Laponneraye had promised news from Paris, which never came to hand; and as time passed on, the disquietudes increased, until the disciples became subject to the most desolating reflections; they feared that they had yielded too easily to representations which might conceal some snare. What a desperate situation for the children of *Icaria*, if the words of an intriguer had led them to doubt their father, and even perhaps betray him!

Under the weight of such overwhelming anxiety, the Toulousians and their brothers of the vicinity held a grand council, and resolved to dispatch an emissary to Paris who might, with his own eyes, see how matters stood, and thus relieve them from their load of troubles. The emissary chosen was a young man of Agen, by the name of L'Héritier. He came pat upon a man who could give him authentic information of all that he desired; that man was myself. We had served in the same regiment together, and hence the preference which he showed me.

I could not refrain a shrug of the shoulders at the recital of the great troubles of the *Icarians*. The mawkish sort of sentimentalism which they showed for their Messiah; the title of father, which they seriously accorded him; the terror that they were in from having perhaps sacrificed to false gods without knowing it—all this excited very great pity. The poor envoy learned how matters stood at once. I informed him that there was no association in Paris in a condition to take arms; those directly in favor of revolution composed but a very insignificant battalion; the communists of various sects were made up of imperceptible fractions; M. Cabet was looked upon as an old pimp beating up for imbeciles, and M. Laponneraye as a very suspicious dealer in political operations who had not thirty partisans in all Paris. Such was the bill of fare that he had to offer to the patriots of Toulouse, and if they did not like it, they might choose for themselves.

The emissary set out on his return filled with consternation.

Oh, what a cloud of desolation swept over the *Icarians* of Toulouse when they came to learn the truth! They launched maledictions upon M. Laponneraye, and hastened to make a confession to the father of *Icaria*, based upon the purest sentiments of contrite repentance; henceforth their zeal should be proof against every seductive attempt—their faith immovable against every shock. And they kept their resolution. The ardor of proselytism redoubled; excitement arose to the highest pitch, and an assembly was held in which the miserable state of society which *Icarianism* was going to set to rights, was so very patriotically described that the attorney general of the king had to moderate the zeal of the most ardent by sending them to a retired place for reflection. They extended their arms towards their father, calling upon him to assist them in the depths of their captivity, and prayed him to come and raise his voice in their favor. M. Cabet could not abandon such devoted disciples in their distress; he went, having first announced himself so as to secure a brilliant reception, and displayed all the treasures of his eloquence in the service of the accused; but as the eyes of the judges were not yet open to *Icarian* lights, his arguments had no other effect than to cost his children a several months' longer term of imprisonment.

Such, towards the close of 1842, were the transactions in the regions of communism; and it has been necessary to relate them in order to give the subject its true physiognomy; but they are characterized by a degree of folly which has appeared to me to render them unworthy of any serious narration.

Not long afterwards, an event of some note also occurred in the secret army of Paris; M. Flocon requested an interview with the four chiefs, expressing the desire to become one of the committee. The combination of Saint Agnès coffee-house having miscarried, and the isolation of the stenographer weighing upon him more and more, he had recourse to an enterprise already under way, and in which he thought he had only to make his appearance in order to assume the supreme authority. The acquisition of the authority appeared to him the more easy inasmuch as the four revolutionary agents had no reputation in the party. I myself was the only one of any note, but I was regarded as a patriot of little ambition and not of the first rank. One evening M. Flocon was led to a meeting of the committee where he made known his wishes. The concurrence of such a man, well known in former conspiracies and renowned for his finesse, could not be refused; but I well knew how to disgust him very quickly with the part which he wished to play, viz: by checking his pretensions and wounding his pride. I had given my colleagues to understand beforehand that our power must remain intact, even for the sake of the association itself, and that in receiving M. Flocon among us, it was as an equal and not as a chief; it was necessary to let him see this at the outset, for otherwise, if we seem to have need of him, he would not fail to absorb all the influence. M. Flocon, then, was admitted, but only as a fifth member of the committee. This condition was stipulated at several different times, so that he could not possibly be ignorant of it. It appeared rather impertinent to the illustrious patriot, without doubt, but he could not take offence at it without showing a total want of tact.

A general review was decided upon for the following week, in order to show the forces of the association to the new chief. It took place at the barrier, upon the Boulevard Rochechouart. The groups were assembled in the environs, and on the announcement of the arrival of the dignitary the chiefs gave the order to file past. The sectionaries passed three by three and arm in arm, being thus distinguished from the other passers by. M. Flocon, accompanied by M. Noyer as cicerone, took his stand at the window of a wine-seller's shop, and from a balcony there, solemnly held his review. His four confederates were at the head of their men, thus showing by their presence the arrival of the different sections. The effective strength was not great; the total of the society was reckoned at eight hundred men, of whom probably about two-thirds would respond to a call; the total present did not exceed three hundred men. They were all in the blouse; for the conspiracy had sunk deep and deeper into the lower strata of the party.

To this review, and to an attendance three or four times upon the meetings of the committee, was limited the part played by M. Flocon in the secret society. With the position that had been granted him, and to which he was closely subjected, he was but little satisfied. Although of a temper not well calculated for sympathy with the masses, being in fact rather unpopular, yet his antecedents were such that he might have imparted some vigor to the conspiracy, if his self-love had been flattered. With the power and the efforts of M. Dourille, the society in his hands would have been restored to its former importance; it would have attracted a few of the old, and some new conspirators, which, however, the government would have been able to put down at their first attempt; and nothing would have been more easy than, by encouraging the stenographer, to lead him on to this result. But the police, by offending his pride, followed a different course; and thus proved that there was no need of giving provocations for repressing the republican faction.

CHAPTER X.

History of the establishment of the *Reform*—Tyranny exercised over M. E. Baune—The poor M. Grandménil—M. Flocon becomes dictator of the Journal.

Little satisfied with renownless and divided glory, M. Flocon sought some means of getting the lead of the democracy, a position that belonged to him of right according to his own opinion. The best means seemed to be that offered by the press, and towards the press were bent all his most cherished desires; but as his talents were only known to himself, the journals showed but very little readiness to admit him as a contributor. Hence he conceived the idea of establishing a newspaper for himself. But the undertaking was by no means an easy one; to draw from a poor writer and a poor party the funds intellectual and financial for sustaining a daily paper, is indeed a difficult problem. The genius of the Republic, however, aiding, the problem might be solved.

At that time M. Grandménil had been washed, as it would appear, from the accusations made against him in 1821, and was thinking of getting up an organ of the veritable interests of the country. Several deputies of a reddish color were to have furnished the necessary funds, but on coming to think the matter over, they left the enterprise in the lurch. The conception remained for a long time in a state of embryo, and M. Grandménil was beginning to despair, when M. Flocon, in company with M. E. Baune, another great man of disposable services, presented themselves and offered to set the work going. The trio soon came to an agreement, and a society of exploitation was immediately formed, to which each one contributed all that he had, viz: an ardent desire to find some one to lend them the necessary money. They assembled their friends, made fine speeches, gave fair promises, and finally succeeded in obtaining the wherewith to set the paper going. Bail was given, all the preparations made, and the *Reform* was launched into publicity one fine morning with 10,000 francs borrowed money in pocket, which was destined never to be returned.

Arrived at the position which he had so ardently desired, that of editor in chief—he was third in fact, but his two co-adjutors gave him no trouble—M. Flocon found himself far above the miserable part of fifth chief of a secret society. He made known then, to the revolutionary agents, that his responsibility as the first publicist of the democracy would prevent him thenceforward from having any relations with them; but as the little insurrectionary army might become of some use to him, he took me into the office with him, hoping, through my agency, to have the control of the association. I very easily penetrated this little scheme, and resolved to thwart it. I had charge of the columns devoted to foreign affairs, at a salary of 1200 francs a year, and during nine months I received about a hundred crowns. Becoming tired of the foolish pride of the ex-stenographer, I abandoned this brilliant position.

The management of the *Reform* was to be shared equally by its three founders; but the establishment of this equilibrium of powers met with a great many more difficulties than did the constitutional equilibrium which the editors scoffed at so divertingly. But a few months had passed away when the prose of M. Baune became banished to the second page, and even had much difficulty in keeping its place there; for it was found to be deplorably turgid and heavy. But it is very true that M. Baune had his opinion, too, with respect to his coadjutor, and could not grant him, by a long shot, a degree of merit equal to his pretensions. He had to content himself, however, by showing his spite among his intimate friends, without daring to proceed to open resistance. Privations, disenchantment, and a life spent in grog-shops, had given him a languid, broken-down character, over which M. Flocon triumphed without pity. Receiving the offer of travelling agent for the paper, he accepted it willingly, asking nothing better than to get rid of a colleague who haunted him like a ghost. As to M. Grandménil, a fat, good-natured man, with a sanctified face, and a gluttonous disposition, the very reverse of a lofty mind, he was crushed flat under the despotism of his co-director.

Having thus acquired the dictatorship, M. Flocon exercised it with all the imperiousness of a Roman emperor. M. Louis Blanc is considered as knowing how to write; but having been invited to give his collaboration to the paper, he was subjected, like all the rest, to the ferule of the master. One day he was remonstrated with in a very learned manner with regard to one of his articles; and finding the criticism to be very just, he considered himself incapable of collaboration with such a powerful man, and immediately cut himself off from all participation in the *Reform*. A singular instance of fraternity, perhaps, the slanderers will say, but it was not the business of the *Reformers* to practise what they preached.

The *pure* patriots had hailed the appearance of the new paper with joy. During the first few weeks they were seen hastening forward by platoons, some for the purpose of subscribing, and others for offering articles or good advice. M. Cahaigne came with a manuscript romance, which he had already presented to a dozen papers; M. Dupoty brought Paris sketches recopied from his *Journal of the People*, and as to street poets and statesmen of the grog-shops, they landed at the door of the office by coach-loads. But M. Flocon sent them all packing, with that peculiar urbanity of his which turned their milk of kindness into the bitter gall of enmity. The confiding patriots who had advanced their funds and could not get a cent of them back, joined the offended crowd of unknown geniuses, and such complaints! they clamored, they styled M. Flocon an aristocrat, and, in short, deserted the office in all quarters. Before making its appearance, the *Reform* had got two thousand subscribers;

and six months after its first issue there remained some six hundred.

The merits of the editorship had certainly contributed to this result, but the insignificance of the republican party had also a share in it. At this period, commencing with the year 1844, the *Journal of the People* was dead, the *National* had three thousand subscribers, and the *Reform* less than one thousand. The strength of the party may be estimated by these numbers.

The affairs of the new paper soon sank to the lowest ebb; the chest sounded empty, and patriots having money to lose were becoming very rare—a perfect dislocation ensued. M. Grandménil, affirming that the enterprise had consumed the remnant of his fortune, was thrust out of doors. His successor, a confectioner, by the name of Charrousse, was a man of too little enthusiasm to play the fool for the *Reform*. He brought a great deal of good-will to the concern, but very little money; which was by no means to the purpose. Fortunately, unexpected assistance came to relieve the embarrassment.

M. Ledru-Rollin, having distinguished himself among the democracy by a roaring manifesto, had made no noise since, and becoming tired of his obscure position, he concluded to enter upon that grand career which was destined to such a magnificent conclusion in the conception of the Arts and Trades. The *Reform* had need of funds, and he had need of newspaper articles, hence a bargain might be struck. An interview was had, and the matter so arranged that the tumidity of the journal was thereafter secured. But the confectioner, M. Ledru-Rollin, and the other capitalists of the concern, finding that their money was not sufficiently secured by the merits of M. Flocon, concluded to give him an assistant, or rather a chief; and they chose one of such a character as could not be objected to without evident presumption. They chose M. Godefroy Cavaignac. Money was the law, and the editor-in-chief had to succumb, and receive a master.

Since his return from exile, M. Godefroy Cavaignac had entirely abstained from revolutionary proceedings. He felt that France had well merited her repose, and he was convinced, moreover, of the weakness of the republican cause. His opinions remained the same, because they were the result of conviction and family inheritance; but the republic appeared to him at such a misty distance, that his thoughts reverted to it with melancholy tenderness rather than with lively hopes. He was still young (45 years), but there was an air of languor and chastened sadness in his appearance, which indicated but too plainly the approach of death. The conflicts of force, blood, and disasters—all these things had become hateful to him; and, as ardent as he had been in exciting to violence poor men, who are always as ready for acts of heroism as for acts of folly, he now entertained for such work only the feelings of abhorrence. Having been informed of the reorganization of the *Seasons*, and the rank which I held in it, he made me promise, with the view of preventing new sacrifices, never to excite, nor permit any attempt at an insurrection; a promise which I found no difficulty either in making or performing.

The *Reform* was not edited a long time by M. Godefroy Cavaignac. He was seized with a rapid consumption, which, after a few months of intense suffering, hurried him to the tomb. I must again repeat that he was a sincere republican, and in every way worthy of respect. With such men as he, the austere form of government which he meditated would have been possible, and even natural; but in the background of the scene—behind that noble figure which stood forth for a moment, and then disappeared forever, what a crowd of degraded, cowardly, and trifling characters were writhing in the darkest shades of democracy! How many reptiles slavering with hatred, envy, and debauchery, and aspiring with a frenzied thirst after gold, pleasures, and honors! How many men, in fine, who rendered impossible what he would have rendered easy and simple!

M. Flocon was reinstalled in his functions. He took as an assistant a professor of rhetoric, who had one of those southern styles of eloquence which can be turned to anything in a country of talkers. This man, after having killed several journals under his direction, and finding himself on the point of returning to his former condition of schoolmaster, took advantage of the revolution, to transform himself into a representative of the people; and he is now one of the flies of the republican coach. His name is Paschal Duprat.

If I have deviated from the current of my narration, and entered among the affairs of the *Reform*, with which it might seem I had but little to do, it is because we are approaching the revolution of February; an event in which it is proper to have a clear idea of the respective parts played by the actors. It is the general opinion that the *Reform* had taken possession of all the revolutionary elements of the country, had commanded the secret societies, and directed the provinces; so that by a mere signal it was able to overthrow the throne of July; but it is not exactly so. The Montagnards have pretensions, which it may be well enough, for the general edification, to demolish; every one of them, according to their own accounts, having procreated and brought forth the revolution of February; a revolution which is nothing but a bastard, it is true, but which has not quite so many fathers as they would wish us to believe.

CHAPTER XI.

Don Quixote-Lagrange—His great enterprises—His decadence—The rather queer but very edifying commercial transactions of M. Caussidière.

As M. Baune, that victim of the despotism of M. Flocon, had been bound over by the Court of Peers to keep the peace, he might justly have been confined to any one of the provinces, and not tolerated in his anxious efforts on behalf of the republic; but such was the tyranny of the government, and, it must be confessed, such was the importance which it attached to M. Baune, that it condescended to look after his proceedings. And was the government wrong in so doing? What! when M. Baune is one of those who say so complacently, "The revolution which we have made!" But to tell the truth, however, the edifice of July lost only about a brick and a half by his efforts.

M. Lagrange, another of the heroes of Lyons, under the supervisions of the police, also made his appearance on the Parisian stage about this period. One should know M. Lagrange. He has the parrot nose, hollow cheeks, sunken eyes, martial bearing, and all the melancholy seriousness which characterized the illustrious knight of La Mancha. He is not wanting, either, in that lofty extravagance which rendered the hero of Cervantes so comically lugubrious. Like his predecessor, too, he took it solemnly into his head to redress the wrongs of outraged humanity. The Red Republic was his Dulcinea del Toboso; and as he pictured her with a brilliance of imagination that went little beyond the sublime, he maintained her to be more supremely radiant than any other beauty of the world. Mounted upon his rickety, democratic and socialistic hobby horse, the equal in every respect of Rosinante, he dreams only of giants to be cleft asunder, nations to be delivered, and on he goes, straight ahead, right or wrong, his eye on fire, nose lifted into the air, and the impending necessity of manifest destiny at work in his head.

Pardoned, together with his confederates in 1837, and casting about for some position in society equal to his abilities, he directed his thoughts towards the higher branches of industry. He put himself at the head of a railroad, which, to be set in operation, had need only of being constructed; but as the capitalists combined against him in order to stifle his industrial genius and keep their money, he was obliged per force, and in self-defence, to keep the road in his own head. His next enterprise was the sale of one of his own inventions; which was, to extract the spirit from anything whatever. It would have made the fortune of the speculators if they could have got hold of it and understood it; but it was lost somewhere, perhaps upon his railroad.

M. Lagrange then struck his forehead; and it appeared clearly that the difficulty lay in the limited sphere of his operations; for the police kept him away from his true centre of action, Paris, and to Paris, therefore, he must go, come what might. He made his appearance there in an open, manly, faceless way, and was arrested. Not discouraged by this, he returned to the charge again several weeks afterwards, and was again imprisoned. On being asked the reason of such notable obstinacy, he replied that a man like him was perfectly exiled when out of Paris, the capital of industry and the arts; that his talents were not properly appreciated in the provinces, and that he might as well be among a parcel of savages as to live there; while at Paris, all the elements of fortune were laid open to him. The government might justly have replied to these representations of the hero, by sending him to the correctional police; for as he had repeatedly broken his bonds, he had rendered himself liable to a severe penalty; but instead of pursuing this course, the authorities said to the insurrectional chief: "You wish to work—be it so; the capital is open to you. Go and make known that the only object of the government is persecution, and that all its efforts are directed to the ruin of the country."

In the midst of a genial element at last, and free to display that great practical ability for which the patriots are so noted, he set to work and went about from person to person, the colporter of great ideas and the prophet of solemn annunciations. He was looked at over the shoulder, and that was all. The fact, too, that the pot must boil, began to make itself felt; and his lofty projects dwindled down under it by degrees, until at length they assumed very much the character of the most ordinary labor. This demigod of revolt, this Murat of insurrection, this *lion* of the Court of Peers, finally found his glory reduced to what?—to peddling wines by the bottle about Paris. But it is not the trade that makes the man; God forbid that I should impute to M. Lagrange as a shame, a calling which gave him an honest livelihood; but it is well enough to show who these great men of February are, and what they were under a real, positive government, which, whatever else may be said of it, knew how to give every one his proper place.

Since the remission of his sentence, he had not occupied his attention with politics except incidentally, feeling assured that he might attain to a social position which would permit him to await the future; but when he came to see that the science of barricades was no longer a title to public confidence, and that his importance as the hero of the *Place des Cordeliers* had had its day, he thought it high time to mount the cockade again and return to the ranks. A condition of things that reduced M. Lagrange to peddling wines was evidently fit for nothing else but to be overthrown. Unfortunately his theatrical bearing, tending somewhat to the ridiculous, finally gave rise to doubts, not only as to his industrial merits but also as to his political value. He used to intimate that when the new insurrection should break out, he would be chosen for the general-in-chief; an idea which gave the shrug of the shoulder to a good many. The wine dealer also gave hints of pretensions to the civil power, as well as to the military, and seemed ogling the presidential chair, in spite of its reservation by so many others. All this appeared to be very presumptuous to the people of the *Reform*, among whom M. Lagrange was included; and in the region of the *National*, where even the lowest office boy entertained a perfect contempt for the whole set of the rival paper, the vanity of the Lyonnais was qualified simply as buffoonery.

Finding himself so little appreciated by the upper stratum of the party, that he could not even allude to his hopes without exciting a smile, he began to delve into the popular societies, hoping that there, at least, his ancient prestige would have left some traces; but the little communist churches, to which he offered himself, were headed by chiefs who had no intention of allowing themselves to be dethroned; and as to the new *Seasons*, the indifference which they showed him amounted to downright irreverence. We were consulted with regard to him, and by my advice he was decided to be a foundered patriot, and a fit subject for the retired list.

The leanness of the poor man was so much increased by this deplorable state of things, that he became a sort of skeleton, which even outdid that of the knight of La Mancha himself. He wandered about the streets with his samples in his pockets, and showing, by his concerned looks, to what a degree of decadence he had fallen. At night, accompanied by a large gray dog—

> Whose mournful mien and wistful look,
> His master's mood and humor took,

he went to drown his cares amidst the excitements of gaming and hard drinking. The coffee-houses of Saint Agnès and Mandar were his habitual resorts. As the profits of his profession were very small, he gnashed his teeth and cursed the fates if he lost more than two stakes of an evening. Such was the condition to which this great man became reduced.

Besides his resemblance to the hero of Cervantes, M. Lagrange might also be compared to one of those large haggard looking birds which are seen in menageries; they are of a peaceful aspect, and exceedingly austere and mournful; but on a closer look, it is seen that their eye is bloodshot, and that over their inclosure is inscribed the word—Vulture.

Before M. Lagrange's arrival in Paris, and at the same time that M. Baune made his appearance, there came also another distinguished person—a sort of giant, with the neck of a bull and the shoulders of a Hercules, presenting upon a broad expanse of face, pierced with two little intelligent eyelet holes, a mingled expression of good nature and cunning —his name was Marc Caussidière. He had been one of the category of Saint Etienne in the persecutions of April. Son of an old soldier without fortune, he had embraced, while still young, the profession of designer of ribbon-prints, in which he had attained to a considerable degree of skill. It is stated of him that he soon showed a bent for industry by selling the same designs both to Swiss and French manufacturers, a proceeding, however, which is hardly admissible in trade, if I am not mistaken. At that time (towards the close of the Restoration), democracy, and socialism, and the red flag had not yet been invented; but the work of anarchy was carried on under cover of the charter. The patriotism of M. Caussidière smacked of his age; it was rather romantic. The war of Grecian independence having broken out, a great many young men, who stood in need of making a noise, hailed with joy a conflict which brought several nations into collision. The ribbon-designer and some of his comrades, Messrs. Tiphaine and Vignes among others, were of the number. They resolved to march to the aid of Hellenic liberty; but instead of enrolling themselves in some regiment, like the common run of the defenders of Greece, they proceeded in the following way. There existed in the country a pentagruelic society, of which they were the founders, and which bore the name of the *Lime-kiln Society*. Its object was nothing terrible, tending merely to develop the faculties of ingurgitation, and perfect the art of practical joking. The qualification for admission consisted in swallowing down extraordinarily large potations of anything whatever, and when this was done, to have the quantity increased by means of a veterinary syringe, applied by one of the members in a manner which it is unnecessary to describe.

It was agreed, then, that the principal members of the society should march to the deliverance of the Greeks, not as private citizens, but as representatives of the very honorable company. M. Caussidière was appointed grand master of the expedition, M. Tiphaine contractor general, and M. Vignes almoner. The army, including the general staff and soldiers, amounted to a dozen persons. They set out, marauded right and left, and arrived at Marseilles, the rendezvous of the liberating army. There they presented themselves to Colonel Fabvier, and made known to him their generous resolution; but the colonel, as it appears, placed but a low estimate upon such a reinforcement. The manners and dress of the *Lime-kiln* folk rendered them suspicious-looking characters. He thanked them for their favorable intentions, but assured them that Greece could get along without their services; and the country of Homer was actually liberated without the assistance of these brave men.

Such was the commencement of M. Caussidière's political career. He is a great joker; and it is from this point of view that all the acts of this singular man must be regarded. If serious at all, it is only in an unquenchable thirst for drink, and a perfect enthusiasm for juicy dinners.

After the amnesty, M. Caussidière returned to Paris, and was tolerated there like M. Baune, with whom he entered into partnership in a manufacturing concern, which still remained in embryo. They met with better luck than M. Lagrange had in finding some one to advance the funds; for having learned that M. Ledru-Rollin had just made a rich match, they knocked at his door, and were not badly received. The Montagnard chief, being solicited by two patriots, who promised, by their great industrial abilities, to render France as glorious by their skill in commerce as they had by their efforts at insurrection, allowed himself to talk, and then opened his purse. He advanced thirty thousand francs for the concern.

But the hopes inspired by the high sounding words and flattering promises of the partnership came far short of being realized; the funds, however, soon disappeared. M. Ledru-Rollin was informed of the failure, and called on again for further assistance; for, all that the concern wanted was to be set going; but finding that the capital had melted away rather rapidly, and that the dividends from the operations of the patriots were not very brilliant, he refused another advance, declaring that the sum lost was quite sufficient.

I cannot pretend to give positively the causes of the failure. It is very certain, however, that the partnership were often at breakfasts which did not end with the setting of the sun, and that the last of all places they were seen at, was their manufactory; but this is not a sufficient reason. Impartial judges will attribute their want of success to the wretched state of society which was then existing. It is well known that the policy of the government of July was to ruin individuals as well as the country; for it has been proved by M. Garnier-Pagès and a dozen others besides.

But be this as it may, the eminent industrial abilities which M. Caussidière boasted of having in the Constituent Assembly, were not displayed in the enterprise in question. Must it be inferred, then, that M. Caussidière has no such abilities? Not at all; the fault lay in the *Lime-kiln*, or rather in the tyranny of the government—anywhere else than in M. Caussidière.

But he was not to be frightened by one failure, for he has a philosophical turn of mind which doubts nothing and believes but little. His next industrial efforts were at merchandise. He formed a new company, with M. Lagrange as junior partner, for the sale of silks. The two friends had not a cent to begin with; and how to get the necessary credit was a question accompanied with difficulties. They succeeded, however, in finding several courageous manufacturers who were willing to risk a first consignment. It may readily be guessed what became of it. The outlays of the establishment and other expenses absorbed the profits as soon as they were made, so that the share of the consignors was reduced to zero. This result was inevitable, and I am very willing to admit that all the abilities of M. Caussidière could not have prevented it; but the question is whether one has any right to exercise such abilities. The house of Caussidière and Lagrange, then, like the house of Caussidière and Baune, proved a failure.

Not in the least disheartened, the *Lime-kiln* man cast about in search of a third partner. He found a good young man, a former clerk, well versed in mercantile affairs, who promised to advance a pretty round sum. They were to sell cravats and other fancy articles. The preparations were made, the store hired, and everything brought to a state of readiness for commencing operations, when a terrible difficulty arose; one of the two partners failed in his engagement, and was not forthcoming with the money. This partner was not M. Caussidière, by any means; for he was to furnish only the essential funds, the industry, which he had already at hand; but his partner who was to have supplied the money, had none, or at least for a partnership with the hero of Saint Etienne. For the want of this trifle, the sale of cravats was abandoned, and hence it is impossible to have a due appreciation of M. Caussidière's genius in that line.

The last enterprise that he engaged in seemed rather an affair of personal convenience than a speculation. He conceived the idea of lighting the numbers of houses at night, and took into company with him for this purpose, M. Berthaud, the brother of the poet of the *Charivari*. M. Caussidière was given to noctambulation; he liked to go to supper at two or three o'clock in the morning at the cook Joissan's or at the wine-sellers' shops of the Halle; and doubtlessly on returning home he had mistaken the door so often, that at length he got the idea of his luminous invention. However this may be, the capitalists were not dazzled by it, and Paris remained enveloped in darkness.

At last, an industrial career seemed entirely closed to him. His former business of designer of ribbon prints still remained open to him, but that was a tiresome and wretched pursuit for a man of his genius; he preferred to abandon himself to the hazards of a *lime-kiln* life. To follow out his history from this moment would be a delicate task. When a man, having nothing, and gaining nothing, passes his days and nights in all kinds of public places, where wine costs money, however sour it may be, it is to be presumed that he has generous friends; but as friends get tired, at last, we may suppose that in the course of time he resorts to the art of living without paying; and when that art becomes exhausted, we may then imagine what we please. As the criminal code is much more chaste than was Boileau, not permitting us to—

Call a cat a cat, and Rolet a knave,

I will go no further. Besides, we ought, perhaps, to excuse certain weaknesses in a soil over rich. M. Caussidière's democracy is epicurean and fantastic; he has introduced patriotism into the grog-shops of the Halle, and is the inventor of the Tyrolian hat. All due honor, then, to the artist.

CHAPTER XII.

The democratic press before February—The *National* and M. Marrast—The man who never pays his debts, and the toothless lion—The *Charivari*—M. Altaroche—M. Albert Clerc—M. Félix Pyat.

About the year 1846, the period when the commercial enterprises of M. Caussidière had borne their fruit and reduced this great man to the most hazardous expedients, the republic was not in a very flourishing condition. Conspiracies still showed themselves now and then, according to old habit, but the important men of the party, or those who styled themselves as such, remained quietly in their tents; a few of them only continued the conflict in the two republican sheets of that time, the *National* and the *Reform*.

The principal editors of the National were Messrs. Marrast, Dornès, Bastide, Duclerc and Vaulabelle. M. Marrast, the editor in chief, exercised a sovereignty acquired by a superlative want of principle, and palliated by a rather remarkable talent for pamphleteering. A singular analogy, and one which will not appear far fetched to those who know the two men, is that M. Marrast is merely another Caussidière polished over; the same eagerness for pleasures, the same scepticism, the same system of cunning, and the same ambition distinguish them both; but while all these qualities are exhibited in the grossest way by the latter, they are exceedingly refined with the former.

M. Marrast has a higher opinion of himself under his frizzled hair than any sovereign under his crown; the empire of the world belongs to him of right. And let it not be imagined for a moment that there is the least shade of democracy amidst that scornful manner and Mephistophelic smile of his. He wishes to be the first in the state; and as he cannot reasonably aspire to the crown, the crown must therefore be got rid of in order that he may reign in France under any title whatever. It will be remembered what ridiculous manners he endeavored to bring in vogue at the commencement of the republic, which had been established, they say, for the improvement of our morals. A single word has done justice to these impertinences; M. Marrast is now called the *Marquis* of the republic. Alas! the good sans-culotte of the *Tribune*, the great insulter of the *National*, the great Aristophanes who brought so much ridicule upon honest men, figures now before the public only as a character of the Carnival! His prints fill the windows of the caricaturists, and even the children, in passing by, salute his spangled dress with an ironic pun. This terrible mocker is now mocked at just as the poor George Dandin was for endeavoring to place himself on an equality with M. de Sottenville; and justly too. France well knew his cold, heartless perfidy, and in the election of 1849 she set her foot upon his neck and drowned him like a cat—the sad destiny of a man who had rendered himself detestable to all parties, and chiefly so to his own.

M. Carrel, the former editor of the *National*, was frank and open, never fearing to throw off the yoke of the populace and wage war with visor up, and with sword, or with lance; but with the editorship of M. Marrast the politics of the paper became cunning, tricky, and underhanded, adopting the Italian system of fence. They consisted in instigating the passions, spurring them on, while retaining a safe distance in the rear, and having a due care for white hands which must not be soiled by too close a contact with the dirty people; and then, if some fine day the republic gets knocked on the head, as it did in 1839, what course think you, is followed by the *National*, that paper which considers itself at the head of republicanism? Why, it very aristocratically shows the debris of the party the doors, and gets rid, as soon as possible, of the poor devils who have been led to their ruin by its pernicious cunning. Ask M. Napoleon Gallois and friends, whether this is true or not; they will doubtlessly remember the fine setting down they got when they went to the office to ask for a few lines of consolation on behalf of the democrats who had just been killed. But why had the unfortunate wretches the impudence to fail! Ah, but if they had succeeded, though, the *National* would not have waited to be asked for eulogies; its dithyrambics would have flowed in streams.

The scorn for those who are called little folk exists nowhere in so insolent a shape as at the *National*. The ancient princes of the blood never considered themselves so lofty by a hundred cubits, as the paragraphists of Lepelletier Street; never did a blackguard parvenu treat his valets half so bad as these democrats treat the popular crowd; and hence, between the people whom they despise and by whom they are in turn despised, and the upper classes whose disdain is far above the reach of their hatred, they form a sort of intrenched camp among the brambly regions of the bourgeoise, which resounds with empty capacities and tumid bombast. They are pedants like M. Genin, sensualists like M. Pagnerre, bullies like M. Charras, and roués like M. Recurt. The estimate placed upon the latter gentleman in French affairs is seen by the result of the last elections.

The *National*, which knows itself well enough not to indulge in self-flattery with regard to the sympathies which it inspires, has repeatedly endeavored to find adherents in the army. And this is a point of view which should not be lost sight of; to gain possession of the public force, and establish its own domination at all hazards—such is its fixed idea. At this very moment, I venture to say, it is intriguing among the regiments; I do not know it positively, but I would bet on it as a dead certainty. Its secret connivances, however, will miscarry, for our soldiers are not the servants of cliques, and they remember moreover the provisional government which sent them away from Paris, which government was made up by two thirds of the men of the *National*. But no defeats discourage these Florentine politicians; they are always in action, always on the watch, reckoning upon surprises as well as upon connivance, and ever the more avaricious of power, inasmuch as they have relished its sweets for a moment and then lost it in a way almost ignominious.

The *National* had looked upon the establishment of the *Reform* with a very unfriendly eye; the pretensions of the new paper towards sharing in the republican subscriptions and in putting itself at the head of the party, seemed to the *National* to be very much out of place. The corps of writers for the *Reform* were not terrible; but its agents showed sufficient freshness and activity to cause the rival paper some alarm. A deep feud arose between the two cliques. Several disinterested patriots, and especially M. Guinard, endeavored to reconcile the parties; but as the *Flocon* paper felt no compunctions in belaboring the *National*, in debauching its subscribers, and even those who advanced it their funds, the task was impossible. The attacks of the *Reform* were replied to by some nice little bits of calumny which M. Degouve de Nuncques contrived to slip into his correspondence from the departments. Things grew worse and worse, until the quarrel became so low that even such men as M. Baune and his fellow travelling agents were attacked; certain drunkards and political charlatans were pointed out as making a great display in the provinces in favor of a paper of ill-fame. But for the want of an antagonist more worthy of his ire, the editor of the *National* assailed M. Ledru-Rollin, well known at that time as the chief patron of the *Reform*. Recriminations loud and quick passed between the two parties; M. Marrast accused M. Ledru-Rollin of allowing his notes to be protested; and *M. Flocon* replied for his file leader, calling M. Marrast a toothless lion. Both sides were right, and this public bucking of democratic foul linen proved quite amusing to the lookers-on.

These two journals, one year before the affair of February, composed the entire republican press of Paris. They shared between them some five or six thousand subscribers for all France, and thus preluded, as we have just described, the advent of the reign of fraternity.

Some, perhaps, will set up claims for the *Chararari*, conceiving that that paper ought to be classed among the democratic organs; but I must undeceive them. The *Charavari*, then, as now, belonged chiefly to M. Louis Perrée, one of the most zealous writers of the *Siècle* in favor of monarchy. Its principal editor, M. Altaroche, a good man who has been considered witty for the last fifteen years, very quietly confected the matters of the journal, and has never dreamed for a long time of adding the least republican spicing to it. Some of the more susceptible democrats even, considered that his illustrations, in which the figures of the people smacked of wine shops and the bawdy-house, were the proof of a want of patriotism. The fact is that the *witty* journal was existing at that time upon a capital of old jokes, which it exhibited in a peaceful way, and offered in all candor to its subscribers, who were persons very easily pleased. It had, especially, about half a dozen conceits, adapted to every taste, which were sure to make their appearance in every number—such as the joke upon M. Arnal, that illustrious friend of the editor in chief; the witticisms of Bibloquet the mountebank; the anglomania of M. Guizot; the stinginess of the civil list, and the charges against Carpentras. This last piece of malice, which consisted in fastening upon the name of Carpentras everything trivial or ridiculous, appeared so exceedingly ingenious to M. Félix Pyat that he could not refrain, one day, from regaling the National Assembly with it.

The editor next in importance to M. Altaroche was M. Albert Clerc, whom the republic has made a consul. He was charged with the department of riddles, rebuses, and charades; and it was in the pursuit of these matters that he acquired his knowledge of international law. But it is known that at the time when his appointment as consul was made, the government amused itself—not in choosing men for the place, but rather the place for the men, and that the reputation of patriot was sufficient for anything. When M. Sentis, a tailor, M. Emmanuel Arago, a fourth rate lawyer, M. Léon Favre, an insolvent bankrupt, M. Savoye, a pedagogue, and M. Thions, an interdicted priest, were invested with diplomatic functions, M. Albert Clerc, maker of conundrums, might certainly aspire to the same dignity. There is this difference, however, in the two cases—the above-named citizens offered themselves as candidates with a reputation of democracy perfectly dyed in the wool, while the editor of the *Charavari* could have no such pretensions. He is a kind of gentleman of the press, mounting his horse and going to the office booted and spurred, and, in spite of a suspicious looking dress and a doleful air, having claims to *lionry*. The worthy man would have been very much astonished to have heard fifteen days before February that he was going to receive the favors of the government as a good republican.

The remainder of the editorial corps consisted of what are called men of letters, pure and simple, that is to say, of young men whose principles, like those of M. Bareste, lay in their bread and butter. To give some idea of the conscience of these fine writers who tore up whatever fair character or good name their patron set them to work upon, a single fact may be mentioned. The *Epoch*, in designing to get up a system of defence, thought of raising a corps of volunteers for firing away upon the smaller papers. The idea then occurred to it of choosing one and the same writers for making alike the attack and the defence. In this way the blows from one side would be as good as those from the other. And the *Epoch* had the pleasure of being a close spectator of this interesting conflict. Having made advances to several of the editors of the *Charavari*, they were enchanted with the proposition, and accepted it without scruple; and these gentlemen very quietly set to work to breakfast upon the *Epoch* and dine upon the *Charavari*.

I entered the office of the *Charavari* in 1840, and remained there five years, furnishing weekly a piece of verse signed by my name, and occasionally articles in prose. When the witty journal felt itself bound recently to declare that I had never formed a part of its editorial corps, it was certainly not joking with me so much as with its readers. These readers might well ask in what the editorship of a journal consists if I were not an editor of the *Charavari*. However, I set up no claims; for having voluntarily sacrificed in 1846 the title which is now denied me, I should be wanting in good sense to seek the recovery by force of what I had thrown aside in disgust. I must confess that I was tired of playing the part of democratic jester.

Besides, Messrs. Altaroche, A. Clerc, Caraguel, Delorde, and another writer of a glutinous style called Huart, who had become part proprietor of the journal in order to have his articles published in it, the *Charavari* reckoned as an editor M. Felix Pyat, who, although he railed at the poor sheet, nevertheless made it an instrument either of his interest or his hatred. He edited the theatrical part; and thus had the double advantage of crying down the productions of his brethren of the drama and extolling his own. The patriots are doubtlessly unaware of the prodigious passion of M. Pyat for a sort of manufactured glory, which is acquired through the journals and which is called puffing; and we may therefore inform them that this *Montagnard* excels in this respect the most renowned quacks of the age. About three months before the representation of one of his dramas, he would let drop a word to his intimates, who would carry it to all the opposition papers, and immediately it would become the blast of Fame's trumpet, conjuring up a small mint of money in honor of the forthcoming master-piece. From the character of the man he could count upon a few friends, but as he had a corner in the two republican journals as well as in the *Charavari*, his brethren of the press took good care not to offend him for fear of reprisals. But this great noise by which his dramatic pieces were heralded in, a privilege which was also enjoyed by another writer of the same class, M. Anthony Thouret, could not stun either the judgment of the public with regard to his works, or especially that of certain writers whose fear of the revolutionary author was not such as to prevent them from saying what they thought of him. He could not, however, well understand raillery when applied to himself; for, having acquired the sole right of attacking everything respected in the world, any assaults made upon him were intolerable insolence. A man of a little more sterling talent than he possessed, M. Jules Janin, having ventured to point out some large spots on the face of his bright sun, was replied to by the democrat in a pamphlet which was so black and acrid with bile that it gave all Paris the heart-burn. It became necessary to administer, by way of a sedative to the ferocious author, a pretty considerable term of imprisonment, including costs and damages. As the gentle M. Jules Favre, his lawyer, insinuated as much poison as possible into the wound already made, the judges had no scruple in awarding a severe sentence.

But amidst all these various elements, the *Charavari* had in fact but one serious object, and that was the getting of subscribers. In virtue of a compromise made previous to the year 1840, by which all attacks against the elder branch of the Bourbons were prohibited, M. Dutacq had acquired for the picture-paper a large list of subscribers among the legitimists; and M. Perrée, the successor of M. Dutacq, religiously respected the compact. The entire editorial control of the paper had to conform to this little arrangement, which might have been respected as a matter of conscience, but which the necessities of the till rendered imperiously necessary. The austere M. Pyat himself had to submit to the rule; for, as he was part owner of the paper, the income of which was very considerable, the poor man had to yield to the obligation of receiving his share of the legitimist's money.

Such was the character of the *Charavari;* in which it is not easy to recognize many traits of democracy.

CHAPTER XIII.

Systematic enfeeblement of the *Seasons*—A new committee—Messrs. Caussidière, Léoutre, Grandménil, Leroux—An effort at reorganization—The reason of its failure—An extraordinary contest.

As M. Flocon had brought nothing but his personality to the new *Seasons*, his retirement therefrom was of no consequence. Things still went on for some time in the old way, without enthusiasm or zeal, and in a state of half organization which, though it permitted the men to consider themselves members of a secret society, yet gave them no influence as such. The members of the respective groups frequently met together, but rather for drinking and singing than for working at conspiracy; excepting that from time to time they were assembled to listen to the reading of an order of the day. The duty of confecting these pieces of eloquence still remained imposed upon me, and I crammed them with as many hollow words as possible. The men, however, applauded, declaring that *the thing was done up brown*. At the end of every order I invariably returned to the old refrain which I had adopted and established, and which was—no ostensible recruiting operations—no politics in public places—no depots of arms or ammunition. It is true that a conspiracy without arms or munitions seemed at first as something wholly extraordinary; but I succeeded in overcoming all objections. The following may serve as a specimen of the orders of the day containing a summary of the ideas which I had caused to prevail. "The association must no longer become compromised in disastrous undertakings. The committee has decided to await the advent of some great popular commotion before making a display of its power; it will then come forth, throw its sword into the balance, and achieve a triumphant victory. But, in the mean time, let us wait—let us envelop ourselves in impenetrable discretion and unswerving prudence. When the supreme hour shall arrive, then muskets and ammunition will be got ready, and your chiefs themselves will furnish them to your terrible arms. Trust, then, to the patriotism of the committee even as the committee trusts to your valor, and beware of fettering its action by inconsiderate rashness. We must accustom ourselves to a difficult but an indispensable virtue, the virtue of resignation; but at that price the victory is ours."

However great was the difficulty in subjecting to this regime of inertia a class of men habituated to the strongest excitements, I succeeded, with the assistance of my colleagues, in effecting it. A general lassitude contributed to this end, and all these old lions of the mob were left biting their nails in the cage. They were deceived to their advantage, their own safety being assured, as well as that of the public.

The orders of the day were no longer printed at my house. During the time of M. Dourille, the clandestine printing-press had been transferred to the house of a chief of group, called Bocage, at Grenelle. I was informed, from the prefecture, that it was in good hands, and hence made no efforts to recover it. M. Gueret made a journey to Brussels at about this period, and had an interview there with M. Imbert, who had left France in consequence of a political prosecution; and having mentioned the embarrassment that the committee were in with regard to the orders of the day, M. Imbert undertook the charge of printing them. It was in this way that the regular publication of these pieces was continued. They were still read according to the old method, that is to say, in the wine-shops, and at the barrier.

Had the police devised to get rid of the association, it is evident that a very simple means presented itself; by transmitting an order of the day to each of the chiefs, and sending a commissary to take both the order and the man, the disorganization of the secret society would have followed as a matter of course. And why was not this course adopted? it may be asked. Because France would thus have learned that there were secret associations still in existence; because the mobbers, who had become lulled into a state of inaction, would have aroused again; because many a young fool, then without a thought on the subject, would have conceived the idea of becoming a conspirator; because the existing association was in a fair way of becoming quietly smothered to death, whereas, if it had been publicly destroyed, a dozen active societies would have arisen in its place. It may be objected that it was at least useless to continue the orders of the day, the bearers of which might become dangerously implicated, either through imprudence or treachery. It has been said that these productions inspired more confidence than mere oral communications; but it was precisely for this reason that they were made use of, serving as the most efficacious means for inculcating a temporization and prudence, which were necessary to a quiet dissolution. It will be seen that they were discontinued as soon as they failed to accomplish this end. I prepared the way of their abolition by discontinuing their periodicity. Originally, an order was issued every month; I first doubled, and then even tripled this period, following a systematic course of irregularity.

This method of latent and gradual dissolution produced its effect; the bond of connection between the members and between the chiefs of groups and the committee became visibly relaxed; the meetings became merely mechanical, and conspiracy a mere matter of fiction. And this state of dissolution was still further increased by the withdrawal of two of the revolutionary agents. M. Dutertre lost a compromising letter, which forced him to retire, and M. Gueret, finding that the republic was too long in coming, threw the handle after the hatchet, and went into the provinces to sell the books of M. Louis Blanc. I was left pretty nearly absolute master of the society, M. Boivin, who remained with me, deferring entirely to my decisions.

Such was the condition of the society when M. Caussidière, forced back to his former trade of conspirator by the hardness of the times, held an interview with me, testifying a desire to become a member. He was accompanied by two friends, Messrs. Grandménil and Léoutre, who also offered their concurrence. M. Caussidière, like M. Flocon, brought nothing but his own person to the society. The *Gypsy* democracy, amidst which he lived, no longer cared for secret affiliations, on account of the attending danger, and as to the people at large, they knew him only by a vague remembrance of his name; his entrance, therefore, into the society was by no means a remarkable event. I knew the man well; and finding him at the end of all his expedients, and that his only resource lay in revolutionary machinations, I was not sorry to get him under my hands, and therefore advised his admission.

M. Léoutre had left but a short time since a regiment of cuirassiers, and not knowing what to do, he became intimate with M. Caussidière, sharing with him his broken down condition. The republic, however, was the last thing in his thoughts; it was only at the invitation of his friend, and for the want of something better to do, that he became a conspirator. He was wholly unknown to the patriots. M. Grandménil stood in the same relation to the ex-prefect of police of February; he was but little recommended by his antecedents, but he had a thorough knowledge of the statistics of wine-shops, and that was enough.

Besides these three personages, a fourth came forward for admission, a M. Leroux, manufacturer of mats and a poet, who gave himself out as one of the leaders of the suburb of Saint Martin. The facts being examined into, it was perceived that he indeed had some influence in that quarter, and was accepted.

The four new-comers and the two ancient chiefs came to an agreement, and constituted themselves as a committee to push forward the labors of the association with activity. It was evident that a new organization had become necessary, and it was attended to immediately. A plan was brought forward, discussed, and definitively settled. It was an imitation of Carbonarism; a chief was to choose his lieutenants, these lieutenants would choose their subalterns, and the subalterns were to make up the sections. The old members were first to be incorporated, and then new battalions formed. M. Boivin and myself kept our old sections, so that our legion was easily made up. M. Leroux also succeeded in raising a small corps. As to the other chiefs, they set about theirs, but the work required a degree of labor inconsistent with their habits. I was fully aware of this, and hence had kept the old sections under my orders, remaining in this way pretty nearly absolute master of the association.

The committee continued punctual in attendance at the rendezvous during a month; then absences took place, and finally the meetings became wholly irregular. At every assembly M. Caussidière swore that he would be punctual, but then, the streets of Paris abound in so many tempting places, how could he attend? And besides, his friends seemed to be setting snares for him in the way of invitations to dinner. He would accept, promising to leave the table at the hour of the rendezvous; but vain hope! the poetry of wine by the quart overcame his resolution. Lost in sweet emotions, he would relate the wonders of his *Lime-kiln* life, or perhaps practise at harangues for the future constituent assembly, by some beautiful discourse highly seasoned and peppered with blows of the fist. Hence, his revolutionary duties naturally became a sacrifice.

Mention has been made in some published work of the gigantic contest that took place one day between M. Grandménil and M. Caussidière. It was on one of the meeting days; and from such a contest it may readily be conceived that they might have forgotten everything. The question was, which of the two could come nearer to gargantua; and the affair came off at the house of *Father* Richard, a wine-seller of Montmartre Street. The champions commenced the bout by a pot of tripe, which disappeared at two jerks of the fork. The next essay was upon a rare done shoulder of mutton reeking with garlic enough to suffocate a Spaniard; it was swallowed down without winking. The adversaries moistened their lips for a few minutes, and then recommenced the attack simultaneously upon a goose and a tray of salad, the whole of which went to join company with the mutton and tripe. At last the decisive morsel was brought forward in the shape of seven or eight pounds of cheese. After several pretty reasonable slices M. Caussidière began to give out; but M. Grandménil still kept on with admirable ease. How could such a formidable athlete be overcome? The future prefect of police thought of various expedients, and finally hit upon one which was truly extraordinary, he took off his boots! Nothing would do however; for M. Grandménil came out conqueror by a pound of gruyère.

CHAPTER XIV.

Continuation of the history of the *Reform*—The Polish subscription—The talents of M. Caussidière—Impuissance of the journal.

THE principal travelling agent of the *Reform*, thus far, had been the worthy M. Baune, who, in order to avoid M. Flocon, his particular tyrant, never returned to Paris when he could possibly help it. During a period of two years, he had circulated among a class of courageous patriots whose purses he had periodically phlebotomized, but who were becoming tired of such continued depletions. The collections gradually grew less and less, until the agent finally had to return empty. He was refused his tax, percentage, or expenses, for all the world just as if he had been a bad government.

The director, M. Chanousse, had had enough of the concern. The small amount of money which he had expended in it weighed heavily upon his heart; and instead of turning a thought towards extricating the paper from its embarrassment, he accosted the folk of the press with a doleful air, explaining to them how many hundreds of times better it would have been for him to have remained in the direction of his own shop, and not have undertaken that of M. Flocon. and company; and when the cashier informed him of some new debt that could not be staved off, he would make a gesture of despair, repeat for the thousandth time the immense sacrifices which he had made for the *Reform*, and then rush to the door and go away. His disillusion was at last complete. Recourse was then had either to M. Ledru-Rollin, whose signature so often came before the tribunal of commerce, that his paper was not very greedily accepted, or to M. Schœlcher, the abolitionist, whom the *Reform* compelled to pay a round sum, and not without reason, for his interminable long articles upon our brethren the blacks; or, in fine, to M. Lemasson, a millionnaire banker of Rouen, who, with the greatest simplicity imaginable, encouraged principles which tended to the ruin of men of his profession. From one or another of these gentlemen a few bags of five franc pieces were extracted, and thrown to the most avaricious of the creditors; and this served to stop up one of the leaks for a few days. But the unfortunate paper resembled very much an old coat, which, when mended in one part, immediately breaks out in another. Want and wretchedness had soon reached a degree that was utterly lamentable.

What was to be done? The most skilful would have been embarrassed by this question. Very fortunately Poland conceived the idea, about that time, of shaking the world again by another convulsion. Subscriptions were immediately got up in aid of the unfortunate people, and the part collected by the *Reform* amounted to some fifteen thousand francs. The handling of this money proved to be a very thorny matter; for as the insurrection in the mean time had been suppressed, leaving it undecided as to what disposition should be made of the funds, these funds might, perhaps, be appropriated in part to a great patriotic necessity, it being understood, of course, that the part thus appropriated should be restored as soon as possible. Messrs. Ledru-Rollin, Flocon, Lemasson, and Etienne Arago, members of the directing committee, all thought so. Hence, one draft was first made upon the Polish money, then another, and then another, until finally the bag became very nearly empty. But lo and behold! the *National* got wind of it, and made haste to call its rival to an account, being justified in so doing by forming a part of the commission instituted for making a repartition of the subsidy. The *Reform* found itself in a pretty predicament truly. It could not say, as did the merchant in the fable, that the rats had eaten the deposit; and even if it had said so, M. Marrast would have replied with a very knowing look, that he very well knew who the rats were. The only course left was to replace the money somehow, and the sooner the better, for the secret was in very bad keeping among the folk of the *National*. M. Ledru-Rollin and others, who had furnished their funds, perceived that the moral existence of the enterprise was in question, and submitted, but not without a grimace, to the repairing of the breach. Two of the editorial corps, however, Messrs. Francois Arago and Recurt, feeling but ill at ease in a concern where such kinds of forced loans were made, thought it best to retire.

With the restoration of the Polish funds, honor came off safe, but the affairs of the *Reform* were in no way bettered by it. The good paper had two very serious causes of trouble, an absence of receipts and the greatest difficulty in coming by a few bags of dollars, on the one part, and a wonderful facility of dissipating the money of the patriots on the other. It was observed that some of the poor editors went to the office fasting and down at the heel, while the director (M. Léoutre at that time), alighting from his cabriolet with a smiling face and sparkling eye, had all the appearance of a man who had had a comfortable breakfast. In this state of things a council was held, not to busy itself with the articles of the paper, by any means, for M. Flocon would not permit that, but to take seriously into consideration the subject of coining money in some way or another, and of putting an end to the wastefulness of the administration. But as the chest was found to be in the last stages of a collapse, the question of filling it up certainly took precedence of that of regulating the uses to be made of it. To this end, a new travelling agent was looked for, some one who might be able to rekindle in the hearts of the patriots that fire of enthusiasm which seemed to be entirely extinct. M. Caussidière was within reach, but in the background, not offering himself, and no one thinking of him, so little fit did he appear to represent the virtuous principles of the democratic paper. However, the great dearth of men proper for the employment and the urgency of the case prevented too close a scrutiny, and it was finally concluded, though not without great reluctance, to intrust him with the destinies of the concern. Contrary to every expectation, he accomplished his task with success. By means of that peculiar eloquence, of which he gave us such beautiful specimens in the constituent assembly, he· succeeded in restoring the phthisical paper to an appearance of health.

He ran over—in fact dug into France in every sense of the word, and had the adroitness to hunt out patriots whose purses thus far had remained unexplored. The means which he put in practice varied according to men and circumstances, but the most common was this: Furnished with a letter of introduction, he presented himself to some of the greenest of the democrats, and addressed them nearly as follows: Directed to you by the most honorable republicans of France, I come to inform you that the welfare of French society is threatened in the existence of the *Reform* newspaper. Every true hearted citizen, without exception, has already contributed towards its support, and your subscriptions are the only ones now to be gained, and surely you would not let a paltry sum of money stand in the way of the happiness of the people, the grandeur of the country, the triumph of virtue, or, in a word, you would not let the worthy and patriotic *Reform* go down. I am convinced, then, that your signature will be given, etc. etc. A share of stock in the paper already prepared and slipped into the hands of the auditors served as a peroration to his discourse; a confederate close at hand sustained his arguments, and if the patriots happened to have a considerable allowance of good nature, everything succeeded well, and the desired signature was acquired.

But this was a very simple operation; M. Caussidière had organized a system of exploitation on a grander scale, and which was practised as follows: On arriving in a city where there were a considerable number of democrats, he spread the report that one of the most illustrious patriots of the capital, happening to be in town, would take the occasion to propose a friendly meeting with his brethren. Several friends to whom he had been recommended, lent their assistance to prepare the *brothers* for the occasion; and these brothers, esteeming themselves highly honored in having the opportunity to become acquainted with a person of so much distinction, made haste to accept the invitation. The meeting took place at the house of some democrat whose cellar would be well supplied with wine, and who would give effect to the ceremonies by numerous bumpers. When the enthusiasm of the brothers had been got up to the proper pitch, M. Caussidière launched at once into the affairs of the *Reform*—that organ of patriotism, so pure, so devoted, so courageous, etc.; and declared boldly that all his sympathies were with it, and that (a favorable occasion then presenting itself) he believed it to be his duty, as a good citizen, to bring to the knowledge of the assembly an unpleasant item of information, which he had but that moment learned, and which was, that the inappreciable organ was reduced to a condition of distress. He had no hesitation in adding that it was the duty of every republican to give it his support. He was aware of the poverty of the party, and, hence, felt some reluctance in calling upon poor men, who had already given so many proofs of their devotion; he could not, however, refrain from making known to them the afflicting intelligence which he had received.

At these words, M. Caussidière stopped, giving the cue to one of his friends, who added, in a doleful strain, that it was impossible that the precious journal could be allowed to go down; it would be a disgrace to the party, and it must be sustained at all hazards. For my part, I subscribe five hundred francs.

Another friend, also in the secret, subscribed an equal sum; and then another subscribed; their subscriptions being either in earnest or not, but serving, at any rate, the same purpose that bird-calls do, in the hands of the fowler. Caught between the cross fires of vinous enthusiasm on the one hand, and ardent self-love on the other, the worthy men who went to the meeting, expecting to be only the auditors of the republican apostle, found themselves subjected to the inevitable condition of becoming stockholders in the *Reform*. One's neighbor had subscribed, everybody had subscribed, and hence there was nothing to be done but to subscribe.

M. Caussidière knew his trade well, and never left a moment's time for reflection. A poor, half decided patriot, on being presented with a pen filled with ink, must either subscribe or be considered a bad citizen. In other respects, the *Reform* was very accommodating—terms of payment made easy, three months, six months, and even a year; the main point being to have the paper of solvent men, which it discounted at any rate whatever, generously abstaining from trifles where its patrons were so liberal. It may readily be conceived that the name of stock, given to the paper thus acquired, was nothing less than a figure of rhetoric. Neither M. Caussidière nor the *Reform* ever thought it worth their trouble to furnish certificates. The stockholders were transformed, as if by magic, into so many donators; and they might help themselves the best way they could; that was no concern of the patriotic *Reform*.

It very often happened that the men who had thus been entrapped, would give the matter a maturer consideration, by the time that their notes became mature, and would refuse to pay them; but there were always some who, out of regard for their obligation, would wince, and pay down their money.

Such was the very laborious trade which M. Caussidière followed during a period of two years; a proof certainly that his industrial abilities have not always been fruitless of success; but when he spoke to the Chamber of his talents as a man of business, he omitted to state in what kind of business he had exercised them. From what has been said, it will be seen that the display of these talents was made in the *higher branches of industry*, as understood by Bilboquet.

From time to time the patriotic travelling agent returned to Paris, and held interviews with his colleagues of the committee. He entered into minute details of what he had seen and done, not omitting to state that he had formed numerous affiliations in the provinces. This, however, was false; for nothing that might be considered as secret societies existed out of Paris, except, perhaps, those of Lyons, Toulouse, and Marseilles; and even the associations there, were neither held together by any substantial bond of union, nor possessed of any real power. Since the conspiracy of 1842, M. Callés and his confederates of Lyons had lost confidence, and, like the conspirators of Paris, no longer pursued their work with interest. The little cliques of communists, at Toulouse and Marseilles, were rather ridiculous than formidable.

It may well be believed that the mere pleasure of crushing M. Caussidière, who is already down as low as he can be, and not likely to commence his career of prodigious mystification very soon again—is not the object which I have in view in recording all this; nor is it from the miserable love of retailing a scandalous history that I expose the secrets of the *Reform*. I do it because it is indispensable to show the characters of that man and of that newspaper which had the disposal of France, on the 24th of February, and which remained our masters for a period of several months.

I pretend to prove that the event of February was not, and could not have been, the work of the republicans, and above all, that the *Reform* was not the sole cause, as has long been believed, of the overthrowal of the monarchy of July. At the period of which I am speaking, towards the close of the year 1846, besides the pitiful condition in which that concern found itself, existing upon the proceeds of fifteen hundred subscriptions and the craft of M. Caussidière, there were numerous other causes of enervation and impuissance originating even in its own party. In the first place, the imperial haughtiness of M. Flocon had made a perfect desert of the office; the numerous subsidies drawn from the patriots, no longer rendered it safe to have anything to do with it, and finally the secret societies were perfectly independent of the control of Messrs. Ledru-Rollin and Flocon. The little communist sects, whom the latter had anathematized, considered him nothing less than an exploiter. Among the *Seasons* all relations with the *Reform* were prohibited. M. Léoutre, become the director, and M. Caussidière the purveyor, of the paper, paid but very little attention to the society; and as for myself, I had decided to keep it clear of the paper. It is true that, in order to make his court to M. Ledru-Rollin, M. Grandménil kept him informed of what was going on among the groups, and from time to time gave some few vague hints in reply to the inquiries of M. Flocon; but this was all the connection that existed between the society and the *Reform*. That paper had no influence or control over the little army of conspirators. Now this paltry, embarrassed, and wretched condition of the *Reform* was the same in 1848 as in 1846. It can be imagined, then, whether the fall of a formidable government was owing, under such circumstances, to a newspaper clique so small and infamous.

CHAPTER XV.

M. Albert becomes one of the committee—Orders of the day abolished—The dissenting society—Its chiefs—Patriotic theft—Another dismemberment—A plan of insurrection.

THE organization attempted by the new committee of the *Seasons* was not carried out, and the committee itself became very nearly dislocated by the departure of M. Caussidière and the connection of M. Léoutre with the *Reform*. The latter having become conspirator only from the want of other employment, withdrew without reluctance. He was moreover instructed to refrain from every act that might compromise the journal, since it already had troubles enough at home without the addition of others from abroad. And such was the condition of every one connected with the *Reform;* M. Flocon, notwithstanding his desire to retain a sort of patronage over the society, feared to inquire after its proceedings, and M. Ledru-Rollin was still more circumspect. These gentlemen are very willing to have it believed now, that they were conspiring at that period with might and main; but as is seen, they were, in fact, thinking of anything else than conspiracies.

M. Leroux, seeing the society going to ruin, soon lost courage and retired, leaving of the new members only M. Grandménil, who was of but little account. Harassed by troublesome affairs, but which, nevertheless, could not prevent him from engaging in speculations of the most colossal character, he paid no attention to the society, and the society paid but very little attention to him. Hence, it follows that M. Boivin and myself had become again the only chiefs of the sections, or at least the only ones who had any direct influence over them. This state of things continued for the space of several months, and then another modification took place. M. Boivin had for lieutenant a man who gradually came to possess a very considerable degree of influence. A conspirator wholly unknown until that period, but being one of those who persevered in his faith and devotion, he soon gained an ascendency over his chief and entirely supplanted him. He became the pivot of the association. The position to which this individual thus arrived, without noise or contention, merely from the indifference or discouragement of his confederates, proved to be the commencement of a career which was to end in his becoming one of the dictators of France. It will be perceived that I allude to M. Martin, surnamed Albert.

I can say with impartiality that, as a type of honesty among the laboring classes, the provisional government might have made a much worse choice. M. Albert, a mechanic by trade, is a simple-minded man, of regular habits, skilful and industrious in his profession. He was foreman to an engineer, and assisted him in the construction of several curious machines, one of which, among others, was for the fabrication of porcelain buttons for linen, an invention which he can partly claim as his own. As to his education or knowledge, beyond the sphere of his profession, there is but little to be said; such as he had, came from the reading of newspapers and revolutionary pamphlets. His ideas tended to communism; but as he adhered to principle rather than to any particular doctrine, he accepted neither the tenets of Cabet, nor those of Babeuf. He was moderate in his views, not claiming, like many of the cracked-brains of the time, the immediate and absolute establishment of his principles. He was neither intemperate in his revolutionary zeal nor ridiculous in his ambition. If his subsequent elevation appeared to be unreasonable, that was not his fault. There was need of an instrument—he was ready at hand and was taken; but I doubt if he had ever dreamed of the singular lot that awaited him. He has set an example, however, which doctors in blouses and statesmen in shirt sleeves would do well to follow, viz: to remain silent upon matters which they know nothing about, and observe a becoming modesty in positions where they find themselves out of place. Before February he had never been seen to abandon his tools for the purpose of driving the quill, nor had he ever taken to the stump, preferring a good trade which he knew, to a bad one of which he knew nothing. When raised by a freak of fortune to the highest point of the wheel, it was observed that he wore his honors with an unaffected ease, free from pride or giddiness; a fact which cannot be said of many of his colleagues to whom modesty would not have been the less becoming.

I had made M. Albert understand that the people were affrighted by the ideas of the communists, and that these ideas, therefore, ought to be kept out of the association. And in order to avoid all dissension and the visitations of the police, the discussion of principles and collecting of arms and ammunition remained prohibited. In short, the old course of things was pursued with the exception of one single point, and that point was an important one; I proposed to my colleague the abolition of the orders of the day. A state of tranquillity which promised to continue for a long time; the implicit obedience of the groups; the confidence which M. Albert had in me—everything, in fine, seemed favorable for the realization of a measure which I had had for a long time at heart. I demonstrated the uselessness of such dangerous productions in the existing state of things; the seizure of one of them might compromise a large number of persons and throw the whole party into disorder; their importance had become very much diminished by a paucity of events compelling them to run always upon the same text; and, besides, they might easily be resorted to again if circumstances should render it necessary. M. Albert approved of these arguments; they were transmitted to the chiefs of groups and accepted by them, and, in short, the proposition was adopted. In order to supply the place of written instructions, it was agreed that the principal members of the association should be assembled monthly, and receive oral communications which they were to make known to their men. It could be foreseen that these assemblies, although directed by the same chiefs, could not have either the importance or the solemnity which the reading of the orders of the day would have given them, and that the bonds of union would become proportionally relaxed. Such, in fact, proved to be the case. The chiefs of groups still repaired to the assemblies as usual; but as they no longer felt that there was a serious committee concealed behind the orders of the day, they lost interest in their work; and the men, being deprived of all communication except with their immediate chiefs, were left without a stimulus, and gradually loosened from the bonds of union which constituted their force.

The hopes of the republic at that time were so faint and unpromising that the greater part of the members submitted peaceably to this dilapidation of the society. The resignation, however, was not general; for some of the *Gypsies*, accustomed to live upon the chances of democracy, saw with alarm the disappearance of secret societies; it seemed to them that their bread and the very air itself were withheld from them. They were happy in the importance of the parts which they were playing; in the dreams of vulgar ambition which rendered the grog shop a palace—and the idea of returning to the common hum-drum life of ordinary, industrious men, was to them exceedingly afflicting. As their views were narrow and their principles consisted in adopting the most exorbitant doctrine as the most patriotic, they were of course in favor of communism, absolute, entire, and immediate. Subjected thus far, though much against their will, to the regulation which prevented all controversy and equalitarian propagandism, they created a schism, formed a small group by themselves, and entered upon a career of the wildest projects and the most abominable hopes. A crack-brain doctor of physic, M. Lacambre, was their chief. He had lost his reason, and seriously proposed to attack the Tuileries by means of scaling ladders and carry it by assault. In order to cure him of such follies he was arrested ; but his partisans became none the better for it. Seized with a kind of madness, they intrepidly admitted the most monstrous consequences of their pretended principles, and finally came to declare, that, as their object was the deliverance of humanity, they might make use of any means for that purpose, even of theft.

This is not a mere insinuation—a way of saying that such and such crimes might be committed because of the theory that was maintained; the case was argued, the consequences regularly deduced, and the application made, viz: that the property of one's neighbors might be taken for the purpose of effecting a revolution. It is evident that the instincts of the malefactor were here at work, and that they were mingled, too, with a very considerable quantum of imbecility. But be this as it may, the appropriation of property was decreed and executed. Unfortunately, however, for our humanitarian distributors of property, rascality is much easier in theory than it is in practice. A very edifying trial took place, in which Messrs. Coffineau, Javelot and other socialists of the free and easy school, were called to an account for their conduct. Some of them denied the theft, and others intrenched themselves behind their good intentions. But the judges, giving but little weight to denials contradicted by proofs, and having but a small appreciation of such intentions as wherewith, it is said, hell is paved, sent these gentlemen to rejoin their companions in the cells for robbers.

Still another dismemberment of the principal society occurred about the same time. Several of the chiefs of groups and some of the members, thinking that the organization of the society was decidedly too weak and the colors too pale, undertook to get up something better. Messrs. Culot, Flotte, Chenu, and Louis Gueret, were the leaders of the dissenters. They formed a crew of about a dozen babblers, drunkards, and subaltern agents of the police, among whom I may mention Messrs. Courtin, Turmel, Gibaut, Barbast, Vitou, senior and junior, Champagne, Moustache, Vellicus and

Pottier. These gentlemen were of the opinion that they could use up the government without a moment's delay. M. Gueret, ex-revolutionary agent, had not made his fortune in selling patriotic books, and hence found it necessary to return to the trade of conspirator. M. Turmel, a wine merchant, made his shop the permanent meeting place of a band of stupid brawlers, to whom he gave the tone. The others, including M. Vellicus, whom we know, were nothing but ordinary hair-brains, who had some influence over a small number of conspirators of the barriers. Partly from instinct, and partly with the view of playing a trick upon the old association, they got up a tremendous excitement, intrigued and caballed right and left, made enlistments, and finally succeeded in drawing together some four or five hundred men. But they had no organization, consisting merely of groups who recognized their chiefs, and of chiefs who had an understanding with each other. With the view of giving themselves some distinction, the chiefs endeavored to add to their class a number of notabilities. M. Lagrange, less and less known by the big guns of the party, and the very excellent M. Baune, always tyrannized over by M. Flocon, were two of the notables whom they wished to decoy. Several thinly attended banquets were given to these gentlemen, at which they displayed their eloquence, but without any great success. As the band of scape-graces which surrounded them were much better qualified for getting a chief into difficulties than for flattering his pride, they excused themselves from taking the command, and shunned the society of their friends as much as possible. This scorn, or this prudence, or whatever else it may be called, had no effect in checking the fervor of the *dissenters*. Their chiefs had taken an oath to lead them to battle, and to battle they must go. The festivities of July were approaching, and this occasion, though repeatedly chosen for an outbreak, and always proving a failure, yet always appearing a favorable one, was fixed upon, and the blow was to be struck on the 28th. It was arranged that the groups should meet at the column of the *Place Vendome*, then repair to a depot of arms in Saint Antoine Street, and immediately commence a discharge of fire-arms. M. Turmel was designated as generalissimo of the expedition. This chief requested an interview with us for the purpose of planning a combined and general movement of the two armies. We replied that we had neither communications nor combinations to make with M. Turmel, and that he and his men might go to prison or lose their lives if it were their pleasure to do so. As the pretended depot of arms had no existence, and as the desire of taking to the streets was opposed by a prospect of success more than doubtful, the affair stopped where it was.

But it was only adjourned over. Heads became inflamed again; the lightnings of excitement and exasperation flashed through the streets, and thunderous war-cries reverberated among the grog-shops. The chiefs, pushed on to the foot of the wall, declared again that they were ready to mount. M. Vitou set out for Rouen, in order to get from M. Lemasson the necessary money for the movement; but the banker conspired only under the blanket, and with his own men, and took good care not to furnish funds. M. Gueret then went to captain Vallier, an old Bonapartist republican, who resided in a village of the environs of Paris, and had shown some generosity towards the party. It was thought that he would prove to be more accommodating than the Rouen millionnaire; but no, a subsidy from that quarter was refused too. Such stinginess on the part of opulent patriots rendered the revolutionists indignant, and even desperate. Since they were left to themselves alone, they would act alone—they would show that they could do without assistance.

Hence, three or four hundred bandits, commanded by Captains Turmel, Moustache, and Champagne, seriously set about taking Paris and the government by assault! This may cause a smile; but we must reflect, that the affair of February was brought about in part by this honorable troop. These are the men who always imagine that they have only to come forth in order to upset the country. It can hardly be conceived to what an extent of infatuation passionate men are borne, by indulging continually in excitement, with glass in hand, dwelling forever upon one and the same idea.

M. Albert and myself were fully informed of all these projects, and he, being a communist, often showed an impatient desire to come to an understanding with these mad men, and risk the delivery of a battle; but I persuaded him from it. After due reflection, he agreed with me, not only in censuring, but in trying to prevent, at all hazards, the sanguinary *coup-de-main* which was premeditated. We made known our disapproval in emphatic terms, and an order of the day was disseminated among the groups, announcing that a detestable project had been formed, in which the members were prohibited from taking any part. At a meeting held at Montmartre, where several chiefs of the *Dissenting Society* were present, we made known the reasons of our disapproval in a way not to be mistaken. The reasonable men listened to our arguments; others perceived their own weaknesses, and in short, the insurrectional army was reduced to a state of dissolution.

This took place in 1847, only a few months previous to the affair of February; and certainly, for a government in the habit of making provocations, a finer occasion had never been presented. An affair undertaken under the conditions which, and by the men whom we have mentioned, must have inevitably proved a miserable failure. And what would have been one of the consequences of this failure? Why, evidently, the impossibility of a revolution in February. The Left, rendered prudent by the miscarriage, would not have opened its disastrous campaign of banquet giving, or have inspired the public mind with that degree of super-excitement which was so successfully taken advantage of by a handful of intriguers to carry out their designs.

But, however this may be, the late government has not to reproach itself for permitting bloodshed so long as it could possibly be prevented.

CHAPTER XVI.

The bomb plot—M. Caussidière forms a revolutionary congress—The check given him—Interview of members of the congress with M. Ledru-Rollin—Their disappointment—Portrait of M. Ledru-Rollin.

From this army hastening to its dissolution there became detached a small corps of wrong headed men, who, seeing no longer any prospect of a regular attack, reverted, as usual, to the idea of a sudden surprise. A nephew of M. Grandménil had sent from Nantes the receipt of an incendiary bomb, the effect of which was to be thoroughly devastating. Messrs. Culot, Viton, Vellicus, Courtin, and Gibaut made a common stock of their chemical knowledge, and undertook to fabricate the projectile. What they were going to do with it when once made was not fully decided upon. Circumstances favoring, they would blow up the Tuileries with it, or the Chamber of Deputies, or perhaps set the four quarters of Paris on fire. These three projects stood at the head of the list of sure and expeditious means for effecting a revolution. The other means of destruction upon the list, though ruminated upon in the dens of the democracy, would be too long for repetition. At certain periods there seemed to be a perfect rage for this sort of inventions; everybody wished to have one of his own. A few intimate friends would be assembled; the walls of the meeting room carefully examined; the exterior premises guarded by sentinels, and then the author of the engine would give a description of it with a suppressed voice and unquiet air, as if it were something which was going to change the face of the world. At one time the design would be to throw a phial of prussic acid upon the king; at another, a mine of fulminating powder was to be so laid at some dinner of the functionaries as to send them all up to the rafters. One of the schemes was to saw the wood work of the roofs in such a way, that a movement might be commenced by throwing the roofs into the streets. Another still, was to persuade the soldiers to massacre their officers and proclaim the republic, and so on. The greater part of these ferocious designs immediately became known to the police; their authors were watched, and at the first attempt towards carrying them into execution, were thrown into prison.

M. Pinel, secretary general of the prefecture charged with the political service, was very well informed of the bombs of M. Culot and company, and kept posted up with regard to their fabrication. Learning one morning that the conspirators were going to Bellville in order to make the trial of some of them, he sent his agents there to lay hands both upon the projectiles and the projectors.

A dozen conspirators were implicated in this affair—were brought to justice, and sentenced to a variety of penalties; and this completed the disorganization of the little army which had set itself up as a rival of the *Seasons*. Until February, this army remained without mission or cohesion, made up of demagogues and communists of every hue and complexion, and lost from view among the darkest dens of the capital.

M. Caussidière was then absent in the provinces; but hearing of the discovery of the bomb plot, and of the excitement which had been exhibited among some of the groups, he fancied that everything was in a blaze in Paris, and, fearing to be anticipated by his colleagues, who testified but a mediocre esteem for him at any rate, he took it into his head to assemble his friends of the departments, and hasten on to Paris in order to decree the insurrection. About the month of October, 1847, M. Albert and myself were informed of his return; and on the same day he gave us a rendezvous at the house of M. Ledouble, a wine-seller of Croix-des-Petits-Champs Street, the object of the interview being, as he intimated, of the very highest importance.

We met at dinner at the wine seller's, Messrs. Caussidière,

Grandménil, Léoutre, and Baune, frequenters of the house, and four delegates from the provinces—Messrs. Rocher, of Nantes, Buvigner, of Verdun, Lorentz, of Nancy, and a fourth from Metz. After the repast was over, the master of the house withdrew, and one of the delegates broached the subject by expressing a desire to be well informed upon the state of things, and as to what would be expected of them. M. Caussidière made a long, studied speech, in which the condition of Paris, which he knew nothing about, was set forth with consummate impudence. He concluded by declaring that everything was ready for a decisive affair, and that all that was wanting was an understanding with the representatives from the provinces. M. Albert and myself were taken aback by this declaration. We were wholly unprepared for it, and, having exchanged looks with each other, I immediately asked how such a conclusion had been arrived at without our concurrence, since we alone were in such relations with the men of the societies as to know their dispositions. The delegates were very much astonished at the strange want of harmony which this incident revealed among the patriots of Paris, and called for explanations. M. Léoutre wished to have it understood that the action taken, so far as it concerned us, had been in good faith, and without ulterior design, and that the gravity of circumstances alone had dictated the conduct of M. Caussidière. But I observed that it was not for M. Caussidière, slightly connected as he was with the association, unknown to the men, and without influence over them, to be as forward as he had just been, and that M. Albert especially ought to have been consulted, since, from habitually mingling with the men of action, he alone knew something positive of their spirit. I said nothing but the truth; but I was glad to insist upon it in order to arouse the susceptibility of my colleague, and dispose him unfavorably towards the project. And I succeeded; for M. Albert declared that the enterprise was inopportune, and expressed his regret that the delegates had been led into a useless proceeding. These gentlemen did not conceal their disappointment from M. Caussidière.

He had represented himself to them as the principal chief of the secret societies, having only to speak to be obeyed. A little presumption might be excused; but to put men to so much trouble as to call them together from the extremities of France, was no trifling degree of levity.

"Oh! the devil, now," exclaimed M. Caussidière humorously, "things are not in so bad a state but that we can go on if we choose."

"Since it has become necessary," I replied, "to portray the wretchedness of our condition, I am going to do it in all frankness. The forces of the democracy militant are as follows: The *Society of the Seasons*, six hundred disorganized men; the *Dissenting Society*, four hundred men in a state of disbandment; add to these about five hundred old conspirators, ready to take arms; the whole amounts to fifteen hundred men, who promise to take to the streets, but one-half of whom will not make their appearance at the given signal. We should have to undertake the affair, then, with seven or eight hundred men, enough to hold out about two hours. Besides, are the necessary measures taken? Have we arms, or ammunition, or plan of attack? Have the chiefs of the party been informed, and have they given their word? Is the new system of government prepared? Are we agreed as to the men who are to be invested with the power? Nothing of all these matters has been attended to. In order to deceive no one, there is but a word to be said, and that is, that the party was never in a weaker condition for undertaking a movement than now."

More and more surprised, the delegates directed inquiring looks towards M. Albert: and he, perceiving the justness of the exposure which I had made, gave it a simple, unqualified confirmation. The emissaries began to think that they had been the subject of a hoax.

From the wine-shop where we dined, we repaired to the estaminet of Sainte Agnès. There, Messrs. Caussidière and Léoutre endeavored to work upon us by sentiment.

"You lose everything," said the future prefect of police to me; "we can make nothing more out of those men; you don't reflect what bad effect your words may produce in the provinces."

"I see but one danger," I replied, "and that is in deceiving men and leading them to believe in imaginary forces. An attack is impossible, and we will have nothing to do with it."

Attempts were made to render M. Albert more accommodating. What they wanted of him was, not an adhesion to a project thenceforth decided on, but simply a few words in order to save the reputation of M. Caussidière. But this consolation was refused him; I stuck close to my confederate, and did not leave him until the conference was ended.

M. Caussidière had assured the delegates that M. Ledru-Rollin had a part in the affair and patronized it warmly. They, therefore, repaired to the house of the tribune in order to have the matter cleared up. They found a man who was at least as much astonished as they themselves were; he told them, drily enough, that no insurrection was going to break out, and that consequently he could not be the patron of one. The poor provincials were astounded; they had got enough this time, and they returned to their homes, entertaining a singular idea of M. Caussidière, of M. Ledru-Rollin, and of the patriots of Paris generally.

If they were not highly charmed with the reception given them by M. Ledru-Rollin, he, on his part, was not more so with their proceedings; for he had by far too many tribulations to deal with already to become implicated in affairs of *coup-de-main*—something for which he had no liking. It may well be believed that the roses were not without thorns in his brilliant career of patriot in chief, tribune of the people, and, above all, protector of the *Reform*. M. Ledru-Rollin is generally thought to be a furious revolutionist, ferocious and indomitable, while, in fact, he is merely a man of sanguine temperament, a lover of noise, fame, and enjoyment. He is a miniature edition of the irregular and gluttonous Mirabeau. The *Reform* one day, wanting a standard bearer, and especially some one to advance the needful, set him up as chief of the republican party; and as Madam Ledru-Rollin, an enthusiastic Irish woman, who had married her husband from political inclination, urged him forward to assume a brilliant position, he yielded to the double pressure as well as to his own impulses, and rushed at all hazards into a revolutionary career. The history of a man stumbling headlong down a mountain's side towards unknown precipices was his from that moment. It was in vain that he cast a piteous look amidst the darkness and dangers that surrounded him, for the impulse had been given, and flounder on he must, shutting his eyes in order not to see, and uttering loud cries to drown his fears.

In the Chamber of Deputies he endeavored to make himself terrible, roaring and panting in the most rarified atmosphere of democratic opinion. The auditor would listen to him for a moment with curiosity, and then shrug his shoulders. He gave forth emphatic harangues, of which the press never published two words, always excepting the *Reform*, which, it was well understood, received a consideration for singing his praises. But the adulterated incense of the hungry journal blinded the eyes of the poor orator; every swing of the censer hit him a stunning blow. He sold his place as advocate at the Court of Cassation in order to defray the expenses of his artificially acquired glory. The proceeds of the sale were soon swallowed up in all sorts of political gulfs. He then had recourse to speculations in land; but these proved a failure, and consumed the rest of his fortune. To avoid intrenching upon the fortune of his wife, he gave his signature to the usurers and gambled in the stocks, making use for this purpose of the services of the respectable M. Grandménil. It was on account of this irregular mode of life that his rival, M. Marrast, let fly a well barbed arrow at him, the arrow being sent back to the *Marquis of the Republic*, tipt with poison, and thus tapping the gall-bladders of both of these magnanimous democrats.

The *National* attacked him not only as a speculator overwhelmed with debts, but ever as a patriotic notability; chuckling with malicious glee over the airs of the *Captain*, and the empty rhetoric of the *Tribune*. With the men of the *National*, this great man was nothing less than a mere intriguer, seeking for his own personal advantage, to ruin a rival newspaper.

Nor did his title of chief of the republic pass current among the other fractions of the party; he gravitated around a common centre with some half dozen of sects, but there was no attraction between himself and them. As to the gentlemen of the suburbs, they knew that he kept liveried lacqueys, an equipage and a large train of domestics, and hence regarded him as very much of an aristocrat. And as he had rejected, on various occasions, every idea of communism, the apostles Cabet, Pierre Leroux, Raspail, etc., had excommunicated him.

And even among the men of the *Reform*, though they decorated his temples with garlands and pointed him out for the adoration of the faithful, his infallibility was not admitted by a very long shot. M. Ribeyrolles, second editor, considered him a very worthy man, whose five franc pieces were very useful. M. Flocon looked upon him as a passable sort of an orator, but a very small sample of a statesman, and allowed it to be seen very clearly that without his services the illustrious democrat would have been just nothing at all. The influence of the pretended chief in the councils of the *Reform* ranked only as third best with that of these two editors; it was in money matters alone that he took precedence, for there it was his own purse which was principally concerned. The advisers are not the payers, says the wisdom of nations; but the proverb hardly proved true in this case.

The rather low estimate which was thus formed of M. Ledru-Rollin cannot be considered as wholly unjust. If to be a man of eloquence it is only necessary to open wide a large pair of scornful looking eyes, maintain a lofty bearing, and go buttoned up to the chin in the Canning style, just unbuttoned enough to allow the hand to be always carried in the bosom—if it is only necessary to have appearances, a pretty large head, broad shoulders, and all the evidences of a sound constitution and a happy temperament—why then M. Ledru-Rollin would be one of the first of our orators; but, unfortunately, all these things do not constitute talent, they are but the mere externals of it.

A portrait of the famous democrat, displayed in the windows of the picture-sellers, seems to affect the air of Mirabeau; the head being arrogantly thrown back shows great pretensions to energy and domination. This portrait is in fact something very ridiculous; its affectation is shocking. It may be seen at a glance that the person who sat for such a portrait had a great deal more pride than merit.

In examining the two portraits of Mirabeau and Ledru-Rollin, the differences of organization are perceived at once. The first has a natural wildness of expression which evinces a power confident of itself, while the other shows a constrained effort at the display of uncertain energy. Mirabeau tosses his head upwards like the enraged bull, while M. Ledru-Rollin draws his back with arrogance in order to intimidate the adversary of whom he stands in fear. In his great boldness there mingles neither aggression nor defiance, but simply the necessity of giving an imposing idea of doubtful strength.

The character of the man may be seen in these traits. The repartee, the unmasking of his adversary—such is his forte. He is a man of intellect, but without much reach of thought, of varied but superficial acquirements, and naturally bold, but slow of conception. He makes up for his defects with audacity, and, as he never really ventures beyond the limits of prudence, he appears always to have the initiative. Like all the other politicians of his sort, he is quick in discovering the faults of others, but takes good care never to suggest remedial measures of his own. Possessed of incontestable intelligence and of a degree of tact much greater than is believed, he alone knows where the shoe pinches him. From this knowledge of himself arises that circumspection which he shows with regard to parties. He will venture with temerity upon the faith of others; he will parody Cambon or some other equally illustrious revolutionary character, but from his own stock of ideas he will hazard nothing. Fearing to advance upon unknown grounds lest he might meet with some of those slip-ups which kill an orator dead, he waits until the question, proposed by others, has become well set forth; then, having a clear perception of the subject, he enters the lists and conducts the attack by a well-known process at the bar—that of assailing the weakest point of the enemy. When once upon a clear road where there is no fear of stumbling, he gives the rein, and, while under full headway, gives out a few phrases of good alloy, and which may well pass for eloquence. But even then, the effect is very much impaired by an enunciation which is rendered difficult from his organs of speech being too much cloyed with fat.

These higher flights, however, are mere exceptions to a general rule, his speeches consisting usually of nothing but words, characterized by redundancy and presumption. There is nothing in them indicative of originality, or even of peculiarity; they are the ordinary verbosities common among men of the gown—the current coin of the oratorial art.

In short, audacious in words but circumspect in action; ever ready to throw pellets of the brain, but never ready to throw those of the musket; often brought before the tribunal of commerce, but with no desire to come before that of the assizes; declaring his party invincible, but knowing to the contrary—M. Ledru-Rollin took no part in conspiracies and had no ambition for the title of conspirator; and hence the cause of the ungracious reception which he gave to the friends of Caussidière. Subsequently, when before the Court of Bourges, he purposely threw out a theory upon *coups-de-main*, such, that it was inferred that he had been the originator of the Machiavelic affair of 1848; but the facts are that until the month of February inclusive he formally denied, disapproved, and rejected insurrectional measures. It was the accident that gave France into the hands of demagogues that led him to change his opinions as well as to present the democracy with the mortifying spectacle of the 13th of June. If the spectators of the principal scene in that drama had known the tribune face to face when assuming his Olympian airs, what a reverse of the medal they must have seen when, in making his escape, he got jammed into the windows of the conservatory!

CHAPTER XVII.

Profiles in charcoal—Messrs. Proudhon, Louis Blanc, Considérant, Thoré, Sarrut, Miot, Xavier Durrieu, Bareste.

HAVING arrived thus far in the history of the republican party as it existed under the government of July, the reader will be surprised, perhaps, at not having met with certain characters who have recently taken such a decided stand, and whose influence ought, according to their own pretensions, to be all prevailing either with the press or the conventicles of the faction. I am now going to say a few words with regard to these men; and the reason why I have not done so before, is because they have had nothing to do with the events which I have related.

Among these characters M. Proudhon is the one of most importance; but even his reputation dates as it were but from yesterday. From the writings of this famous socialist and the caricatures given of him by the smaller prints, there is no one who has not formed some idea of his physiognomy and his character. To finish the picture, therefore, we have but to add a few off-hand strokes. M. Proudhon is a man of thirty-five years of age, of a robust constitution, and with a large head firmly set upon his shoulders; his prevailing trait being a strange sort of avidity, consisting of half and half of the energies of the bull and the greediness of the ostrich. His greediness, however, counts in the devouring of adversaries' arguments and objections. Unpolished, negligent in his dress, and laboring as he goes along with a heavy, awkward gait, his gaze is always peering through a pair of lunettes, and wandering off in search of paradoxes and economic humbugs. Venus herself might brush by him without his seeing her. The true riches of this wretched world, such as women, works of art, and magnificence of all kinds, he values about as much as he does the heavy prose of the poor M. Pierre Leroux. He is original, mystic, gross, and murderous. He is a greasy monk, a German philosopher, an unkempt boor, a sectarian, but proud withal, and infatuated beyond all conception. He delves into science like an ancient Benedictine; he wields fulminating doctrines like his friends Fucurbach, Mauerer, and the brothers Bauer; he launches forth audacious truths like the peasant of the Danube, and would, like Omar, destroy the faith of his rivals by fire and sword. He would set fire to the temple of Ephesus if Erostratus had not got the start of him.

As to notions upon the nicer elements of life, he has none whatever; what is called the world is to him an unknown land. If you tell him that in order to make laws for men it is necessary to know something of human nature, he will stare at you and shrug his shoulders. Individuals are to him but the mere figures with which he works out his problems, and if his operations are correct, that is all that he cares for; it is no consequence whether the data are right or wrong. It is pretended that his logic is exceedingly acute and his philosophy arch-profound; whereas, his logic consists in the mere method of mathematics and his philosophy in forced efforts at precision. All the elements of his calculations are brought together with wonderful exactness and symmetry, but unfortunately they are wholly wanting in a very important matter—in the principle of life; they are nothing but useless mechanism. A false proposition being stated, M. Proudhon will undertake to prove it true even to the most infinitely small fraction of a hair's breadth, such is his art and such his character.

This extraordinary man was originally a simple type-setter of Besançon, his native city. Having contended for a prize of the academy, he won it, and thus commenced his career of glory. With a natural bias towards questions of political economy, he looked about among the various schools of the day to discover to which he should belong. An idea struck him. To invent a new system was not an easy matter; to become the disciple of another master was too repugnant to his genius; but he might become the demolisher in chief of all economical science and all social tradition up to that time. Such then was to be his mission. Resolved to strike a blow at the outset that would make his name ring through the world, he wrote at the head of a book a combination of letters in comparison with which the incendiary torch is a mere rushlight. These letters are as follows:—

"PROPERTY IS THEFT!"

He had not the remotest doubt but that the utterance of these three words would bring his name down upon the astonished world like a clap of thunder in a fair day; but in this he was disappointed. For at that time the most towering bonfire of socialism excited but very little curiosity—no passion whatever; and the government having the good sense not to throw oil, in the shape of anathemas, upon that of M. Proudhon, the consequence was, that it flared up and then flared out, becoming extinguished of itself. Not till some six months after its appearance did a few amateurs, in search of something to blow up the old world with, remember this beautiful piece of pyrotechny. The learned, especially, showed an outrageous contempt for the famous book which the author had so imperiously thrown among them as a bone of discord. The Utopian was therefore hurt to the heart. A few Fly-catchers, it is true, considered the work as perfectly sparkling; but M. Proudhon, doubtful whether he understood it himself, was quite sure that they didn't understand it. And, who would believe it! this ferocious amateur of ruins had the weakness to fish for the opinions of the very men whom he had used up. To be quietly scorned by a set of wretches to whom he could give five arguments for one, was something intolerable. He must be revenged, and emphatically too, and without delay. His revenge consisted in a work entitled—*A System of Economical Contradictions*. He took up the chiefs of school, one after another, and gave them a terrible lamming, leaving them as flat and hollow as an old tile. But even this magnificent execution made no noise; or if any at all, it was heard only by the great men whom it demolished. No one was spared by it; not even M. Louis Blanc the radical, nor M. Michael Chevalier the conservative. As the author passed for a republican, people were astonished to see him wage war against his own party; but how little did they know of M. Proudhon! He a republican! why what can folks be thinking about? Is the republic anything new under the sun? Could the innovator stop for a moment at anything so fossiliferously old as that? Not he; annihilation—that is the word with him. If anything had an existence dating back before his day, that is enough to damn it to all eternity. As to what is called his *doctrine*, that consists in establishing religion without a God, society without property, and a state without a government. The rest of his works he has borrowed from M. Joseph May, and a few German philosophers in their dotage, with whom he has been made acquainted by M. Charles Grün. Before February, he declared, with all the seriousness imaginable, that every government is a downright usurpation, that every individual is his own sovereign, and that the delegation of sovereignty should be prohibited. No executive, no legislature—nothing, absolutely nothing! Men would live together in perfect freedom, like the Mohicans of Cooper; such is his doctrine, a very difficult one to be invented truly. The inventive genius of M. Proudhon, however, shows itself to a much better advantage when engaged in exterminating his confederates.

In the mean time, the socialist destroyer thought of establishing himself in the capital. He had thus far made but short visits there, and one fine day he set out for Lyons, where he had some friends whom he wished to see, being resolved to push on to Paris. But his books had not yet procured him a livelihood, and the uncertainty as to the pot's boiling, forced him to remain at Lyons as the clerk of a steamboat company. It was not until the close of 1847 that he made his entry into that Parisian Babel, to whose confusion he was going to add his own. At the outbreak of the revolution, he was preparing, together with Messrs. Pilhes,

Pyat, and Thoré, to establish a journal, the idea of which I had conceived for the purpose of increasing the discord among the patriots.

Hence, M. Proudhon, being wholly unknown to the people before February, and having his light kept under a bushel by the doctors of democracy, who probably foresaw in him an undisciplinable character and a terrible confederate, had no influence, either personal or moral, in bringing about the revolution.

And one of his rivals of those days, as he is still, M. Louis Blanc, had no more to do with the insurrection than he had; although his books, better known and more practised, in appearances at least, may have decided or confirmed several persons in a course of revolutionary agitation. The person of M. Louis Blanc consists of two large black eyes, miraculously underscored by a pair of thick lips, and fixed upon a body about the height of an hostler's boot. It is an eternal source of despair with this great man to find that his glory is shut up in an envelop not more than four feet eight inches in height. He has, however, the most refined manners, the most aristocratic distinction, and knows very well how to put on the insipid smile of dealers in court holy-water. On witnessing his gentle elegance, mixed always with a certain degree of personality, one suspects a character not exactly symmetrical, and that within that little body there lies a little man. A workingman, on hearing him make a speech once, said to a comrade: "That's a malicious little fellow, that!" And I am of the workingman's opinion; M. Louis Blanc has never shown anything else but malice. Since the production of his *History of Ten Years*, which gave him a pretty high stand in radicalism, he has carefully abstained from becoming connected with any coterie, well knowing that the entrance into one would close the doors against him of all the others. The men of the *Reform* displeased him by their vulgarity, and those of the *National*, by their aristocratic bourgeois pretensions; but, whenever one of his volumes was to make its appearance, he had a very affectionate shake of the hand for both. The tactics of this little man were to raise himself by means of the papers, but without connivance with them. His plan was to dazzle the upper classes by his brilliant works, and the lower classes by appearances of communism; and his object was, anything or everything, so that he was not confounded among the crowd. As M. de Lamartine prevented M. Victor Hugo at that time from sleeping, so M. Thiers gave wakeful nights to M. Louis Blanc; he was passionately jealous of the historical, oratorical, and statesman-like abilities of that celebrated conservative. Like the foolish serpent in the fable, he gnawed away upon the steel of the bourgeoisie, merely because M. Thiers was the personification of that capital force of modern society. The intercourse of M. Louis Blanc with the people having been limited to a few interviews with the more learned of the workingmen, who called upon him with congratulations for his historical and social doctrines, and his reserve with regard to the papers having kept him removed from an active part in intrigues, he could not well have, nor indeed had he, any direct influence in the events of February.

There is nothing to be said with regard to M. Pierre Leroux; he remained at Boussac Hollow, in charge of a little printing establishment, the emanations of which were pretended to be understood by half a dozen disciples.

As to M. Raspail, since his disappearance from our pages, his history runs as follows:—

About the year 1834, he established the *Reformer*, a paper which propagated the principles of the author both in politics and chemistry. It was an implacable diatribe against both the government and the faculty. Its odor was so intense and 'pungent, that the reader, while perusing it, might readily imagine himself in a drug shop. It was one of those concerns which the police call unhealthy. M. Raspail is the incarnation of sulphuric acid.

The collaborators of the terrible chemist led a miserable life; never were recruits so cavalierly treated by their corporal. The candid M. Dupoty, who cultivates conundrums and little girls, was so outrageously maltreated by him, that he left the office one day, determined to clear out, but he was called back by the ferocious editor-in-chief, collared, and maltreated for being an agent of the police.

But though the *Reformer* was conducted by such an extraordinary man, it did not prosper; it met with but a wretched support, hardly enough to cover the two sides with ink; and the inheritance of the *Tribune*, which soon fell to it, effected no change in this state of things. The ancient journal of M. Marrast had died from starvation, leaving nothing but fines and lawsuits, which certainly do not enrich a legatee.

M. *Raspail* made a vigorous appeal for the support of his doctrines upon the subjects of government and arsenic; but his partisans were either not very numerous, or not very devoted; for he didn't get a dollar. At such unworthy conduct as this, M. Raspail launched out into awful imprecations, and then packed up his baggage.

Dating from that day, a single word, the word camphor, exhibits the whole history of his career. He took refuge at Montrouge, barricaded his door, refused all intercourse with humanity, and delivered himself up to the elaboration of his famous system of hygiene and therapeutics. After immense researches upon the subject as to what diseases camphor cured and what others it prevented, he arrived at a very simple formula which included everything, viz: camphor cured all and prevented all.

Four large volumes soon made their appearance, every page, every line, and every word of which proclaimed, repeated, and rung out in every variety of change—that camphor was a universal remedy. Do you want a universal remedy? then take camphor!

Adding practice to precept, he camphored himself, his wife, his little ones, his neighbors, and all his acquaintances; whoever didn't smell of camphor was his declared enemy. As he could not give advice himself, not being a regular physician, and having too great a contempt of the faculty of Paris to ask for a diploma, he employed a worthy practitioner, who, willing also to preach by example, swallowed so much camphor that he gave up the ghost. But this didn't stop the new Hippocrates; he replied, like the doctor in the comedy: "The patient died according to rule, and there was nothing more to be said on the subject."

In spite of all his precautions, he had a crow to pick with justice—he was accused of the illegal practice of medicine. A fine accusation, my faith, to make against a man who set himself up as above the whole faculty! M. Raspail's tongue is not wanting in glibness; he pleaded his own case, and lost it. It was in vain to demonstrate that he was the victim of ignorant confederates, and especially of M. Orfila—nothing did it avail him.

But by the check thus given him he was by no means disconcerted; the preaching of the new doctrine went on as usual, and lawsuits followed as a matter of course; lawsuits against doctors, lawsuits against druggists, and lawsuits against the editors of medical works—M. Raspail bearing the brunt of the whole. He pleaded and repleaded, time and again, until the judges became so much accustomed to his presence that they addressed him as they would have done one of the regular advocates of the bar, thus: "You have the floor, MASTER Raspail."

This joke was not unpleasant to him; in fact, justice had had so much to do with him that he might well permit her a little diversion at his expense now and then. Speaking of the amusement of the court, by the way, reminds us of an incident which, as it is not altogether out of place here, we may be permitted to relate. It is concering M. Emmanuel Arago, ex-ambassador of the Republic. Before February, M. Arago was an advocate, but as he always lost his causes, being called on that account *M. Maximum*, as indicating the usual result of his pleadings, he declared a strike for the greater part of the time, and did nothing. To keep his faculties alive, however, he exercised them upon the ingenious combination of the game of dominos. He became as great at this game as he was inferior as an advocate. Once in a while some stray cause would happen to stop at his door, but the impressions of his favorite game led him into the strangest inconsistencies with it. Having got hold of one of these causes one day, he repaired to the Palace of Justice in order to plead it. Coming directly from a fine game of dominos, his thoughts were anywhere else than with the matters in hand. As the advocate for the king offered him the floor, Master Emmanuel, who preferred speaking second, in order at least to know something about the question, replied very naively:—

"No, Mr. King's advocate, it is your *lay down!*"

The title of *Master* applied to M. Raspail, though not so effective as the *lay down* of M. Arago, is still not without its salt or appropriateness. This illustrious man, in fact, had become deplorably given up to chicanery, and it was while poring over old musty records that he was surprised by the revolution of 1848; certainly, if he was expecting anything, it was not a revolution. Until the evening of the 24th of February, he declared openly that the affair was nothing but a trick of the police.

Let us pass on to several other characters who have become out and out socialist-democrats, but with whom nothing of the kind had been previously suspected. The first who offers himself to the view is M. Victor Considérant, the grand priest of Phalansterianism. Thus far the world had discovered nothing in Fourierism except a mixture of ideas, lascivious, benignant, foolish, and absurd. It was very evident that the application of the Phalansterian system would require a perfect removal of the ancient foundations of society; but M. Considérant and his fellow faithful were very confident that they could demolish everything pacifically, without disorder, and in the most amicable way in the world; were these gentlemen sincere? I am half inclined to believe that they were, for when the Fourierist pleasantry is once admitted, why not admit anything else—the taking of the moon by the horns, for instance, or the destroying of the faith, the morals, and the interests of the world, without a murmur or a complaint? But whether sincere or not, the Fourierists in the train of M. Considérant were openly in favor of *pacific* progress, and fully admitted the monarchical principle—this is incontestable. Now either these Utopians were jesting with the world, or else they have made a decided recantation. There is no more similarity between their ideas of 1847 and those which they entertain now than there is between white and black. The revolution has had more effect upon M. Considérant and his followers than they have had upon the revolution.

A man whom it is surprising to meet with in demagogic diggings is M. Etienne Arago. Is *he* a bad man? No, unless the habits of a millionnaire without any income might be considered as rendering him so. The truth is, he is overwhelmed with debts, and the monarchy offered him no means of paying or increasing them. M. Etienne Arago is wanting in everything to constitute a literary genius, and he has never passed as such, although, being a brother of the great Arago, he of course must have an intellect. Hence, he had a sort of notoriety in the world of letters, but as his talents did not pass very currently with the sold papers, that is to say, with those that had the means of paying, he was obliged, perforce, to content himself with the *pure* papers, the only inconvenience of which was that they left their editors to die with hunger. He was a theatrical reporter to the *Reform*, a position which qualified him for postmaster-general at the revolution. His influence in Paris was absolutely nothing, the part which he took in events being merely personal.

M. Ribeyrolles, the lieutenant of M. Flocon, is a man of intellect degraded by distress and the usual career of unprincipled young men. He had but one consolation in his physical maladies, and that was to jest at the moral miseries which he had directly under his eyes—such, for instance, as the infallibility of M. Flocon; the legerdemain of M. Caussidière; the misfortunes of M. Baune, who had taken to the bottle; the dilapidation of M. Lagrange, and a thousand other little scenes as lamentable as ridiculous. One day the scene presented would be the arrival at the press of M. Jeanty Sarre, now a representative of the people, but then the bearer of the prose of M. Etienne Arago, and of such a quantity of absinth, too, as to be wholly oblivious of what had become of one-half of the manuscript—left somewhere on the road. On another occasion it would be a court of honor instituted for trying M. A. Dangeliers, another representative of the people, for having pawned the watch of M. Watripon; and so on.

About this period M. Dupoty had been called to have a hand in the *Reform*, with the view of getting the assistance of his relations in favor of the till. But as it was soon discovered that he had been squeezed dry, and that his friends had no money to lose, he was left to languish in the office for some time without receiving anything to do, and finally was compelled to retire by force of insult and outrage, being told, by way of an explanation, that he had lost his head, and should go and take care of himself. The worthy man is no more of a warrior than M. Ribeyrolles, and neither of them has knocked tyranny on the head.

M. Thoré, whose pretensions are nothing short of reading lectures to all the patriots, and who modestly entitled his paper—*The True Republic*—is he, perhaps, one of the Samsons who have pulled down the columns of monarchy? I think probably not. About the year 1840, M. Thoré had attempted to establish a journal, to be called—*The Democracy;* but shortly afterwards venturing upon a pamphlet leprous with socialism, he became introduced into the precincts of Sainte Pelagie. Since then he occupied himself exclusively with the arts, which are his profession. He was a reporter of the *Constitutional*, a bourgeoise paper, and hence but a faint idea could be formed of what socialistic ferocity he was going to exhibit in the *True Republic*. M. Thoré is a man to be pitied. He had sense enough, as it would appear, to perceive that the diggings of 1848 were located on a wrong prospect, and that he ought to move elsewhere; but no, into the dirt he went, up to his neck; and now, the artist, the man of delicate and elegant tastes, lies, and perhaps for life, the inmate of a prison. The immediate cause of his loss is what is ruinous to us all, viz: jealousy. He saw many of his comrades becoming representatives of the people—such as M. Altaroche, a poor man, M. Pyat, a bad man, and he, who is neither foolish nor wicked, wanted to become one as well as they. And as the quickest way in these ill times of arriving at such destruction is to become the mountebank of the populace, he donned the socialists livery, and brought up at the fine pass in which we now see him. May the favors of the social republic rest gently upon him.

The name of M. Thoré was never pronounced, and he himself had not made his appearance before the events of February.

But at least, it will be said, such is not the case with M. Sarrut, who declared in the Constituent Assembly, that he had meddled in some hundred and odd conspiracies—such a man as he must certainly have turned the scale in the three glorious days of 1848. Gentle reader, M. Sarrut is a man of the South, full of ardor and imagination. There is no doubt but that he has conspired a hundred times and upwards, since he says so, but it was only in imagination, for the only real conspiracies which he can claim the honor of having been engaged in, are reduced to two or three, viz: those of the *Friends of the People*, and the *Rights of Man* on behalf of the republic, and, perhaps, a small affair on behalf of the Bonapartists. His other conspiracies are not known to men who, however, very well knew M. Sarrut. He was not even counted as a unit in the revolution, but rather as a cipher on the left hand.

M. Miot, a member of the legislature, in a speech which caused his expulsion from that body, mentioned the fights that he had had with the Municipal Guards on the 24th of February. This lofty minded citizen must have had a carbine of more than ordinary range, for at that time he was at Moulins Engilbert, in the Morvan, some sixty leagues from the scene of combat. I do not deny that the minions of tyranny may be hit at that distance; but certainly no one but a montagnard could do it.

Shall we speak, then, of M. Xavier Durrieu, who, taking a skilful advantage of the disbandment of the 13th of June, became for several months the shepherd of the socialist flock? Some five or six years ago, M. Durrieu won the cross of Spain by means of some very gallant articles in favor of Queen Isabella. At the commencement of the revolution he was editing a dynastic newspaper. When the republic came in vogue he became a republican; when socialism was invented, he became a socialist, and a man who conforms so readily to the course of events will probably become anything else when the occasion offers. It is useless, then, to speak of him as the maker of revolutions; he is satisfied with making his profit out of them.

There are still other great men from whom the smoke of February is not yet cleared away, but who are seen clearly enough to receive a hit or two for the diversion of the reader. We might, for instance, signal out M. Bareste, and question him about that translation of Homer which he gave out as edited by himself, but which he bought for a hundred crowns of a German by the name of Wolf, who, coming to him sometime afterwards for the loan of a hundred sous, was sent away empty. We might also ask him to inform us if while at the office of the *French Courier*, before February, he did not smile with a pleasant naivete at some men who were talking politics, and say that it was utterly ridiculous to have any opinions at all; but this would be a loss of time, and a useless indulgence in pasquinades. I shall, however, relate an anecdote of him a little further on, which will show in what estimation he was held by his fellow patriots at the period of the revolution.

CHAPTER XVIII.

The effective strength of the republican party in the beginning of 1848—The bourgeoisie and the royalty of July.

THE account which we have thus far given of the republican party differs so much from that which is usually spread before the public, that our readers may doubtlessly ask in surprise—Have not M. de Lamartine, and M. Louis Blanc both written histories of February, and have not these heroes of the revolution known what they were writing about? Have they been jesting with the public? Partly both. The revolutionary part of republican history was either not well known by these gentlemen, or else they have deemed it too paltry to be recorded; and hence have embroidered, embellished, and invented, arranging their romances in such a way as to aggrandize the heroes, said heroes being the authors themselves. M. de Lamartine speaks of the sections of the *Rights of Man* and the *Families* coming down on the 24th from Bellville, sombre, filling the streets like a swollen flood, and giving themselves the word of order. This might do very well for newspaper writers, but is simply absurd in a book which has the serious pretensions of history. Nothing compelled him to give designations; and in the whole course of his work it is easily perceived that he knew nothing of facts with the exception of those which concerned himself; and even they are so denaturalized by a puerile vanity as hardly to be recognized. The *Rights of Man* had been dead for fourteen years, and the *Families* had been merged in the *Seasons* since 1836. With regard to M. Louis Blanc, the few important scenes which he touches upon are probably better known to him; but the little man has arranged everything in such a way that it is difficult to perceive the truth in what he says.

Thus, the elevation of M. Albert as a member of the government, which was decided upon at the office of the *Reform* by about thirty persons, becomes changed under his pen into the immense acclamations of combatants, assembled in the court of the establishment. But I am not making a literary criticism, and this is not the place for exposing all the errors, absurdities, and boastings of these two writers. By comparing their books with the one in hand, it will be readily perceived on which side the truth lies.

The effective strength of the republican party, in February, may be stated as follows: The *National* had 4000 subscribers, one-half of whom, at least, had become dynastic under the lead of Messrs. Carnot, Garnier-Pagès, and others. It will be remembered, that these gentlemen made a confession of faith, much to the ire of the *Reform*, in which monarchy was declared sufficient for the march of progress. Of the 2000 remaining subscribers, we may put down 600 as belonging to Paris, and of these, about 200 as disposed to fight for their cause. The *Reform* had 2000 subscribers, 500 of whom were of Paris, and the whole 500 in favor of a revolution at all hazards. This makes 700 combatants among the subscribers to the newspapers. The two secret societies, the *Seasons* and the *Dissenting Society*, amounted together to 1000 men, 600 of whom belonged to the old society, and 400 to the new. But this army was very much broken up and scattered, and could not have furnished, probably, more than 600 men; but let us put it down at 1000. All the revolutionary communists had joined the *Dissenting Society*, so that of the sectarians there remained only the Cabetists, numbering some four or five hundred. It is known that by the articles of their creed, violence was not admitted as a means of success; but let us pay as little attention to their pacific declarations as they do themselves, and count them as among the number of the combatants. There remain now, four or five hundred old conspirators, whom the noise of muskets would call back to their ancient trade, together with a medley of republicans, unaccustomed to conspiracies, which may be estimated at 1500. These fractions, when added together, give a total of 4000 men. I am positive that the effective strength of the republican party of the capital did not exceed this number; and I defy any one to prove the contrary.

In the provinces, there was but one single secret society of any note—that of Lyons, and even that had led a precarious sort of an existence for a long time, like those of Paris. Toulouse, Marseilles, and two or three other cities had the semblances of associations, but they were of no importance. I believe that I give full measure when I state the number of republicans in the provinces as fifteen or sixteen thousand. We see, then, that for all France, that is to say, for a male adult population of ten millions of inhabitants, there were some twenty thousand republicans, or about one five-hundredth part of the whole! The least grain of common sense would teach us that such a small minority as this could not have overthrown a formidable government.

However, it is true that the revolution has taken place, and the republicans have claimed it as wholly their work. It is more like a dream than a reality, and to our cost we are made to credit it; but the question is, how was it brought about?

On that head, we may be permitted to make a few observations.

The third estate, or the bourgeoisie, which is not, as Siéyès said, everything, but which is at least the heart, the true pivot of our modern society, based upon industrial force, was very accurately represented by the family of Orleans. From the popular king, who was the head of their house, Henry IV., down to our days, this family have always sympathized with the movements of the middle classes. This fact is shown by the history of two centuries and a half. Allied to the throne, and attached to the middle classes, when the course of things had led to the establishment of a popular monarchy, this family was unanimously invested with the sovereignty. And has not the monarchy thus established, satisfied the exigencies of the times? Has it not perceived that the greatness and power of states no longer consists in chivalric renown or great military exploits, but in studying the safe and peaceful occupations of national industry? There can be no doubt of this; the impulse given to our national industry dates from the monarchy of July; the throne became, as it were, an immense counting-house. This last expression will doubtless offend a certain class of men who look upon the bourgeoisie as synonymous with weakness and folly. But these gentlemen should remember that there is a country—England—the population of which is principally made up of this class of citizens, the object of their scorn, but which, nevertheless, makes a considerable figure in the world. There is another country—the American Union, not without its importance, the whole population of which is occupied with trade. There are, moreover, such states as Prussia, which increase daily in power and strength, because of cherishing the interests of commerce. And there are other states, like Spain, on the contrary, whose existence is reduced to a mere vegetation by the loss of their merchants. France has always been the equal of the most powerful of these states in war, and has taken the lead of them in the arts; but what must inevitably be the result of not following their example in that new field of enterprise, called the market? Why, she will become comparatively weakened, just in proportion as the others gain strength; she will gradually fall back into the condition of a second or third rate power; and that event may take place much sooner than we think for. To use the word bourgeois as a term of contempt, is very easily done, but this bourgeois does not therefore the less occupy the place of the knight of the Middle Ages, and of the hero of our martial period of history. He is as correct a representative of the genius and grandeur of France at the present day, as the knight and the hero were in their day. I am aware that a certain class of fancy politicians will consider these views as unbecoming the dignity of France; but then, a course of policy which has for its object the well-being of the individual and the tranquillity of the state, is, after all, not so very deplorable.

But notwithstanding a community of interests and views, a misunderstanding arose between the monarchy of July and a part of the bourgeoisie. Indoctrinated by blind or interested advisers, by the coterie of the *National* on the one hand and by the leaders of the *Left* on the other, the lower order of merchants began to suspect that the designs of royalty were to subject them to a species of feudalism, of which they were to become the serfs. This feudalism, as it was called, consisted in nothing else than the elevation of a few individuals among the masses, an event of ordinary occurrence everywhere, but to whom the name of moneyed aristocracy, being once applied, became repeated by every one. It was one of the weapons made use of in the political contest of the period, just as the Roman question and the tax on drinks have been since. At bottom, there was a maturely formed and very reasonable desire on the part of the lower order of business men to have a voice in the election of deputies. Their services were often required as national guards, and since they defended the government by their arms, why not also by their votes? To keep them removed from the polls showed either contempt or a want of confidence, and they were deserving of neither. That was true. Had the qualifications been lowered from two hundred francs to fifty, it would have firmly attached the great mass of the bourgeoisie to the Orleans family, and taken away every pretext for popular commotions for a long period of time to come. The qualification of fifty francs would have placed the right of voting, in fact, within the reach of every one; for any workingman of the least energy or skill could have attained to it. The main object of the laboring man is to rise above his condition. It was considered immoral, before February, to base a right upon money; but money represents the spirit of order and conservatism, and these two qualities are indispensable elements in every form of government. If an individual has not the intelligence or energy to attain to a comparatively low position, what can he be expected to do with the affairs of state? If a man possesses nothing, his bonds of connection with society are very slight, however honest he may be; but the moment he becomes possessed of property he begins to perceive its corresponding duties. It is evident, therefore, that duties should be performed before rights are demanded. It is my opinion that a property qualification of some kind or another should be established; it may be as small as you please, but one should be fixed.

The government of July, forced into a merciless conflict which continued during the period of five long years, had become too much accustomed, perhaps, to see nothing but enemies and snares in everything. But be this as it may, it is certain that the government abstained from every act towards constitutional reform from the sincere conviction that the attempt would only lead to anarchy. The example of the English government, yielding to popular pressure at the proper time, did not appear to it as applicable to our country; and it believed that duty as well as its dignity rendered it necessary to resist. Events have shown that it was mistaken. The reform of the electoral law—all that was wanted—would have been an act of justice, and that act, although properly refused to party dictation, could have been granted after 1840, consistently with every principle of honor. I would not undertake to lecture men who are rendered illustrious by a high order of intelligence and exalted character, but I have ventured upon these remarks simply because they have been traced out by facts in characters of light.

The parliamentary opposition, headed by M. Odilon Barrot, had assumed the position of patron and advocate of the bourgeoisie, whom it defended with ardent and sincere, though not unseldom, exaggerated zeal. Nothing, however, was more remote from the intentions of this opposition than the destruction of the monarchy of July; for a revolution would naturally lead to its own ruin. This opposition, in fact, held the power in its own hands; but being dissatisfied with what appeared to be a badly adjusted equilibrium, it claimed a more decided preponderance in its favor.

The government persisted in a resistance which it considered wise, but which only served to stimulate the opposition to urge its claims with more vehemence, and thus gave rise to hot and angry disputes, in which the contending parties were generally hurried by passion into imprudences, which neither of them should have committed. By dint of mutual recriminations, repeated in a thousand various ways, the public came at length to regard the ministry and the leaders of the opposition as men who were engaged in a violent contest for power. Hence, it often happened in these passionate contests, that the blow aimed merely at the abuses of the government, would fall wide of the mark, and strike the very government itself.

It was thus that, by progressive degrees, that state of things became developed which led to the revolution. It arose from a struggle between the government, and a large, respectable, and influential class of citizens; a struggle, not for principles, but simply for a balance of power. And had this struggle been conducted with wisdom and moderation, it would have led to an arrangement satisfactory to both parties; but as it is, it has proved doubly catastrophous. Neither party has benefited by it; while contending for the oyster, the third party of the fable has stepped in and repeated his scurvy trick.

This very simple manner of viewing the question will not please certain men of yesterday, who are fully convinced, or rather are fully interested to have it believed, that the people alone have brought about the revolution, because they had no rights, were dying from hunger, and longing wistfully after socialism. But I think that I know the people, the true people, those who labor, as well as their pretended chiefs. This people are more occupied with gaining a livelihood than with the affairs of state; they have never died of hunger until the advent of the beautiful government, which promised them everything, and as to socialism, the true name of which is communism, they consider it simply as a humbug, or something even worse, an impudent foolstrap.

CHAPTER XIX.

The banquets—What the republicans first thought of them—Great wrath of the Left—The banquet of the twelfth arrondissement—The disdain of the *Reform*—Assemblying of the students—The decision that they came to—The committee of the banquet—The backing out of the Left.

THE result of the elections of 1846 is well known; the conservatives carried it by a large majority. They presented themselves in the Chambers compact and triumphant. The opposition of the Left, unabated in their zeal, took an unexpected course; they appealed to the generosity of their adversaries, and urged them to propose the reform themselves. The proposal seemed to the ministry as one of simplicity at least. Convinced that the electors represented the true interests of France, they were surprised to find themselves called upon to propose a change in the policy which had just been so solemnly confirmed. The legal means of ascertaining the opinion of the country had been employed, and the opinion thus ascertained was in favor of the cabinet. What more could be said on the subject? Were the nation to be told that they had been mistaken? If so, what were the proofs? Were they to be told that their opinions had not been properly ascertained? What better mode was there for ascertaining these opinions than the one which had been used? If the opposition possessed any great influence in the country, they were at liberty to show it—the ministry asked nothing better than to see the proofs.

Many of the members of the opposition, less wise than excitable, took fire at this, and swore that the proofs should be given. They set at work and succeeded in persuading their constituents that they were treated with contempt, and that energetic measures had become indispensable. Hence the organization of banquets was decided on. The first of these banquets took place at the tea-garden of Chateau-Rouge, and was got up with considerable eclat. Every shade of opposition, dynastic as well as radical, was invited to be present, and all were represented except the *Reform*. The directors of that sheet considered the manifestation as wholly insignificant, and below their notice. This conduct may appear surprising at the present day, but it can be accounted for by several reasons. The *National*, which the *Reform* accused of monarchism, patronized the banquet, and the *Reform* had no notion of appearing in the wake of a detested rival; then it was believed that no agitation of the country would arise from mere parliamentary opposition, and, in fine, there was not the remotest suspicion of the tremendous clap of thunder in which this sport was going to terminate. The recusance of the *Reform* gave the lead to the men of the *National*. M. Recurt was their spokesman. His speech, though mild in terms, contained several passages that went considerably beyond the limits of the programme, and made some noise in the ministerial journals. The leaders of the opposition were cautioned against their factious proceedings, and advised to reflect well before going any further. A single fact was adduced which might serve to enlighten them; by a decision of the organizers of the banquet, the toast to the king had not been given—an act of open disrespect and hostility. The leaders rejected this imputation; for such was not the design either of M. Barrot or of his lieutenants, Duvergier de Hauranne, de Malleville, and others. They were in a huff, it is true, and wished to give emphatic evidence of it, but without the least disrespect. Their presence alone, they said, was enough to give the banquet a character perfectly proper and constitutional. The conservatives perceived in these remarks something more than a mere gasconade; there was a mawkish style of cynicism in them that made them tremble. But as they had thrown defiance to their opponents, they felt bound to let them go on; not, however, without vague presentiments of disastrous consequences.

The good faith of the agitators, however, showed itself more explicitly a short time afterwards, at a considerable manifestation given at Lille. When they saw a large number of republicans present, and among them those of the *Reform*, perceiving that their own presence would give but little of a dynastic character to the meeting, they demanded that the toast to the king should be given as a proof of adherence to the constitution. But, as usual, this attempt at moderation came a little too late; for the democrats are not men to give up the ground that they may have won. Situated as the democracy were between the alternative of M. Barrot's presence *with* the toast, and his absence *without* the toast, they could have no hesitation; and hence, the consequences were that the chief of the Left had to make a very sorry retreat, leaving the banquet wholly to the republicans.

The presentiments of the conservatives became more and more realized, and more solemn warnings were given to the promoters of agitation; but the stakes were down, and self-love carried the game beyond all good advice or prudence. The opposition continued their banquets in city after city, harping in their speeches upon corruption as the rallying cry of reform, and complaining against the ministry that its duration threatened to be eternal. At every one of these banquets several voices were heard exclaiming against all connection with the dynasty; these voices gradually became more numerous, until at last the assemblies of Dijon and Châlons were purely and unqualifiedly republican. But these two famous banquets, of which stunning reports were given by the *Reform*, consisted, after all, only of a few hundreds of republicans, mostly of the vicinity, and drawn together by every possible means.

The initiative taken by the Left having thrown open the doors to the anarchists, these would have considered themselves foolish not to have taken advantage of so favorable a circumstance. Besides, the *Reform*, which had been so disdainful of these manifestations at first, had thought the matter over, and come to the conclusion that they might be turned to a good account in filling the till. The two patriotic collectors, Messrs. Baune and Caussidière, no longer served this purpose; the first had had his time, and the other was used up; their stories had become stale, and their fine speeches like crocodile's tears—nobody would trust them. Thanks to the banquets, the *Reform* could dispense with such subordinate measures, and bring forth its chiefs themselves. What patriot could refuse to come up to the mark when the tam-tam should be sounded by M. Ledru-Rollin in person?—or how show reluctance when the dish should be presented by so great a man? The *Tribune* then was dispatched right and left into all those places where the subsidies had become small. The cloth being removed, he would resort to his eloquence, and succeed in charming several out of a part of their money. But to be made use of in this way, like a walking-puff, was a game of which he soon grew tired. The chest still sounded hollow, however, and there was no excuse. He tried several times, like popular actors, to escape by pretending indisposition, but nothing would serve his turn. When the hour for the departure of the diligence arrived, Messrs. Baune, Grandménil, and Caussidière would go and get him, bundle him into the carriage, and pack him off in spite of himself. He had the consolation of listening to the maudlin conversation of these good fellows while inhaling the grog-shop perfumery with which they were infected. At the banquet of Dijon, however, he must have kept at a considerate distance from M. Grandménil, on account of that gentleman's showing symptoms of sea-sickness.

The Left was not only outdone by M. Ledru-Rollin and his band, but also by the familiars of the *National*, who were half republicans, and who, while submitting to the patronage of the Left, were seeking to impose upon it their own. In a country like ours, too, where the revolutionary fires are so easily enkindled, words of resistance went much further than was intended by the orators themselves. However much inclined towards monarchy the intention might be, the fact, that is to say, the struggle in a public place instead of parliamentary debates, could not fail to push measures to the extreme of anarchy.

Such was the state of things on the opening of the session of 1848. The agitators made their appearance with an air of triumph, like men who had victoriously accepted a challenge; but, what was not their astonishment on hearing the throne fulminate against them a crushing decree. They had become tired in a long course of preaching, and the men whose eyes they had tried to open, disdainfully scorned them by calling them blind themselves! The republicans were honored by being styled as enemies, but they on their part were treated with a shrug of the shoulders, as much as to say—poor fellows! you have lost your senses. The *Journal des Débats* had already told them so, in fact, in plain words; but to hear it to their face, in full chamber, and from the mouth of the king, was to the last degree offensive, and of course productive of a storm.

They contended against the address with obstinacy. They believed that the Chamber would not dare to carry things so far as to ratify the decree of the government; but, they were mistaken; for a majority gave it an unqualified confirmation. The wrath that then seized upon them was no fiction; believing that the design was to overwhelm them with disgrace, they held a consultation and decided upon an audacious course. The banquets, which had just been censured by a significative vote of the Chamber, they resolved to continue. One of these banquets was being got up by the 12th arrondissement of Paris, and they openly took the management of it, declaring that they assumed all the responsibility. This was in direct opposition to the legislative will.

The course of the agitators astonished the public, and occasioned considerable trouble to the men of the government. The members of the centre, the office-holders, the bankers and large proprietors—old men for the most part with rigid ideas of discipline—were astounded by such temerity. The aids-de-camp showed impatience mingled with defiance. The ministry were in frowns, but had no doubts of the victory; as councillors of the king they felt themselves adequate to a much greater emergency. And they believed, moreover, as was indeed the truth, that M. Barrot would be stopped by a prospect of danger to the dynasty.

The government, however, could not fail to perceive the critical condition of things, and while holding itself in readiness for every event, it neglected no means for checking the foolish vehemence of the opposition. It is an incontestable fact that the organs of the ministry showed a sincere spirit of reserve and conciliation, and that the sentiments of violence were all on the side of their adversaries. The government saw danger, and coldly and sadly pointed it out; but, M. Odilon Barrot and his followers replied that the design was to frighten them. It had become good taste to laugh in scorn when the government spoke to them of demagogism, of clubs, and invasions of the populace; such talk was considered as an old tale, which had become ridiculous. A month later, however, the laughers had occasion to change their principles of good taste very materially.

For the moment, the course of things in the future was in suspense. The *National* foresaw at most the success of the

Left; and the *Reform* discovered nothing of any interest; all that it could see was a bonfire of the opposition which would go out of itself—a dynastic game which was below its dignity. Having been invited to take a part in the manifestation, it replied by a refusal full of fatuity. This is but the history of yesterday, and can be easily verified.

The banquet had been proposed before the vote of the Chambers upon the subject. It had been moved by several subaltern leaders of the 12th arrondissement, among whom were M. Bocquet, a pretended student, M. Collet, subsequently condemned by the councils of war of June, M. Watripon, editor of the *Advance Guard*, a small journal for young students, and about a dozen other citizens of the same sort. The committee formed of these men was to be merged in that of the parliamentary Left; but the latter, containing personages who considered such a fusion as beneath their dignity, resolved to expel their new colleagues. The committee having been sifted was composed, under the presidency of M. Boissel, deputy of the 12th arrondissement, of the habitual undertakers of the Left; that is to say, of men who were half for the *Siècle* and half for the *National*, attached to the *Siècle* by opinions and to the *National* by submission. M. Pagnerre was one of the great guns of this intrigue.

They appointed delegates, collected subscriptions, and made all the usual preparations. But the former committee, which had yielded with a good grace, soon repented that they had done so; for, on coming to weigh the matter fully, they found that the men of the Left were too moderate; and besides, were they not as capable of organizing a banquet as anybody else? The editors of the *Advance Guard* became the propagators of this schism. They held several meetings where the question was discussed whether the purely republican party, that is to say, the *Reform*, ought not to take the direction of the affair. The decision was for the affirmative. Strengthened by this decision, Messrs. Watripon, Bocquet, and company got together a large meeting of Scholars, in order to give a more solemn solution to the difficulty. The meeting took place in a large workshop in the suburb of Saint

Marceau; three hundred young men were present, of whom about a dozen were members of the *Seasons*, led there by M. Albert and myself. One of those scenes of disorder took place of which we have since had such fine specimens under the Republic of Clubs. The persons present were divided into two parties, which were nearly equal, one in favor of giving the management to the *National* and the other to the *Reform*. They stamped, cried and vociferated until they were tired out; the partisans of the *National* yielding at length to the stronger lungs, and abandoning the ground to the *Reform*. It was voted that the banquet should be held under the patronage of M. Ledru-Rollin, and that a committee of well-tried democrats should be charged with preparing the toasts.

All this was done without the knowledge of the *Reform* and of M. Ledru-Rollin, who were not informed of it till the following day. They saw nothing in it worthy of their attention. The ferocious journal liked to decorate itself with the youth of the schools, as it were with a pretty trinket, but no other importance was attached to it.

The parliamentary committee heard of the decision of the students, but it in no wise altered their course; they continued their preparations, looked about for a place which it proved rather difficult to find, and finally, after many delays, fixed upon the 22d of February as the day for the banquet, to be held on the premises of private property at Chaillot. Things remained in this condition until the eve of the great day.

About a hundred deputies, together with Messrs. de Boissy and d'Althou-Shée, peers of the realm, had subscribed, and, from all appearances were determined to be present. They could easily do so in consequence of a compromise which had been consented to by the ministry. As the agitators had on several occasions referred to the law, not an article of which, according to their own interpretation, prohibited the right of holding meetings, M. Duchatel declared that he was ready to test the question by bringing it before the courts. It was agreed that no preventive measures should be taken against the deputies, but that a verbal process might be instituted upon the spot to serve as the basis of a trial by the police courts which should have a final decision in the case. But this was very great condescension on the part of the government, for the courts in fact, offered a very advantageous ground to its adversaries for the continuance of their course of agitation. The government might hope to gain time and perhaps lessen the pressure of the question by the detailed formalities of judicial proceedings; but in the long run, the advantage to be gained by this course was decidedly on the side of its opponents.

On the evening of the 21st, at a time when the agitators were congratulating themselves upon the great concessions made by the government, they were startled by a sudden piece of news; the authorities had reconsidered the matter and had posted up threatening proclamations throughout the capital. One of these, issued by General Jacqueminot, enjoined upon the National Guard to abstain from taking a part in all public meetings without superior orders. Another from the prefect of police, was an injunction against the banquet. A third, also, from M. Delessert, called attention to the ordinances against riots. Disposed to test the question as to its legality, the government still consented that cases might be brought before the courts; but as the banquet would serve as the pretext for a large gathering, and as in particular a manifesto had been published in the morning announcing that the National Guard had been called on to be present, and prescribing the order of their arrangement in regular martial array—which was nothing short of downright anarchy, it was judged indispensable that the manifestation should have some regulating supervision. The injunction then was given to every guest to repair individually to the banquet, and to retire immediately on the first evidence of infraction. In case of resistance, the authorities would be compelled to have recourse to legal measures.

And in taking this course the government certainly made only a moderate use of the right of self-defence—of its attribute as the maintainer of order and respect for authority.

In fact, the manifesto referred to assumed a form of officiality which no statesman in any country could possibly have tolerated. We give the principal part of it for the edification of the public. At the present day, when dangers are no longer made light of by the impertinences of inexperience or passion, the enormity of this production will be clearly perceived.

"The committee of arrangements have thought proper that the manifestation should take place in a quarter of the capital where the width of the streets and public squares is such as to permit the assembling of the people without their being crowded. With this view, the deputies, the peers of the realm, and other persons invited to the banquet, will assemble next Tuesday at eleven o'clock at the ordinary place of meeting of the parliamentary opposition, *Place de la Madeleine*, 2. The subscribers to the banquet who form a part of the National Guard are requested to assemble in front of the church, and to form two parallel lines, between which the invited guests will take their place.

"The procession will be headed by such superior officers of the National Guard as shall be present to take a part in the manifestation.

"Immediately after the invited and other guests, will follow a body of officers of the National Guards.

"Then the National Guards, in the order of their corps.

"Between the third and fourth columns, the young men of the schools, under the direction of marshals appointed by themselves.

"Then the other National Guards of Paris and the vicinity, in the order above designated.

"The procession will move at half-past eleven o'clock and proceed by way of the *Place de la Concorde* and the *Champs-Elysées*, towards the place of the banquet."

M. Odilon Barrot, on being questioned with regard to this extraordinary production, replied that he neither approved of it nor disapproved of it, having nothing to do with it. And such indeed was the fact. It came from the members of the committee who were under the control of the *National*.

These men, endued with a large share of prudence and cunning combined, had managed to evade the responsibility of the manifesto, by leaving it to hover over the chiefs of the Left. It is thus that under these unfortunate circumstances the parliamentary agitators added to their own faults those of others.

The effect of the proclamations upon the deputies, however, was decisive. A meeting which immediately took place among them, showed that they were not yet wholly bereft of reason. Out of about a hundred of them, some ten or a dozen alone resolved to continue in their revolutionary course of action. Among the latter, M. d'Althon Shée, a peer, declared that he was ready to go all lengths, and to repair to the banquet at the head of the people. To these sentiments, however, he found no response. But the course pursued by the deputies, under the circumstances, showed a degree of rancor that was perfectly puerile; against a ministry which was so averse to being destroyed without some resistance, they resolved to bring an accusation; the men whose wrong consisted in efforts to prevent the authority with which they had been legitimately invested from being trampled in the mud, they pronounced traitors.

This was the last scene of the drama in which the Left made their appearance. With honest intentions at bottom, but deplorably misguided as to means, and traitorously implicated by underhanded machinations, the deputies had thus suspended over the country one of the most terrible storms which it had ever yet endured.

CHAPTER XX.

State of the public mind on the 21st of February—A council of war held at the Reform—The strange opinions of M. Louis Blanc, and M. Ledru-Rollin—A wonderful decision—The revolution is a trick of the police.

SOME degree of agitation had been felt among that part of the busy bourgeoisie, who believed themselves under the lead of the *Siècle*, but who were, in fact, under that of the *National*. They had a tormenting thirst for political rights; but with no ulterior designs, without suspicion, and especially without a wish for a change in the form of government. The rest of the middle classes, that is to say, the great masses, looked on without displeasure, at a course of things which seemed tending to their advantage; but they were content with a system of policy firmly devoted to peace, favorable to credit, and protective of their interests. They awaited patiently the progress of affairs, and were but little disposed to trouble the existing order by their claims. The working people listened with indifference to the great noise which was being made above them. They were moved solely by that excitement which precedes some extraordinary event; the curiosity of the suburbs was aroused. Among some of the workshops there was a disposition to be present at the manifestation, partly from the instinct of opposition common among inferior men, and partly from a desire to see the sight. There was to be a procession of deputies and peers in the midst of the people; it would be a grand spectacle, and it is well known whether the inhabitants of Paris are indifferent to spectacles or not.

As to the secret societies, they felt the public emotion from the first; but as their chiefs declared that it was only an affair of the bourgeoisie, in which they could have no interest, their excitement subsided. There were a few turbulent groups of the *Dissenters*, who talked of barricades, musketry, and all that, but as they had no declared chiefs, no organization nor agreement among themselves, what could they do? Many of the members, moreover, were of the opinion that it was best to leave the Left to its own affairs, and to abstain from having anything to do with them. This course was the one which had been adopted by M. Albert and myself. Our men had promised not to go to the manifestation in a body, but those who wished to go individually, were at liberty to do so. The chiefs were to be on the look-out, and to give other instructions should there be an occasion for it. As the only journal reputed republican also followed this course, the groups made no objection to it.

The excitement produced by the *Presse* and the deputies of the Left, was a matter of indifference to the *Reform*, but the part played by the *National* in the affair gave it some trouble. Fearful of being supplanted by the rival paper, and of thus losing the direction of the revolutionary forces, it decided, two days before the banquet, to come forth from its proud reserve. An article, by M. Flocon, brought this fact to the knowledge of its subscribers. It was announced that the *Reform* would sustain the legal opposition of the deputies, being unwilling to incur the reproach of indifference, in a question where the interests of the country were at stake. It may well be imagined that this declaration appeared very insignificant to the public. The superb pretensions of the Jacobin sheet occasioned a laugh with a great many, and imposed only upon a few.

But when this resolution had been once taken, as it might happen that the position claimed by the *Reform*, in the manifestation, might not be conceded to it, and as, on the other hand, the suburbs, whose intentions remained unknown, might resort to some unexpected course of action, it was decided to call a meeting of all the familiars of the concern, in order to act with concert and unanimity. A circular letter was immediately prepared and sent round, under the seal of the *Journal*. It ran as follows: "In view of the condemnation of the chief editor, and of the manager of the *Reform*, we appeal to your patriotism; a meeting will be held to-morrow, Monday, at precisely 7 o'clock of the evening, at the office of the *Journal*, in order to consult upon the circumstances in which we find ourselves."

The reason assigned for this proceeding, was one of those finesses often practised by M. Flocon, and of which everybody knows him to be exceedingly fond. It was very natural that the meeting should be called; it was very desirable to have an understanding on an occasion like the one in question. Nevertheless, it was generally conceded that the banquet was merely a movement of the bourgeoisie, and that it had no bearing in favor of the republican party. The day passed off pretty quietly; the deputies, their confident promises, and their probable conduct on the morrow, were the subjects of conversation; no one ventured a forethought beyond this. But towards night, on the reading of the proclamations, a feeling, not of wrath or of hope, as might have been expected, but of surprise, took possession of the leaders. They said that the act of the government was a declaration of war; and by such an evidence of energy, they were considerably disconcerted. Perceiving that the fanfaronade of speech, and the pen, were much easier than a regular battle against a power armed with troops and cannon, a great many of them shook their heads, and concluded that they had been played a bad trick. It was under this impression that the frequenters of the *Reform* arrived at the office. About 8 o'clock, some fifty republicans, editors, stockholders, and subscribers, had come to the meeting. Their names were as follows:—

 Messrs. FLOCON, editor-in-chief,
  RIBEYROLLES, coadjutor-editor,
  E. BAUNE, agent of the Journal,
  M. CAUSSIDIÈRE, agent of the Journal,
  GRANDMÉNIL, ex-manager,
  PASCAL DUPRAT, editor,
  ETIENNE ARAGO, editor,

Messrs. Louis Blanc,
   Hibback, pastry-cook (l'Echiquier Street),
   E. Guillemot, gentleman,
   F. Adam,
   J. Gouache, manager of the Journal,
   Leboeuf, clerk,
   Fournier, lithographer (Dauphine Place),
   Charles Lagrange,
   Martin, surnamed Albert, mechanic,
   De La Hodde,
   Pilhes, travelling clerk,
   Jouanne, keeper of an eating-house, Montorgueil Street,
   Pelvilain, grocer (Mogador Street),
   Bruet, bath keeper (Quatre-Vents Street),
   Core, mechanic,
   Augier, editor of the Journal,
   Chesneau, merchant (Montmartre Street),
   Louchet, grain-merchant,
   Tiphaine, business agent,
   Garnaux, cashier of the Journal,
   Sedail, editor of the Journal,
   Yvon-Villarceaux, captain of the National Guard,
   Detourbet, captain of the National Guard,
   Lesseré, captain of the National Guard,
   Tisserandot, employee of the stage-coach office,
   Demougeot, horologist,
   Dupuis, currier,
   Desirabode, dentist,
   Aubert-Roche, physician,
   Chancel, contumacious, at the trial of Bourges,
   Favreau, employee of the ministry of war,
   Chambellant,
   Rey, ex-commandant of the Hôtel-de-Ville,
   Bocquet, ex-adjunct of the mayoralty of the 12th arrondissement,
   Desgranges, wine seller,
   Duseigneur,

Messrs. DAUPHIN, painter,
    MONGINOT, captain of the National Guard,
    LECHALIER, placer of assurances,
    GALLAND, inspector of markets,
    MANGIN, student.

Messrs. Ledru-Rollin, Edgar Quinet, and many others, did not make their appearance till after the opening of the meeting.

In order not to lose time in formalities, M. Flocon stated that he would act as president himself. After a few words upon the condemnation of the *Journal*, the pretext for the meeting, he announced that they were ready for discussion; to say upon what subject was useless, for everybody understood the case.

M. Baune spoke first; he attempted to make an exposition of the state of things, and point out the course that ought to be followed. He was not very clear, and his indecision was evident. Sharing in a sort of numbness with which the meeting had been seized, and fearful of going astray, he carefully evaded everything positive; but, true to his gasconade habits, he indulged in high sounding words, and intrepid tosses of the head. This, however, was not satisfactory; for everybody felt the necessity of something decisive—of a line of conduct clearly marked out.

The next to speak was M. Grandménil. He came forward with the air of a man who felt that his opinion was expected as one of great weight; an illusion of his which no one shared in but himself. The viscous style and mighty intellect of the man were, in fact, something to be dreaded. M. Flocon, whose nerves were all in a flutter on seeing him arise, permitted him to give utterance to two or three absurdities, and then gave him to understand clearly that there was not time to listen to any more.

At this moment M. D'Alton Shée arrived, bringing news from the parliamentary Left. The deputies had held a caucus with regard to the proclamations, and the young peer, who had just come from the caucus, announced that it was a complete back-out. As to himself, he had agreed, together with seven or eight of his confederates, to go all lengths, and he intended to stand by his agreement; but to this end, he must be assured of an earnest support.

A burst of bravos followed the recital of M. Alton; he had conducted himself valiantly, and should not be deceived in reckoning upon the republicans. Sustain him, hey! why, everybody was ready to do so; his promise ran no risk of a failure; they would give him the means to keep it. And while they were thus encouraging him, their faces lighted up, their heads assumed a proud, firm set upon the shoulders, and a patriotic shiver ran through the crowd. M. Louis Blanc caused silence to be restored, and then pronounced the following words:—

"After the deputies of the opposition have agitated the country even to its very bowels, do they now back out! I feel the blood curdling in my veins. Were I to listen only to my indignation, I should say at once, in reply to such felonious proceedings, let us raise the war-cry and advance! But humanity restrains me. I ask if we have the right to dispose of the generous blood of the people without benefit to the cause of democracy? If the patriots should take to the streets to-morrow, abandoned as they are by the men who had put themselves at their head, they would be inevitably crushed, and democracy drowned in a sea of blood; such would be the issue of a conflict to-morrow. And do not deceive yourselves; that National Guard, which displayed its uniform from banquet to banquet, would join in with the army and deal upon you its grape-shot. You may decide upon insurrection if you please, but if you so decide, I will return to my house, cover myself with crape, and mourn over the ruin of democracy."

This speech was certainly nothing else than the expression of the general sentiment. It explained very clearly the relative positions of the republican party and the government. A revolt in the existing state of the democracy would only have ended, beyond a doubt, in a catastrophe; and the fact that it has ended otherwise, is due to one of those interpositions of providence which set all human wisdom at naught. However, reasonable as this speech seemed to be, it produced but a sorry effect. The more illiterate patriots generally think that their chiefs, whose tongues are so well hung on ordinary occasions, ought to exhibit in the moments of crisis, something else than mere words of resignation. Such was the case in the present instance; murmurs of disapproval fell upon the ears of M. Lagrange, and brought the knight-errant to his feet. His opinion was, that in case the popular lion should give a growl, then to display the banner and grasp the scymitar. But the question was whether the lion would growl or not. In case of silence on the part of said lion, M. Lagrange didn't explain what he would do.

The secret of this indecision was as follows. The plebeian democracy were perfectly confident in the power of their cause; but, when a battle was in question, they wanted some influential voice to make an exposition of the resources of the party, and prove that the affair could be safely undertaken. With respect to the leaders, they either deceived themselves or very adroitly deceived their followers; in the first case, they expected, like the others, an *exposé* to confirm them in their illusions; in the other case, they remained silent, leaving their comedy until the moment in which it should assume the aspect of a tragedy.

The speech of M. Louis Blanc did not offer the encouragement which was felt to be needed; and that of M. Lagrange did not appear to be more conclusive. M. d'Alton Shée followed M. Lagrange, and was of the opinion that the only course to be taken was to address the people a formal recommendation to abstain.

With the view of ascertaining whether the chiefs had any ulterior designs, I took a part in the discussion, and asked what was to be done in case that the people, of themselves, should decide upon the attack, or should find themselves pushed on to it by some aggression. Persons talked of advising them not to move, but, besides that the people had but few real representatives in the meeting, there was no proof that the recommendation would be listened to. And, moreover, there was but a night's time to give the notice in, which was not sufficient. The meeting were not aware of the fact, perhaps, that in some of the workshops the men had promised themselves a holiday on the occasion of the banquet, and was it expected that a simple notice, imperfectly given, would check the suburbs and dissuade them from a spectacle which they had so long anticipated?

At these questions, which went to the heart of things, some old mobbers aroused, and then the talk of revolution began to be heard in this assembly of revolutionists. M. Rey, who has since been called Colonel Rey, was explicitly in favor of battle. "If the people take the streets, said he, our place is at their head; if they are ready to throw up barricades, we, on our part, ought to move the first paving stones, and fire the first shot. Such occasions as the present one have become too rare to be neglected. Let us show that our trade of republican is no child's play, and that when the time comes we know how to do our duty."

This was a new shock of electricity sent through the crowd, and the men of action exchanged looks of animation and excitement. M. Caussidière, who was waiting like the others for explicit words, then entered into the discussion. He stated that, together with M. Albert and myself, he had just passed through the suburbs (which was false), and that a threatening disposition had been observed there. "I cannot swear," said he, "that they will take the bull by the horns, but there will be a row, and if we don't want to come in at the end of the feast, we must plant our batteries. Let us take some little measures; it can do no harm; if there is no fuss, we can go to bed; if there is one, the people will see that we are occupied with the affair; that won't hurt us in any case."

M. Caussidière, it will be perceived, never lost sight of the interests of the house; his speech was half warlike and half industrial. M. Rey, who was less calculating, spoke again, confining himself this time to the point of honor, and declaring that the honor of the chiefs of the party had become implicated in the question. It was then that a voice which had been waited for with impatience, made itself heard; M.

Ledru-Rollin came forward to give his opinion. With an air rather disdainful, like that of the pedagogue who sees his pupils engaged upon a difficult problem, he let fall these memorable words: "In the first revolution, when our fathers were about entering upon a conflict, they had prepared for it a long time beforehand; but as to ourselves, are we prepared? Have we arms, ammunition, and organized men? The government, indeed, is all ready, and its troops are only waiting for the signal to crush us. It is my opinion that an affair undertaken under such circumstances, is the extreme of folly."

Coming from a man who has since assumed such a high stand with regard to the affair of February, this speech will appear inconceivable, and one might readily conclude that he was playing a comedy, as he subsequently endeavored to have it believed when before the court of Bourges; but I have already said that his theory given out on that occasion was the invention of an after thought, and that in giving himself out as a roué, the celebrated montagnard was doing himself an injustice. The fact is he had had a close view of the picture presented by his party; had seen its immorality, its laziness, its foolish pretensions, its malignant rivalries, its utter disorganization, and the smallness of its numbers. The idea of leading all this wretchedness and all this turpitude into a conflict against the great nation of France, made up of honest, brave, and laborious men, appeared to him as an act of veritable madness. I may go still further, and say, that in the existing condition of things, the prospect of an unexpected triumph of his cause filled his mind rather with a sentiment of fear than of joy. In fact, with but a handful of republicans, greedy and inefficient, he perceived that the establishment of a government would be rendered impossible; and, on the other hand, he could hope for no support except in those bad elements of the country which would be shaken up by the revolution. The position of chief under such circumstances possessed nothing very flattering or even reassuring, and the Tribune had but little ambition for it. I render this justice to M. Ledru-Rollin, and let him not attempt to belie me, for it is useless; but when the revolution of 1848 shall be spoken of again as conceived, organized, directed and executed by him and his lieutenants, let him silence the speakers, and tell them that that joke has been carried quite far enough.

The meeting, wholly composed of the men of the *Reform*, had nothing to do but to remain silent after the master had spoken. A few objections, however, were hazarded, but without any success. M. D'Alton Shée had already gently rejected the palms of martyrdom; and M. Edgar Quinet breathed not a word. M. Flocon made a few remarks under a diplomatic reserve, and, in short, the question of war was completely abandoned. The only decision come to was the resolution to give the people orders not to make their appearance in the streets, and in case of disobedience, which did not appear probable, to mingle with them and observe the course of things.

The recital which we have thus given may appear an unbecoming raillery. What! on the evening of the great day the montagnards declared an affair impossible, and interdicted every movement on the part of the people! What! that revolutionary oracle, the *Reform*, had not the least expectation of a revolution! Did M. Louis Blanc say, that to attempt it would prove a disaster? and did M. Ledru Rollin say, that to think of it was folly? What! the secret societies had orders not to have anything to do with the manifestation, as something too insignificant! What! the general staff of the republican party conducted themselves in this way on the 21st of February, the eve of that famous movement, the glory of which they now so loudly claim. Let those who are in doubts upon this subject, question the fifty witnesses whose names are above given; or even read the *Reform* of the following day. M. Flocon published the determination of the chiefs, in which occurs the following phrase, and which ought to be stamped upon the page of history in letters of a cubit's length:—

"Men of the people, beware to-morrow of being hurried

into rashness, do not furnish to the authorities the desired occasion for a bloody success."

The desired occasion! this time, good people, you will doubtlessly be enlightened as to the despicable impudence of the charlatans who beset you. Thus, that glorious national manifestation, that irresistible impulse towards revolution and the republic, was—what? Why, a provocation of the police! It is not I who say it, it is the *Reform!*

CHAPTER XXI.

The *Dissenting Society* begins the movement—The morals of this Society—Scenes at the *Place de la Concorde*—The gamins of Paris—Barricades—An attempt at assassination—Opinion of the chiefs—Council of war—Pillage—A conflagration—Result of the day of the 22d.

HENCE, there is no longer room either for errors or falsehoods with regard to the following points: 1st. On the 21st of February, the eve of the revolution, the two republican chiefs, Ledru-Rollin and Louis Blanc, rejected the idea of an attack, the one as a folly, and the other as an inspiration of ill fortune; and with their advice, the general staff of the party decided to abstain and to prohibit the people from taking to the streets. 2d. The *Secret Society* of the *Seasons*, the most considerable and the most serious of all the others, had orders not to move, because the movement was below them. And, exclusive of these two categories, what was there remaining to the republicans? The men of the *National* could not be reckoned of the party, for almost all of them had abandoned the idea of a conflict of arms, and none of them was expecting the catastrophe which followed. The *Icarian* communists paid but little attention to the movement, being convinced that their Utopia had nothing to gain by it. Once single fraction had made no engagement, and had received no orders; this was the *Dissenting Society*, which was ready for anything. It contained, as I have said, about four hundred members, without organization or discipline, and was commanded by chiefs of the most suspicious characters. Some idea may be formed of their morals, by the following instance : A dozen of them were in the pay of the police; they would go directly to the prefecture, give their information, and receive in return several pieces of a hundred sous. Since they spent their money more freely than the condition of simple workingmen would admit, they guessed each other out, and subjected themselves reciprocally to a hideous species of black mail. They would station a watch in the vicinity of the prefecture, in order to keep a look-out upon the premises; and when one of their number was seen coming out, they would suddenly set upon him, twit him of having imparted a secret, and then force him to foot the bill of some disgusting orgie. It may readily be conceived, that the loyalty of these worthy citizens was exactly in proportion to the liberalities of M. Pinel, who threw them their husks; so that, when one of them was thanked for his pains, he would immediately set to work conspiring in good earnest—becoming out and out a democrat. Their patriotism was not wholly free from accusations, it is true, but as all the chiefs of the very honorable *Society of Dissenters* were of the same stamp, no one paid any attention to that. This army, in short, was in every respect worthy of its chiefs, having the honor to reckon among its numbers, drunkards, keepers of girls, vagabonds, and even robbers—all excellent communists, by the way, and boldly declaring that the reign of corruption should cease.

It was this *Dissenting Society*, made up of such men, and commanded by such chiefs, that spread itself through the suburbs, and induced many of the workshops to take a holiday; not that the industrious workingmen were under the control of these wretches, but the banquet was going to be an extraordinary ceremony; persons of all sorts would pass in procession—peers, deputies, journalists, great patriots, &c., and the people had the curiosity to be present.

Whether this view of things may please the inventors of epics or not, it is nevertheless true that the revolution sprung materially from such elements as these—from the dregs of society and from popular curiosity. I must confess, that it is impossible for me not to show temper at that opinion which is so openly advanced, and so foolishly admitted, that the affair of February was a great national and republican movement. What! national, when the glorious *Dissenting Society* caused it to break out! Republican! When Messrs. Ledru-Rollin, Louis Blanc, and Flocon, on the one hand, the chiefs of the *Seasons* on the other, and the *National* and all the leading men of the party formally disapproved and interdicted it! Of what consequence were the faults of the late government? If the initiative of a band of scape-graces and the curiosity of the people, had not commenced a mob in Paris on the 22d, would there have been any mob at all? No, for the chiefs of the republican faction had perceived their impuissance, and had prohibited not only an attack, but even a manifestation; and if the 22d, had passed off quietly, Paris and France would have been saved; that great national impulse so much talked of would not have occurred, and the illustrious republican party would have been left in all its infirmity and insignificance. By no possible means can this fact be annulled, and the country will, ere long, come to recognize it. Pompous pretensions and interested declamation have had their day. To say that the fall of the government of July, was owing to this, or to that fault, committed during a period of eighteen years, is an old woman's tale. It fell because at a moment when stoical energy was necessary, it observed a course of imprudent generosity; it fell as even the mightiest may fall, by a false step, in a moment of disconcertment, and no one can attribute its fall to any cause but the inscrutable and sovereign decrees of Providence!

At about eleven o'clock on the 22d of February, the men of action of the *Reform* and the chiefs of the *Seasons* set out for the Madeleine in order to observe the movement. After having examined the masses which were stationed upon the Place de la Concorde, and undulating along the boulevards, they perceived that their men were not among them. The population in the streets consisted of nine-tenths of the amateurs of public spectacles interspersed with squint-eyed patriots and exploring bandits. The blouses were in a majority upon the place, forming groups here and there, while the bourgeois were moving to and fro. There was no noise nor excitement; and much less any settled plan. The policemen had orders not to appear in their uniform—one cause less for agitation; and had it not been for certain signs which are known by men experienced in such matters, no one would have suspected that the crowd contained any elements of disorder. One of these signs exhibited itself at about mid-day: some weather-beaten patriots, blue in the lips and three sheets in the wind, fell upon a poor devil and began beating him, calling him an agent of the police. I was but a few paces distant, in company with M. Cheneau, a rope merchant of the suburb of Montmartre, and I managed to wrest the unfortunate man from the hands of his assailants. Who he was I do not know; and they who were beating him were certainly no better informed on that point than I was.

Previous to this incident, an attempt had been made against the Chamber of Deputies. The students, led by the editors of the *Advance Guard*, had set out from the Latin quarter arm in arm, hat cocked over one ear, pipe in mouth, and, being joined on the way by a group of workingmen, made their appearance upon the Place de la Concorde. Seeing nothing extraordinary there, they resolved, by way of giving animation to the picture, to penetrate the Palais-Bourbon by escalading the iron fence. Several of them carried this project into execution. This was only one of those pretty ways familiar to our bright young men, but the example happened to be a bad one under the circumstances. Troops came up, drove away the students, surrounded the chamber, and posted a guard at the bridge.

At about the same time a mob was got up by men of the suburbs around the ministry of foreign affairs. They shouted forth the old rallying cry of the virtuous journals—"Down with Guizot! Down with the man of Gand!" and then set to throwing stones into the windows. A messenger, who was coming out on horseback, had like to be stoned. Troops arrived at this point, too, and drove back the crowd, which flowed off towards the Champs Elysées.

These demonstrations were nothing surprising; the Parisians had not had a mob for the space of nine years, and their itching for disorder was very explicable, especially when they found themselves in numbers upon the pavement. The population of Paris, when assembled on some political occasion, is hurried away into aggression as naturally as the swollen Seine rushes to the sea; and this is a fact which the guardians of public order ought never to lose sight of.

Though the dense crowds of the Place de la Concorde vexed and annoyed the authorities who were dispersing them with the cavalry, there was still nothing threatening in their attitude. The most turbulent were at the entrance of the Champs Elysées, near the river, and they were swept back several times among the trees, but with no success in dispersing them, for they would immediately reform again and press back upon the place. There was among them a number of those morose and shameless children who are called the *gamins* of Paris, and who form the advance guard of sedition. When the cavalry were returning to their post after a charge, these little wretches would assail them in rear by a discharge of stones. And true to their paternal blood, they soon took the chairs that were along the borders of the avenue and piled them up across the road. This was the first barricade; but there was nothing serious in it, the passers by kicking it down as they passed along.

When the *gamins* had finished this work, they then moved upon the fortified guard station upon the line of the main avenue. Armed with a supply of stones, they assailed the men of the guard, who prudently took refuge within their station; then approaching the inclosure, from which a discharge might have cut them in pieces, they kept up a shower of stones upon the station during the space of a quarter of an hour. As the guards made no movement, a youngster in a blouse, about fifteen years of age, mounted the inclosure, climbed up the front of the edifice, and tore down the colors, which he carried off in triumph. The mounted guards being occupied upon the place did not make their appearance during this scene; but an incident soon occurred which brought them to the spot; a cloud of smoke, arising from behind the station, showed that the little wretches had set the edifice on fire.

The crowd continued until five o'clock in the same state, at the entrance of the Champs Elysées and around the Madeleine. Dispersed at one point, they would immediately reassemble at some other. This contact with an armed force; the excitement communicated from one to another among men who had come together without hostile designs, but who gradually became accustomed to the impression of being in face of an enemy; the gleam of the sabre as it was flourished from time to time above the crowd, and then the sly instigations thrown in by demagogues thridding the mass in all directions; all this finally gave quite a tingling of the nerves to the more excitable. I was accosted by many asking to know what was to be done.

"The committee is on the look-out," I replied; "make no movement without receiving instructions."

"But if anything should occur, where shall we meet?"

"This evening, at the Palais Royal, at nine o'clock."

I took it upon myself to appoint this rendezvous for some dozen chiefs whom I met with upon my way. All of them complied with my recommendation, and abstained from aggressive acts. But the example given by the *gamins*, and that detestable electricity which pervades a mob of the populace, soon led to the commission of more culpable acts. A group of the *Dissenting Society* threw up a barricade in Matignon Street, from the materials of a house which was being built; and in Faubourg Saint Honoré Street, omnibuses and other carriages were upset. The instinct of disorder soon gained the interior of the city, and the pavements were torn up in Rivoli Street, in front of the Hôtel des Finances. In Saint Honoré Street the crowd had time to erect a pretty strong barricade. At a few paces from there a gunsmith's shop was pillaged; and at the same time that of Lepage, in

Richelieu Street, having been broken in and invaded, was defended by a body of troop.

By the close of day it was evident that the band of patriotic scape-graces which we have designated, had begun to be decidedly emboldened. In Saint Honoré Street one of their number threw himself upon old Colonel Bisfeld, who was passing with a detachment, wrested his sword from him, and tried to assassinate him. Others uttered seditious clamors and appeals to revolt. These, it is true, were only isolated facts, and were received by the crowd with evidences of fear rather than of sympathy.

At the moment in which the act of Saint Honoré Street was being committed, I met with Messrs. Caussidière and Albert, from whom I had willingly separated. The first shook his head.

"All this is not clear," said he; "there are a great many people here, and that is all; there is nothing that looks like the work of the musket."

M. Albert was of the same opinion; he had discovered but a small number of patriots among the crowds of the Place de la Concorde, and confessed that there were no signs of a republican manifestation.

As night closed in, the men of the suburbs gradually evacuated the vicinity of the Madeleine and returned to their quarters. The idle and curious returned to their houses, and the mobbers dispersed among the wine-sellers' shops and at the corners of dark and narrow streets, where anarchy is wont to prepare for its work. At the Champs Elysées, that night, there was still another deplorable spectacle. Throughout the day, that unusually peaceful quarter had been frightened by the clamors of the mob; and to its fears of the day there was now to be added that of a conflagration by night. The wretched street boys who had begun the disorder, gave the finishing touch to their work by making an *auto de fé* of the seats of the promenade.

The day past, the impressions of the republican chiefs were everywhere about the same. They perceived that the government had given proofs of extreme moderation; that it would hence be authorized to act with the greater vigor on the morrow; and that in view of its resources energetically employed, a movement of the people would be checked at once. Such was the opinion of M. Ledru-Rollin, who slipped into the office of the *Reform* in the evening, showing himself provoked that an affair had been undertaken in spite of his orders, which he considered supreme, and especially since the responsibility would probably fall upon him, notwithstanding his perfect innocence. This particular concern was, and he showed it repeatedly, that the *Reform* might be broken up and all its editors and patrons placed in arrest. M. Flocon did not see things in a more favorable light; he confessed that the affair might end in a death blow to the cause.

At the *National*, where the intervention of the suburbs was as much feared as it was at the Tuileries even, the events of the day appeared as an enormous fault; they cursed right earnestly the wretched people who had allowed themselves to be hurried into such compromising rashness.

The men of action, such as Messrs. Caussidière and Albert, were not so much frightened; but even they showed but little confidence. At nine o'clock they arrived at the rendezvous at the Palais Royal, agreeably to the notice which had been given. The meeting consisted of about a dozen individuals—Messrs. E. Baune, Grandménil, Fargin-Fayolle, Chancel, Caussidière, Albert, Pilhes, Chenu, and myself, all more or less engaged in secret societies, besides several familiars of the *Reform*, who had nothing to do with conspiracies, among whom were Messrs. Cheneau, Demougeot, and Boissier. The stops were closed, the lights extinguished, and a sullen silence reigned throughout the palace. We arranged ourselves in a circle under the colonnade in front of the Lemblin coffee-house, and commenced a confused and embarrassed discussion, in which nothing positive was advanced by any one. We must wait, we must see; such was the summary of the opinions. Finally, wishing to know where to find the dangerous men on the following day, I proposed as a place of meeting the boulevard of Saint Martin. I knew that the revolutionists would seek the central quarters of the town, and my object was to assemble them as far as possible in an open place. My proposition was adopted; remaining subject, however, to the course that might be pursued by the men of the suburbs. They had taken to the streets themselves on that day, but perhaps on the morrow they would not make their appearance. In this case it was understood that no one was to move. Such was the decision come to by those intrepid chiefs to whose supreme direction the public attributes the events of July.

In the mean time, the conspirators of the *Dissenting Society*, together with a crowd of mysterious characters whom the excitement of the day had drawn together, were shouting at the wine-shops and swearing extermination against the government on the following day. Some of the old patriots who had retired from the secret societies were yearning towards the musket and becoming very busy. Among their number was M. Sobrier, whom I met with about eleven o'clock at the Post Coffee-House, Montorgueil Street, in company with M. Pilhes and several others. The feverish organization of this person being powerfully acted on, broke out into frenzied words and gestures. He, at least, had no hesitation; barricades, battles, proclamations of the Republic, immediately, on the spot—such was his opinion.

"Do you want arms?" said he; "come on, I've got 'em!"

The crowd followed him to his lodgings, Mazagran Street, where he laid open an arsenal of arms of all sorts—muskets, carbines, pistols, swords, sabres, and one blunderbuss; the whole in a bad condition enough. Every one seized the first weapon at hand, and returned to the streets. Arrived in the midst of the Saint Martin quarter, the crew were stopped by a discharge of musketry, which came from Bourg-l'Abbé Street. Some of the mobbers had made their appearance in arms in that quarter, and had a slight engagement with the Chasseurs of Vincennes; and this was the concluding scene of the day in Paris. As M. Sobrier and his friends were not sure of their arms, and had, moreover, no ammunition, they beat a retreat, and, after strolling some time through the suburbs of Saint Martin, came to the conclusion to go to bed.

A little earlier in the evening, scenes of pillage and devastation, committed under the very eyes of the authority, had occasioned the people much alarm. At Batignolles a band of audacious men disarmed the guard of the barrier, and set fire to the guard-house. In Saint Honoré Street, opposite Coq Street, a shop of military equipments was pillaged. At a hundred paces from there, the door of Beringer's gun-shop was forced open. A strong patrol happened to be passing at the time, and the pillagers, ceasing their work for the moment, cried out at the top of their voices—"Hurrah for the troops of the line!" The commanding officer passed on without noticing, or without wishing to notice anything, and the noise of the hammer and crow-bar, which were immediately applied again upon the face of the shop, fell dead upon his unperceiving ears. A degree of laxness in the orders for repression had been remarked from the first, and it was already producing its effect. The greatest evil of the hour was the impression which this laxness had made upon the troops; the events of themselves, though sad enough, had nothing in them very alarming. With resolute men and vigorous measures the authority would easily have been maintained on the following day.

CHAPTER XXII.

The intrigue of the *Reform*—All the patriots don the uniform of the National Guards—The bourgeoisie of the *Siècle*—Disastrous mediation—The *Seasons* in the boulevard of Saint Martin—Arms given!—M. Albert accused of treason—Concession to the revolt.

At ten o'clock on the morning of the 23d, a dozen familiars of the *Reform* had assembled in the office, when M. Flocon entered exclaiming:—

"You must go and dress yourselves in the uniforms of the

National Guard; those who have not got them must get them from among their friends, from the pawnbrokers, no matter where; tell all the patriots to do the same. As soon as you are dressed, go to the mayoralties and shout 'Hurrah for Reform!' Then put yourselves at the heads of the detachments and interpose everywhere between the people and the troops. Go, hurry! the republic depends upon it, perhaps."

M. Flocon, though a ridiculous man, is a very serious revolutionist, and he said the truth: for the republic lay in this manœuvre. A thousand causes, it is true, might have rendered it a failure, such as, especially, a firm determination to repress every act of sedition from whatever quarter it might come; but as the government made no use of its natural means of defence, it followed that a gross piece of trickery was to triumph over immense forces and beyond all expectation.

It was on the evening previous that this idea of disguising the patriots as National Guards, and of misleading the bourgeoisie by simple cries of reform, had been proposed; it had been discussed by Messrs. Flocon, Etienne Arago, Monginot, and Lesseré, and by the morning of the 23d was fully adopted. The two latter gentlemen, being captains of the militia and on good terms with the *National*, had undertaken to communicate the plan to the people of that paper, and get their concurrence. They found their men very ready to listen, and in a very accommodating tone of mind. To accept a part in a fine intrigue when not too compromising, is a piece of good fortune which those diplomates have never neglected.

But it is well known by every intelligent man that without the intervention of the middle classes no revolution is possible. At the beating of the recall on the previous day, but very few of the National Guards had paid any attention to it; they yielded to that carelessness which shifts one's duties from his own shoulders to those of his neighbors, without reflecting that in moments of crisis every faithful citizen should be at his post. Perceiving this absence of the men of order, the anarchists conceived the idea of taking their place, of making use of their influence, and of passing off their own sentiments as those of the bourgeoisie. A fraction of the middle classes, who were represented by the *Siècle*, took a part in the trick; kept in a constant state of demi-aggression by men of sterile rhetoric and paltry ambition, they were ready to become instrumental in every clever machination. With the word *reform*, the summary of the some dozen of phrases which constituted their *vade mecum*, they might be led blindfolded into anything, no matter what. The *roués* of the radical party had discovered this, and were going to make use of it to their own advantage.

On the morning of the 23d, the drum had called together as yet only a small body of conservatives, when the radicals invaded the mayoralties with the cry of reform, and installed themselves there as masters. The plain men like M. Altaroche, and the jugglers of the opposition, such as Messrs. Perrée and Pagnerre, rushed in with their ambition all on fire, and ready to commit all kinds of folly. The patriots immediately commenced their part, fraternizing to the rallying cry, as had been agreed upon; claiming the expulsion of *the man of Gand*, and declaring that a contest between the people and the troops was an abomination that ought to be prevented at all hazards. The conduct to be observed was directed to a single point, viz: to prevent all collisions. The National Guards of the Left consider this idea an admirable one. In their innocence, the people whom they were going to let loose by a detestable connivance, would stop at the precise point fixed upon by them; they were to wrest the portfolio from the hands of M. Guizot, present it respectfully to the chiefs of the opposition, and then ask for nothing more than to repose upon their laurels. What an inconceivable absurdity!—not in believing in the wisdom of the true people, but in not perceiving that the movement, being undertaken by the dregs of the suburbs, and pushed on by intriguers, would rush into anarchy for want of repression, and lead to the triumph of demagogism! The whole revolution lies in these three facts—in the blindness of the opposing bourgeoisie, in the frightful drama of the boulevard, and finally, and above all, in the generous weakness of the government.

At about eleven o'clock, M. Altaroche, at the head of a company of the 2d Legion of National Guards, perambulated Montmartre Street, shouting for reform. Detachments of the 8th and 9th Legions came from the suburbs uttering the same cries. Some companies of the 3d Legion, assembled in the vicinity of the mayoralty of Petits-Pères, also conformed with the word of order. All the platoons marched escorted by a crowd of people, inoffensive at some points, but sinister at others, panting for disorder and shouting in passion. By these latter signs could be recognized the savage bands of conspirators from the barriers. All these men had entered the streets, prowling like wolves amidst the storm, and only waiting for a signal to rush on to the work of blood and devastation. Scattered through the four quarters of the capital, without chiefs and without instructions, they followed only their own instincts of hatred and rapine.

One of the first acts of that strange mediation which consisted in tying the hands of the troops while the populace were at work demolishing the monarchy, took place at the corner of the street of the Bank. Some of the mob had endeavored to disarm the post there, but had been prevented by a detachment of dragoons; a party of the National Guard came up, and, deciding that the dragoons had been in the wrong, charged bayonets upon them. Similar scenes occurred at fifty different places. In Bourtibourg Street, where a fire of musketry was opened for a moment, the National Guard intervened; in Royale Saint Martin Street, at the commencement of a fire of musketry there was the same haste on the part of the National Guard to check the public force in the execution of its duty. The few patriots who had slipped among the platoons, audaciously took the initiative of this manœuvre, and the whole detachment, either from being duped or from weakness, abetted or let things go on. It must not be imagined that I am here arranging the details of history to suit preconceived theories as other writers have done; the miserable imbroglio which I mention really had an existence, and was the web and woof of the day of the 23d. The effusion of blood was avoided almost everywhere, but solely to the advantage of anarchy; it was a disastrous re-enactment of the fable of Bertrand and Raton.

Towards mid-day, the men of the secret societies arrived at the boulevard Saint Martin, agreeably to the orders which had been given the preceding evening, and finding the position strongly guarded, fell back into the neighboring streets and commenced throwing up barricades. This work was accomplished in the most perfect security, and during the space of two hours several bands remained in absolute possession of the quarters of the Temple and Saint Martin. They were surrounded by a crowd who were animated as much by curiosity as by sympathy. Thus far the mob, with rare exceptions, had no arms. When the barricades were finished in the streets of Neuve Saint Laurent, Notre-Dame, and Nazareth, many of the suburbans, half drunk, foul mouthed, and evil eyed, cried out that they must enter the houses of the *bourgeois* and get their muskets. One of them had a crow-bar, and others large clubs; they knocked loudly at the doors, and made known their wishes in a brutal manner, threatening to sack the houses in case of a refusal. The affrighted families brought forward the arms which they possessed, and the pillagers wrote upon the doors in chalk—"Arms given!"

On every like occasion, the revolt traces its passage by this formula, which is like a seal of defeat impressed upon the houses. Nothing can present a sadder or more demoralizing spectacle than this of bandits despoiling peaceable men of their arms, and turning them against that society which they were designed to defend. And it is always in this way that the first corps of insurgents get their equipments, and find the means of arraying themselves against the supporters of order. If asked what remedy I would propose for this disastrous state of things, I should say at once, that every citizen armed by the government should be at his post when the government is attacked, and not wait to be disarmed in his house; and after every rebellion, it appears to me that every member of the National Guard should be compelled either to produce his musket or prove that it has been taken from him by superior force; and in case of not satisfying one of these two points, he should be subject to punishment by a council of discipline. If these means should prove insufficient, then have recourse to what are called measures of public safety; for it is highly improper that the anarchists should be permitted any longer to use as an instrument of revolutions, what ought to be only an instrument of public peace.

The true theatre of public action was the place which I have just indicated, that is to say, the higher points of the quarters of Saint Martin and the Temple. The fermentation there was great, but as to combats, properly speaking, there were none. A strong line of troops closed up all the issues of the square of Saint Martin, but they did not fire a gun. Some Municipal Guards, occupying the street a little lower down, delivered one fire, solely, into Grenéta Street. Messrs. Caussidière and Albert came up at this moment to the rendezvous of the *Seasons*, and had liked to be hit by the discharge. The few armed insurgents whom the Municipal had attacked, made their disappearance, and as the others were inoffensive, the affair had no consequence.

At the same moment, a group of the men of the *Seasons* arrived in Old Temple Street, in front of the house No. 131, where M. Albert resided. They came to summon him to furnish them with muskets and ammunition as he had agreed to do. Not finding him, they burst out into cries of rage, and resolved, by the advice of one of their number, to erect a barricade in front of his house, solely with the view of compromising their chief, whom they accused of treason. It may be seen from this fact that the more reasonable republicans had not as yet the least hopes of success. The barricade was constructed by the mobbers without their receiving any interruption. But an hour afterwards, as this rampart, which rose as high as the first story of the house, seemed rather annoying, two pieces of artillery of the Boulevard were brought up to destroy it. A great noise was heard, and two balls came to bury themselves in the mass of stones. This was the only place where artillery was heard during the day. The dozen of insurgents who were behind the barricade, made their escape in a hurry.

In Croix-de-la-Bretonnière Street, an engagement also took place between a dozen mobbers and a platoon of Municipals, the first having three of their men put hors du combat.

Such, with a few events of less note, was the day of the 23d until two o'clock. It was at that moment that royalty, deceived by false reports and fatal advice, decided upon a first concession, the consequences of which were to end in a frightful catastrophe not only for France but for all Europe.

In view of this immortal lesson, all reflection and all recrimination is useless; it is now written in letters of fire and blood, that the authority ought never to yield one inch to a rebellion. Though a rebellion may have the best of excuses, the advantages of its success are always a thousand times less than its evils.

It may be said that there was no reason for such an astonishing measure as that of capitulating to a revolt. Whatever certain writers may have said, there had been no conflicts of arms worthy of notice on that day, and in the first skirmishes which had taken place, the government had met with no notable check. It is well known, moreover, that only a few platoons of Municipals had been engaged. That a regular attack, if made by the troops at about two o'clock, would have proved successful, no man of intelligence and good faith can doubt.

The king was fully aware of the incalculable importance of the act to which he became resigned. That from this moment a reform might have appeared to him necessary, can readily be believed, but that from his own free choice he yielded at a time when it was almost dishonorable to have done so, cannot be credited. He found himself in a network of hesitation, false appearances, cowardice and intrigue which disturbed his mind and enchained his will. He regarded the movement of Paris as the result of an occasional disorder seized upon by the populace—a fact below the anticipations of a statesman; and partly from a reminiscence of opposition among the National Guards—something to be regretted, but of no very serious tendency. The course of conduct to be observed in such a state of things ought never to descend, the king thought, to an act like that which was proposed to him, that is to say, a backing out of the authority. If he yielded, it was because he had none of that obstinate vanity which the ignorant have imputed to him, and hence he feared that by rejecting the sincerest advice of his reputed friends, who were all agreed upon counselling him to a deplorable measure, he might incur the blame of foolish presumption.

Let other governments profit by this example; it is in times of crisis and danger that the true servants are seen; those who, in such moments, have only words of sadness and counsels of concession, have no regard for their master, they look out only for themselves.

CHAPTER XXIII.

Ferocity—The popular wolf let loose in Paris—The *Reform* and the *National* organize a catastrophe—A seditious peregrination—M. Lagrange—The pistol-shot of the Boulevard des Capucines.

The result of the change of ministry seemed to restore the counsellors of the king to their senses. The news was spread at about three o'clock through the popular quarters of the town, and the excitement there almost immediately subsided. The part of the National Guard who were under arms, an army of which the friends of the palace were so much afraid, but which after all consisted of only about six thousand imprudent men, held in tow by a few dozens of republicans; this National Guard, a very small fraction only of the bourgeoisie which they pretended to represent, had not in fact any design of going beyond a change of ministry, and having accomplished this, something which they certainly had no expectations of doing, they were fully satisfied, and had no stronger desire than that of appeasing the people. And as this people had also yielded to the itching for asserting their authority against the authority, they hailed the change with enthusiasm, and claimed nothing more. The fall of M. Guizot, especially, whom they had been taught to hate, appeared to them as a magnificent satisfaction.

But just in proportion as the wishes of short-sighted men were gratified, the fears of the far-seeing men became realized; the bands of anarchy which had been let loose upon the capital were not disposed to abandon their prey. While Paris was indulging the belief that it had been saved, all the men of rapine and blood, vagabonds, communists, men of ruined fortunes, robbers, members of secret societies, and bandits of all kinds, still clung to the work of disorder, and opened the eyes at last of the most blind. The Municipal Guards, particularly, were the objects of their rage. In Bourg l'Abbé Street, at the store of Lepage, a detachment of these brave soldiers, having been pressed upon by a crowd of roaring blood-thirsty men, owed their safety solely to the interposition of the mayor of the sixth arrondissement, and the colonel of the seventh legion. M. Etienne Arago, who happened in just as these men were leaving the store, revenge slumbering in their looks and their fists clinched in wrath, undertook to conduct them to the Hôtel de Ville and be responsible for their safety. But in spite of his efforts, the tigers of the suburbs had liked to glut their rage upon them, for, at the Place de Grève, they rushed upon the unfortunate guards, uttering the sinister cry, "To the river with them!"

At the moment when the Municipal Guards were returning to the suburb of Saint Martin, all the populace of that quarter set upon them in a fury, overwhelmed them at the entrance of the barracks, and took possession of the edifice; and had it not been for the arrival of a company of the National Guards, a horrible massacre would have been the consequence. Everywhere the same ferocity was displayed against these admirable supporters of public order, against this corps of honor, the very type of military fidelity.

And this took place, let it be remembered, after the change of ministry had been made known; a fact which proves that the reptiles of the lowest mud had become stirred up, and that the retreat of the National Guard had not restored order to Paris. These butchers of Municipal Guards and the ragged bands who were seen passing through the streets panting for blood and pillage like so many apparitions from hell, were the outpourings of the caverns of conspiracy and the dens of robbery; they consisted of some thousand patriots of the secret societies, and about as many robbers who shouted reform at the top of their voice, while their faces lighted up with infernal fire at the idea of overthrowing society and fastening their yellow tushes upon its very entrails. These men had no chiefs except themselves; for, as is always the case under like circumstances, the hierarchy was broken. Neither M. Albert nor the other members of the committee of the *Seasons* could find their men again; they were wandering in the storm and merged among the groups of the *Dissenting Society*. A third part of the *Seasons* had retired with the National Guard; but the rest remained upon the pavement, in pursuit of the quarry which they were determined should not escape them.

Such was the happy state of things brought about by the mediation of the National Guard acting under the combined influence of the *Siècle*, the *National*, the *Reform*, and a few mock militia men! The rankling sediment of gay and sprightly Paris, exposed to the light by political agitation, had infected society with a disease that nothing short of the most violent remedies could eradicate. The bandits who came forward that day, and who had already on the preceding day fanned the fires of disorder among the crowd, were to have free scope until France herself should arise to exterminate them. They were allowed to gain their end on the twenty-third; a conflict with them was shunned on the twenty-fourth, and their next step was to become our masters! They rushed to the work of pillage, ruin, and assassination, and on the twenty-fifth they demanded that a new reign of terror should be signalized by the adoption of the red flag. On the fifteenth of May they dictated through one of their organs the confiscation of wealth; and, finally, in the days of June, it was in a sea of blood of their own digging that they were overwhelmed by outraged society. How much misery, wretchedness, and disgrace would have been avoided if Marshal Bugeaud had taken the same course in February which was followed four months later by General Cavaignac!

Power then had capitulated; the bourgeoisie of the left triumphed, and the populace opened their cry upon wounded monarchy, like the eager pack when about to seize upon the exhausted quarry. There were other passions, too, brought in play; the most brutal appetites were accompanied with the lowest jealousies, and the most ridiculous ambition. The pretended chiefs of the party, those men who had prohibited the movement on the twenty-first, perceiving that the weakness of the government gave room for ulterior designs, and counting upon making up for a deficiency in influence by audacity and chance, fomented the discord with all their might. The roués of the *National*, throwing wide the doors to all kinds of hopes, racked their brains in trying to conjecture the issue of things. The two patriotic journals gave vent to the same idea, viz: that the mob must be resuscitated and agitation carried to the very heart of the populace. The fall of the government, which had appeared impossible on the preceding day, and even on that very day, had, by nightfall, begun to appear possible to everybody; its moral force was gone.

M. Flocon on the one hand, and M. Marrast on the other, each surrounded by his own familiars, held eager councils in order to hit upon the desired expedient, while some of the amphibious patriots, such as Messrs. Etienne Arago and Louis Blanc, passed to and fro from one conventicle to the other, seeking to harmonize efforts, and giving the news which they picked up on the way. They discussed, they clamored, they made a thousand motions, but no one could find the word for cutting this new gordian knot. Some one at the

Reform was proposing an open appeal to the people, when M. Ledru-Rollin happened in, and, more irresolute than ever, adverted with bitterness to the sad attempt at authority which they had made on the twenty-first. When they asked him for his opinion, he replied as he had done the day before, by shaking his head, and saying, we must see, we must wait. Such were the instructions which were given by this chief of the party to his own men!

At the *National*, the idea of putting itself at the head of the people could not have occurred to any one; for the coterie were too well aware of their own unpopularity; and besides, such is not the way of proceeding with these folk of Lepelletier Street. To attack a powerful enemy openly, to his face, is altogether too gross—catch them at anything of the kind! The most timid or the least greedy men of this cavern of intrigues, were of the opinion of M. Ledru-Rollin, that they must let things take their course, and wait; but the great guns, such as Messrs. Marrast and Recurt, for example, were impatient for the issue. They believed that a reliance on Providence would do only for dupes, and that well timed measures might give a direction to destiny itself.

I do not pretend to say, that at a given moment, and under such or such circumstances, these men would have decided upon a massacre for the purpose of electrizing the mob; neither the time nor the means was fixed upon; but that they were determined to provoke a conflict, and only wanted for this purpose an occasion and a proper man, I boldly affirm.

While these councils were being held at the two journals, M. Sobrier arrived at the coffee-house des Postes, Montorgueil Street, swinging his arms, tremulous with fever, his features all on fire, and his eyes rolling in frenzy. Messrs. Pilhes, Cahaigne, Boivin, Zammaretti, and three or four other obscure conspirators, followed in his train. Hats, daggers, and pistols were thrown upon the table, and then M. Sobrier exclaimed: "Bring some punch, beer, and brandy, and let every one make copies of the proclamations which I am going to dictate; proclamations to the people, proclamations to the National Guards, proclamations to the army. We've let the revolution escape us; but we must not lose everything; write!"

Although known as a crack-brained man, he showed such a degree of ardor and resolution that he was obeyed without hesitation. He dictated the fritters of several haggard and windy phrases, and they were copied down; but, after a moment, on reading over his work, he immediately abandoned it; another idea struck him.

"We are losing time," said he; "it is upon the barricades and with *viva voce* that we must speak to the people; follow me! Let the men of the *Reform* scratch their ears and brew their notions—*action* is the word for us."

The houses were illuminated from top to bottom, and gave out their floods of light upon groups who were passing in the streets, arm in arm, and chanting victory; that man, the scapegoat of every calumny and of every odium, M. Guizot, had been overthrown; power had been humiliated and mangled, and now, the joy of the crowd was at its height. The joy was sincere in many respects, and might have served at that moment to distinguish the blind misguided from demagogues and malefactors.

M. Sobrier stopped one of these groups as they were passing along preceded by *gamins* bearing torches, and, addressing himself to the *gamins*, said:—

"Give us your light, for I am charged with reading a proclamation to the people."

The boys mounted with him upon the first barricade; silence was restored, and the madman then howled out the following harangue:—

"Citizens: The satisfaction given to the people is nothing but a derision. Molé or Thiers in the place of Guizot, what matters it to us! The people have been massacred by the police and the Municipal Guards, and these two corps must be discharged! The rights of the people have been disregarded for fourteen centuries, and they must be solemnly recognized!

Citizens, you are all summoned to assemble to-morrow at the Chamber of Deputies to demand justice."

Though but a few evidences of applause followed this discourse, yet the instincts of disorder, which it is so easy to arouse on such occasions, were actively at work; the idea of remaining masters of Paris another day, and of again treating with power on equal terms, was very flattering and agreeable. But there was not, I repeat it, any ulterior designs on the part of the mass; the republic was thought of only by a very small minority, and even they still regarded it as almost impossible.

Followed by a crowd, which grew larger as he passed along, and preceded always by the torches, M. Sobrier perambulated the principal streets of the quarters of Montmartre, Montorgueil, Saint Denis, Saint Martin and the Temple, and at every barricade stopped to repeat his harangue. This exercise, added to numerous libations and a sort of epileptic loquacity which had seized upon him since the preceding day, had so much exhausted him that his lungs were no longer capable of giving forth any but a few inarticulate and wheezing sounds. His companions, who were obliged to relieve him from time to time, were no better off, saving and excepting M. Pilhes, whose lungs had proved equal to every test and whose rough voice, breaking out in sharp quick jerks, sounded like claps of thunder amidst the churme of the hurricane.

By the time that M. Sobrier had reached the extremity of the Marais, his eyes were out of their sockets, and, panting and extenuated, he entered a drinking house and fell motionless to the ground. His comrades followed him; and the crowd, being left without orators, pursued their way and gained the boulevard.

Other assemblages had also perambulated the city during the evening, seeking to reanimate the mob by their cries and excitations; but that of M. Sobrier was the most considerable and the one which left upon its way the most detestable impressions.

That crowd, by turns increased and diminished after the

disappearance of its chiefs, followed a direction leading towards the Madeleine, and arrived, at about ten o'clock, in front of the office of the *National*. There it came to a halt, by the advice of several National Guards who had but a short time previously joined it. M. Marrast made his appearance in the balcony and harangued it, in prudent terms, but in such a way as to exasperate it against the public force. He was grieved at the loss of those brave citizens who had been massacred by the troops, and he demanded, like M. Sobrier, that those impious myrmidons should be disbanded. The crowd were at liberty to understand that he meant either the army or the Municipal Guards, just as they pleased.

When the discourse was finished, a man came forward, to put himself at the head of the crowd, and exclaimed:—

"Come on, my friends, forward!"

The impression made by this man has remained fresh in the recollection of a great many witnesses. He wore a drab-colored overcoat, and his meagre frame, as it swayed right and left, under an awkward gait, caused his shoulders to be swept by a head of long, brown hair. These traits are enough to designate M. Lagrange. It is certain that this patriot left the coffee-house of Saint Agnès at about nine o'clock, and repaired, not to the Latin quarter, as has been said, but to the boulevard; and it is not less certain that he had a conference that evening with the men of the *National*. There are many significant facts, moreover, connected with this sinister moment. Tumbrels were noticed in Lepelletier Street, not far from the *National;* and when the column began to move, at the command of the man in the drab-colored overcoat, it was observed that the red flag was floating over the leading ranks; something which had not been seen before the arrival of the crowd at the office; and finally, the assemblage, which had been inoffensive thus far, exhibiting only a few bad sabres, now contained a great many men armed with all kinds of weapons. All this cannot be denied, and it gives rise to reflections, the importance of which can be easily comprehended.

Commanded by a chief from the *National*, overshadowed

by its red flag, and lighted by the torches, which showed the gleaming steel of their arms, the crowd arrived in front of the Hôtel des Capucines, where, it is known, a battalion was stationed, charged with the delicate and rigid duty of defending a man who had been marked out for popular vengeance. Though the troops may have allowed themselves an imprudent fraternization at every other point, they could not do so here. Instead of perceiving and respecting the position of these soldiers, the column of mobbers, with the red flag at their head, and the musket in hand, moved straight upon the battalion, apparently with the design of forcing it to yield, and all the while uttering the judaical cry—"Hurrah for the Line!" The commandant declared that his orders were to prevent their passage; and he urged them not to force him to measures of rigor. The man of lantern jaws parleyed with him for a moment; then, raising his arm aloft, the report of a pistol rung upon the ear, and one of the soldiers of the battalion fell dead.

There is a case here which may still prove of incalculable consequence, although it has already been productive of immense disasters. Let us give it a moment's consideration. In face of a large crowd of armed and excited men, who, with the red flag displayed, were assuming an attitude of open aggression, and who had actually begun to make use of their arms, can it not be readily conceived that the more impatient, or the more immediately threatened among the soldiers, might well have fired without orders, that others may have thought that the order to fire had been given, and that the fire might thus have become general?

But, on the other hand, that man who gave the signal, the consequences of which were to be a frightful massacre, the annihilation of the act of conciliation of the day, and a redoubling of hatred against the government—has he the excuse of the soldiers? Can he say that he acted under an impulse, and in self-defence? Can he expect to be believed if he claims that his conduct was exempt from machination and malice aforethought? No! the design was to fasten the stain of blood upon the front of power, and that blood, as usual, was drawn from the bosom of the people.

The corpses had hardly fallen, when a tumbrel arrived upon the scene of the drama, and gathered in the funeral harvest. The driver, one Junioux, held the reins, while a troop, headed by the man in the drab-colored overcoat, placed the torch-bearers in front of the carriage, and shouted out—" To the *National!*"

It was, indeed, there that the *good news*, the *lucky* issue of the pistol shot, must first be carried!

The *National* had not taken a decided stand thus far; it had been content to raise the cry of reform and to compromise the National Guard; but as this explosion of the boulevard des Capucines had shattered the throne, it immediately set to work to deal the finishing blows. Compositors and employees were, forthwith, sent into the streets. "To the barricades! To the barricades!" became the general cry; all the familiars and partisans, were informed—the hour for the general assault had sounded.

At the *Reform*, where the tumbrel arrived about midnight, after having exhibited its sinister appeal to vengeance through the quarter of Montmartre, the same furious hopes seized upon the mind. "The satisfaction shall be terrible," exclaimed M. Flocon; "let every family see the frightful havoc that has been made, and let tyranny be annihilated by public execration!"

The tumbrel then resumed its march, and trundled all night amidst the affrighted capital.

CHAPTER XXIV.

The course that ought to have been pursued on the 24th—Hesitation at the barricades—Royalty takes measures for safety—General Bedeau—Disastrous concession—The Hôtel-de-Ville taken—Combat of the Palais-Royal—Heroism and ferocity—Scene at the Tuileries—Abdication—The palace abandoned.

THE catastrophe of the boulevard des Capucines filled the heart of the king with profound grief. Besides the blood that had been shed—besides the infernal spirit of hatred which that machination made manifest, the event in itself was big with consequences. It especially rendered impossible that peaceful issue towards which such a serious sacrifice had been made on the previous day. Paris indignant or in consternation; the republicans burning with ardor and hope; the gypsies, vagabonds, and bandits alighted upon the capital like so many vultures upon the staggering quarry; pavements torn up; the streets striped with barricades; the trees of the boulevards cut down; arms pillaged; balls cast; bivouacs smoking at the corners, and cries, detonations, and the quick hurried peals of the tocsin calling together the soldiers of the revolt—such was the terribly significant spectacle that met the eye, and showed beyond a doubt that the time for battle had arrived. What then was to be done? It was a sad, but nevertheless an irresistible fact that war existed, and that the conduct of affairs ought to be turned over to the men of war. If there was still room for further management and conciliation it should have consisted only in issuing a proclamation to the people expressive of these three ideas. The government considered the event of the boulevard as a great misfortune, but the responsibility of which it entirely rejected. The electoral reform would be proposed to the Chambers within a period of three months;

Paris is in a state of siege, and the armed force will re-establish order at all hazards.

Everybody would thus have been warned, friends as well as enemies, and especially that class of men who were neither one nor the other, but who were unawares aiding and abetting in disorder. These being decided would have shown clearly how opinion stood; the friends would have pressed around the throne with renewed confidence, forming a powerful fasces of strength, and there would have remained to the disturbers only the demagogues and malefactors, a small, insignificant band, incapable of resistance and unworthy of pity.

And such was the opinion of the king. In the existing state of things his course was clearly marked out, and he was not wanting in resolution to pursue it; but a confused medley of counsellors, laboring under variant impressions, animated by intentions not wholly loyal, and the greater part of them struck with alarm, had invaded the palace, and were entangling the mind of the monarch in a snarl of words without order, energy, or even dignity. To the urgent requests which he made to be precisely informed upon the true condition of things, very few either knew how or were willing to answer. The fallen ministry had retired in a huff, excepting M. Guizot, who, in a melancholy mood, was less affected by his fall than by the embarrassment which resulted from it. The new ministry had not yet been formed. As no one held the position of official adviser, the will of the king remained in suspense, between the silent reserve of statesmen on the one hand, and the contradictory statements of a crowd of courtiers on the other. But finally, a man made his appearance who pronounced some decisive words. Nothing was clearer to him than the evil and the remedy; there was a revolt in Paris, it must be fought and suppressed. The middle classes, it was pretended, supported the movement; but a few hair-brained and ambitious men did not constitute the middle classes. And besides, a rebel is but a rebel, whether of the National Guard or anything else. The eye of the king glowed with joy; he had found a man of his own way of thinking, and fit for the emergency. Marshal Bugeaud then was appointed commanding general of the troops of Paris. This was a fault, say the good men even still; for the marshal was unpopular, and could be of no use towards conciliation. A pretty argument, truly! As if the enemy were to have their choice of the general to be sent against them; and as if conciliatory measures had not been carried a great deal too far already! There was no longer room for diplomatizing with the sedition in any way whatever; it had already gained too much ground, and all that remained to be done was to give it a vigorous defeat, and for that purpose a vigorous man was needed.

It was three o'clock in the morning. The marshal had twenty-five thousand men under his command, and he immediately took measures which were as simple as they were energetic: two columns, one commanded by General Bedeau and the other by General Sebastiani, received orders to force their way, the first to the Bastile, where General Duhot was already encamped, and the second to the Hôtel-de-Ville, occupied by General Taillandier. A ministry—Thiers, Odilon Barrot—had just been appointed; this would soon be made known by proclamation, and the generals were to announce it while on their way. It was decided that this condescension should be the last, and that at break of day arms should be employed against all resistance.

In the execution of these measures lay the safety of France —nothing is more certain. And not so much blood would have been shed as is thought; for General Sebastiani reached the Hôtel-de-Ville without striking a blow, and General Bedeau drew an insignificant fire only at the entrance of the suburb of Montmartre. At bottom, and notwithstanding the almost general demonstrations of hostility, it was stupor and fever that pervaded the mass rather than bad intentions. The republican leaders showed themselves almost everywhere, but as they acted under the pretence of reform, the National Guards and the crowd who considered them in earnest, without ulterior designs, did not exhibit that ardor for a fight which threatened to go to extremes. A large part of the men who were occupying the barricades had no serious belief, even, that a fight would take place; the idea and the desire existed only with those bands of old conspirators, and the men of rapine whom I have pointed out. The chiefs of the *Reform* and the *National* anticipated, without doubt, the fall of the throne, but not as the result of a conflict of arms; their chief hopes lay in the concessions into which the government had so inconceivably allowed itself to be hurried, and in the Machiavelic machinations by which they had thus far so well succeeded. From a regular pitched battle men of intelligence could expect only a catastrophe.

General Bedeau advanced to the top of the boulevard Poissonnière, passing by barricades the defenders of which shouted "Hurrah for the Line!" and parleyed with vehemence but without showing open resistance. This conduct threw the general off his balance, and caused him to hesitate in his duty. He believed that a mere misunderstanding existed between the people and the government, and that to push things to extremes would be a fault. This idea, and the indecision to which it gave rise, may be considered as among the gravest faults of that day. The resolute march of the general as far as the Bastile would have imparted to the government the only force in which it had been wanting for two days, viz: moral force. The men of good faith would have understood that the authority, after all, must retain the ascendency; the knowing ones of the republic would have seen their unprincipled rascalities exposed, and the troop of demagogues would have found that a hot reception was in store for them. In adding another evidence of weakness to all those which had thus far been shown by the government, the general gave a wider scope to that rash audacity and to those criminal hopes which a display of energy might have quelled, or at least very much weakened.

But, that fatal blindness which seemed to seize upon the general was not alone experienced by him; it obscured the vision also of men who were reputed the most far seeing of all others. The honorable M. Thiers, charged with the government together with M. Odilon Barrot, also conceived that things might still be brought to a peaceable issue. He did not see that the hour had come for asserting the position of the government by vigorous and decisive acts; he had no suspicion that behind the manifestation of the bourgeoisie there lay a diabolical intrigue, plotted and managed by the republicans. Informed of the hesitation which was shown by the men of the barricades, and knowing that the cry of reform alone was raised against the government, he decided his colleague, and got the consent of the king to recall the columns which were engaged, and even to withdraw the command from Marshal Bugeaud—two new concessions. It would seem that there was a determination to yield until the very last, without perceiving that by thus giving way, the danger became more imminent. Several of the officers of the National Guards, some through good faith, and others with the view of carrying out their plans, spoke to the generals, and promised a prompt re-establishment of order if they were permitted to treat with the *people*. They were listened to, the city was given up to them; and from that moment anarchy had its foot upon the neck of royalty.

General Bedeau being informed of the decision of the government, countermarched with his column. The National Guards of the *Reform* and the *National*, supported by a band of republicans in blouses, followed up the retreating troops, and, while shouting "Hurrah for the Line!" and bestowing a thousand ironical caresses upon the soldiers, despoiled them of their cartridges, compelled them to reverse their muskets, and took away from them two pieces of artillery. Never was a more disgusting spectacle exhibited, or a more impudent farce played off under the eyes, and at the expense of men of experience.

At the same time a scene of more serious consequence was taking place upon the Place de Grève. Some of the men of the suburbs, leaving the barricades where they had nothing to do, moved upon the Hôtel-de-Ville, which had been abandoned by the troops; took possession of several pieces of artillery, and invaded the apartments, killing the poor Municipal Guards who had been left without defence. The second position of Paris was thus occupied by the insurgents without hardly the snap of a gun! Such success could not be otherwise than perfectly infatuating, and why indeed should not these honest worthies, fresh from their demagogic dens and "lodgings for the night" at the barriers, rush furiously upon a prey that lay so fully exposed to their voracity? The Hôtel-de-Ville once taken, a bright idea occurred to all—they must take the Tuileries too! And as from the Place de Grève, from the boulevard, from the quarters of the centre, and from all parts of Paris the amazed soldiers were seen returning to their barracks, this army of disorder rushed howling upon the seat of royalty.

Never will the lugubrious spectacle that followed be effaced from the memory of those who saw it; and never can it be explained how a government, reputed formidable throughout the world, should end in such a cataclysm as this—yielding suddenly to a factitious pressure, cracking and giving way in every joint and falling in fragments like a castle of cards.

And not one chief of valor, not one seriously directive act in all this extraordinary movement. The committee-men of the *Seasons* were wandering through the city without finding their men, who were lost among the crowd; the members of the *Dissenting Society* were apart, among the wine-sellers' shops near the barricades, and the only controlling influence that could be perceived was that of a few *roués*, shouting reform and hurrying the credulous National Guards into the trap of the republic.

As soon as the Hôtel-de-Ville was occupied, one of the chiefs of the *Seasons* arrived at the *Reform* with the news. M. Flocon's dignity fairly fell prostrate at this—he could hardly believe in such good news. On being informed that the people had remained masters of the cannons of the Place de Grève, he exclaimed: "But if we are the masters of the Hôtel-de-Ville, we must take possession of the Tuileries; bring up the cannons to the palace, and all of us go there!"

The chief of the *Seasons* returned to the Place de Grève where he found the populace indulging in the most hideous saturnalia. Some of those frightful little monsters, the *ga-*

mins of Paris, were mounted astride of dead horses and playing leap-frog over them; naked bosomed heroes were staggering along, arm in arm, holding each other up and howling out couplets of the Marseillaise; thousands who had just armed themselves from the Hôtel-de-Ville were firing into the air in honor of their victory; a public woman, mounted upon a cannon, was haranguing the crowd in indecent language—numerous, in short, were the signs of joy, a joy that signified as plainly as words themselves could imply—we are the masters here; on, then, with shamelessness and debauch! When the envoy of M. Flocon endeavored to take away the pieces of artillery, the public woman opposed it, crying out treason and myrmidons of tyranny; they wanted, she said, to give the cannons to Marshal Bugeaud. The men who were around her sided with her, and gave the chief of *Seasons* such ill-omened looks that he thought it best to beat a retreat.

Since the morning the men of the *Reform*, barricaded in Jean Jacques Rousseau Street, were passing between the office and the drinking shops of the street, rigged out in a panoply of war which attracted the attention of their neighbors. M. Flocon made his appearance from time to time, and with the air of a general listened to the news and gave bombastic instructions; he carried his National Guard musket suspended from his shoulders by the sling. Messrs. Baune, Fargin Fayolle, and Tisserandot had fowling-pieces, M. Albert a musket, and M. Caussidière a carbine, together with a large sabre of '93 hung from his waist by a piece of string. M. Grandménil, the Sancho Panza of the troop, carried the wine which he had drunk at the various stations of the patriots. All these furious warriors had taken no part in the skirmishes of the day. At the moment when the crowd were being hurried by the instinct for ruin towards the royal abode, and the first reports of fire-arms were sounding from the Palais Royal, the band then moved towards the theatre of action, excepting the editor-in-chief, who considered his office as the centre of the movement, and seemed to be afraid to leave it. It will hence be seen what importance is to be attached to the idea that the *Reform* was the pivot upon which events turned; it had about as much to do with the whirl of events as it had with the diurnal revolution of the earth; some few familiars and the above-mentioned band constituted the only army under its orders. Its influence was felt solely through the few dozens of National Guards which it could reckon among the legions. The secret societies had long since thrown off all subjection and obeyed no one.

The *National*, at this moment, was in a great agitation; not that the direction of the popular bands gave it so very much to do, for the revolution was as far beyond its controlling influence as it was that of the *Reform*, but the knowing ones of the establishment saw the waters becoming more and more disturbed, and feared that they might lose their share of the fish.

It was about ten o'clock when the various armed bands arrived in the vicinity of the Place du Palais Royal. One of them was commanded by M. Considère, the incendiary; others by unknown chiefs, brought out like reptiles by the storm. Learning that the post of Chateau d'Eau was occupied by Municipal Guards, these men resolved to go and massacre them before proceeding to further measures. M. Etienne Arago, that fly of the coach buzzing about the vicinity, arrived there and endeavored to force the garrison to a shameful capitulation. One of the officers of the post replied that that could not be done, that he and his men would die before consenting to dishonorable terms. While they were parleying, some soldiers of the 14th who were on duty in the court of the palace, being assailed from the interior, fell back upon the main post and delivered their fire. They were supported by their comrades, and a shower of balls was poured in upon the insurgents, which caused them to disappear in the twinkling of an eye behind the barricades and in the court of the palace. The men of the *Reform*, who had just arrived, were on the side of Coq Street; M. Etienne Arago took shelter behind the façade of the court, together with a platoon of the National Guards, who were taking a part in the invasion of the palace. Major Poissat, Captains Lesseré, Fallet, Greinezer, Jouanne and

Thomas, and about forty of the patriots of the National Guards, were present. The assailants altogether might have numbered five or six hundred men.

A hot fire of musketry was opened. The National Guards were followed by a band of pillagers, who busied themselves in alternately pillaging the furniture and firing upon the post. During the space of half an hour the issue remained uncertain, for the combatants on both sides were sheltered from each others' balls. However, the garrison was much the most exposed; they fired from the windows, and not a soldier advanced to deliver his fire without receiving a whole volley in return. The besieged, expecting assistance, but finding that time passed away without bringing any reinforcement, began to grow desperate. They made repeated sorties in order to drive back those of their assailants who ventured out upon the place, and if possible to break through their enemy, but at every outlet they met with overwhelming showers of stones and balls. They resolved to hold out, then, as long as possible, and die with honor.

At this moment one of the insurgents conceived a horrible idea. "We must grill them," said he; "let us go and get straw and set fire to the building."

And was there not one single brave man there to chastise that wretch? the reader may ask. *Chastise* him!—on the contrary, his idea appeared admirable, and was hailed with acclamations of ferocious joy. Immediately some of them ran to the stables of the king near the spot and returned in triumph with bundles of straw. The soldiers could do nothing against them; in order to deliver their fire they had to lean out of their windows and expose themselves to receive five hundred shots for one. The incendiaries piled up the straw against the walls, set it on fire, and the flames soon arose to the top of the roof. The heroes of the barricades shouted with delight at this spectacle; and their clamors rose still higher, when some of the other insurgents made their appearance dragging up the king's carriages which they had found in the court of the stables.

"To the fire! To the fire with them," was the cry from all quarters.

Bundles of flaming straw were thrown into the carriages and their rich hangings disappeared in a moment. The strange moderators who had thus delivered up Paris to the populace, might now appreciate their work; the royal carriages were being destroyed, and the turn of royalty itself, would come next.

The last hour for the heroic defenders of monarchy drew near; all hope was lost, and a terrible fate awaited them. They had borne themselves like brave men; but they had to deal with men whose conduct was that of cannibals. Already the hot walls were reeking like a heated stove; the wretched soldiers felt their muskets dropping from their burning hands, and soon they began to fall themselves under the suffocating heat. They reassembled their remaining forces, and poured a last discharge upon the enemy—as it were their dying malediction. At the same moment a great noise was heard —the roof was giving away; and it fell, burying beneath its burning fragments more than half of the garrison. The rest opened the door and came out, covered with blood, black with powder and fire—a band of brave men whom the savages themselves would have respected; but the rascals who had endeavored to burn them alive, rushed upon them and massacred them without pity. Not one soul escaped. One of their officers, who had at first been spared, was assailed by one of the wretches and run through with a bayonet!

And while this butchery was going on, the palace was being sacked by the bands who had invaded the apartments, and the furniture and precious objects were either stolen or thrown into the gutters. One of the invaders had even set fire to the apartments.

During this combat of the Palais-Royal, a fact that made a deeper impression than either the ferocity of the assailants or the heroism of the besieged, was the astonishing inertia of the government. What possible motive could it have for withholding assistance from those brave men who were meeting with such a wretched fate? Alas! here, as well as in every other act of the government for the three past days, we see that fatal spirit of error which was leading royalty inevitably to its loss. Because a few concessions had been made, the opinion seemed to be that it was necessary to make others. The opposing National Guard had been yielded to in the sacrificing of M. Guizot. Very well! It was imagined that this portion of the National Guard, though very small, and by no means of much intelligence, had a sovereign control of the agitation, and that by leaving them the masters of the pavement, they would make haste to re-establish order; and, in consequence, the command of the troops was withdrawn from Marshal Bugeaud. Let us admit even this as reasonable and politic; but a fact of very significant importance then took place; an important post, within a few paces of the Tuileries, was attacked with peculiar fury; the Palais-Royal was devastated, and the royal carriages were given to the flames. Was it not high time, therefore, to recognize past errors, and perceive that energetic measures had become necessary for the salvation of the monarchy? Does it not seem that even the most blind ought to have comprehended the folly or weakness of that portion of the middle class which were allowed to predominate, and that it was full time to give another direction to the course of the government? But, no! the fatal misconception was to continue until the last. Even at this late moment, a mere word, restoring Marshal Bugeaud to the command of the troops, might have saved everything; but, instead of adopting that course, see what was done, and observe what took place.

At the very time when the peals of musketry at the Palais-Royal were sounding, as it were, at the doors of the Tuileries, like a horrible summons, the authority was amusing itself in posting up the following proclamation:—

"CITIZENS OF PARIS:—

The order has been given *to suspend firing*. We have just been charged, by the king, with the formation of a new ministry. The Chamber will be dissolved. An appeal is made to the country. General Lamoricière is appointed commander-in-chief of the National Guard of Paris. Messrs. Odilon Barrot, Thiers, Lamoricière, Duvergier de Hauranne, are ministers.

Liberty, order, reform!
ODILON BARROT, THIERS."

Concession upon concession, and nothing but concession! And to show what importance the crowd attached to it, M. Odilon Barrot was hissed upon the boulevard, where he had gone to have himself recognized; and M. Lamoricière, while renewing his attempts at conciliation in Saint-Honoré Street, was wounded. Since the people continued their firing after this last act of condescension, it proved that they were bent upon disorder at every hazard; and, since the National Guard did not retire, it was evident that they were either factious or incurably blind; and hence, there was no other course left to the government than to muster up its resolution, make an appeal to the men of heart, and to assume a bold and unyielding attitude in the face of the rebellion. M. Guizot would have done it; so would Marshal Bugeaud, and so would the king, who was only waiting good advice, and men of action, in order to decide upon a course which, alone, of itself, would have resulted in safety; but fatal counsels and false information continued to beset him. All etiquette was done away with; every one was talking at one and the same time, and contradictory propositions were clashing and conflicting in every quarter. In the midst of this babel-confusion—this pell-mell of impressions, by which the king was harassed and worn out, a man of adventures, M. De Girardin, made his appearance, and brutally dealt upon him this knock-down argument—"Sire," said he, "you must abdicate." And everybody, excepting the queen, a saint-like, and courageous woman, urged him to sign the act of abdication.

"But that is not possible," exclaimed the monarch; "it is not possible that the National Guard can require that of me."

"No, no!" said a courageous deputy, M. Piscatory; "they

deceive you, sire; we must fight, for the course which they propose to you leads to the republic!"

The king arose and was about to tear up the paper which was presented to him, when suddenly new ill-starred counsellors arrived. Among them was a man of suspicious character, and of gluttonous ambition. M. Crémieux, who was listened to because he was not a friend of the family, and because it was not conceived possible that one could be guilty of perfidy or levity at such a moment. He announced that the National Guard was moving in mass upon the palace, and that not only abdication, but flight had become necessary. Marshal Bugeaud, who happened in, blushing with wrath and shame, and cursing that foolish rabble of courtiers who were so pitifully murdering the monarchy, could not arrest the hand of the king, which had already been extended over the fatal paper.

"Marshal," said the monarch, "the crown was peacefully offered to me by the people, and especially by the middle classes, and I do not wish to keep it at the price of a sanguinary conflict—my mind is made up."

And he signed the abdication.

Together with this act of magnanimity an evil of incalculable consequence was also accomplished. The principle of authority was decapitated!

The king had been told that this sacrifice, finally, would be enough; but within an hour afterwards he was informed that he must think of flight. In fact, the army of burners and devastators of the Palais Royal, together with the fraction of the National Guard, upon whom had devolved the care of restoring order, moved upon the Tuileries, in order to finish their work. Everything had been granted to them thus far, except the possession of the royal abode, and they now demanded that. .All idea of resistance having been abandoned, the gates were thrown open, and that old palace of our kings was delivered up to the populace.

CHAPTER XXV.

The true heroes of 1848—The nomination of three Provisional Governments.

THE revolution, then, was accomplished, and the monarchy destroyed. To suppose that after the abdication of the king, the abdication of royalty would not also be demanded, were absurd. Hence, when the people had got possession of the palace, the democrats began to venture their cries of "Hurrah for the Republic!" A great many seemed to be aroused from a dream by this. While entering the palace among others, I distinctly heard a party of the National Guard say, as they were coming out—"What have we done?" The republic, in fact, was hailed only by that honorable class of patriots whom we have already sufficiently described, and by whom every political catastrophe is regarded as good fortune. The ovation made by the Cossacks on their entrance into Paris, has been very much talked of, but, there is no doubt about it, the crowd which applauded at that time, with the exception of a few fanatics, consisted of the same elements as that which bestowed its salutations upon the republic. There are always to be found in Paris some ten thousand knaves, who would overthrow the existing government, and shout, hurrah for the republic, for the empire, for the monarchy, or for anything else you may please, so that they might gain by it, some a week of anarchy and licentiousness, and others, the gratification of some ambition, hatred, or cupidity. And every revolution, as I have said, repeated, and will repeat even to satiety, comes from this class of men. The faults of the government are the pretence, the impulses of the middle class the motive power, but the real machine that catches our governments, good or bad, in a horrible combination of wheels within wheels, and tears them in pieces, is this class who have become gangrened, leprous, and ulcered in the sinks and gutters of Paris. I think that I have demonstrated this fact; if not, I could show statistical details which would convince the most obstinate.

Who, then, were this rabble howling through the apartments of the Tuileries after the departure of royalty, breaking, destroying, pillaging, drinking wine by the hogshead, setting fire to the vaults and rendering a place, respectable from so many considerations, the theatre of such hideous scenes that even the bacchanalian revels of a gang of galley slaves could alone give any idea of them? What men were those who were carrying off jewels, precious objects, titles of rents and effects of all sorts? What individual was that who was shouting out upon the place of the Palais Royal—"I must kill somebody?" Who were the men who wished to open the doors to the robbers of the Roquette, and were marking the houses designated for plunder? By whom were the palace of Neuilly, the railroads, the bridges of Louis Philippe, Asnières, and hundreds of other structures set on fire? What nameless *thing* was that which took aim at an officer of the Invalids, M. de Saint Grielde, and, without saying a word, endeavored to assassinate him? And that woman, on the arm of an insurgent, who stopped a lady passing by, saying—"Citizen, lend me thy gold bracelet!" Who were all these? Were *they* the French people? No, certainly not! but they were the people of our revolutions, and it is they who have the right to claim the paternity of the revolution of 1848!

The part played by the *Reform*, and *National*, thus far, has been seen. It consisted in maintaining a cautious attitude and in playing off a few tortuous tricks, some of which resulted in blood. Let us now look at the course pursued by the two journals after the *victory*.

At about two o'clock, whilst going in a melancholy mood, towards the office of the *Reform*, I met M. Flocon escorted by Messrs. E. Baune, Caussidière, Albert, Tissérandot, Fayolle, and many others, hurrying along at a rapid pace and in a great state of excitement.

"Where are you going?" said I.

"To take the Tuileries," proudly replied M. Flocon, who had not left his office during all that day.

"But you are too late, it is already taken; I have just seen a rag-picker rolling upon the cushions of the throne."

What news! An emotion of tenderness took possession of the crowd; they embraced each other upon the spot; then, as all farther dissimulation became unnecessary, they sent up a loud shout of Hurrah for the Republic! This done, they hastened back to the office in order to prevent the revolution from being pilfered, that is to say, to cut it up into pieces while still warm and reserve the best parts for themselves.

A fact which proves the mediocre influence of the journal and its men is, that at this moment when the result was known by everybody, the office was nothing less than embarrassed by it. By and by some of the patriots come in— M. Louis Blanc in uniform; M. Thoré, cane in hand; M. Sobrier, armed to the teeth and wilder than ever, and finally, the most of the *Familiars*. The popular element was represented by M. Albert and M. Chenu. The latter came in at the head of a band of mobbers who were draped, begrimed, and equipped according to the most approved fashion— musket in the fist, cartridge box upon the hip, breast laid bare, blouse dirty, face smutty, the eye on fire and the head seething with wine. The names of the men composing this glorious assembly which was about to dispose of the destinies of the empire were as follows:—

Messrs. Louis Blanc, Flocon, E. Baune, Caussidière, Etienne Arago, Cahaigne, Sobrier, Fargin-Fayolle, Albert, de la Hodde, Tisserandot, Chenu, Pont, Garnaux, cashier of the Journal; Jeanty Sarre, copyist to M. Etienne Arago; Augier, cutter of the Journal; Vallier, a retired captain; Gras, travelling clerk; Bocquet, a tutor; Boivin, copper turner; J. Ledoux, cobbler; Zammaretti, chimney doctor; Boileau, a mechanic; Gervais, a mason; Dupuis, a currier; Delpech, a founder; Tissot, a carpenter, and Gaulier, a vine-dresser.

There were besides, the servants of the establishment and several employés and subaltern editors.

They were all standing up around the green baize of the editorial table. M. Flocon, the natural president of the meeting, declared that the state of things required the nomination of a truly popular government, and that it was for the *Reform* to take charge of that duty; that important matter should be attended to without a moment's delay, for persons of suspected patriotism were already busy upon the subject, and thus, a mongrel democracy might get the upper hand of the real pure. The members of the future government, then, would be put to the vote.

"I ought in the first place," continued M. Flocon, "to bring to your knowledge this list which has just been sent to me; it is the provisional government decreed by the *National*. See whether the names which it contains are satisfactory to you or not."

He then began reading the names, and called out in a loud voice that of M. Odilon Barrot.

"Good!" exclaimed the retired captain; "I recognize the intrigues of the *National* there."

"M. Odilon certainly counts for something in the revolution," replied M. Flocon in a sly manner; "the question is to know whether he is wanted to govern the republic or not?"

A formidable No! emphasized by the butts of muskets, was the response of the whole assembly.

"I propose M. Ledru-Rollin."

"Bravo! hurrah for Ledru-Rollin! Agreed! agreed!"

"Francois Arago."

"Yes, yes! Hurrah for Arago!"

M. Flocon presented for the suffrages of the grand electors the names of Messrs. Louis Blanc and Lamartine, which were accepted without an opposing voice; then those of Messrs. Garnier Pagès and Marrast, which were tolerated. The *National* had had the impertinence not to enter the name of M. Flocon upon its list, and the *Reform* gave a lesson to the rival sheet by accepting its editor in chief. M. Flocon thought, perhaps, that in overlooking this error, the same good turn would be done him the next time; as to this, however, I can't say.

The famous government, then, was nominated. Highly satisfied with their work, these palatines were thinking of going to install their elected, when M. Baune showed that he wished to be heard.

"Citizens," said he, "we have an important vacancy to fill up; the government consists only of black coats; it is indispensably necessary that a blouse should be added. That would give the revolution its sanction and force."

M. Gaulier, a vine-dresser, made a bound of surprise and admiration.

"Famous!" cried he; "that's what I call an idea! Let us nominate a citizen of the people; I am one of them!"

This zealous devotion to the cause came very near procuring to M. Gaulier the honors of the government; many of his comrades were showing signs of approval, without venturing, however, to express themselves openly, when M. Flocon settled the question, by saying: "I believe that citizen Albert is a fair representative of the laboring classes, and that it would be proper to nominate him."

"Albert! Albert!" shouted the laboring men, who knew him as a chief of secret societies—"Hurrah for Albert!"

The election of this statesman in blouse, which M. Louis Blanc has poetized in such a ridiculous way, was made without any further ceremony. There was neither acclamation in the court, which was empty, nor a flow of tears, nor inexpressible emotion; such grimaces were wholly out of place, and certainly, the persons present were occupied with anything else.

When the meeting was on the point of breaking up, M. Caussidière remarked, that it would be well to provide for two important branches of the service—the prefecture of police and the post-office. "We should have there," said he, "solid good fellows, and we ought not to leave their nomination to others." The meeting was perfectly of his opinion, after the supreme chiefs nothing was more natural than that the inferior dignitaries should be nominated.

M. Caussidière was proposed for the prefecture, and he made a great display about accepting it; it was not a trade to his liking; he was a soldier, not an administrator; he would be much more suitably placed at the head of a legion of volunteers than at that of a legion of employés, etc. etc. All of which was very true; but what was not less true was, that the good man, vexed at not having a seat in the provisional government, had no design of allowing the offered compensation to escape him. His resistance was not carried too far. M. Sobrier, who was in a great perturbation about this time, proposed himself as the second of M. Caussidière. He was neither accepted nor refused; and the poor fellow owed his nomination to that axiom which says—Nothing said is consent given.

As to the post-office, M. Flocon offered it to M. Etienne Arago, who accepted it with great eagerness.

And here, this immortal ceremony came to an end. The characters of the farce were thus cast, and the actors went to learn and play their parts.

Arrived at the post-office, M. Etienne Arago presented himself with that *aplomb* which characterizes his race, and demanded the investiture of the administration. The men of the guard looked at him askance and put him out of doors; and M. Chenu and his band had to go and communicate to the rebel soldiers the orders of the sovereign diet, and compel them to admit the new director of *packages*.

At the *National*, towards one o'clock, the whole communion were assembled in full consistory, Messrs. Marrast, Recurt, Dornès, Thomas, Garnier Pagès, Marie and Vaulabelle were there, and also M. Louis Blanc and E. Arago, cautious men, who were glad to have a foothold in both camps. They had just learned the result of the combat of the Palais Royal, in which neither of these gentlemen, properly speaking, had taken a part, and it was well understood that the existing state of things could not continue much longer. But the weakness exhibited by the government, however, was something so inconceivable that they still had to fear that it might arouse, and were prepared at any moment to hear some terrible news. But presently a messenger arrived. Did he bring the bad news anticipated? Had the troops finally become engaged? The triumphant air of the messenger left them in but a moment's suspense; he threw in upon the palpitating assembly these few words:—

"The Tuileries are taken, and the king has fled!"

Quick—without loss of time in congratulations, the list of a provisional government, already drawn up, was decreed, copied, and sent off to the *Reform*, the chamber, and the multitude. It bore at its head the names of Messrs. Marrast, Marie, Garnier Pagès, and Recurt—four men belonging to the establishment! The next were those of Messrs. Francois Arago, Lamartine, Ledru-Rollin, Louis Blanc, and Odilon Barrot. The work was dispatched with less ceremony even, than at the *Reform;* the new dignitaries literally and positively nominated themselves.

People, be assured! the men who thus shamelessly invested themselves with power, are those puritans who have never ceased harping for a period of eighteen years against the proclamation of the Duke of Orleans by 229 legitimately elected deputies!

There, then, we have two governments nominated! But this is not all; we are going to see a still more lamentable display at the Palais Bourbon.

The Duchess of Orleans, with the Count of Paris, arrived at the Palais Bourbon at half past one o'clock. Greeted by loud acclamations, it seemed for a moment that the courageous mother and the orphan were going to retrieve the cause that had been lost. M. Dupin, and after him M. Odilon Barrot, had warmly set forth the reasons of state in their favor as well as the touching position of the woman and the child who confided in the devotion of the deputies. In spite of some opposition from a member of the Right, the sentiments of the Chamber were evidently tending in favor of the regency; but in the then existing state of things, could the authority of the representatives survive the ruin of the other powers? Those who entertained such hopes were very soon undeceived. A catch word had already been thrown to the populace, warning them against a surprise.

Remember the jugglery of 1830, said the roués, who were engaged in executing the jugglery of 1848. Hence, a band from the Tuileries repaired to the Palais Bourbon, invaded it at the moment when M. de Larochejacquelein was demanding that an appeal should be made to the nation. The advocates Marie and Crémieux had already spoken before him in favor of a provisional government. The invaders, armed and bearing flags, interrupted the session, shouting out: "It is forfeited! it is forfeited! no regency!" M. Ledru-Rollin had not breathed a word thus far; but encouraged by the presence of the insurgents, he made ready to speak.

The reader has had no news of this great man for two days; but let him feel no uneasiness on that account; for the tribune, he may be assured, notwithstanding his terrible reputation to the contrary, is a man of admirable prudence, and will see that his precious person is not lost to the party. During the whirl of events he never set foot in the streets except to steal quietly two or three times to the *Reform*, and even then casting a look at all the corners of the court of the office to see that there were no commissaries of the police stationed there. As the position of nothing was defined, he had no desire to define that of himself. His opinion, however, had not varied—everything would end in a disaster for his party, and the principal weight of it would come upon the *Reform*. It is even asserted as a positive fact that on the evening of the 23d he designed to take to flight.

He did not recover his *aplomb* until the 24th, after the abandonment of the Tuileries. On repairing to the Chamber with the conviction of finding everything there in a state of dissolution and of meeting with a triumphal reception, he was very much astonished to hear enthusiastic cries in favor of the Duchess of Orleans, and at finding himself as wise a man of Gotham as before. He took his seat and waited.

When the first band of invaders arrived, he began to feel symptoms of courage. However, among the uniforms of the National Guards and the black coats before his eyes there were as yet but a few blouses; and these were not his men— not the men who sack and pillage and carry their arguments at the point of the bayonet. To occupy time, he entered into a regular lawyer's plea upon the subject of the regency. Some of the insurgents had already raised their voices for a provisional government; M. Marie had formally supported the demand, as also had that truculent man, the advocate Crémieux, whose conduct throughout these events is so miserable. M. Ledru-Rollin still pleaded round and round, until at length some of the legitimist members themselves suggested to him the logic of his position; M. Berryer crying out to him: "Conclude, then, for a provisional government!" Besides the excitations which he received from various quarters, a great noise and clamor were now beginning to be heard at the doors announcing the presence of the real men of the barricades. Led by a chief of Bellville, one Bussy, several hundreds of sinister looking suburbans forced their way into the hall; caused the Duchess of Orleans to retire; dispersed the deputies, and put the great and courageous tribune very much at his ease. There remained as representatives only those who had either been republicans or who had suddenly become such in view of the great and glorious spectacle of the sovereign populace. In presence of this chosen people M. Ledru-Rollin remounted the tribune, and, radiant and intrepid, proceeded to an operation of which I shall give an exact report.

M. Dupont (de l'Eure) and M. Lamartine had endeavored, amidst the noise and confusion, to form what was called a government, and, satisfied with a pitiful semblance of an election which gave him a part in the dictatorship, the poet had gone to mount the capitol at the Hôtel-de-Ville. M. Ledru-Rollin was determined to render the affair more grotesque still. Addressing himself to the populace, a disgusting mass of passion and drunkenness, which was assuming the investiture of sovereign power—

"Citizens," said he, "you understand that you are performing an act of grave importance in nominating a provisional government. What all the citizens ought to do is to grant silence and lend attention to those men who wish to *constitute themselves* as their representatives; therefore, listen to me. We are going to perform an act of great importance. It has been demanded this very moment. A government cannot be nominated *in a trifling way*. Permit me to read you the names which seem to be proclaimed by the majority. As I read them out, you answer Yes or No, accordingly as you are satisfied or not. (Very well—Listen) and in order to have it in some way official, I beg the gentlemen stenographers of the *Moniteur* to take note of the names as I shall read them off, because we cannot present France with names which shall not have been approved *by you*."

This might appear to have been drawn from a piece of Odry, but it is literally exact; the *Moniteur* bears witness to it.

The question having been stated in this grave manner, M. Ledru-Rollin proceeded to call out the names in the following order:—

Dupont (de l'Eure). (O Yes! yes!)
Arago. (Yes! yes!)
Lamartine. (Yes! yes!)
Ledru-Rollin. (Yes! yes!)
Garnier Pagès. (Yes! yes! No!)
Marie. (Yes! yes! No!)
Crémieux. (Yes! yes!)

A voice from the crowd—Crémieux, but not Garnier Pagès. Yes! yes! No! He's dead, the good man!

M. Ledru-Rollin—Let them who are opposed to him raise their hands. (No! no! Yes! yes!)

Great confusion ensued, the ayes and noes conflicting; but without stopping at this slight disagreement, M. Ledru-Rollin resumed in these words:—

"Gentlemen—

"The provisional government which *has just been nominated*, has great and immense duties to perform. We are under the necessity of dissolving the meeting in order to repair to the bosom of the government and take all the measures necessary for the consecration of the rights of the people."

And accordingly, the meeting was dissolved, and the Tribune set out in triumph for the Hôtel-de-Ville.

There existed formerly a celebrated sort of elections, by the practice of which the people of Paris used to be highly diverted—those for the king of revellers and the king of fools; and what would not have been the diversion of these three elections of the patriotic race if behind this stupendous mockery there had not been seen tears and blood, ruin, disgrace, and wretchedness!

CHAPTER XXVI.

The Hôtel-de-Ville—The delegates of the people—A new provisional government—General Lagrange—The prefecture of police—M. Sobrier—The companions of the prefect—Order for the arrest of the Duchess of Orleans—Organization of the Montagnards.

Through the inertness of a fraction of the National Guard and a fatal generosity on the part of the government the monarchy had been destroyed, and the republican wolves, prowling in rear of the combatants, had rushed upon the prey to devour it. By republicans I do not mean those legions of imbeciles or intriguants who became republicans from the 25th and who would become royalists to-morrow should the monarchy be restored again; I refer solely to that faction which took its rise in 1830, whose frenetic efforts were vainly directed against royalty during a period of five years, who then relapsed into a state of impuissance which continued for thirteen years, and which was about putting an end to their existence, when they were again resuscitated by an unexpected turn of fortune.

Four important points were occupied by the revolution; the Hôtel-de-Ville, the prefecture of police, the Luxembourg and the Tuileries. I shall give a sketch of these four centres, and then draw to a close, having reached the limits which I had assigned for this work.

The persons who had been elected by the three conclaves made their entrance into the Hôtel-de-Ville without any parade or display, for the crowd were not only strangers to their grandeur but the place was in the most terrible state of confusion. The arrival of M. Ledru-Rollin alone, who made his appearance escorted by Messrs. Felix Piat, Laviron, Jules Favre, the faithful Grandménil and others, produced some sensation. M. Grandménil bawled his throat sore in shouting—"Here is Ledru-Rollin, the friend of the people; hurrah for Ledru-Rollin!" As this name had some notoriety among the people, rough voices applauded, and a triumph, in a small way, accompanied by incidents not exactly triumphal, was got up for the Tribune. Penetrating as best he might into a hall of the first story overlooking the square, he succeeded in mounting upon a table which, by repeated efforts, was kept from being upset while silence was being restored. The thundering noise finally ceased and the orator delivered his harangue. It has been said and repeated that on this occasion M. Ledru-Rollin proclaimed the republic; but this is false, as hundreds of witnesses can testify. Still stunned by an inexplicable victory which he dared not to consider as decisive, he pronounced a devious and wordy discourse, in which even the word republic was not once mentioned. His text was, that the nation had recovered its rights, and was called upon to assume a form of government. This was certainly not very compromising; not so much so that a proclamation of the regency would have found M. Ledru-Rollin out of the way. I was present, and can affirm the exactness of my version.

A little before the appearance of M. Ledru-Rollin at the Hôtel de Ville, Messrs. Dupont (de l'Eure), Lamartine, Crémieux, and Garnier Pagès had arrived, and after having been hustled about by the crowd for a long time, had succeeded in getting into a room by themselves. M. Ledru-Rollin joined them, and they commenced their deliberations. It must be said to the honor of these men, who had been thrown as it were by a hurricane into a position which was the more terrible as it was an elevated one, that the fears of anarchy had seized upon them all; the word regency was at first upon the most of their lips. M. Garnier Pagès pronounced it without occasioning any surprise; however, they dared not to venture far upon that ground. The arrival of Messrs. Marrast and F. Arago produced no change in the direction of ideas. And in fact, every one felt that the inspiration of such a moment came neither from reason nor experience, but from the brutal force which was making the very place tremble with its disorders. It was a hard necessity, but they accepted it because power was at that price. In the midst of these impressions, three new sovereigns made their appearance, the delegation from the *Reform*, Messrs. Flocon, Louis Blanc, and Albert. They took their seats without ceremony and entered into the deliberations. The men of the *National* and the improvised republicans of the Chamber, looked at them with knit brows.

"What intruders are these? Whence come they?"

"We are nominated by the people," said M. Flocon.

"What people?" demanded M. Marie.

"The true people, those who have fought," replied M. L. Blanc. "Do you intend to put us out of doors? Quotha!"

"Yes, sir; we cannot deliberate in your presence," said M. Arago, coldly.

The little man clinched his fist in a rage.

"I know you," said he, "you are the Lafayettes of 1848; but you will go out by the windows before we go out by the doors, you may depend upon that."

Crimination and recrimination followed until the illustrious assembly had like to come together by the ears as a prelude to the reign of fraternity and self-denial. After a long parleying, in which the bitterness gradually gave way to the reflection that the legitimacy of their powers was as liable to suspicion in one case as in another, they finally came to an understanding, every one admitting the sovereignty of his neighbor in order to preserve his own. It was in this way that the quarrel between the blues and the reds commenced. Simple minded men were inquiring upon what grave subject of public interest the new government were then occupied; —their first care was to try to devour each other!

The sovereigns had not yet come to an understanding

when new powers by the dozens rose up around them. In the first place there were the *Delegates of the People*, who, taking the hint from the mechanism of the elections of which they had been witness, got up a little election for their own benefit. Several hundreds of individuals, without distinction of any kind, republicans of the hour, thought that if the new government had the right to decide the fate of the nation, they, in their turn, had the right to impose their decisions upon the government. Why not? They nominated, no one knows how, fourteen delegates who were to be nothing less than the sovereigns of sovereigns. One of them was a man by the name of L. Devins: a citizen by that name has been condemned for robbery; is he the same one?

At the same time that this committee of public safety was formed, another government was instituted, which differed in no way from the rest except that it was more open and frank. It originated among the heroes of the *Dissenting Society* and the frequenters of the Court of Assizes.

"'They are going to *nig* us,' said one of them; 'this is not the way that the people are to be dealt with. Let us nominate for our governors some good fellows who will agree to share with their comrades.'

"Agreed," cried the crowd; and they proceeded to a new election, the result of which was a dozen honest fellows chosen as masters of France, who scorned egotism and swore not to forget their friends.

Besides these governments, there was the power of *General Lagrange*, a power that admitted of no rivalry; it stood alone. The knight of the rueful countenance had wandered through the streets since the preceding day, in a wilder mood than ever, exclaiming: "It is I who have saved France; it is I." Learning that a government had been installed at the Hôtel-de-Ville, he hastened thither, forced his way into the hall of deliberation and cried out: "It is I, Lagrange! Yesterday I saved France. You want a governor. I nominate myself! Fear nothing, you are under my protection!"

The *Eleven* were amazed, but allowed him to go on. He got some epaulettes, a cocked hat, and, posting himself at the door of the council, he replied to the inquiring and stupefied looks that were directed upon him—"It is I, General Lagrange! It is I who have saved France!"

I am not exaggerating. Every body at the Hôtel-de-Ville either heard him boasting of his exploit, or were aware that he did boast of it. At the prefecture of police, where he went to congratulate M. Caussidière, he repeated the same words. This continued during four days, when it was discovered that reason had entirely abandoned him. He fancied that conspirators, concealed in the Hôtel-de-Ville, were trying to destroy both him and his government. He presented a miserable spectacle, which had liked to end in a tragedy, and the consequences of which were expulsion and the loss of his honors.

During these hatefully grotesque incidents, the disorderly bands of the place who were fearing measures averse to anarchy, howled with fury and threatened to sack the Hotel if they were not assured on that point. The Eleven, with the exception of the four dictators of the *Reform*, were in consternation; they must either abandon their power or yield; in order to remain the masters of France they must become the slaves of the populace of Paris. The word republic, then, was let loose; not freely and in a decided tone, but in a tortuous, circumlocutory manner, amidst the empty, high-sounding phrases of a proclamation. "The provisional government is in favor of the republic, provided that it be ratified by the people, who will be immediately consulted." Such was the formula.

As the masters of the Hôtel-de-Ville were unknown to the conspirators, the phalanxes of the *Seasons* and *Dissenting Society* did not make that place their rallying-point; they assembled at the prefecture of police, where M. Caussidière received them with open arms.

The prefecture was evacuated at about three o'clock. About six hundred municipal guards were in the court when a loud discharge of musketry upon the quay was heard, fired by a battalion of the line out of complaisance on the arrival of the insurgents. It was known that all was over, and M. Delessert, who maintained his post until the last hour, thought only of securing the lives and the retreat of his soldiers. At the head of the band of invaders was a company of the National Guards, some of those who had evoked the republic in the name of reform. Terrified at what they had done, they had come to endeavor to save the garrison of the prefecture. One of their number, the Adjutant Caron, came to the gate to parley with the garrison, and advised them urgently to yield the place in order to avoid being massacred. "All Paris had surrendered," he said, "resistance would be useless, and a capitulation not dishonorable."

"Be it so," said the commandant, "if they will leave us our arms."

"That is impossible," replied the adjutant; "these men here will never permit it."

"But when we are disarmed the wretches will assassinate us. . . . . What say you, my friends," said the commandant addressing his men; "will you surrender your arms?"

At these words a sombre and terrible expression might be seen coming over the features of these brave men. "Death," cried they, "but in fighting."

The time was pressing; the crowd were already surging at the gate and beginning to roar like the storm. Some course or another must be pursued. The commandant asked the National Guards if they would be responsible for the lives of his men; and on being answered in the affirmative he gave orders to disarm.

A spectacle of lugubrious grandeur and thrilling dramatic interest was then exhibited. The guards broke their muskets upon the pavement, and, tearing off their uniform and equipments, trampled them under foot. Some were seen embracing and shedding tears of shame, while others endeavored to kill themselves. What an inconceivable fatality that a government with such men as these should fall without offering any resistance!

The municipal foot guards, the most of them with their arms and heads bare, filed out between the two lines of National Guards, who had the good fortune to secure their retreat to the Barracks of Tournon. As to the mounted guards, who were also with their heads bare and without their arms, they were permitted to leave the prefecture; but they had not reached the quay when a discharge of musketry pitched many of them to the pavement. Bravo! was the cry; and these heroic men, whom capitulation had invested with a sacred character, were shot down like dogs by the infamous populace!

Such was the prelude to the saturnalia of the prefecture. A moment afterwards, two men, one having pistols in his belt and a carbine in his hand, the other trailing along a huge sabre, bustled into the establishment.

"Citizens," cried the first, with a rough voice and in a wild, haggard manner, "by the will of the people we have come to take possession of this place; I am Sobrier and this is Caussidière!"

Very few of the men of the establishment knew them; but under such circumstances one does not look closely, and their acquaintance was soon made. Sobrier—Caussidière, so be it! They were accompanied to the office of the Secretary General, where they installed themselves, and immediately set to work in drawing up a proclamation. It was that famous production, written in suspicious French, in which occurred this phrase, so worthy a prelude of what was going to follow: "It is expressly recommended to the people not to quit their arms, their positions, nor their revolutionary attitude, etc." The proclamation finished, M. Sobrier, whose exaltation had gone on increasing during the last three days, was finally in a burning fever, and he fell upon a couch in a state of unconsciousness.

At the news of the greatness of M. Caussidière, all his pothouse companions hastened to join him. Among the number were M. Mercier, his brother-in-law, Messrs. Caillaud, Lechallier, Morisset, Gras, Louchet, Core, Tiphaine, etc., the latter taking with him his whole family. These individuals and many others, among whom was a fencing-master, who was accused, two days afterwards, of pilfering arms and plate, led a course of life not above suspicion, and from which they had strong hopes that their illustrious friend would raise them. Besides these chosen men, the advance guard of that famous phalanx who were going to immortalize the place, began to make their appearance. The first was M. Chenu, who organized the first fraction of Montagnards. Then came M. Gallaud, an old conspirator, recovered since from his illusions, and who contributed towards restoring some order to the establishment; and finally, the captains of barricades, Beaume, Peccatier, and Helie, the latter accused of antecedents more than suspicious. All came forward in a murderous greediness, their first care being to find out the rack and drinking trough. The illustrious M. Pornin did not make his appearance till the day following; for, having been jugged on the 21st, he could not be with the insurgents during the three days except in spirit.

M. Sobrier recovered his senses; but not his composure or reason. A vertigo had seized upon him; his movements were furious; his words foaming. Either from jealousy or frenzy, he was haunted with the idea of the provisional government.

"Marrasts, Lamartines, and Garnier-Pagès," cried he, "it is infamous! If we wait till to-morrow before putting those men out of doors, we are lost."

M. Caussidière assented very readily to the unworthiness of some of the members of the government; but the ambition of his colleague appeared to him rather dangerous. He had a pretty good place after all, and prudence required that he should not risk it foolishly.

"A little patience," said he; "what the devil! we must have time to look about us. Let us first count our forces and get firmly fixed in our position. It will go very hard with us if in the end we do not blow up those gentlemen."

"Art thou afraid?" replied the madman; "then let me alone and I will act by myself."

"Let you alone," grumbled the prefect in a low voice; "that is not exactly the way that I understand things; I'm thinking in fact, that it isn't I who leaves these premises first."

The fact is, the division of the prefectorial authority pleased him but little, and he was determined from the first to eject his colleague. There was not much difficulty in the way of executing his wishes, inasmuch as Garnier-Pagès, who came to the prefecture, found in M. Sobrier a fit subject for Charenton.

The proclamation of the two prefects was sent to the *Moniteur*, but did not make its appearance the next day; an evidence of disrespect by which M. Caussidière was deeply wounded, and particularly as he learned that it had been brought about by orders from the Hôtel-de-Ville. He perceived that he had been appreciated, and was not highly esteemed; an opinion which was confirmed by the offer that was soon made him by his superior, the mayor of Paris. M. Garnier-Pagès advised him to accept the government of the palace of Compiègne, which the munificence of the Eleven deigned to offer him. But this proposal met with no success. The ex-*Lime-kiln* man replied with his little flute-like voice that contrasted so strangely with his large shoulders:—

"It is impossible that I should leave this place; I am needed here. There are already below some hundreds of fine lads who are working well; and I am expecting as many more of them. Should good-will or courage fail you at the Hôtel-de-Ville, I will come to your assistance. And the revolution will do a neighborly turn, eh! eh!"

"The revolution! why, it is over."

"Bah! it hasn't commenced."

The puritanism of M. Caussidière, in fact, was never of the ferocious kind, and he would be one of the most accommodating men in the world if no attempt were made to wrest the prey from his very teeth; but he was determined from this hour to hold demagogism unmuzzled and embroil everything in order to have a better chance to dictate his terms.

I arrived at the prefecture on the 25th at about three o'clock. Notwithstanding the danger, it appeared to me as my duty to penetrate that gulf of confusion where I might possibly be of some use in giving a check to anarchy. I had reasons for believing, moreover, that the originals of my letters had been destroyed, and I felt that I might make a good figure under any suspicions that the existence of mere copied extracts might excite. On seeing me, M. Caussidière, who was burning to show his tact to the provisional government, exclaimed—

"Ah, come in then! you know well that I am in want of some good fellows here; if the prefecture doesn't show itself, we are flats. Here, take this mandate and execute it immediately."

He handed me a paper upon which I read—"Order for seeking out and apprehending the body of the ex-Duchess of Orleans, and of the ex-Count of Paris, who are probably at the Invalides."

"You understand," added the prefect, "that with such hostages as these, if the counter-revolution budges an inch, we'll show them that we've read our history of '93."

M. Miot, who was at that time in his woods of Morvan, and who ventures to speak of things which he knows nothing about, has denied that this order of arrest was given. I refer him for the facts to M. Beaurain, No. 16, Notre-Dame-des-Victoires Street, who was joined with me in my mission. M. Beaurain passes for an honest man; and I may add, moreover, that on this occasion he showed himself to be a man of heart.

On returning from this expedition, which was managed in a way to be of no serious consequence to the illustrious proscribed, even though they had been at the Invalides, which was not the case, the prefect took me aside and said—

"Install yourself in the office of the secretary general, and let it be known that the rendezvous of the true patriots is at the prefecture; we must have here all the old conspirators and the men who know how to handle the musket; we can then hold the frying-pan by the handle. Ledru-Rollin, Flocon, Albert and myself understand each other; the question is to overthrow the *National;* that done, we will republicanize the country will he nill he! Be assured, we have to do with shy fellows, but we'll teach them a thing or two."

The idea of M. Caussidière was very clear. It was to surround himself with a corps of Janissaries drawn from the dens of the capital; set up this hideous phalanx as a scarecrow before the majority of the Eleven, and as occasion offered, to throw them upon the Hôtel-de-Ville. This plan was executed; and it is known that during three months its success fully answered the expectations of the terrible good man.

From the 27th the prefecture became the head-quarters of the revolutionary populace. The court, the offices of the employés, the halls, all were thronged by a wild-looking set of men, hideous, offensive to the very smell, lounging upon the cushions, or howling among the drinking pots. Nothing can give any idea of the spectacle unless it is a camp of drunken and rampant Cossacks.

M. Caussidière was hail fellow well met with his worthy friends, fraternizing and bandying jokes with them, and from time to time inviting the most knowing ones of them to his table. That table, which he has since calumniated, was worthy of a much finer if not more gluttonous palate than his. It was furnished by the cook of M. Delessert, in a very aristocratic style, and plentifully moistened with the wines of the ex-prefect. I speak with some knowledge of the fact, having had the sad honor of occupying a seat in it for fifteen days. At first, the desire of exhibiting something of Lacedemonian virtue, had led him to have recourse to the ragoûts of a neighboring cook; but he soon got tired of that regimen, and by the end of eight days had come to the conclusion that extra heating wines and superfine dishes were nothing too good for his honorable self and company. Enchanted with the manners of their chief, the old soldiers of the prefecture conceived a tender regard for him, and swore to defend him to the last gasp.

In order to derive all the advantage possible from their devotion, he thought of giving them an organization. M. Pornin, whom he had appointed governor of the establishment, received the title of Commandant of the Montagnards, with directions to form a regular battalion. He made up a battalion of three companies, of which the designations and the chiefs were as follows:—

1st company, *The Mountain*, commanded by Captain Menant, and Lieutenants Javelot and Davoust. M. Menant is the frequenter of obscure drinking shops; M. Javelot is one of the honorable chiefs of that band of *Robbers* called the *Materialists Society*, and M. Davoust is a patriot of the wrong complexion, as it would appear, since he was requested to take his discharge and not make his appearance at the prefecture again.

2d Company, *The 24th of February*, Captain M. Leon and Lieutenants Paquette and Badieux, three hair-brained men who were characterized by nothing in particular, and who were all killed, it is said, upon the barricades of June.

3d Company, *The Rights of Man*, its officers Messrs. Dormes, Butte, and Guibourg. The first was a ticket taker at the Theatre Historique, and the others were bandits of the ordinary stamp. M. Guibourg has rendered himself liable to prosecutions which have forced him to expatriate himself.

M. Pornin appointed as Adjutant Major of this honorable legion the very honorable M. Helie.

Not satisfied with having this army at the prefecture, M. Caussidière established other companies of the same kind in various quarters of Paris. One of them was stationed at the barracks of Tournon, where M. Coré commanded; another at those of Petits-Pères, governed by M. Martin, who had under his orders M. Chenu and several other officers.

CHAPTER XXVII.

Records of the prefecture—The secret tribunal of the Luxembourg—The eight barrelled revolver—Poison—Orgies at the Luxembourg—The band of the Tuileries—Finale.

These dispositions had been made, when a thunderbolt fell upon the greatness of M. Caussidière. M. Sobrier, who considered himself a man of first-rate importance, and believed that all the denunciations of the police must have been directed exclusively upon himself alone, had got from the keeper of the archives the files of papers pertaining to politics; and his surprise may be imagined when he found nothing in them relating to him except a few notes which were as insignificant as himself. The files relating to the prefect, however, were very full and complete, and on being opened they were communicated to him without delay. M. Caussidière fairly bounded with amazement and wrath; the infamous fellow who had unmasked him, had given a detailed account of his life from day to day, and, instead of exhibiting him as a formidable man and a matchless patriot, had represented him as an impudent charlatan, a speculator of suspicious character, an habitual drunkard, and a conspirator of no importance. I am quite certain that had M. Caussidière foreseen the curious disclosures that were going to be made from those records, he would have posted his most trusty Montagnards over them with orders to shoot the first one who should venture to touch them. But as it was, the blow had been given, and all that remained was to have vengeance of the traitor.

I can very readily say, in reply to a passage in the memoirs of M. Caussidière, wherein he states that he had never held me in any esteem—I can readily say that I have always paid him back liberally in the same coin, and that I have never sought his society nor accepted his services—something which he cannot say with regard to me. I have freely expressed my opinions to hundreds of the patriots with regard to him. I made no efforts to induce him to enter the association of which I was the principal chief; and I defy him or any one else to prove that I have pursued any other course than that of getting possession of the moral influence of the conspirators with the view of undermining and destroying it. I have had no intimate relations with any one in the way of demagogism excepting M. Pilhes; I have been in his company daily for a period of three years, but without saying a word of secret societies; I believe that M. Pilhes is loyal enough not to deny this fact, which however can be proved without his testimony.

The original copies of my letters and other documents were not destroyed; the private secretary of the ex-prefect, M. de Lachaussée, held them under lock and key in a chest which was in his office. During the events of the 25th, he succeeded, with the assistance of M. Nabon, chief clerk of the office, in conveying the contents of the chest to the archive keeper, who put them in a sack that had been taken from among the old papers of no importance. This measure would have secured me against all danger, had not an employé of the office, M. Martorey, given information of the removal of the papers to M. Elouin, chief of the municipal police. M. Elouin, who would not have even deigned to look at M. Caussidière the day before, now made haste to tell him everything, making, for a smile, a cowardly sale of secrets which in no way concerned him. Although I had not once visited the prefecture during a period of eight years, yet my name and the part that I was playing were known, as it would appear, to M. Elouin; another employé also knew that I had formerly manifested the design of aiding the police in destroying the republican party, and both of them had already directed the suspicions of M. Caussidière upon me. They were charged with making researches concerning me. After a long exploration, the missing file of papers was discovered. I was well aware that there was a certain distrust hanging over me; but convinced, as I was, of the destruction of my original papers, I had taken the resolution of holding out to the last.

One night, at about eight o'clock, I was taken to the Luxembourg—for reasons that I could not possibly conjecture. On entering the office of M. Albert, I found myself in the presence of individuals whose names are as follows: Messrs. Caussidière, Grandménil, Monnier, Caillaud, Bocquet, Chenu, Pilhes, Bergeron, Lechallier, Tiphaine and Mercier. They began by forming a tribunal, which, though it occasioned me some surprise, was not so very astonishing when I reflected that it was a formality frequently had recourse to by the patriots in many cases of no importance. M. Caussidière opened the proceedings; and at the very first words which he uttered I was relieved from all uncertainty. He made a positive charge against me, without, however, mentioning the material proofs which he had in his possession. Leaning with my back against the chimney, I listened to him, and made preparations for my defence. When he had finished speaking, I made a few paces forward, and as he thought that I was going to take to flight, he threw himself between me and the door in order to prevent it. Drawing out an eight barrelled revolver and levelling it at me, he declared that if I made any attempt at violence or evasion, he would blow my brains out. I had no idea of making my escape, and I told him to put up his artillery, for it was useless. I had taken such prudential measures with M. Pinel, and my position appeared so favorable in some respects that I succeeded without much difficulty in destroying the first effect of the accusations against me. M. Caussidière allowed me to go on, keeping his little eyes fixed upon me, full of venomous irony. Finally, stopping me by a gesture of impatience, he announced that since I was so sure of my cause, he, on his part, was going to show that he had not accused me without due consideration; and he immediately exhibited the whole bundle of my letters. One of them was signed in my own name; and it gave such details that I could not say a word in defence. I was overwhelmed; the thought of the scandal which would come upon my name and family, tore my heart; and the more so as I could see no possible means, very soon at least, of making known my real position.

M. Caussidière declared that the assembly was transformed into a council of war for the purpose of trying me.

"My life is at your disposal," said I, "you can do with it as you please."

I stood resting my elbow upon the chimney, whilst they were deliberating upon my fate. The general opinion was that I ought to be condemned to death. This sentence was put to vote and carried. The next step to be considered was the manner of its execution. Various opinions were expressed; some were for shooting me upon the spot, others for removing me for that purpose to the garden; but as an executioner was necessary, and as the trade was rather a dangerous one, they concluded that it would be best to make me perform that office myself. One of the free and accepted judges was of the opinion that the pistol should be given to me for that purpose. I replied that I would not kill myself. The whole *tribunal* then assailed me with furious invectives, and declared that I should not leave the Luxembourg alive.

"Ah, well! you may assassinate me," said I, "but I shall not kill myself."

M. Bocquet, who was foaming with rage, took the pistol from the hands of M. Caussidière, and thrusting it into my very face, exclaimed:—

"Here, coward that thou art, take this and blow thy brains out, or I will do it myself!"

A shuddering sensation ran through my frame; I raised my hand to take the weapon, determined that the head of that miserable pedant, who would have trembled before me if we had been alone, should receive its contents before mine, when one of the assassins cried out to him not to let go the pistol.

"A murder must not be committed here," said M. Albert, "especially by means of fire-arms; the report would throw the whole palace into disorder, and that would be a terrible affair."

"However, he must die," said the prefect; "he knows too

much; what he has seen, first and last, might ruin us forever. Instead of the pistol we may use poison; I've brought some."

M. Bocquet leaped with joy.

"I have said that I would not kill myself," I replied; "will you make me take poison by force?"

"Yes, if necessary," said M. Caussidière; "thou canst not live much longer."

The moment had arrived when the scoundrels were going to bind me in order to force me to swallow the mortal drug. Without means of defence or escape, I gave up and recommended my soul to God.

But the unbridled fury of some of the free and accepted judges had begun to produce a reaction among the others; M. Albert was the first to say that I must be let alone and that the affair should be carried no further. As the majority, though still making preparations to massacre me, could not regard the consequences of their criminal intentions without terror, the ideas of death began to subside; and the prefect announced that I should be taken to prison and turned over to justice.

This resolution appeared to me more horrible than all the rest. A trial—the scandal of the affair when brought before the courts, under the existing circumstances wherein every attempt at defence would be in vain—all this frightened me, and I was in despair.

"You have no right to imprison me," said I; "the law has nothing to do with the case; I do not wish to go to prison, and I will not."

The ferocious tribunal hesitated. Seeing that they began to consult, I went to M. Caussidière and besceched him to revoke his decision. He repulsed me brutally; but as I appeared determined to offer resistance, he agreed to detain me only a few days and keep the affair secret in consideration of my family.

On leaving the palace, he offered me his arm, doubtlessly for the better making sure of me.

"There is no need of your holding me," said I; "since you have promised to avoid scandal, I am ready to follow you."

I was led to the depot, and from there to prison, where I was kept during the two months and a half which elapsed before the fall of the prefect of February. I was subjected to an examination which no one dared to continue, so absurd did it appear, and so deserving of the scorn with which I treated it. As to the promise of the loyal M. Caussidière, he kept it by placarding me that very night in the *Commune* (newspaper) of M. Sobrier, as the hero of an adventure, but, taking good care, however, to arrange the scene of the Luxembourg in such a way as not to compromise himself.

Such is the truth with regard to the affair of the Luxembourg; I have neither exaggerated nor extenuated, but have given the facts.

The scenes that took place afterwards at the prefecture, the gay light-hearted rascalities, the ambitiously stupid plans and Homeric boon companionship of M. Caussidière, of M. Pornin and his patriotic crew—all this is beyond my assigned limits; it has already been portrayed by a masterly hand, in bold touches and of frightful verity; I could neither better it nor render it more exact.

Before taking leave of the prefecture, I must relate a single anecdote connected with it. M. Sobrier, being obliged to give up his share of the prefectorial authority, immediately set to work to invest himself with a power of a different kind. He assembled a dozen old patriots, and got up together with them a handbill, of which the substance was as follows: "The ancient measures of Marat must again be brought in force; a system of delation and epuration must be organized, and the government compelled to admit our creatures. To this end, a committee formed of old conspirators, has just been nominated and is already occupied with its labors; every citizen is invited to bring his denunciations before it."

The signers of this document were Messrs. Sobrier, Bergeron, Pilhes, Felix Pyat, Cahaigne, and seven or eight others. It was posted up in Paris, occasioning some alarm to the peaceable citizens, and not a little jealousy among the intriguants, who, if they could only get their names upon such an instrument as that, fancied that the road to honors would be opened to them at once. The next day, as M. Sobrier was reading his master-piece over again upon the walls, what was not his astonishment to find that a name had been inserted among those of the signers which he had had no idea of having there. It was that of M. Bareste, the editor-in-chief of the *Republic*. This honest man, as it is left to be inferred, had had some new copies of the document struck off in which he had interpolated his own name. But to show the mock patriot that he was known, orders were given to tear down all the placards, and others were put up, from which the intruder's name was ignominiously stricken out.

All the birds of prey of the secret societies had alighted upon the prefecture. But when M. Albert had established himself at the Luxembourg, a party of his old companions joined him there, and had the satisfaction of a demagogic regency there too. Festivities without name were got up at the Petit Luxembourg, which was placed at the disposal of these wretches. The Pornin of the place was an ancient chief of group of the *Seasons*, by the name of Barbier. During the day he led his men to listen to the preaching of Louis Blanc, and at night, he presided at the diversions upon the grass-plots of the garden. The wine of the grand referendary, brought by the pitcherful, moistened the palates of the patriots and their poetic mistresses, dames taken from the harems of the city or from the barriers. M. Albert yielded to the torrent through weakness. One day, M. Henry, that mercenary idiot who simulated a regicide by way of a speculation, called on the dictator in blouse, and reminded him of that exploit; and M. Albert gave him a note for 1000 francs. A chest was established at the Luxembourg, supplied with public funds, for the payment of claims for political services; and crowds of persons, of whom the sharpers were not among the last, were dipping into it, morning, noon, and night. Messrs. Grandménil, Barbier, and L'Heritier (de l'Ain) drew up the bills, which M. Albert decorated with his signature without looking at them. Finally, he even signed his name for blank amounts. To every patriot who presented himself with dirty hands, a hoarse voice, and the look of a runaway galley slave, sums of 100, 200, or 500 francs were thrown out with princely generosity. M. Albert, it must be said to his credit, finally put an end to this lavish waste of the public money. But as to the exploits of M. Barbier and his myrmidons, they continued until a later period, until the orgies of the republicans began to bring the blush of shame to every honest cheek.

The Tuileries, which were also occupied by a band of these men for about a dozen days, were made the theatre of scenes not less ignoble. The commandant appointed by the provisional government, M. Saint Amand, had no authority over his garrison; the real chiefs there, were M. Imbert on the one hand, nominated superintendent of the *Civil Invalids*, and on the other, Captain Dormes, the ticket-taker. The characters of men who were under the orders of such chiefs, may be imagined; they were not even old conspirators; they were a dirty rabble, drawn together from the lowest dens of the capital. Their saturnalia excited such an indignation that M. Caussidière received orders to put a stop to them, and he had to obey. The company of Dormes was expelled from the palace; but M. Caussidière, in order to express his regrets to these excellent citizens, took them to himself, and formed a company of Montagnards of them.

From that day the contingent of idle and worthless men were found under the orders of M. Albert at the Luxembourg, and of M. Caussidière at the prefecture. These men and their chiefs, so long as they were permitted to tear at the quarry and dishonor France by their way, wallowed in pleasures and indulged in the most brutal excesses; but when the country had finally aroused from its stupor and they saw their power threatened, they took to the old road of conspiracy again, and came to an end on the 15th of May, and the 23d of June.

Since the 10th of December, the government is entirely rid of them; and it is high time that all France should be so too!

In writing this book, I have complied with a severe duty towards men whom I regard as obstacles in the way of private interests as well as of public greatness. Without either vanity or boasting, I would say to every man of law and order that he should follow my example, and take a decided stand against anarchy even when roaring the loudest! The clubbists of '93 were asked: "What hast thou done to be hung should monarchy be restored?" And the question at the present day to every man of order should be: "What hast thou done to be hung if socialism should triumph?" When this shall be clearly understood, and when no one will any longer fear to withhold his censer from the nostrils of demagogism, the monster will be seized with terror, convinced of its impotence, and fall crushed to the earth beneath public indignation and scorn!

THE END.

www.ingramcontent.com/pod-product-compliance
Lightning Source LLC
Chambersburg PA
CBHW051848300426
44117CB00006B/305